ESSENTIALS OF COMPARATIVE POLITICS THIRD EDITION

ESSENTIALS OF COMPARATIVE POLITICS

THIRD EDITION

PATRICK H. O'NEIL

University of Puget Sound

W. W. NORTON & COMPANY

New York • London

W. W. Norton & Company has been independent since its founding in 1923, when William Warder Norton and Mary D. Herter Norton first published lectures delivered at the People's Institute, the adult education division of New York City's Cooper Union. The firm soon expanded its program beyond the Institute, publishing books by celebrated academics from America and abroad. By mid-century, the two major pillars of Norton's publishing program—trade books and college texts—were firmly established. In the 1950s, the Norton family transferred control of the company to its employees, and today—with a staff of four hundred and a comparable number of trade, college, and professional titles published each year—W. W. Norton & Company stands as the largest and oldest publishing house owned wholly by its employees.

Editor: Aaron Javsicas
Assistant Editor: Carly Fraser
Project Editor: Kate Feighery
Design director: Rubina Yeh
Production manager, College: Eric Pier-Hocking
E-media editor: Dan Jost
Ancillary editor: Rachel Comerford
Composition: Matrix Publishing Services, Inc.
Manufacturing: Quebecor World—Fairfield division

Library of Congress Cataloging-in-Publication Data
O'Neil, Patrick H., 1966–
    Essentials of comparative politics / Patrick H. O'Neil—3rd ed.
      p. cm.
    Includes bibliographical references and index.
   ISBN: 978-0-393-93376-5 (pbk.)

   1. Comparative government. 2. State, The. 3. Capitalism. 4. Democracy.
5. Post-communism. I. Title.

JF51.O54 2009
  320.3—dc22   2009015082

    ISBN: 978-0-393-93376-5 (pbk.)

   W. W. Norton & Company, Inc., 500 Fifth Avenue, New York, N.Y. 10110
www.wwnorton.com

W. W. Norton & Company Ltd., Castle House, 75/76 Wells Street, London W1T 3QT

  3 4 5 6 7 8 9 0

CONTENTS

9 LESS-DEVELOPED AND NEWLY INDUSTRIALIZING COUNTRIES   230

LIST OF MAPS

ABOUT THE AUTHOR

Patrick H. O'Neil is professor of politics and government at the University of Puget Sound in Tacoma, Washington. Professor O'Neil's teaching and research interests are in the areas of democratization, conflict and political violence. His publications include the books *Revolution from Within: The Hungarian Socialist Worker's Party "Reform Circles" and the Collapse of Communism* and *Communicating Democracy: The Media and Political Transitions* (editor). His current research focuses on Iran. He is coeditor with Ron Rogowski of *Essential Readings in Comparative Politics*, Third Edition, and coauthor with Karl Fields and Don Share of *Cases in Comparative Politics*, Third Editon, both published by W. W. Norton & Company.

PREFACE

The past twenty years has seen the dramatic transformation of comparative politics: the end of the Cold War and the collapse of the Soviet Union, the spread of democracy around the world, the rise of new economic powers in Asia, and the deepening of globalization. For a time, many looked upon these changes as unmitigated progress that would bring about a decline in global conflict and produce widespread prosperity. Recently, however, there has been growing doubt, as the uncertainties of the future seem to portend more risk than reward, more conflict than peace. It is increasingly difficult to sustain the notion that a nation can function without a good understanding of the billions of people who live outside of its borders. We ignore the world at our peril.

This textbook is meant to contribute to our understanding of comparative politics (the study of domestic politics around the world) by investigating the central ideas and questions that make up this field. It begins with the most basic struggle in politics—the battle between freedom and equality and the task of reconciling or balancing these ideals. How this struggle has unfolded across place and time represents the core of comparative politics. The text continues by emphasizing the importance of institutions. Human action is fundamentally guided by the institutions that people construct, such as culture, constitutions, and property rights. Once established, these institutions are both influential and persistent—not easily overcome, changed, or removed. How these institutions emerge, and how they affect politics, is central to this work.

With these ideas in place, we tackle the basic institutions of power—states, markets, societies, democracies, and nondemocratic regimes. What are states, how do they emerge, and how can we measure their capacity, autonomy, and efficacy? How do markets function, and what kinds of relationships exist between states and markets? How do societal components like nationalism, ethnicity, and ideology shape political values? And what are the main differences between democratic and nondemocratic regimes, and what explains why one or the other predominates in various parts of the world? These are a few of the questions we will attempt to answer.

Once these concepts and questions have been explored, subsequent chapters will apply them directly to various political systems—advanced democracies, communist and post-communist countries, and newly industrializing and less-developed countries. In each of these, the basic institutions of the state, market, society, democratic or nondemocratic regimes all shape the relationship between freedom and equality. What basic characteristics lead us to group these countries together? How do they compare to one another, and what are their prospects for economic, social, and democratic development? Finally, we will conclude with discussions of political violence—looking at terrorism and revolution in particular—and globalization, linking what we have studied to two of the most central areas of concern today.

There are several changes to the Third Edition of this book. One major change has been in the order of the chapters on democratic and nondemocratic regimes, moving the former before the latter. The rationale for this change was to use the democratic regimes chapter as a template to show the origins and structures of these systems, which will then allow for a more focused comparison with nondemocratic regimes. This allows for the two chapters to be more explicitly comparative, rather than viewing nondemocratic systems as a "residual category" of idiosyncratic institutions. In addition, the chapter on globalization has been moved to the end of the text, immediately following the discussion of political violence. This allows for the discussion of globalization to benefit from the earlier investigation of political violence and also lets us look at how the two might be related. In addition, the globalization chapter considers to a greater extent the ways in which comparative politics as a field of study might be affected by the blurring between domestic and international politics. Finally, throughout the book, supporting examples and evidence have been updated, and recent influential work in comparative politics is noted and discussed.

The format of this text is rather different from that of most textbooks in this field. Traditionally, books have been built around a set of country studies, with introductory chapters for the advanced, post-communist, and less-developed world. While such a textbook can provide a great deal of information on a wide range of cases, the trade-off is often a less thorough consideration of the basic grammar of comparative politics. We might know who the prime minister of Japan is but have less of an understanding of political culture, mercantilism, or state autonomy, all ideas that can help us make sense of politics across time and place. This text strives to fill this gap and can be used alongside traditional case studies to help draw out broader questions and issues. By grasping these concepts, arguments, and questions, students will better understand the political dynamics of the wider world.

This thematic approach to the essential tools and ideas of comparative politics is supported by a strong pedagogy that clarifies and reinforces the most important concepts. Key concepts lists and "In Focus" boxes in every chapter highlight important material that students will want to review. Numerous figures and tables illustrate important concepts and provide real world data related to the topic at hand. Timelines and thematic maps show important political developments over time and around the globe. The importance of institutions is emphasized by "Institutions in Action" boxes.

Essentials of Comparative Politics is designed to offer instructors flexibility in creating the course that they want to teach. In addition to the core textbook, a corresponding casebook and a reader are also available. *Cases in Comparative Politics*, coauthored by Karl Fields, Donald Share, and myself, applies the concepts from *Essentials of Comparative Politics* to thirteen country studies. In *Essential Readings in Comparative Politics*, my coeditor Ronald Rogowski and I have selected key readings to accompany each chapter in the textbook. Norton also offers the textbook and casebook in e-book format. Support materials for instructors, including a Test Bank and PowerPoint lecture outlines, are also available.

Many people have contributed to this work. The text itself is inspired by Karen Mingst's *Essentials of International Relations*. When Norton released Mingst's book in 1999, I was struck by its concision and came to the conclusion that comparative politics would benefit from a similar kind of text. At Norton, Peter Lesser first encouraged me to submit a proposal for this textbook, and Roby Harrington encouraged me to develop the initial chapters, supported its publication, and provided important feedback at many stages. As editor, Ann Shin held me to a high standard of writing argumentation in the First Edition. For the Second Edition, Peter Lesser took over editorial duties, helping to further improve the work. In this Third Edition, Aaron Javsicas guided me through a number of complicated revisions. I am grateful to all three of them for their investment in this work. Thanks, too, to Elizabeth Kaster for her research assistance.

In addition to the people at Norton, many academics have helped improve this work. Most important have been my colleagues at the University of Puget Sound, in particular Don Share and Karl Fields. Over the past few years Don, Karl, and I have team-taught introductory comparative politics, and it was my work with these two outstanding teachers and scholars that helped generate many of the ideas in this book. Don and Karl were also kind enough to use draft chapters of this text in their courses and provided a great deal of feedback and numerous suggestions. I am fortunate to have such colleagues. Another important source of input has come from those reviewers who provided input in advance of the Third Edition: Emily Acevedo (California State University, Los Angeles), James Allan (Wittenberg University), Josephine Andrews (University of California, Davis), Alex Avila (Mesa Community College), William Heller (Binghamton University), Robert Jackson (University of

Redlands), Ricardo Larémont (Binghamton University), Eric Leonard (Shenandoah University), Mary Malone (University of New Hampshire), Pamela Martin (Coastal Carolina University), Philip Mauceri (University of Northern Iowa), Mark Milewicz (Gordon College), John Occhipinti (Canisius College), Anthony O'Regan (Los Angeles Valley College), Paul Rousseau (University of Windsor), Emmanuel Teitelbaum (George Washington University), and José Vadi (Cal Poly, Pomona).

Finally, I would like to thank the students of the University of Puget Sound for their questions and insights, the administration of the university for its support of this project, and my family for their patience.

Patrick H. O'Neil
Tacoma, Washington
June 2009

Africa

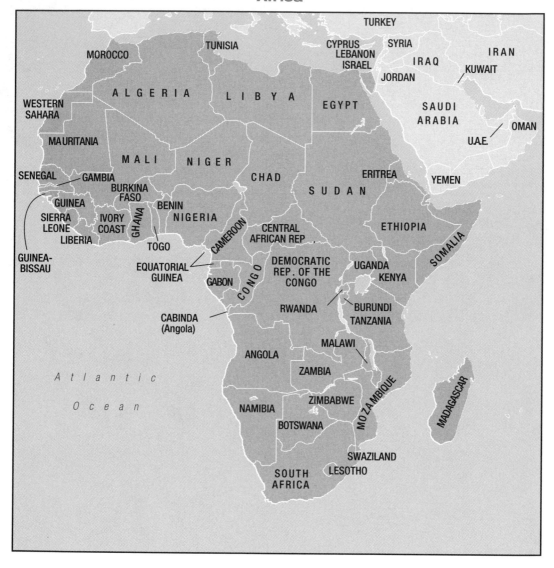

Asia

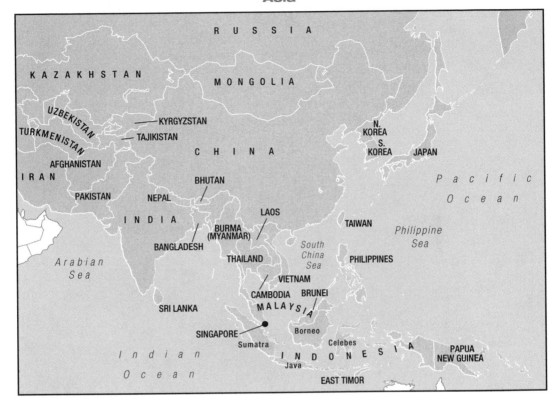

Europe

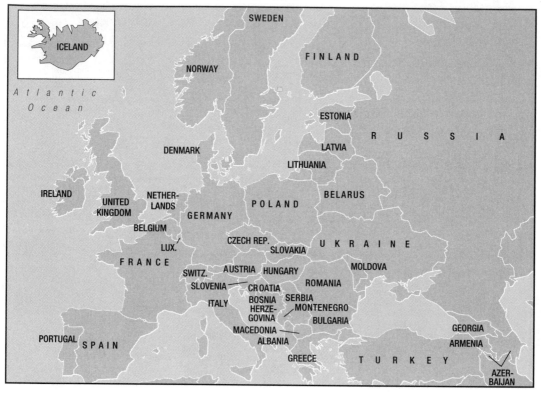

Central and South America

North America

ESSENTIALS OF COMPARATIVE POLITICS

THIRD EDITION

1 INTRODUCTION

KEY CONCEPTS

- Comparative politics relies on a comparative method in order to construct and test hypotheses.

- There are long-running debates over whether we can make comparative politics more scientific—better at explaining or predicting politics.

- One concept to guide our study is political institutions: self-perpetuating patterns of activity valued for their own sake.

- One ideal to guide our study is the relationship between freedom and equality, and how politics reconciles the two across countries.

During the past two decades, the world has seen an astonishing number of changes: the rise of new economic powers in Asia, the retreat of communism and the advance of capitalism and democracy, the return of religion to politics, the spread of the Internet and wireless technologies, the deepening of globalization. As a result, many of the traditional assumptions and beliefs held by scholars, policy makers, and citizens are open to question. New centers of wealth may reduce poverty, increase inequality, or both. Democracy may be an inexorable force, or it may founder on the obstacles of nationalism, economic instability, or culture. New forms of electronic communication may bind people across societies, creating shared identities, or fragment communities, generating a backlash.

Debates over ethnic conflict illustrate these issues. Why does this form of political violence occur? Is it a response to economic or political inequality or bad government? A function of cultural differences, a "clash of civilizations?" Is it abetted by globalization? Perhaps the explanation lies somewhere else entirely, beyond our purview or comprehension. How can we know what is correct? How do we scrutinize a range of explanations and evaluate their merits? Competing assumptions and explanations are at the heart of political debates and policy decisions, yet we are often asked to choose in the absence of reliable evidence or a good understanding of cause and effect. To be better citizens, we should be better students of political science and **comparative politics**—the study and comparison of domestic politics across countries.

This chapter will lay out some of the most basic vocabulary and structures of political science and comparative politics. These will fall under three basic categories: *analytical concepts* (assumptions and theories that guide our research), *methods* (ways to study and test those theories), and *ideals* (values and beliefs about preferred outcomes). Analytical concepts help ask questions about cause and effect; methods provide tools to seek out explanations; ideals provide a way to compare what we find in political life to what we would prefer. Concepts and methods can help us reach our ideals by revealing what we don't know and when our assumptions are wrong.

Our survey will consider some of the most basic questions: What is politics? How does one compare different political systems around the world? We will spend some time on the methods of comparative politics and how scholars have approached its study. As we shall see, over the past century, political scientists have struggled not just with the challenges of analyzing politics but also with whether this can actually be considered a science. Exploring these issues will give us a better sense of the limitations and possibilities in the study of comparative politics. From here we will consider comparative politics through the concept of **institutions**—organizations or activities that are self-perpetuating and valued for their own sake. Institutions play an important role in defining and shaping what is possible and probable in political life by laying out the rules, norms, and structures through which we operate. Finally, in addition to looking at institutions, we will take up the ideals of freedom and equality. If institutions shape how the game of politics is played, then the objective of the game itself is the optimal mix of freedom and equality. Must one come at the expense of the other? If so, which is more important? Can both freedom and equality be achieved? Or is perhaps neither desirable in place of some other ideal? With the knowledge gained by exploring these questions, we will be ready to take on the complexity of politics around the world.

What Is Comparative Politics?

Before we go any further, we must identify what comparative politics is. **Politics** is often defined as the struggle in any group for power that will give one or more persons the ability to make decisions for the larger group. This group may range from a small organization up to an entire country or even the entire global population. Politics can be found everywhere there is organization and power; for example, we may speak of "office politics" when we are talking about relations and power within a business. Political scientists in particular concentrate on the struggle for leadership and power for the larger community. Politics is the struggle for the authority to make decisions that will affect the public as a whole. It is therefore hard to separate the idea of politics from the idea of **power**, which is often defined as the ability to influence or impose one's will on others. Politics is thus about the competition for public power, and power is about the ability to extend one's will.

Within political science, comparative politics is a subfield that compares this struggle for power across countries. The method of comparing countries, it is believed, can better test our assumptions and theories than simply looking at our own country or by making arguments about cause and effect without any comprehensive evidence drawn over space and time. For example, one important puzzle we will return to frequently is why some countries are democratic while others are not. Why have politics in some countries resulted in power being more dispersed among the people while in other societies power is concentrated in the hands of a few? Or to be more specific, how come South Korea is democratic while North Korea is not? Looking at North Korea alone won't necessarily help us understand why South Korea went down a different path or vice versa. A comparison of the two, perhaps alongside similar cases in Asia, may better yield explanations. As should be clear, these are not simply academic questions. Democratic countries actively support the spread of like-minded regimes around the world, whether through diplomacy, aid, or war, but if it is unclear how or why it comes about, democracy becomes difficult or even dangerous to promote and perhaps foolhardy to take as inevitable. It is important to separate ideals from our concepts and methods and not let the former obscure the latter. Yet even as comparative politics can help inform and even challenge our ideals, it can provide new ways of thinking by highlighting alternatives to what we see and know, questioning our common assumption that there is one (right) way to organize political life.

The Comparative Method

If comparison is an important way to test our assumptions and shape our ideals, how we make those comparisons between cases is important. If there is no criterion or guide by which we gather information or draw conclusions, then our studies become little more than a collection of random details. Researchers thus often seek out puzzles—questions about politics with no clear answer—as a way to guide their research. From there, they rely on some **comparative method**—a way to make comparisons across cases and draw conclusions. By comparing countries or subsets within them, scholars hope to draw conclusions and make some generalizations that could be valid in other cases.

To return to our earlier question, let us say that we are interested in why democracy has failed to develop in some countries—a big puzzle if ever there was one. This argument was central to debates over going to war with Iraq and remains a contentious issue with different groups marshaling their own evidence or beliefs to make their case. We might begin our answer to this puzzle by looking at North Korea. Why has communism persisted in North Korea, even after it has declined almost everywhere else?

A convincing answer to this puzzle could tell scholars and policy makers a great deal, even guide our tense relations with this country in the future. But this kind of research also has its limitations. The study of one country alone can generate interesting hypotheses, but it alone is not enough to test those hypotheses. We call the single-case approach **inductive reasoning**—the means by which we go from studying a case to generating a hypothesis. Thus, we might study North Korea and perhaps conclude that the use of national-ism by those in power has been central to the persistence of authoritarian (nondemocratic) rule. In so concluding, we might suggest that future studies look at this relationship between nationalism and authoritarianism in other countries around the world. Inductive reasoning can therefore be a "building block" to greater theories in comparative politics.

From the other direction, comparative politics can also rely on **deductive reasoning**—starting with a puzzle and from there generating some hypothe-sis about cause and effect which will then be tested against a number of cases. Whereas inductive reasoning starts with the evidence as a way to undercover a hypothesis, deductive reasoning starts with the hypothesis and then seeks out the evidence. To contrast, whereas in our example of inductive reasoning we started with a case study of North Korea and ended with some general-ization about nationalism to test across other cases, in deductive reasoning we would start with our hypothesis about nationalism and then test that hypothesis by looking at a number of countries. By carrying out such stud-ies, we may find a **correlation**, or apparent association, between certain fac-tors or variables.[1]

Neither inductive nor deductive reasoning is particularly easy. First, polit-ical scientists are unable to control the variables in the cases they study. In other words, in our search for cause-and-effect relationships, we are unable to make true comparisons because each of our cases is quite different. By way of illustration, suppose a researcher wants to determine whether increased exercise by college students leads to higher grades. In studying the students who are her subjects, the researcher can control for a number of variables that might also affect grades, such as the students' diet, the amount of sleep they get, or any factor other than exercise that might influence the results. By controlling for these differences and making certain that many of these variables are the same across the subjects with the exception of exercise, the researcher can carry out her study with greater confidence.

But political science offers very few opportunities to control the variables because the variables are a function of real-world politics. Countries are amazingly diverse in terms of economics, culture, geography, resources, and political structures, and it is difficult to control for these differences. Even in a single-case study, variables change over time. At best, we can control as much as possible for variables that might otherwise distort our conclusions. If, for example, we want to understand why gun possession laws are so much less restrictive in the United States than in most other industrialized countries, we would be well served to compare the United States with those that have similar historical, economic, political, and social experiences, such as Canada and Australia, rather than Japan or South Africa. This allows us to more effectively control our variables, but it still leaves many variables uncontrolled and unaccounted for.

This leads us to a second problem. Political scientists are often hampered by a limited number of cases. In the natural sciences, research is often conducted with a huge number of cases—hundreds of stars or thousands of individuals. This breadth allows researchers to select their cases in such a way as to control their variables, and the large number of cases also prevents any single unusual case from distorting the findings. But in comparative politics, we are limited by the number of countries in the world—fewer than 200 at present, most of which did not exist a few centuries ago. If we attempt to control for differences by trying to find a number of cases that are similar (for example, industrialized democracies), our total body of cases will be relatively small.

A third problem in comparative politics concerns how we access the cases we do have. Even with the limited number of countries available to study, research is further hindered by the barriers that make countries unique. The information that political scientists seek is often not easy to acquire, necessitating "work in the field," conducting interviews or studying government archives in other countries. International travel requires time and money, and researchers may spend months or even years in the field. Interviewees may be unwilling to speak on sensitive issues or may distort information intentionally or unintentionally. Libraries and archives may be incomplete, or access to them restricted. As you might imagine, doing such research in more than one country is extremely challenging. A researcher may be able to read Russian and travel to Russia frequently, but if he wants to compare communism between the Soviet Union and China, it would be ideal to be able to read Chinese and conduct research in China as well. Few comparativists have the language skills, time, or resources to conduct field research in a number of countries. Almost none, for example, speak both Russian and Chinese. As a result, comparativists often master knowledge of a single country or language and rely on deductive reasoning. This limits the kinds of comparisons they can make. The specialization of comparativists also tends to congregate around those regions that can be easily studied at home and abroad. There are many comparativists who study Europe—not so many who study Indonesia, even though it is the fourth most populous country in the world. This also means that comparative politics is slow to shift its focus when new challenges and questions arise; just as intelligence agencies lack Arabic speakers, so too political science has few practitioners with necessary language skills.

Finally, the problems of variables and case selection are further muddied by issues of bias. By this we don't mean political bias, though sometimes that can be a problem as well. Rather, it is the question of how we select our cases. In the natural sciences, case selection is randomized to as great an extent as possible so that those cases under observation have not been chosen in advance to support one hypothesis or another. But for the reasons we mentioned above, such randomization is not possible in political science. Single-case studies are already influenced by the fact that comparativists study a country because they know its language or would prefer to travel there. Yet even if we rely instead on deductive reasoning—beginning with a hypothesis and then seeking out our cases—we can easily fall into the trap of **selection bias**.

For example, say we want to understand revolutions and we hypothesize that the main cause is a rapid growth in inequality. How should we select our cases? Most of us would respond by saying that we should find as many cases of revolution as possible and then look for whether they were preceded by such a change in inequality. But by looking only at cases of revolution, we miss all those cases where inequality may have grown but revolution *did not* take place. Indeed, there may be many more cases of inequality without revolution than those where revolution has taken place, disproving our hypothesis. So, better that we concentrate on what we think is our cause (growth in inequality) rather than what we think is our effect. While this may now seem obvious, it is a frequent mistake among scholars, who are often drawn to particular outcomes first and then work their way backward. To sum up, the study of comparative politics is limited by the direction in which we do our research (inductive versus deductive) and the range, quality, and selection of cases we have to do that research.

These are significant obstacles but they are not necessarily impossible to overcome. Though variables can't be perfectly controlled, certainly similar countries can be studied; secondary sources or other data can be used where language skills are lacking; and careful construction of our research can make certain we don't fall into the trap of selection bias. This done, we may draw some interesting conclusions, but we must be modest in what we may claim. Say, for example, that careful research finds that countries with a low rate of female literacy are less likely to be democracies than countries where female literacy is high. Why this would be the case is still not clear; our correlation, even if strong, still does not mean causality. For example, female literacy and authoritarianism may both be driven by some other variables, like poverty or inequality or ethnic diversity.

Even if we are confident enough to claim that in fact there is a causal relationship between female illiteracy and authoritarianism—a bold statement indeed—another problem looms. Which one is cause and which is effect? Is it perhaps that low rates of female literacy limit public participation such that democracy finds a limited audience, or perhaps that authoritarian leaders (by and large men) take little interest in promoting gender equality? This problem of cause and effect, known as **endogeneity**, is a major obstacle in any comparative research. Even if we are confident that we have found cause and effect, we can't easily ascertain which one is cause and which one is effect. Upon reflection, this is to be expected; one political scientist has called endogeneity "the motor of history," as causes and effects tend to evolve together, each transforming the other over time. Thus, early forms of democracy, literacy, and women's rights may well have gone hand in hand, each reinforcing and changing the others. This makes an elegant claim about cause and effect problematic, to say the least.[2]

Can We Make a Science of Comparative Politics?

We have so far elaborated all the ways in which comparative politics—and much of political science in general—makes for difficult study. In fact, you may well have concluded at this point that the notion of anything like a science of politics is hopeless. But it is precisely these kinds of concerns that have driven political science, and comparative politics within it, toward a more scientific approach. Whether this has or will yield significant benefits, and at what cost, is something we will consider next.

Political science and comparative politics have a long pedigree. In almost every major society there are masterworks of politics, prescribing rules or, less often, analyzing political behavior. In the West, the work of the philosopher Aristotle (384–322 B.C.E.) departed from the traditional emphasis on political ideals to conduct comparative research on existing political systems, eventually gathering and analyzing the constitutions of 158 Greek city-states. Aristotle's objective was less to determine the ideal political system than to understand the different forms of politics that actually existed and their relative strengths and weaknesses. With this approach, Aristotle conceived of an empirical (that is, observable and verifiable) science of politics with a practical purpose: statecraft, or how to govern. Aristotle was perhaps the first West-erner to separate the study of politics from that of philosophy.[3]

Unfortunately, Aristotle's early approach did not immediately lead to any real science of politics. For the next 1,800 years, discussions of politics remained embedded in the realm of philosophy, with the emphasis placed on how politics should be rather than on how politics was actually conducted. Ideals, rather than conclusions drawn from evidence, were the norm. Only with the works of the Italian Niccolò Machiavelli (1469–1527) did a compar-ative approach to politics truly emerge. Like Aristotle, he sought to analyze different political systems—those that existed around him as well as those that had preceded him in history, such as the Roman Empire—and even tried to make generalizations about success and failure. These findings, he believed, could then be applied by statesmen to avoid their predecessors' mistakes. Machiavelli's work reflects this pragmatism, dealing with the mechanics of government, diplomacy, military strategy, and power.[4]

Because of his emphasis on statecraft and empirical knowledge, Machi-avelli is often cited as the first modern political scientist, paving the way for other scholars. His writings came at a time when the medieval order was giv-ing way to the Renaissance, with its emphasis on science, rationalism, secu-larism, and real-world knowledge over abstract ideals. The resulting work over the next four centuries reinforced the idea that politics, like any other area of knowledge, could be developed as a logical, rigorous, and predictable science.

During those centuries, a number of major thinkers took up the compar-ative approach to the study of politics, which slowly retreated from moral, philosophical, or religious foundations. In the late sixteenth and early seven-teenth centuries, authors such as Thomas Hobbes and John Locke followed in Machiavelli's footsteps, advocating particular political systems but on the basis of empirical observation and analysis. They were followed in the eigh-teenth century by such scholars as Jean-Jacques Rousseau and Baron de Montesquieu, whose studies of the separation of power and civil liberties would directly influence the writing of the American Constitution and others to follow. The work of Karl Marx and Max Weber in the nineteenth and early twentieth centuries would further add to political science with analyses of the nature of political and economic organization and power. All these develop-ments reflected widespread changes in scholarly inquiry and were often a blend of political ideals with analytical concepts and some attempt at a sys-tematic method of study.

Thus, by the turn of the twentieth century, political science formally existed as a field of study, but it still looked much different from the way it does now. The study of comparative politics, while less focused on ideals or philosophy, resembled a kind of political journalism: largely descriptive, athe-oretical, and concentrated on Europe, which still dominated world politics through its empires. There was little in this work that resembled a comparative method.

The two world wars and the rise of the Cold War would mark a turning point in political science and comparative politics. There were several reasons for this. First, among universities there was a growing move toward applying more rigorous methods to studying human behavior, whether in sociology, economics, or politics. Second, the world wars raised serious questions about the ability of scholars to meaningfully contribute to an understanding of world affairs. The creation of new countries, the rise of fascism, and the failure of democracy throughout much of interwar Europe were vital concerns, but political scholarship did not seem to shed enough light on these issues and what they meant for international stability. Third, the Cold War with a rival Soviet Union, armed with nuclear weapons and revolutionary ideology, made understanding comparative politics a matter of survival. Finally, the postwar period saw a wave of technological innovation, such as early computers, that generated a widespread belief that through technological innovation many social problems could be recast as technical concerns, finally to be resolved through science. The fear of another war was thus married with a belief that science was an unmitigated good that had the answers to almost all problems. The question was simply making the science work.

Although these changes dramatically transformed the study of politics, the field itself remained a largely conservative discipline, taking capitalism and democracy as the ideal. In comparative politics these views were codified in what was known as **modernization theory**, which held that as societies developed, they would become capitalist democracies, converging around a shared set of values and characteristics. The United States and other Western countries were furthest ahead on this path, and the theory assumed that all countries would eventually catch up unless "diverted" by alternative systems such as communism (as fascism had done in past).

During the 1950s and 1960s, comparativists influenced by modernization theory expanded their research to include a wider number of cases. Field research, supported by government and private grants, became the normal means by which political scientists gathered data. New computer technologies combined with statistical methods were also applied to this expanding wealth of data. Finally, the subject of investigation shifted away from political institutions (such as legislatures and constitutions) and toward individual political behavior. This trend came to be known as the **behavioral revolution**. Behavioralism hoped to generate theories and generalizations that could help explain and even predict political activity. Ideally, this work would eventually lead to a "grand theory" of political behavior and modernization that would be valid across countries.

Major Thinkers in Comparative Politics	
Aristotle (384–322 B.C.E.)	First separated the study of politics from that of philosophy; used comparative method to study Greek city-states; in *The Politics*, conceived of an empirical study of politics with a practical purpose.
Niccolò Machiavelli (1469–1527)	Often cited as first modern political scientist because of his emphasis on statecraft and empirical knowledge; analyzed different political systems, believing the findings could be applied by statesmen; discussed his theories in *The Prince*.
Thomas Hobbes (1588–1679)	Developed the notion of a "social contract," whereby people surrender certain liberties in favor of order; advocated a powerful state in *Leviathan*.
John Locke (1632–1704)	Argued that private property is essential to individual freedom and prosperity; advocated a weak state in his *Two Treatises of Government*.
Charles Louis de Secondat, Baron de Montesquieu (1689–1755)	Studied government systems; advocated the separation of powers within government in *The Spirit of Laws*.
Jean-Jacques Rousseau (1712–1778)	Argued that citizens' rights are inalienable and cannot be taken away by the state; influenced the development of civil rights; discussed these ideas in *The Social Contract*.
Karl Marx (1818–1883)	Elaborated a theory of economic development and inequality in his book *Das Kapital*; predicted the eventual collapse of capitalism and democracy.
Max Weber (1864–1920)	Wrote widely on such topics as bureaucracy, forms of authority, and the impact of culture on economic and political development; developed many of these themes in *Economy and Society*.

Behavioralism and modernization theory were two different things—modernization theory a set of hypotheses about how countries develop, and behavioralism a set of methods with which to approach politics. However, the two were clearly linked by a sense of approaching politics in a more scientific manner to achieve certain policy outcomes.[5] Behavioralism also promoted deductive, large-scale research over the single-case study common in inductive reasoning. It seemed clear to many that political science, and comparative politics within it, would soon be a "real" science.

By the late 1970s, however, this enthusiasm began to meet resistance and significant obstacles. New theories and sophisticated methods of analysis increased scholars' knowledge about politics around the world, but this knowledge in itself did not lead to the expected breakthroughs. Those theories that had been developed, such as modernization theory, increasingly failed to match politics on the ground; rather than becoming more capitalist and more democratic, many newly independent countries collapsed in the face of violent conflict and revolution, to be replaced by authoritarianism that in no way reflected Western expectations or ideals. What had gone wrong?

Some critics charged that the behavioral revolution's obsession with appearing scientific had led the discipline astray by emphasizing methodology over knowledge and technical jargon over clarity. Others criticized the field for its ideological bias, arguing that comparativists were interested not in understanding the world but in prescribing the Western model of modernization. At worst, their work could be viewed as simply serving the foreign policy of the developed world. Since then, comparative politics, like all of political science, has grown increasingly fragmented. While few still embrace the old descriptive approach that dominated the earlier part of the century, there is no consensus about where scholarship is going and what research

---

IN FOCUS

Trends in Comparative Politics

Traditional approach	Emphasis on describing political systems and their various institutions.
Behavioral revolution	The shift from a descriptive study of politics to one that emphasizes causality, explanation, and prediction; places greater emphasis on the political behavior of individuals as opposed to larger political structures and on quantitative over qualitative methodology; modernization theory predominant.
Postbehavioralism	Rejection of a grand theory of politics; criticism of modernization theory as biased and inaccurate; diversity of methods and political approaches, emphasizing such issues as gender, culture, environment, and globalization.

methods or analytical concepts are most fruitful. This lack of consensus has led to several main lines of conflict.

Methodological debates turn on how best to gather and analyze data. Traditional "area studies" scholars continue to emphasize the importance of deep, long-term investigations of particular countries or regions, relying on what is known as **qualitative** evidence and methodology. In their view, the behavioral revolution in many ways led the discipline astray by attempting to oversimplify a complex and culturally diverse world. In contrast, others reject the qualitative approach as failing to contribute to the accumulation of knowledge and being little better than the description that dominated the field a century ago. These advocates of a **quantitative** approach favor a greater use of statistical analysis as well as mathematical models often drawn from economics. For this group, the failing of the behavioral revolution is that this revolution is not yet complete.

A second related debate concerns rationality. Are human beings rational, in the sense that their behavior conforms to some generally understandable behavior? Some say yes. These advocates rely on what is known as **rational choice** or **game theory** to study the rules and games by which politics is played and how we seek to realize our preferences (like voting, choosing a party, or supporting a revolution). Such formal models can, ideally, lead not only to explanation, but even to prediction—a basic element of science. Naturally, many qualitative political scientists are skeptical of this view. They argue that human beings are essentially unpredictable and that the emphasis on individual rationality discounts the importance of historical complexity or idiosyncratic behavior.

As these debates have continued, the world around us has changed. The Cold War came to an end, something neither qualitative nor quantitative scholars anticipated (or really even took under consideration). Religion reemerged

---

IN FOCUS

Quantitative Method vs. Qualitative Method

Quantitative method	Gathering of statistical data across a large number of countries in order to look for correlations and test hypotheses about cause and effect. Emphasis on breadth over depth.
Qualitative method	Mastery of a limited number of cases through the detailed study of their history, language, and culture. Emphasis on depth over breadth.

as an important component in politics around the globe—again, a force that modernization theory (and research focused on Europe) told us was on the wane. New economic powers emerged in Asia, coinciding with democracy in some cases but not others. Terrorism resurfaced with spectacular results. It seemed that political scientists, whatever their persuasion, had little to contribute to many of these issues and were unable to prepare us for their implications.

Where does this leave us now? Does political science or comparative politics matter, or is it simply time to chuck this book in the trash? In recent years there have been some signs of progress. Quantitative scholars recognize that careful scholarship is possible with qualitative approaches, recognizing that simply expressing information in the form of numbers does not make it "scientific," nor does purely qualitative information necessarily lack rigor. Similarly, traditional area scholars are making more use of statistics and more careful methodology to ensure that their research is more than simply description that cannot be built upon by others. New models, like those from game theory, can be employed with both quantative and qualitative material. Some scholars speak optimistically of an integration of statistics, "narrative" (case studies), and formal models, each contributing to the other.[6] Finally, all sides have recognized that the discipline has sometimes lost touch with real-world concerns, become inaccessible to laypersons, and failed to speak to those who make decisions about policy—whether voters or elected leaders. In the past few years there has been an increasing emphasis on reconnecting political science to central policy questions and also reengaging political ideals, something largely discarded in the behavioral revolution as "unscientific."

This new emphasis is not a call for comparativists' research to be biased in favor of some ideal (though some raise this concern); rather, comparative politics should not be simply about what we *can* study or what we *want* to study but also how our research can reach people and help them be better citizens and leaders. After decades of asserting that political science should have an objective and scientifically neutral approach, this call for greater relevance and contribution to the ideals of civic life represents a dramatic change for many scholars, but relevance and rigor are not at odds. They are in fact central to a meaningful political science and comparative politics.

A Guiding Concept: Political Institutions

A goal of this textbook is to provide a way to compare and analyze politics around the world in the aftermath of recent changes and uncertainties. Given the long-standing debates within comparative politics, how can we organize our ideas and information? One way is through a guiding concept, a way of looking at the world that highlights some important features while deem-phasizing others. There is certainly no one right way of doing this; any guide, like a lens, will sharpen some features while distorting others. With that said, our guiding concept is institutions, which were defined at the beginning of this chapter as organizations or patterns of activity that are self-perpetuating and valued for their own sake. In other words, an institution is something so embedded in people's lives as a norm or value that it is not easily dislodged or changed. People see an institution as central to their lives, and as a result, the institution commands and generates legitimacy. Institutions serve as the rules, norms, and values that give meaning to human activity.

Consider an example from outside politics. We often hear in the United States that baseball is an American institution. What exactly does this mean? In short, baseball is viewed by Americans not simply as a game but as some-thing valued for its own sake, a game that helps define society. Yet few Americans would say that soccer is a national institution. The reason is prob-ably clear: soccer lacks the kind of public perception of its indispensability that baseball has. Whereas soccer is simply a game, baseball is part of what defines America and Americans. Even Americans who don't like baseball would probably say that America wouldn't be the same without it. Indeed, even at the local level, teams command such legitimacy that the mere threat of their moving to another city raises a hue and cry. The Brooklyn Dodgers moved to Los Angeles in 1958, yet many in New York still consider them "their" team half a century later. For many Canadians, while baseball is important, it is clearly hockey that is viewed as a national institution, thought of as "Canada's Game" and an inextricable part of Canadian iden-tity and history. In Europe and much of the world, soccer reigns as a pre-mier social institution, with teams provoking such fervent loyalty that fan violence is quite common. As a result of this legitimacy and seeming indis-pensability, institutions command authority and can influence human behavior; we accept and conform to institutions and support, rather than challenge, them. Woe to the American, Canadian, or European who derides the national sport!

Another example is directly connected to politics. In many countries, democracy is an institution: it is not merely a means to compete over politi-cal power but a vital element in people's lives, bound up in the very way in which they define themselves. Democracy is part and parcel of collective iden-tity, and some democratic countries and their people would not be the same without it. Even if cynical about democracy in practice, its citizens will defend the institution when it is under threat and even die for it. In many other coun-tries, this is not the case: democracy is absent and unknown or weakly insti-tutionalized and unstable. People in such countries do not define themselves by democracy's presence or absence, and so democracy's future there is insecure. However, these same people might owe a similar allegiance to a different set of institutions, such as their ethnic group or religion. Clearly, there is no single, uniform set of institutions that holds power over people all around the world, and understanding the differences is central to the study of comparative politics.

What about a physical object or place? Can that, too, be an institution? Many would argue that the World Trade Center was an American institution—not just a set of office buildings, but structures representing American values. The same thing can be said about the Pentagon. When terrorists attacked these buildings on September 11, 2001, they did so not simply to cause a great loss of life but also to clearly indicate that their hostility was directed against America itself—its institutions as they shape and represent the American way of life and the U.S. relationship to the outside world. Israelis and Palestinians similarly struggle over the future of Jerusalem, which Palestinians and Israelis both claim as their capital. The historical, political, and religious significance of the city is what is key—for both groups, the city is an institution that is central to their identity and ideals.

In general, however, institutions are not physical structures. Because they are embedded in each of us, in how we see the world and what we think is valuable and important, it is difficult to change or eliminate institutions. When institutions are threatened, people will rush to their defense and even re-create them when they are shattered. This bond is the glue of society. However, one problem that institutions pose is this very "stickiness," in that people may come to resist even necessary change because they have difficulty accepting the idea that certain institutions have outlived their value. Thus, while institutions certainly can and do change, their very nature is one of great perseverance.

Politics is full of institutions. The basic political structures of any country are composed of institutions: the army, the police, the legislature, and the courts, to name a few. We obey them not only because we think it is in our self-interest to do so but because we see them as legitimate ways to conduct politics. Taxation is a good example. In many Western democracies, income taxes are an institution; we may not like them, but we pay them nonetheless. Is this because we are afraid of going to jail if we fail to do so? Perhaps. But research indicates that a major source of tax compliance is people's belief that taxation is a legitimate way to fund the programs that society needs. We pay, in other words, when we believe that it is the right thing to do, a norm. In contrast, in societies where taxes are not institutionalized, tax evasion tends to be rampant; people view taxes as illegitimate and those who pay as suckers. Similarly, where electoral politics is weakly institutionalized, people support elections only when their preferred candidate wins, and they cry foul or riot when the opposition gains power.

IN FOCUS

Institutions . . .

- Are any organization or pattern of activity that is self-perpetuating and valued for its own sake.
- Embody norms or values considered central to people's lives and thus are not easily dislodged or changed.
- Set the stage for political behavior by influencing how politics is conducted.
- Vary from country to country.
- Are exemplified by the army, taxation, elections, and the state.

Institutions are a useful way to approach the study of politics because they set the stage for political behavior. Because institutions generate norms and values, they favor and allow certain kinds of political activity and not others. As a result, political institutions are critical because they influence politics, and how political institutions are constructed will have a profound effect on how politics is conducted.

In many ways, our institutional approach takes us back to the study of comparative politics as it existed before the 1950s. Prior to the behavioral revolution, political scientists spent much of their time documenting the institutions of politics, often without asking how those institutions actually shaped politics. The behavioral revolution that followed emphasized cause and effect but turned its attention toward political actors and their calculations, resources, or strategies. The actual institutions were seen as largely unimportant. The recent return to the study of institutions in many ways combines these two traditions. From behavioralism, institutional approaches take their emphasis on cause-and-effect relationships, something that will be prevalent throughout this book. However, institutions are not simply the product of individual political behavior; they can and do have a powerful effect on how politics functions. In other words, institutions are not merely the result of politics; they can also be an important cause.

As recent events have shown us, there is still a tremendous amount of institutional variation around the world that needs to be recognized and understood. This textbook will map some of the basic institutional differences between countries, acknowledging their diversity while pointing to some basic features that allow us to compare and evaluate them. By studying political institutions, we can hope to gain a better sense of the political landscape across countries.

A Guiding Ideal: Reconciling Freedom and Equality

At the start of this chapter, we spoke about analytical concepts (such as institutions), methods (such as inductive or deductive, quantitative or qualitative), and ideals about politics. Politics was defined as the struggle for power in order to make decisions for society. The concept of institutions gives us a way to organize our study by investigating the different ways that struggle can be shaped. Yet this begs an important question: People may struggle for political power, but what are they fighting for? What is it they seek to achieve once they have gained power? This is where ideals come in, and we will concentrate on one core debate that lies at the heart of all politics: the struggle between freedom and equality. This struggle has existed as long as human beings have lived in organized communities, and it may be that these are values that are more than ideals, that are part of our evolutionary makeup.

Politics is bound up in the struggle between individual freedom and collective equality and how these ideals are to be reconciled. Of course, these two terms can mean very different things to different people, and so it is important to define each of them. When we speak of **freedom**, we are talking about the ability of an individual to act independently, without fear of restriction or punishment by the state or other individuals or groups in society. It encompasses such concepts as free speech, free assembly, freedom of religion, and other civil liberties. **Equality** refers to a shared material standard of individuals within a community, society, or country. The relationship between equality and freedom is typically viewed in terms of justice or injustice—a measurement of whether our ideals have been met.

Freedom and equality are tightly interconnected, and the relationship between the two shapes politics, power, and debates over justice. What is unclear, however, is whether one must come at the expense of the other. Greater personal freedom, for example, may imply a smaller role for the state and limits on its powers to do such things as redistribute income through welfare and taxes. As a result, inequality may increase as individual freedom trumps the desire for greater collective equality. This growing inequality can in turn undermine freedom if too many people feel as though the political system no longer cares about their material needs. Even if this discontent is not a danger, there remains the question of whether society as a whole has an obligation to help the poor—an issue of justice. The United States, as we shall see, has one of the highest degrees of both personal freedom and economic inequality in the world. Should this be a cause of concern? Is it right?

At the other end, a primary focus on equality may erode freedom. Demands for greater material equality may lead a government to take greater control of private property and personal wealth, all in the name of redistribution for the "greater good." Yet when economic and political powers are concentrated in one place, individual freedom may be threatened since people control fewer private resources of their own. In the Soviet Union under communism, for example, all economic power was held by the state, giving it the ability to control people's lives—where they lived, the education they received, the jobs they held, the money they earned.

Are freedom and equality by nature zero-sum, where the gain of one represents the loss of the other? Not necessarily. Some would assert that freedom and equality can also serve to reinforce each other, with material security helping to secure certain political rights, and vice versa. In addition, while a high degree of state power may weaken individual freedom, the state may also act as the very guarantor of these rights. Finally, the meaning of freedom and equality may change over time, as the definition of each shifts through changes in the material world and in the fabric of our values. For some, managing freedom and/or equality necessitates some, or perhaps a great deal of, centralized political power. Others view such power as the very impediment to freedom and/or equality. We will consider these debates to a greater extent when we consider political ideologies in subsequent chapters.

In short, politics is driven by the ideal of reconciling individual freedom and collective equality. This inevitably leads to questions of power—influencing others or imposing one's will—and the role of the people in political life. Who should be empowered to make decisions about freedom and equality? Should power be centralized or decentralized, public or private? When does power become a danger to others, and how can this be prevented? Each political system must address these questions and in so doing determine where political power shall reside, and how much. And each political system creates a unique set of institutions to structure political power, shaping the role that the people play in politics, and their debates about justice.

In Sum: Looking Ahead and Thinking Carefully

Politics is the struggle for power in any organization, and comparative politics is the study of this struggle around the world. Over the past centuries, the study of politics has evolved from philosophy to a field that emphasizes empirical research and the quest to explain and even predict politics. This approach has limitations: in spite of the earlier desire to emulate the natural sciences, comparative politics, like political science as a whole, has not been able to generate any "grand theory" of political behavior. Yet the need to study politics remains as important as ever; dramatic changes over the past twenty years have called on comparativists to shed light on these developments and concerns.

Political institutions can help us organize this task. Institutions generate norms and values, and different configurations of institutions lead to different forms of political activity. Institutions can help us map the landscape of politics. If institutions serve as a map to political activity, then the goal of that activity is to reconcile the competing values of individual freedom and collective equality. All political groups, including countries, must reconcile these two forces, determining where power should reside and in whose hands. In the chapters to come, we will return to this question of freedom and equality and to the way in which these values influence, and are influenced by, institutions.

A final thought before we conclude on how to use all this information. Much of our discussion in this chapter has been about the controversies in how best to study politics—what method? What concepts? What role for ideals? In all of this it may seem that we have gained little understanding of how to "do" political science well. If scholars can't agree about the best way to analyze politics, what hope do we have of making sense of the world? Recently, the work by the political scientist Philip Tetlock provided some insight. Thinking about the goal of predictability in the social sciences, Tetlock conducted a long-term survey of a number of scholars and policy makers, asking them to forecast the likelihood of specific world events (such as a revolution in particular country or a war between rivals). He also conducted psychological surveys of those same individuals, hypothesizing that certain personal characteristics, rather than ideological or methodological differences, would be most strongly correlated with the ability to predict politics well. The result? Tetlock divided his subjects into two basic categories, borrowed from the late philosopher Isaiah Berlin: hedgehogs and foxes. Hedgehogs know one big thing; they tend to look for a single overarching explanation that can explain many different political events and are more likely to reject information that runs counter to their beliefs. Foxes are less confident in their views, with many small ideas that are cobbled together and subject to frequent revision. As you might suspect, hedgehogs are much worse predictors of world events and are more interested into trying to fit the world into their preconceptions than revise their beliefs on the basis of new information.[7]

We would do well to consider these findings. The most fruitful approach to comparative politics is to be skeptical not simply of others—that's the easy part—but of what *we* believe and take for granted as well. We should be ready to reconsider our beliefs in the face of new evidence and arguments and to remember that every explanation in this book is a conjecture and subject to revision if we can find better evidence. With this approach, by the end of this course you will be able to draw your own conclusions about the contours of politics and what combination of values might construct a better political order.

So, drop your assumptions about how the world works, and let's begin.

NOTES ───

1. Gary King, Robert Keohane, and Sidney Verba, *Designing Social Inquiry* (Princeton, NJ: Princeton University Press, 1994).

2. Adam Przeworski, "Is a Science of Comparative Politics Possible?" in *Oxford Handbook of Comparative Politics*, Charles Boix and Susan Stokes, eds. (Oxford; New York: Oxford University Press, 2007).

3. Aristotle, *The Politics*, T. A. Sinclair, trans. (New York: Viking, 1992).

4. Niccolò Machiavelli, *The Prince*, W. K. Marriott, trans. (New York: Knopf, 1992).

5. For more on the behavioral revolution, see Robert A. Dahl, "The Behavioral Approach in Political Science: Epitaph for a Monument to a Successful Protest," *American Political Science Review*, 55, no. 4 (December 1961), pp. 763–772.

6. David Laitin, "Comparative Politics: The State of the Subdiscipline" in *Political Science: The State of the Discipline*, Ira Katznelson and Helen V. Milner, eds. (New York: Norton, 2002).

7. Philip Tetlock, *Expert Political Judgment* (Princeton, NJ: Princeton University Press, 2005).

2 STATES

KEY CONCEPTS

- The state is a central institution in comparative politics, as the centralization of violence over a territory.

- Regimes guide states by serving as the fundamental rules and norms of politics.

- Government is the leadership or elite in charge of running the state.

- Political legitimacy can take several forms: charismatic, traditional, and rational-legal.

- States can vary in autonomy and capacity, and this can shape their power at home and abroad.

We begin our study of the basic institutions of politics by looking at the state. This discussion is often difficult for North Americans, who are not used to thinking about politics in terms of centralized political power. Indeed, when Americans in particular think of the word *state*, they typically conjure up the idea of local, not centralized, politics.[1] But for most people around the world, "the state" refers to centralized authority, the locus of power. In this chapter, we will break down the basic institutions that make up states and discuss how states manage freedom and equality and distribute power toward achieving that authority. The chapter will define what states are and what they comprise, distinguishing a state from a government or a regime. We will also consider the origins of states themselves. For most of human history, politics was built on organizations other than states, and myriad forms of authority existed around the world. Yet now only states remain. Why? In other words, we can consider states as an effect—what caused them to come into existence?

Once we have discussed the nature and origins of the state, we will look at some different ways in which states can be compared. This discussion will include an analysis of different forms of legitimacy that give a state power and the actual levels of power itself. Can we speak of states as weak or strong? And if so, how would we measure that strength or weakness? To answer this question, we will make a distinction between state capacity and state autonomy, and how this might differ across cases and policy areas. Here, we consider states as a cause, in how they can shape other institutions. With these ideas more clearly in hand, we will return to our theme of individual freedom and collective equality and consider the future of the state itself.

Defining the State

What exactly do we mean by the term *state*? Political scientists, drawing on the work of the German scholar Max Weber, typically define the **state** in its most basic terms as the organization that maintains a monopoly of violence over a territory.[2] At first glance, this may seem to be a rather severe definition of what a state is or does, but a bit of explanation should help flesh out this concept. One of the most important elements of a state is what we call **sovereignty**, or the ability to carry out actions or policies within a territory independently from external actors or internal rivals. In other words, a state needs to be able to act as the primary authority over its territory and the people who live there, setting forth laws and rights, resolving disputes between people and organizations, and generating domestic security.

To achieve this, a state needs power, typically (but not only) physical power. If a state cannot defend its territory from outside actors such as other states, then it runs the risk that those rivals will interfere, inflicting damage, taking its territory, or destroying the state outright. Similarly, if the state faces powerful opponents within its own territory, such as organized crime or rebel movements, it runs the risk that its rules and policies will be undermined. Thus, to secure control, a state must be armed. To protect against international rivals, states need armies. And in response to domestic rivals, states need a police force. In fact, the very word *police* comes from the old French word meaning "to govern."

A state is thus a set of institutions that seeks to wield the majority of force within a territory, establishing order and deterring challengers from inside and out. In so doing, it provides security for its subjects by limiting the danger of external attack and internal crime and disorder—both of which are seen as threats to the state and its citizens. In some ways, a state (especially a nondemocratic one) is a kind of protection racket—demanding money in return for security and order, staking out turf, defending its clients from rivals, settling internal disputes, and punishing those who do not pay.[3]

But most states are far more complex than simply being an entity that applies force. Unlike criminal rackets, the state is made up of a large number of institutions that are engaged in the process of turning political ideas into policy. Laws and regulations, property rights, health and labor, environment and transportation are but a few things that typically fall under the responsibility of the state. Moreover, the state is a set of institutions (ministries, departments, offices, army, police) that society deems necessary to achieve basic goals regarding freedom and equality. When there is a lack of agreement on these goals, the state must attempt to reconcile different views and seek (or impose) consensus. And unlike a criminal racket, which people obey out of fear or pure self-interest, the state is typically valued for its own sake. The public views the state as legitimate, vital, and appropriate: Who can imagine politics without it? States are thus strongly institutionalized and not easily changed. Leaders and policies may come and go, but the state remains, even in the face of crisis, turmoil, or revolution. Although destruction through war or civil conflict can eliminate states altogether, even this outcome is unusual and states are soon re-created. Thus, the state is defined as a monopoly of force over a given territory, but it is also the set of political institutions that create standards through which conflicts related to freedom and equality can be resolved. It is, if you will, the machinery of politics, establishing order and turning politics into policy. Thus many social scientists argue that the state, as a bundle of institutions, is an important causal variable in such things as variations in economic development or the rise of democracy.

A few other terms that are often used with regard to political organization need to be defined here. Although often used interchangeably with the concept of the state, they are in fact separate institutions that help define and direct the state. First, we should make a distinction between the state and a **regime**, which is defined as the fundamental rules and norms of politics. More specifically, a regime embodies long-term goals regarding individual freedom and collective equality, where power should reside and how it should be used. At the most basic level, we can speak of a democratic regime or a nondemocratic one. In a democratic regime, the rules and norms of politics emphasize a large role for the public in governance, as well as certain individual rights or liberties. A nondemocratic regime, in contrast, will limit public participation in favor of

---

IN FOCUS

The State Is . . .

- The monopoly of force over a given territory.
- A set of political institutions to generate and carry out policy.
- Typically highly institutionalized.
- Sovereign.
- Characterized by such institutions as an army, police, taxation, a judiciary, and a social welfare system.

those in power. Both types of regimes can vary in the extent to which power is centralized and the relationship between freedom and equality. The democratic regime of the United States is not the same as that of Canada; the nondemocratic regime of China is not the same as that of Cuba or Syria. Some of these regime differences can be found in basic documents such as constitutions, but often the rules and norms that distinguish one regime from another are unwritten and implicit, requiring careful study.

In other words, regimes are an important component of the larger state framework. Regimes do not easily or quickly change, although they can be transformed or altered, usually by dramatic social events such as a revolution or a national crisis. Most revolutions, in fact, can be seen as revolts not against the state or even the leadership, but against the current regime—to overthrow the old rules and norms and replace them with new ones. For example, France refers to its current regime as the Fifth Republic. Ever since the French Revolution overthrew the monarchy in 1789, each French republic has been characterized by a separate regime, embodied in the constitution and the broader political rules that shape politics. In another example, South Africa's transition to democracy in the 1990s involved a change of regime as the white-dominated system of apartheid gave way to one that provides democratic rights to all South Africans.

In some nondemocratic countries where politics is dominated by a single individual, observers may use the term *regime* to refer to that leader, emphasizing the view that all decisions flow from that one person. Or as King Louis XIV of France famously put it, *L'état, c'est moi* (I am the state). When the Bush administration spoke of its desire for "regime change" in Iraq and Iran, our broader definition can apply as well, because the objective was not simply to eliminate the leadership but to facilitate or install democratic institutions. This returns us to the question of cause and effect. Regimes can emerge through centuries of slow development but can also be the product of sudden revolutionary change. How regimes become institutionalized is not clear; it is easy to write a constitution, as we saw in Iraq, but much harder to make it stick, especially if it is meant to displace a previous set of rules and norms and fundamentally transform politics. If anything, some political scientists have observed that regime change is most effective when there is a general public attachment to the state that can bind people together through such periods of transition.[4]

IN FOCUS

A Regime Is . . .

- Norms and rules regarding individual freedom and collective equality, the locus of power, and the use of that power.
- Institutionalized, but can be changed by dramatic social events such as a revolution.
- Categorized at the most basic level as either democratic or authoritarian.
- Often embodied in a constitution.

To recap, if the state is a monopoly of force and a set of political institutions to secure the population and generate policy, then the regime is defined as the norms and rules regarding the proper relationship between freedom and equality and the use of power toward that end. To use an analogy, if the state is the machinery of politics, like a personal computer, then one can think of a regime as its software, the programming that defines its capabilities. Each computer runs differently, and more or less productively, depending on the software installed.

This brings us to a third term to add to our understanding of state and regime: *government*. **Government** can be defined as the leadership or elite in charge of running the state. If the state is the machinery of politics, and the regime its programming, then the government acts as its operator. The government may consist of democratically elected legislators, presidents, and prime ministers, or it may be leaders who gained office through force or other nondemocratic means. Whatever their path to power, governments all hold particular ideas regarding freedom and equality and attempt to use the state to realize those ideas. But few governments are able to act with complete autonomy in this regard. Democratic and nondemocratic governments must confront the existing regime in the norms and values of politics that have built up over time. Push too hard against an existing regime, and resistance, rebellion, or collapse may occur. For example, Mikhail Gorbachev's attempt to transform the Soviet Union's regime in the 1980s contributed to that country's dissolution.

In part because of the power of regimes, governments tend to be weakly institutionalized; that is, those in power are not viewed by the public as irreplaceable, such that the country would collapse without them (Figure 2.1). In democratic regimes, governments are replaced fairly frequently, and even in nondemocratic settings, those who rule are continuously threatened by rivals and their own mortality. Governments come and go, whereas regimes and states may live on for decades or centuries with a great degree of continuity.

Finally, we have the term **country**, which can be seen as shorthand for all the concepts so far discussed—state, government, regime—as well as the people who live within that political system. We will often speak about various countries in this textbook, and when we do, we are referring to the entire political entity and its citizens.

IN FOCUS

Government Is . . .

- The leadership or elite in charge of running the state.
- Weakly institutionalized.
- Often characterized by elected officials, such as a president or prime minister, or unelected officials, such as in authoritarianism.
- Limited by the existing regime.

Figure 2.1 **STATE, REGIME, AND GOVERNMENT**

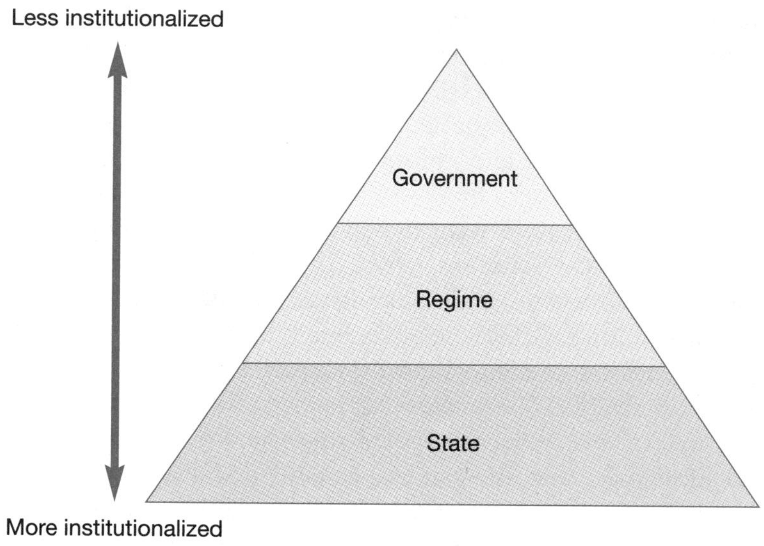

Governments are relatively less institutionalized than regimes and states. Governments may come and go, while regimes and states usually have more staying power.

The Origins of Political Organization

So far we have noted that modern politics is defined by states, which monopolize force and generate and realize policy. This political machinery is given direction by a particular regime and by the government in power. Governments generate short-term goals regarding freedom and equality, which are in part based on an existing regime that provides an institutionalized set of norms and values about politics. This combination, linking state, regime, and government, is relatively new in human history. This is not to say that there is no history of political organization. On the contrary, for thousands of years, human beings have formed collective groups, ranging from relatively simple and fluid gatherings to highly complex systems that incorporated hundreds of thousands or even millions of individuals and lasted for centuries. Complex political forms took root anywhere that people moved from nomadic to sedentary life. But as we look over the face of the earth in this millennium, we see that the various forms of political organization that dominated human history have for the most part disappeared. The globe is now clearly demarcated by only one type of political organization—the state—that has displaced virtually all other political structures, and within the course of only a few hundred years. Every person and piece of habitable property on the face of the earth is the subject of some state.

But where did states come from, and why have they displaced all other forms of political organization? Why are there no longer parts of the world controlled by city-states, tribes, or empires? To answer this puzzle, we first need to go back into human history and discuss the origins of political organization. How human beings have come together and how they have organized their lives will also be a central issue later on as we look at the role of democracy and nondemocratic rule in the modern world. It would appear that states have been able to dispatch all other forms of political organization, in spite of the long history of these other forms. By understanding the origins and power of states, we can better grasp their functions in the modern world. We can also consider that just as human beings once existed without states, states might themselves be replaced in the future by one or more other forms of political organization.

Archeology and history tell us that human beings have long organized into political units, although our findings do not necessarily explain why humans organized in the first place beyond being in a small group. For political scientists interested in current affairs, this original motivation may be of little concern, but for anthropologists and others focused on human history and social evolution, the question is important. There are a number of competing explanations as to why humans organize beyond family or tribe. One important factor is probably environment and agriculture. Where people were able to domesticate plants and animals (a much more difficult process than one might imagine), they moved from a nomadic hunter-gatherer existence to one of sedentary living. Concepts that would have previously been meaningless, such as territory, crops, homes, and personal property, suddenly became life-or-death issues.

In addition, the rise of agriculture and domestication allowed for the creation of food surpluses, again a great change from the hunter-gatherer days. Food surpluses allowed for greater human specialization: some people could forgo farming and pursue other activities, such as making useful goods that could be exchanged for food and other items. But while agriculture and a sedentary existence created property and specialization, it also created, or at least increased, human inequality. In a system of greater specialization that relies on a wide array of talents, some individuals will clearly benefit more than others; wealth and power inevitably become unequally distributed.

This time period is when political organization most likely had its beginning. As societies grow larger, more specialized, and more unequal, they require new mechanisms to handle disputes. Those with economic surpluses seek to protect their riches from theft. Those without surpluses seek a greater share of the group's resources. And both fear attack by outside groups or internal competitors that might covet their lands, crops, and homes. Because of such human innovations as agriculture, the very concepts of individualism versus the collective, of freedom versus equality, probably first arose. Who gets what? Who has the right to do what? And how should these decisions be made and enforced? Having to confront and reconcile freedom and equality in turn raised questions about where power should reside and toward what end. Political organizations formed to reconcile these competing demands and concerns. Once humans could conceptualize the idea of fairness, politics emerged.

Organizations could settle or prevent disputes between individuals, generating early notions of law and justice. Political organizations could also establish rights, punish those found guilty of breaking rules or violating others' rights, and raise a force capable of resisting outside attack. To carry out these activities, though, political organizations required revenue, creating the need for taxation. Clearly, then, many of the elements of modern politics emerged in the distant past, over and over again, around the world.

One thing that remains unclear, however, is whether these political organizations emerged through consensus or through force. In other words, did political systems develop because some people managed to impose their will on others, installing themselves as chiefs or kings and using violence to impose their will? Or did people willingly form political systems as a way to overcome the anarchy that would otherwise result in a world that lacked central authority? In the absence of evidence, philosophers have long debated this issue. Some, like the philosopher Thomas Hobbes, believed that human beings voluntarily enter into a "social contract" or agreement among themselves to create a single political authority to overcome anarchy, where neither freedom nor equality is ensured. In return for giving up many of their rights, people gained security and a foundation on which to build a civilization. In contrast, Jean-Jacques Rousseau believed that human beings were in essence "noble savages" whose lives were compassionate and egalitarian. It was rather civilization, and the rise of the state, that corrupted this life by institutionalizing a system of inequality. Each of these competing visions provides a different interpretation of civilization and political organization, though both emphasize that states must be subject to the people, and not the other way around.

For a long time scholars have assumed that Rousseau's vision of human political development was more accurate than Hobbes's vision of "a war of all against all," and that people lived in relative harmony and equality until technological innovation created more sedentary, more unequal, and more violent lives. In addition, Rousseau's vision often argued that the consequent shift to political organization was largely consensual, a response to these new challenges. More recent research, however, indicates that neither is correct. Pre-state societies were very likely more violent than states in the present. By one estimate, up to a quarter of the population died at the hands of others. States appear to have emerged out of this constant warfare as one set of individuals gained the upper hand over others; at the same time, state coercion also promised an end to endemic violence, which provided a form of legitimacy. Whereas we once speculated that technical innovation, civilization, and human political organization were the sources of violence, it now appears to be the opposite.[5]

Through this mixture of coercion and consensus, complex organizations began to emerge about 8,000 years ago in the Middle East, bearing the political hallmarks of politics that exist to this day, such as taxation, bureaucracy, laws, military force, and leadership. Some of these political units were relatively small, such as the city-states that emerged in ancient Greece some 2,700 years ago. In other cases, large and highly sophisticated empires emerged, as in China, South America, the Middle East, and Africa. Across these political systems, economic relations were based on agricultural production, with more specialized goods and trade as secondary activities. And unlike in modern countries, the borders of these early political systems were often undefined. Beyond their authority, large portions of the inhabited world possessed no form of complex political organization that would resemble a modern state.[6]

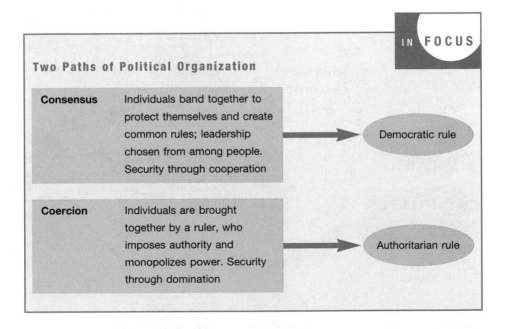

IN FOCUS

Two Paths of Political Organization

Consensus Individuals band together to protect themselves and create common rules; leadership chosen from among people. Security through cooperation → Democratic rule

Coercion Individuals are brought together by a ruler, who imposes authority and monopolizes power. Security through domination → Authoritarian rule

The Rise of the Modern State

This diversity of political systems eventually gave way to the modern state, which first arrived in Europe. Why the modern state first emerged in Europe and came to dominate the world is uncertain, but it may in part be due to historical chance and the curious advantage of backwardness. Two thousand years ago, Europe, like other parts of the world, was dominated by a single large empire—in this case, the Roman Empire. Spanning thousands of miles across western Europe to North Africa and Egypt, the Roman Empire developed a highly complex political system that tied together millions of people and generated an advanced infrastructure of cities, laws, trade, knowledge, and roads. After a thousand years, however, the Roman Empire eventually declined, succumbing to the pressures of overexpansion and increased attacks by rival forces. By the fifth century C.E., Rome itself was sacked by invaders.

As the Roman Empire collapsed, the complex political institutions and the other benefits that had extended across its territory largely disappeared, particularly in western Europe (Figure 2.2). The security generated by imperial

Figure 2.2 EUROPE IN THE TWELFTH CENTURY

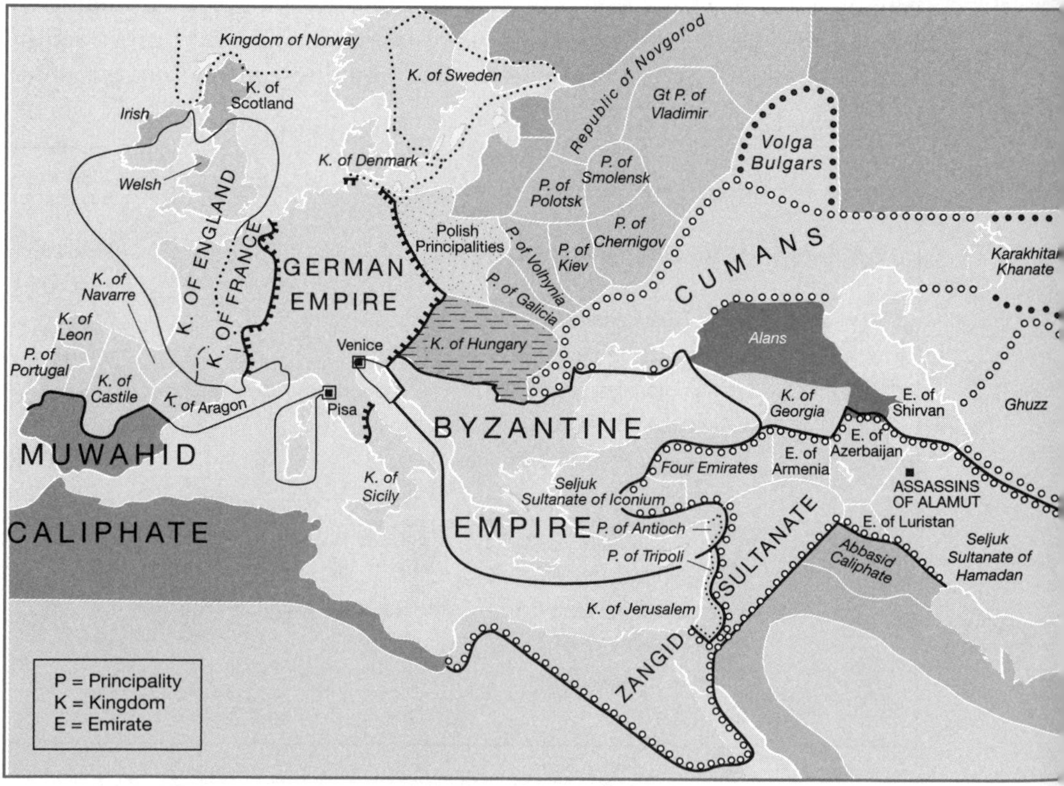

control evaporated, replaced by roving bands of marauders. Roads and the other basic forms of infrastructure that people depended on eroded. Rules and regulations fragmented and lost their power. The knowledge and technology accumulated under the empire was lost or forgotten, and the advanced system of trade and travel between communities came to an end. Much of Europe reverted to anarchy, entering the period commonly known as the Dark Ages, from about 500 C.E. to about 1000 C.E. Europe's rise to power was thus not preordained; as China, the Middle East, and South America each experienced a period of growth and innovation, Europe experienced decline and decay.

Yet paradoxically, this period of dramatic decline and anarchy appears to have set the stage for the creation of the modern state. As the sociologist Charles Tilly has noted, in Europe's highly fragmented, unstable, and violent environment, new political organizations began to develop, in constant competition with their rivals.[7] In some cases, these were simply marauders who realized that they could earn a better living by controlling and taxing one group of people rather than by constantly pillaging from place to place. Warlords staked out relatively small areas of land that they could easily defend and consolidated control over these regions, fighting off rival groups. In other cases, the people banded together themselves to fight off rival groups. As Tilly and others have concluded, the modern state emerged from or in reaction to what was essentially organized crime, with armed groups staking out turf, offering protection, and demanding payment in return.

The constant warfare among these numerous rivals seems to have generated a kind of rapid organizational evolution. Groups that could quickly adapt survived while less successful groups were conquered and disappeared. Rapid development was thus encouraged by a highly competitive and fluid environment.

Not only history but also geography has played a role in the rise of the modern state. The physiologist Jared Diamond has argued that Europe's close proximity to Asia and the Middle East provided benefits in the form of new plants, animals, and technical innovations that were unavailable to peoples in the Americas or Africa. At the same time, Europe's diverse geography hindered political centralization under a single language or culture.[8] Even at the height of the Roman Empire, much of central, northern, and eastern Europe had lain beyond the Romans' reach. Contrast this with China, where political power was centralized and institutionalized already by the third century C.E. Because China was more politically stable and lacked the kind of competitive environment seen in Europe, over time its institutions grew inflexible and resistant to political, economic, or technological change.

Out of the constant warfare of the Dark Ages emerged a new form of political organization—the state—that possessed three important advantages over alternate forms. First, states encouraged economic development. Before and during the Dark Ages, most Europeans lived under an economic system based on subsistence agriculture. Property such as land tended to be monopolized by those in power rather than by those who worked it. Warlords could tie the people to the land (serfdom) and extract their labor and levy heavy taxes on those who produced nonagricultural goods. However, such economic conditions were counterproductive for society as a whole: individuals had little incentive to produce if the fruits of their labor were simply taken by others. Those rulers who created laws, regulations, and infrastructure that permitted and respected private property and individual profit, however, found that production grew, giving the ruler more resources to tax or borrow (and with which to make war). Property rights thus became a hallmark of state development.[9]

A second advantage emerged when some rulers similarly encouraged technological innovation as a means of increasing their own economic and military power. As with private commerce and trade, rulers recognized that new technologies would also stimulate economic development by providing new goods and services. When technological innovation was harnessed to commerce, economic development expanded dramatically. Technological change was thus viewed by some rulers not as a threat to their power but as a means to expand it. Many of the advantages that made Europe powerful as it set off to conquer the world—gunpowder, advanced mathematics, modern mapmaking, paper, astronomy—originated in other parts of the world. But the Europeans absorbed these innovations and put them to new use. What mattered most was not who had discovered these things but rather how these discoveries were encouraged or used. Whether this application of innovation was primarily a function of intense European competition or certain particular values among Europeans is still a source of intense and bitter debate (see Chapter 3).[10] Whatever the reason, technological innovation, combined with the state's willingness to tolerate or encourage private enterprise, set the stage for modern capitalism—a system of private property, free markets, and investment in the pursuit of wealth.

A third advantage came about through the creation of domestic stability, increased trade and commerce, and the development of infrastructure whereby the state assisted in the homogenization of peoples who were originally quite different from one another. The fact that people could travel more freely within the territory of their state encouraged interaction and the development of a shared culture. The state, through printed documents, education, and legal codes, also contributed to the standardization of language. People in Europe began to see themselves as belonging to a common ethnic identity that comprised shared cultural values. Instead of identifying primarily with their trade, clan, religion, or town, people began to see themselves as English or French or German. Ethnicity proved to be a powerful asset to the state, for it in turn fostered nationalism—a shared political identity. This will be discussed in detail in the next chapter.

Although the modern state offered all these advantages, by around 1500, states covered only 20 percent of the globe, the rest belonging to alternative forms of centralized organization or none at all. But this was soon to change. Well organized and armed with technological advances, growing national identity, and economic resources, the states of Europe began to rapidly accrue power. As economic power grew, so did the ability of the state to manage ever greater numbers of people and ever more territory. Increased finances and state organization also allowed for the development of major militaries. Possessing the ability to conquer and control larger pieces of land, states began to defeat and absorb their European rivals. Spiritual rivals also fell by the wayside. The Thirty Years' War (1618–1648), in part a struggle between Roman Catholicism and Protestantism, culminated in the Treaty of Westphalia in 1648. Under this treaty, the authority of the pope over Europe's people was radically curtailed. Without this rival spiritual authority, states were free to direct religion within their own territory, subordinating the spiritual to the political. State sovereignty as we understand it today is often dated from the Treaty of Westphalia.

European states now began to expand their economic, technical, and military powers beyond their own shores. During the seventeenth and eighteenth centuries, Spain and Portugal took control of large parts of the Americas, while the Dutch, French, and British expanded state power into Asia. By the nineteenth century, nearly all of Africa had similarly been divided up among European states and incorporated into their respective empires.

The organizational structure of the state was thus imposed around the world by force. Yet as European control receded in the twentieth century, the structure of the state remained—indeed, states grew in number as these lands and peoples gained sovereignty. Although peoples all around the world resisted and eventually threw off European domination, they viewed the state as a superior—or at least inevitable—form of political evolution, and they adopted it for their own purposes. The world thus became a world of states. States set forth international boundaries and established international rules and were the primary actors in domestic and international politics around the world. Countries like India or Nigeria might throw off colonial rule, but they retained and expanded the state institutions originally imposed by imperialism.

The rapid spread of states may be viewed as the triumph of a form of organization that was able to destroy other political rivals, no matter how sophisticated. But this has not come without cost. Whereas Europe took several hundred years to create the modern state, much of the world has been forced to take up this form of organization more quickly, adopting these institutions out of necessity or force. Yet the historical paths of Africa, Asia, and

TIME LINE / POLITICAL ORGANIZATION IN EUROPE	
10th–9th centuries B.C.E.	Greek dark ages
8th–7th centuries B.C.E.	Beginning of Greek city-states; centralization of political power in Europe
6th–5th centuries B.C.E.	Establishment of Roman republic; first development of democracy in Athens
2nd–1st centuries B.C.E.	Roman conquest of Greece
1st–2nd centuries C.E.	Roman Empire expands across Europe and into the Middle East; zenith of centralized imperial power in Europe
3rd–4th centuries C.E.	Internal decline of Roman Empire; beginning of European Dark Ages; development stagnates
5th–6th centuries C.E.	Rome sacked by the Visigoths; widespread strife among competing European warlords
7th–8th centuries C.E.	Muslim armies enter Spain; Islamic world grows in power during a period of innovation and expansion
9th–10th centuries C.E.	Viking raids across Europe
11th–12th centuries C.E.	European crusades into Middle East; warfare begins to consolidate Europe into distinct political units
12th–13th centuries C.E.	Period of rapid innovation and development: mechanical clock invented; paper, compass adopted from Asia and the Middle East
14th–15th centuries C.E.	Voyages of exploration and early imperialism; early European states centralize; Islamic world stagnates
16th–17th centuries C.E.	Scientific revolution; modern states develop; modern identities of nationalism and patriotism develop

South America were radically different from those of Europe. Many of these new states have lacked the resources, infrastructure, capital, and organization that much older states developed over a thousand years. Consequently, these newer states often face significant challenges, such as establishing sovereignty over territories where a multitude of peoples, languages, religions, and cultures may coexist—problems that most European states solved only over the course of centuries and at the cost of many wars, revolutions, and lives.[11] For better or worse, although Europe no longer directly rules over much of the earth, it has left us with the legacy of the state itself.

Comparing State Power

It is clear from the preceding discussion that political evolution has been a lengthy and somewhat arbitrary process. Where conditions allowed for human beings to settle permanently, complex forms of political organization emerged, with features that reflect basic aspects of modern politics: freedom, equality, and the allocation of power. But only over the past few centuries has the modern state taken shape, forging new political, economic, and social institutions that have made it so powerful. States quickly eradicated all other forms of political organization and laid claim to all corners of the earth.

Still, not all states are the same. As we have already observed, some states are powerful, effective, prosperous, and stable; others are weak, disorganized, and largely incapable of effective action. Moreover, a single state can have a commanding presence in one area but appear ineffectual in another. What explains this range? How do we understand differences in what we might call "stateness"—variations in the quality or powers of states? To answer this question and make effective comparisons, we need a few more conceptual tools with which to work.

Legitimacy

The first concept to address is that of legitimacy. **Legitimacy** can be defined as a value whereby something or someone is recognized and accepted as right and proper. In other words, a legitimate institution or person is widely accepted and recognized by the public. Legitimacy confers authority and power. In the case of states, we know that they wield a great deal of coercive force. But is that the only reason that people recognize their authority? In fact, many people obey the law even when the threat of punishment is slight. Why? They view such behavior as "the right thing" to do. We may pay our taxes, stand at the crosswalk, or serve in the military not because of fear of punishment or a personal benefit but because we assume that the state has the authority to ask these things of us. As states provide security, they can engender a sense of reciprocal responsibility to the state. Legitimacy thus creates power that relies not on coercion, but on consent. Without legitimacy, a state would have to use the continuous threat of force to maintain order—a difficult task—or expect that many of its rules and policies would go unheeded. Legitimacy is therefore a critical component of stateness.

How then does a state become legitimate? Let us turn again to Max Weber, who argued that political legitimacy comes in three basic forms: traditional, charismatic, and rational-legal.[12] Traditional legitimacy rests on the idea that someone or something is valid because "it has always been that way." In other words, this legitimacy is built on the idea that certain aspects of politics are to be accepted because they have been accepted over a long period of time. In some way, they are seen as inseparable from the identity of the people themselves. **Traditional legitimacy** often embodies historical myths and legends as well as the continuity between past and present. Rituals and ceremonies all help to reinforce traditional legitimacy by providing actions and symbols that are ancient, unique, and dramatic. One good example is the legitimacy accorded to a long-standing monarchy, where a particular family holds the office over generations. However, the example of a monarchy may also connote that traditional equals outdated. Yet even modern institutions, like an elected office or a regime, can develop traditional legitimacy if in place long enough. In short, traditional legitimacy is a system built on history and continuity. The longer a traditional political system has been in place, the more institutionalized it becomes, as it has the weight of history on its side. Change becomes difficult to imagine if an institution has existed "since time immemorial."

Charismatic legitimacy is in many ways the very opposite of traditional legitimacy. When we use the word *charisma* in everyday conversation, we usually are describing someone who is good-looking or perhaps a witty conversationalist. But in politics, charisma means much more. Rather than relying on the weight of history and the continuity of certain roles or values, charismatic legitimacy is based on the power of ideas, or what is sometimes called "the gift of grace." Charisma is typically embodied by one individual who can move the public through these ideas and the manner in which she or he presents them. Some individuals possess a certain magnetism that binds who they are to what they say. Jesus and Muhammad are perfect examples of charismatic figures who could gather huge followings through the power of their ideas. In a more modern and more sinister example, Adolf Hitler was a charismatic figure, whose power with ideas and language brought about world war and genocide.

As you can imagine, charismatic legitimacy is not institutionalized and thus is fairly tenuous, since it commonly dies with the individual who possesses it. But charismatic legitimacy can be transformed into traditional legitimacy through the creation of rituals and values that are meant to capture the spirit and intent of the charismatic leader's power. Religions, monarchies, even constitutions and regimes can be examples of this. Weber called this kind of institutionalization "the routinization of charisma."

In contrast to the first two forms of legitimacy, **rational-legal legitimacy** is based not on history or rituals (as in the case of traditional legitimacy) or on the force of ideas (as in charismatic legitimacy) but rather on a system of laws and procedures that are highly institutionalized. Leaders or political officials are legitimate by virtue of the rules by which they come to office. Moreover, people abide by the decisions of these actors because they believe that the rules the leaders enforce serve the public's interest. In this case, it is not the person who is important or even that individual's particular values or

Three Types of Legitimacy

Type	Characteristics	Example
Traditional legitimacy	Built by habit and custom over time, stressing history; strongly institutionalized	Monarch (Queen Elizabeth)
Charismatic legitimacy	Built on the force of ideas and the presence of the leader; weakly institutionalized	Revolutionary hero (Vladimir Lenin)
Rational-legal legitimacy	Built on rules and procedures and the offices that create and enforce those rules; strongly institutionalized	Elected executive (Barack Obama)

ideas, but the office he or she holds. The office is legitimate, rather than the person in it. Once that person leaves office, he or she loses authority.

As you have probably already guessed, the world of modern states is built on a rational-legal foundation. States rely on bureaucracies, paperwork, and thousands of individuals to make daily decisions on a wide range of issues. Ideally, the public accepts these decisions as the proper way to get things done, and they presume that these decisions are reasonably fair and predictable. For example, if there are elections, they accept the outcome even if their preferred candidate loses, and they obey those who won. The 2000 presidential election in the United States is a perfect example of rational-legal legitimacy. After weeks of bitter disputes over who had actually won the election, the Supreme Court's intervention effectively ended the battle, and the Democratic candidate, Al Gore, agreed to abide by the outcome. In spite of denunciations by some that the election was illegitimate, the majority of Americans accepted George W. Bush as their president, even if they had not voted for him (and the majority of voters had not). What's more, legitimacy is not confined to political actors within the state; our own individual legitimacy comes from a rational-legal foundation: our driver's licenses, identification numbers, passports, or voter registration cards all confer a certain form of authority and power that flows between citizen and state.

Note, however, that just because the rise of modern states was built on a rational-legal legitimacy, that doesn't mean that traditional or charismatic legitimacy has disappeared. In almost any country, one can distinguish stateness by looking at the mix of legitimacy across these three sources. Political leaders in many countries throughout modern history have wielded a great deal of charismatic power and have sometimes become the centers of large "cults of personality," which we will explore further in Chapter 6. These cults portray the leader as the father (or, occasionally, the mother) of the nation and imbue him or her with almost superhuman powers. Charismatic leadership, and the power that it places in the hands of one individual, can corrupt, but some charismatic figures have dramatically changed the course of politics for the better: Mohandas K. Gandhi, in India, or Nelson Mandela, in South Africa, for instance. Barack Obama clearly rose out of nowhere to become president of the United States through charisma, not his experience.

Traditional power can similarly be found in a wide variety of circumstances. The United Kingdom, Japan, Sweden, and more than thirty other countries still have monarchs. Although the powers of most of these monarchs are now quite limited, they remain important symbols and attract national and sometimes even international attention. Canada and Australia retain the British monarchy as their head of state, even though it exercises no real authority and is part of its colonial past. Rules and regulations can also eventually take on a kind of traditional legitimacy if they function for so long that people can't imagine doing things any other way. The U.S. Constitution, for example, is not only a set of rules for conducting politics; it is also considered a sacred symbol of what makes the United States unique and powerful. Is the difficulty in modifying the U.S. Constitution due to the procedures involved, or has there developed over time a resistance to tinkering with this "sacred" document? If the latter is true, then it is not simply rational-legal legitimacy but also traditional legitimacy that binds American politics together.

To summarize, a central component of stateness is legitimacy. Traditional legitimacy stresses ritual and continuity; charismatic legitimacy, the force of ideas as embodied in a leader; rational-legal legitimacy, laws, and rules. Whatever the form or mixture, legitimacy makes it possible for the state to carry out its basic functions. Without it, states find carrying out these tasks very difficult. If the public has little faith in the state, it will frequently ignore political responsibilities, such as paying taxes, abiding by regulations, or serving in the armed forces. Under these conditions, the state has really only one tool left to maintain order: the threat of force. Paradoxically, then, states that use the most coercion against their citizens are often the most weakly institutionalized states, for without violence, they cannot get the public to willingly comply with the rules and duties set forth.

Centralization or Decentralization

In addition to varying in the kind and level of political legitimacy they enjoy, states also vary in their distribution of power. As we noted in Chapter 1, individual freedom is typically associated with the decentralization of power whereas collective equality is typically associated with a greater centralization of power.

State power can be centralized or decentralized in a couple of different ways, the first of which is the dispersal of power within the state itself. Under **federalism**, significant powers, such as taxation, lawmaking, and security, are devolved to regional bodies (such as states in the United States, *Lander* in Germany, or provinces in Canada) that control specific territory within the country. These powers are defined within the national constitution and therefore are not easily constricted or eliminated by any government. Here the argument is that federalism helps represent local interests as well as check the growth of central power (which is viewed as a threat to democracy). In contrast, **unitary states** invest most political power at the national level, with limited local authority. The central government is responsible for most areas of policy. Territorial divisions within unitary states (such as Japan or France) are less important in terms of political power. The perceived advantage of a unitary state is that local interests can be represented without recourse to regional bodies and that federalism tends to weaken state efficiency by dispersing power among many local authorities.

In recent years there has been a greater tendency toward decentralization in many states, something we will speak to at greater length in subsequent chapters. This process, called **devolution**, has become popular for a number of different reasons. In some cases, devolution has been viewed as a way to increase state legitimacy by vesting political power closer to the people, a concern as states have grown larger and more complex over time. In other cases, devolution has been seen as a way to resolve problems like ethnic or religious differences by giving certain groups greater autonomy. Often this does not lead to outright federalism but nevertheless a significant movement of power downward from the central state. We will speak more about devolution in subsequent chapters.

Power, Autonomy, and Capacity

Another way in which we can measure stateness is in the relationship between the state and other states and domestic actors. At the most basic level we can make a distinction between **strong states** and **weak states**. Strong states are those that are able to fulfill basic tasks: defend their territory, make and enforce rules and rights, collect taxes, and manage the economy, to name a few. In contrast, weak states cannot execute such tasks very well. Rules are haphazardly applied, if at all; tax evasion and other forms of public non-compliance are widespread; armed rivals to the state, such as rebel movements, organized crime, or other states, may control large chunks of territory or the economy. State officials themselves, having little faith in their office or responsibilities, may use their jobs simply to fill their own pockets through corruption and theft. In turn, economic development is certain to be much lower as a result of this unstable political environment. In general, weak states are not well institutionalized and lack authority and legitimacy. At an extreme, the very structures of the state may become so weak that they break down to a large extent. This is commonly termed a **failed state** (see Table 2.1).[13] Afghanistan prior to 2001 was commonly viewed as a failed state, with no real sovereign authority, even in the hands of the Taliban; in many ways, Iraq remains a failed state, one that effectively collapsed in the aftermath of invasion and now has only limited power and must be backed up by international force.

However, speaking of states as merely weak or strong fails to capture the complexity of state power. In fact, we run the risk of a tautology (something that can't be disproven) if we simply argued that if a state can do something it must be strong and if it can't it must be weak. American elected officials can wage large-scale wars around the globe but can't ban handguns, whereas for Canada just the opposite would be true. Which one, then, is weak or strong? Comparative politics thus further builds on the categories of weak and strong states through the use of two other terms: capacity and autonomy. **Capacity** is the ability of the state to wield power in order to carry out the basic tasks of providing security and reconciling freedom and equality. A state with high capacity is able to formulate and enact fundamental policies and ensure stability and security for both itself and its citizens. A state with low capacity is unable to do these things very effectively. High capacity requires not just money but also organization, legitimacy, and effective leadership. Roads get paved, schools get built, regulations are created and followed, and those who break the law are punished.

In contrast, **autonomy** is the ability of the state to wield its power independently of the public or international actors. In other words, if an autonomous state wishes to carry out a policy or action, it can do so without having to consult the public or worry about strong public or international opposition that might force it to reverse its decision. A state with a high degree of autonomy may act on behalf of the public, pursuing what it believes are the best interests of the country, irrespective of public opinion. A state with a low degree of autonomy will act largely at the behest of private individuals, groups, or other states and will be less able to disobey the public will or the demands of well-organized groups.

Table 2.1 Top Twenty Failed States

Rank	Total	Country	Demographic Pressures	Refugees and Displaced Persons	Group Grievance	Human Flight	Uneven Development	Economy	Delegitimization of State	Public Services	Human Rights	Security Apparatus	Factionalized Elites	External Intervention
									Indicators of Instability				
1	114.2	Somalia	9.8	9.8	9.5	8.3	7.5	9.4	10.0	10.0	9.9	10.0	10.0	10.0
2	113.0	Sudan	9.0	9.6	8.8	8.8	9.3	7.3	10.0	9.5	9.9	9.8	9.9	9.9
3	112.5	Zimbabwe	9.7	9.0	10.0	10.0	9.6	10.0	9.5	9.6	9.8	9.5	9.3	7.0
4	110.9	Chad	9.1	9.2	9.7	7.8	9.1	8.3	9.7	9.4	9.5	9.8	9.8	9.5
5	110.6	Iraq	9.0	9.0	9.8	9.3	8.5	7.8	9.4	8.5	9.6	9.8	9.8	10.0
6	106.7	Dem. Rep. of the Congo	9.6	9.2	8.8	7.9	9.0	8.3	8.3	9.1	8.9	9.6	8.6	9.4
7	105.4	Afghanistan	9.1	8.9	9.5	7.0	8.1	8.5	9.2	8.3	8.4	9.6	8.8	10.0
8	104.6	Ivory Coast	8.5	8.3	9.5	8.4	8.0	8.5	8.9	7.8	9.0	9.2	8.9	9.7
9	103.8	Pakistan	8.0	8.6	9.5	8.1	8.8	6.2	9.5	7.1	9.5	9.6	9.8	9.1
10	103.7	Central African Republic	9.0	8.8	8.9	5.5	8.8	8.4	9.2	8.6	8.7	9.4	9.4	9.0
11	101.8	Guinea	7.9	7.4	8.5	8.3	8.6	8.6	9.7	9.0	8.9	8.4	8.6	7.9
12	100.3	Bangladesh	9.8	7.1	9.7	8.4	9.0	7.1	9.1	7.8	8.0	8.3	9.6	6.4
12	100.3	Burma	8.5	8.5	9.5	6.0	9.0	7.6	9.5	8.3	9.9	9.3	8.7	5.5
14	99.3	Haiti	8.5	4.2	8.0	8.0	8.2	8.3	9.0	8.8	8.9	8.9	8.9	9.6
15	97.7	North Korea	8.2	6.0	7.2	5.0	8.8	9.6	9.8	9.6	9.7	8.3	7.6	7.9
16	96.1	Ethiopia	8.9	7.5	7.8	7.5	8.6	8.2	7.9	7.5	8.5	7.5	8.9	7.3
16	96.1	Uganda	8.7	9.3	8.3	6.0	8.5	7.6	8.3	7.9	7.9	8.1	7.8	7.7
18	95.7	Lebanon	7.2	9.0	9.4	7.1	7.4	6.3	8.0	6.7	7.0	9.3	9.4	8.9
18	95.7	Nigeria	8.2	5.1	9.4	8.2	9.2	5.9	8.9	8.7	7.5	9.2	9.3	6.1
20	95.6	Sri Lanka	7.0	9.0	9.8	6.9	8.2	6.0	9.2	6.6	7.5	9.3	9.5	6.1

Note: Indicators are on a scale of 1–10, with 10 the most severely unstable.

Source: www.foreignpolicy.com/story/cms.php?story_id=4350&page=1.

Each of these concepts helps us to evaluate different states in terms of power. Strong states with a high degree of capacity and autonomy may be able to execute major policies relatively easily. A case in point is China's construction of the Three Gorges Dam, the world's largest such project, despite the technical challenges, enormous cost, and widespread international criticism for its possible environmental impact. High capacity and autonomy, however, may come at the expense of individual freedom. States with a high degree of capacity but lower autonomy may have widespread powers but at the same time these powers are subject to public authorization and oversight. The United States and Canada are good examples of this, further reinforced by their federal structure. Individual freedom may be high, and this can also constrain central authority and consequently hinder national policy making. States with high autonomy but low capacity, meanwhile, may have few limits on their decision making but lack the ability to realize those policies effectively. Russia may fall into this category; during the last decade the state has become more centralized and autonomous, but it still lacks a great deal of capacity in promulgating and enforcing regulations and rights. Finally, states may lack both autonomy and capacity. This is true of many less-developed countries, such as in Africa, where states have been "captured" by dominant elites or groups and are largely unable to fulfill some of the most important national tasks, such as encouraging economic development or ensuring public education. Failed states are extreme examples of situations in which autonomy and capacity have left the state.

In short, speaking of state power in terms of autonomy and capacity can help us better understand stateness: what states are and are not able to do, and why. However, even when we speak of autonomy and capacity, we should note that within these two areas individual states may vary widely depending on the issue or area at hand. An observer of China may conclude from that country's rapid economic development or ability to censor the Internet that this state enjoys high autonomy and capacity. However, China's corruption, proliferation of underground religions, widespread disregard of regulations, and numerous public protests indicate that its autonomy and capacity are in many areas circumscribed. In contrast, North Korea and Iran suffer from limited economic development but can master nuclear technology—no small feat. Autonomy and capacity thus are useful concepts for comparing states but depend on the issue or task at hand.

Finally, we are left some big questions: Why are some states more centralized or decentralized? Why do they have more or less capacity or autonomy? Some of the answers lie in history, particularly the nature of international threats and how this affected the relationship between taxation (to pay for those wars) and representation (to have some say in how the state conducts itself). For more recently founded states, however, this long histor-

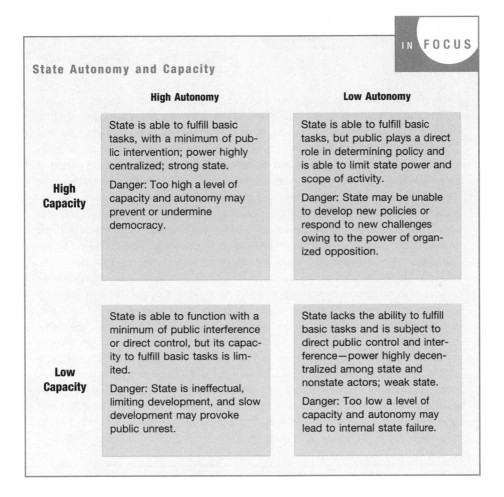

IN FOCUS

State Autonomy and Capacity

	High Autonomy	**Low Autonomy**
High Capacity	State is able to fulfill basic tasks, with a minimum of public intervention; power highly centralized; strong state. Danger: Too high a level of capacity and autonomy may prevent or undermine democracy.	State is able to fulfill basic tasks, but public plays a direct role in determining policy and is able to limit state power and scope of activity. Danger: State may be unable to develop new policies or respond to new challenges owing to the power of organized opposition.
Low Capacity	State is able to function with a minimum of public interference or direct control, but its capacity to fulfill basic tasks is limited. Danger: State is ineffectual, limiting development, and slow development may provoke public unrest.	State lacks the ability to fulfill basic tasks and is subject to direct public control and interference—power highly decentralized among state and nonstate actors; weak state. Danger: Too low a level of capacity and autonomy may lead to internal state failure.

ical explanation is not particularly useful. How do you build a state so that it is viable? Is there an ideal mix of legitimacy, centralization, autonomy, and capacity? Scholars and policy makers are still debating these issues, something we will return to in later chapters.

In Sum: Studying States

This chapter began by defining the state as a monopoly of force but also as the institution charged with transforming freedom and equality from ideas into concrete action. The kinds of decisions made toward this end, however, are shaped by regimes and governments. Regimes are the fundamental rules and norms of politics, providing long-term goals regarding individual freedom and collective equality and the location and use of power toward those goals.

INSTITUTIONS IN ACTION

STATENESS AND THE CASE OF IRAQ

For tragic reasons, Iraq is an excellent example of many of our considerations regarding the nature of states. In the run-up to the war with Iraq, many supporters of the invasion spoke of regime change, believing that a rapid invasion was possible that would essentially "decapitate" the leadership and regime, allowing for an occupying force to install a new regime and government within a relatively short period of time. However, this assumption was predicated on the belief that the state would remain intact—the leadership may fall, but civil servants would head back to work once the smoke had cleared. But this assumption proved incorrect for several reasons. First, it underestimated the extent to which state capacity and legitimacy had eroded under Saddam Hussein and international sanctions since 1991. When the war began, the state quickly failed, leaving in its wake anarchy. This was compounded by the actions of the Coalition Provisional Authority, which further hastened state collapse by marginalizing Iraqis as important players in reconstituting the state and dissolving the Iraqi military. Some of these failures can be traced to American political culture—inasmuch as Americans think about the state, they view it as a necessary evil that must be constrained, not a set of institutions vital to security and prosperity. The question now is how one coaxes a state back into existence after it has been razed: restoring a monopoly of force through military and police, creating laws and regulations that are respected and enforced, and generally creating enough autonomy and capacity so that the state is sovereign, effective, and responsive to the needs of its citizens. There is no simple blueprint for how to do this, especially in the absence of security.

Governments, in contrast, are those political elites in charge of running the state. Influenced and constrained by the existing regime, they attempt to formulate policy regarding freedom and equality that may then be executed by the state. These represent the most basic facets of states everywhere—and indeed, states are everywhere. Although similar political organizations have existed for thousands of years, only within the past few centuries did states arise in Europe and quickly come to dominate the globe. States are the main political players in the world today.

The universal presence of states, and variations in their stateness, compels comparativists to find some way to study and evaluate them. One way is by assessing their legitimacy; different kinds of legitimacy—traditional, charismatic, and rational-legal—all create their own kinds of authority and power. The other is by assessing the actual dispersal of power itself; states may be weaker or stronger, with more or less capacity and autonomy, depending on how power is distributed within the state and between the state and the public. Too much power in the hands of the state risks tyranny; too little power risks anarchy. Finding the right mix is not simply a technical question but one that shapes how states and societies reconcile freedom and equality. This debate over freedom and equality, then, ranges far beyond the boundaries of the state itself. As we shall see in the chapters that follow, it is influenced by society, through ethnic and national identity, culture, and ideology; by economic institutions and the interaction between states and markets; and by democratic and nondemocratic practices.

Since the dawn of human civilization, people have relied on some form of political organization to construct a relationship between individual freedom and collective equality. For the past few centuries, modern states have been the dominant expression of that relationship. We might thus conclude that states now represent an end point in human intellectual and organization evolution. But why should this be so? It seems logical that in future new forms of political organization will displace states, just as states displaced empires, city-states, and other institutions. Perhaps challenges to states—environmental, economic, or cultural—will overwhelm many, and they will revert to empires, city-states, or warlordism. Or perhaps technological innovation will make old forms of political centralization weak or irrelevant, binding humans in communities where sovereignty is virtual, not physical. Perhaps the core debate over freedom and equality that has stretched over millennia will be reconciled once and for all, changing the very nature of politics as we understand it. These questions may seem unanswerable, more amenable to fortune-telling than to research. But as we shall see, they lie at the heart of ideas and conflicts that have transformed the world in the past and may dominate our future.

NOTES

1. In the United States, the word *state* refers to the federal structure of regional government. As a result, for Americans, the word *state* conjures up the idea of local government, whereas for political scientists (and most people around the world), the word *state* refers to national, not local, organization. This confusion stems from U.S. history. During the period of revolutionary struggle and the creation of a federal system, the former British colonies in America viewed themselves as independent political units—in other words, as states. With the creation of a federal system of government, however, their individual powers were subordinated to a central authority. The United States of America, in other words, eventually became a system of national government, with the term *state* left as a remnant of that brief period when these units acted largely as independent entities.

2. Max Weber, "Politics as a Vocation," in *Gesammelte Politische Schriften* (Muenchen, 1921), pp. 396–450.
3. This idea has been developed by Charles Tilly, "War Making and State Making as Organized Crime," in Peter Evans, Dietrich Rueschemeyer, and T. Skopol, eds., *Bringing the State Back In* (New York: Cambridge University Press, 1985), pp. 169–191.
4. Zackary Elkins and John Sides, "Can Institutions Build Unity in Multiethnic States," *American Political Science Review*, 101, no. 4 (November 2007), pp. 693–708.
5. See Azar Gat, *War in Human Civilization* (New York: Oxford University Press, 2006); also Jared Diamond "Vengeance is Ours," *New Yorker*, 21 April 2008, pp. 74–87.
6. S. E. Finer, *The History of Government from the Earliest Times, Vol. 1, Ancient Monarchies and Empires* (New York: Oxford University Press, 1999).
7. Charles Tilly, *Coercion, Capital, and European States: 990–1990* (Oxford, UK: Blackwell, 1990).
8. Jared Diamond, *Guns, Germs, and Steel: The Fates of Human Societies* (New York: Norton, 1997).
9. Mancur Olson, "Democracy, Dictatorship, and Development," *American Political Science Review*, 87, no. 3 (September 1993), pp. 567–576; see also Margaret Levy, "The State of the Study of the State," in Ira Katznelson, ed., *Political Science: The State of the Discipline* (New York: Norton, 2002), pp. 40–43.
10. For the cultural explanation, see David Landes, *The Wealth and Poverty of Nations: Why Some Are So Rich and Some So Poor* (New York: Norton, 1999).
11. Stephen Krasner, "The Case for Shared Sovereignty," *Journal of Democracy*, 16, no. 1 (2005), pp. 69–83.
12. Max Weber, "Politics as a Vocation," in H. H. Gerth and C. Wright Mills, trans. and eds., *From Max Weber: Essays in Sociology* (New York: Oxford University Press, 1958), pp. 77–128.
13. Robert I. Rotberg, ed., *When States Fail: Causes and Consequences* (Princeton, NJ: Princeton University Press, 2003).

3 NATIONS AND SOCIETY

KEY CONCEPTS

- Ethnic identity defines how individuals identify with their community.

- National identity binds people through common political aspirations such as sovereignty.

- Citizenship and patriotism define our emotional and legal relationship to the state.

- Ethnic and national conflict can stem from clashes between these different identities and their goals.

- Political attitudes are views regarding the pace and scope of any political change.

- Political ideologies are specific values held by individuals regarding the fundamental goals of politics.

- Political culture constitutes the basic norms for political activity in a society.

Society is a broad term that refers to complex human organization, a collection of people bound by shared institutions that define how human relations should be conducted. From country to country and place to place, societies differ in how individuals define themselves and their relationship to one another as well as their relationship to government and the state. These relationships are each unique; for all the surface similarities that may exist between societies, each country views itself and the wider world around it in a distinct way. These differences make comparative politics a rich field of study but also a frustrating one, as social scientists seek to find similarities that are often few and far between.

In this chapter, we will look at the ways in which people identify themselves and are identified, both as individuals and as groups, and how these identifications relate to politics and the state. We will start with the concepts of ethnic and national identity, two of the most basic ways in which individuals and groups define themselves. What does it mean to be part of an ethnic group? How is such a group defined? What is the difference between an ethnic group and a nation? We will also make a distinction between ethnicity, nationality, and citizenship. A related question arises in the distinction between nationalism and patriotism: What is the difference between being patriotic and being nationalistic? We will answer these questions by looking at some examples of each and tracing their historical origins. Throughout recent history, the world has seen violent domestic and international conflicts connected to national and ethnic identities. Why do such conflicts occur? Are they a natural and inevitable part of human organization, or are such conflicts manufactured by political leaders to serve their own purposes? In this chapter, we will also look at some of the effects of these different identities when they conflict with one another.

From there we will move on to a discussion of political attitudes and ideologies. Whereas ethnicity, nationality, and citizenship are group identities, political attitudes and ideologies are the values and positions that individuals take with regard to freedom and equality. How should these values be reconciled, and to what end? One thing we will see is that although basic political attitudes and ideologies can be compared around the world, their relative strength or influence differs dramatically from country to country, and we'll discuss why this may be the case.

Before we move ahead, we should make a couple of observations. First is that identities like ethnicity, nationality, or ideology are not a fixed part of our nature. Many social scientists agree that these identities are "socially constructed," generated in the minds of women and men rather than being biological or genetic constructs. That, however, is not to say that these institutions are somehow trivial or easily modified or eliminated. In the past, many social scientists viewed these institutions as forms of identification that would be overwhelmed by modernization. Yet such arguments ignore both the power of these institutions and the basic human instinct to form groups. Constructing society and creating distinct identities—forming ingroups and outgroups and discriminating between them—is as old as human organization. Over time, comparativists have grown more skeptical of the idea that ethnicity or nationalism will become a thing of the past or that collective identities will somehow no longer be a central part of defining who we are. That said, let us consider some of the most powerful societal institutions that shape comparative politics.

Ethnic Identity

People identify themselves in many ways. One way that we identify individuals in society is by their ethnicity, as when we speak of people as German or

Irish, Kurdish or Zulu, Latino or Ukrainian Canadian. When we use the term **ethnic identity** or **ethnicity**, we emphasize a person's relationship to other members of society. Ethnic identity is a set of institutions that bind people together through a common culture. These institutions can include language, religion, geographical location, customs, and history, among other things. As these distinct attributes are institutionalized, they provide a people with a particular identity among members that is passed down over time from generation to generation. This process is called "ascription"—the assigning of a particular quality at birth. People do not choose their ethnicities; they are born into them, and their ethnic identity remains largely fixed throughout life. Ethnicity provides social solidarity and can generate greater equality as well. Groups with a high degree of ethnic solidarity may also be more willing to redistribute resources within the group and, conversely, less willing to share resources with groups that are ethnically different. This is clearly important, as it suggests that redistribution can be as much about identity as about economic policy, and also that highly diverse societies may face greater challenges in reducing inequality than those that are more homogeneous.[1]

Each ethnic group is characterized by its own set of institutions that embody norms and standards of behavior, and a single society can be broken up into numerous ethnic groups. For example, Singaporean society is made up of ethnic Chinese, Malays, and Indians. In the United States and Canada there are indigenous people who further classify themselves as Hopi or Makah or Cree, for instance. In both Singapore and North America there exist broader societies made up of many different ethnic groups. In fact, the majority of countries in the world are not ethnically homogeneous; rarely are society and ethnicity one and the same. Societies are made up of various ethnic groups, in some cases only a few, in other cases tens or even hundreds, each with its own particular identity. It is important to note that ethnicity is at its core a social, not a political, identity; people may identify themselves with an ethnic group without drawing any particular conclusions about politics on that basis. Ethnicity and the solidarity it provides is not inherently political, though it can become so.

Although we have listed a number of common attributes that often define ethnic differences, it is important to stress that there is no "master list" of differences that automatically define one group as ethnically different from another. In Bosnia, for example, the main

---

IN FOCUS

Ethnic Identity Is . . .

- Specific attributes and societal institutions that make one group of people culturally different from others.
- Often based on customs, language, religion, or other factors.
- Ascriptive, generally assigned at birth.
- Not inherently political.

ethnic groups—Croats, Serbs, and Muslims—speak the same language and are similar in numerous other ways. What divides Bosnians is primarily religion: Croats are mostly Roman Catholic, Serbs are Eastern Orthodox, and Muslims practice Islam. Yet we speak of Germans as a single ethnic group, even though some are Catholic and some are Protestant. Why are ethnic groups in Bosnia divided by religion, while in Germany such divisions don't produce different ethnic groups? In an even more confusing case, that of Rwanda (where several hundred thousand died in 1994), the Hutu and Tutsi ethnic groups cannot be easily distinguished by any of the factors we have listed. Both speak the same language, practice the same religions, live in the same geographical regions, and share the same customs. For most outside observers, there is no real ethnic difference between the two, and even Hutus and Tutsis cannot easily distinguish between one another; they rely on such vague and incorrect distinctions as height, facial features, and diet.

Ethnicity, then, is a good example of what we referred to earlier as a social construction, in each case built from a unique combination of attributes. Ethnicity exists when people acknowledge and are acknowledged by outsiders as belonging to a distinct group. Even though such distinctions may be difficult to observe, these ascriptive identities can have powerful effects.

National Identity

In contrast to ethnicity, which may be constructed in a unique manner from group to group and is not an inherently political concept, the idea of a **nation** or national identity is much more consistent across various cases. It is also a much more inherently political concept. If ethnic identity is a set of institutions that bind people together through a common culture, then **national identity** can be defined as a set of institutions that bind people together through common political aspirations. Among these, the most important is self-government and sovereignty. National identity implies a demand for greater freedom through sovereignty, as in a colony's revolt against its colonial master. National identity also involves issues of equality, such as secessionist movements that argue that independence

IN FOCUS

National Identity Is . . .

- Based on the concept of a *nation*: a group of people bound together by a common set of political aspirations, especially self-government and sovereignty.
- Often (but not always) derived from ethnic identity.
- Inherently political.
- The basis for *nationalism*: pride in one's people and belief that they have a unique political destiny.

would eliminate unequal treatment at the hands of some other group. Pakistan's secession from India in 1947 or Kosovo's declaration of independence from Serbia in 2008 can both be seen in terms of arguments for greater freedom (from another dominant group) and equality with others in the international system (through the creation of a sovereign state).

As you can see, national identity often—but not always—develops from ethnic identity. For example, an ethnic group may chafe against the political system under which it lives; its members may feel that they lack certain rights or freedoms. As a result, some leaders may argue that the ethnic group should have greater political control and that the group's own interests would be better served if it controlled its own political destiny. The interaction between ethnicity and national identity can be seen in recent developments in Canada. There, the French-speaking population of the province of Québec constitutes its own ethnic group, quite distinct from the English-speaking citizens of the rest of Canada (as well as from their own French ancestors). By the 1960s, this ethnicity began to develop into a sense of national identity, as some in Québec argued for separation from Canada, where they saw themselves as a minority whose unique concerns were not taken into consideration. Such arguments actually led to national referenda on the issue of secession in 1980 and 1995. In the latter case, the proposal that Québec secede failed by little more than 1 percent of the vote. Thus, ethnic identity has also fostered a national identity among many—although not all—Québecois. A similar process can be seen at work among Palestinians, most of whom seek the creation of an independent Palestinian state out of territories controlled by Israel.

National identity can thus create **nationalism**, a pride in one's people and the belief that they have their own sovereign political destiny that is separate from those of others. In Québec, for example, we find a people uncertain of whether they are just an ethnic group or also a nation—a group that desires self-government through an independent state. This lack of clarity between ethnicity and national identity is also evident in other groups, such as the Scots in the United Kingdom. Some, but not all, members of the ethnic group support the nationalist cause of independence. In other words, although ethnic identity often leads to a political identity built on nationalism, this is not always the case. Just as groups can vary in the strength of their ethnic identification, people may also vary in the degree of their nationalism. Nigerians have strong ethnic identification across numerous groups but at the same time a high degree of Nigerian national identity; in homogeneous Japan, national pride is far lower.

If we can have ethnicity without it leading to national identity, can we have national identity without ethnicity? In other words, must ethnicity always be the source of nationalism? Political scientists have not reached any consensus on this question. At first glance, it would seem logical that without ethnicity, there is no foundation for national identity; people would lack a common identity, source of solidarity, and set of institutions on which to build national pride. But like ethnicity, nationality lacks a "master list" to define it. In the case of the United States, it is easy to conclude that there is no single American ethnic group. But is there an American or Canadian nation? Some might say no, because nationalism is often assumed to require an ethnicity on which political aspirations can be built. Yet Americans and Canadians are each bound by certain common historical symbols, such as flags, anthems, constitutions, and common cultural values (recall our discussion of baseball and hockey in Chapter 1). One could thus argue that even in the face of great ethnic diversity, the United States or Canada is indeed a nation whose people are bound together by a sense of pride in certain democratic ideals. Just as some in Spain may consider themselves ethnically Basque and nationally Spanish, or some in the United Kingdom ethnically Scottish but nationally British, so, too, do many see themselves as black or Korean or Hispanic or Indian but also as American or Canadian. Thus, national identity may be constructed even when a common or dominant ethnic identity is absent.[2] Finally, we should emphasize that nationalism is not inherently bad, as is sometimes implied. Nationalism does not necessarily mean hatred of others, and national identity can serve as a powerful force for binding communities together and achieving political, economic, and societal goals.

Citizenship and Patriotism

Our final form of identification is citizenship. So far, we have noted that ethnicity is not inherently political, although it may develop a political aspect through nationalism. At the other end of this spectrum, citizenship is a purely political identity, developed not out of some unique set of circumstances or ascripted by birth but rather developed explicitly by states and accepted or rejected by individuals. **Citizenship** can be defined as an individual's or a group's relationship to the state; those who are citizens swear allegiance to that state, and that state in return is obligated to provide rights to those individuals or the members of that group. Citizenship can also convey certain obligations, such as the duty to serve in the armed forces or pay taxes. Citizens are therefore defined by

IN FOCUS

Citizenship Is . . .

- An individual's relationship to the state; the individual swears allegiance to the state, and the state in turn provides certain benefits or rights.
- Purely political and thus more easily changed than ethnic identity or national identity.
- The basis for *patriotism*: pride in one's state and citizenship.

their particular relationship to one state rather than to one another. Although citizenship is often gained at birth, citizenship has qualities quite separate from those of ethnic or national identity.

Citizenship is thus a potentially more inclusive or flexible concept than national or ethnic identity or ethnicity. Like those two institutions, however, citizenship can vary in clarity and power. Citizenship may confer a host of benefits, such as education and health care, or relatively few, depending on the state. A state also may not necessarily grant citizenship to all those born on its territory while others may allow citizenship in more than one country. Matters can be further complicated if citizenship is founded on ethnic or national identity. In an extreme example, in the 1950s, South Africa's apartheid regime created internal "homelands" for blacks as a means of stripping them of their South African citizenship.

Citizenship, in turn, can give rise to **patriotism**, or pride in one's state. People are patriotic when they have pride in their political system and seek to defend and promote it. When we think of patriotism, some of the things that may come to mind are our flag, important historical events, wars, anthems—all images that people associate with politics and the state. Incidentally, here we see some of the confusion in thinking about nationalism in cases like the United States or Canada, since some would assert that what we see in these cases are examples of patriotism, not nationalism. States that are weak or illegitimate often have difficulty instilling patriotism among their citizens, which makes tasks like defending the state in times of war very difficult. Being a citizen does not automatically make you patriotic, nor does a strong ethnic or national identity.

To sum up, ethnicity, nationality, and citizenship are institutions that define groups in different ways and that carry different political implications. Ethnic identity is built on unique social attributes among people, such as language or culture, whereas national identity implies political aspirations, specifically sovereignty. Although an ethnic identity often leads to a national identity and nationalism, it does not always do so, nor does the absence of a single dominant ethnicity prevent nationalism from developing. Finally, citizenship is an identity built on a relationship to the state. As should be clear, none of these identities is exclusive; all of us possess different combinations of ethnicity, national identity, and citizenship, with each contributing to how we see the world and our role within it.

Ethnic Identity, National Identity, and Citizenship: Origins and Persistence

Now that we have distinguished among these three identities, it is worth considering the origins of each: Where did they come from and why do they exist?

Contrary to most people's assumptions, ethnic and national identities are relatively recent concepts that emerged in Europe toward the end of the eighteenth century. For example, in the Roman Empire, its people did not think of themselves as "Romans" in the way we might imagine today. Nor did those living in the Chinese Empire imagine themselves to be "Chinese." Citizenship, too, has relatively recent origins: although the concept can be traced back to ancient Athens and to the Roman Empire, this disappeared with the fall of Rome, only to resurface centuries later.

The emergence (or reemergence, in the case of citizenship) of these identities had much to do with the formation of the modern state.[3] As states took form in Europe in the fifteenth and sixteenth centuries, asserting sovereign control over people and territory, people could travel greater distances within their own country's borders, enjoying the security provided by the state. This mobility in turn increased commerce, which was often centered around the city where the state leadership was based. These fortified capitals served as centers for trade, information, and new social relationships. Such interaction in turn fostered increased homogeneity. Languages and dialects began to merge into a common tongue, further standardized by the state through written laws and other documents. Common cultural and religious practices also developed, often created or supported by the state (as during the Protestant Reformation). In other words, new social institutions began to take shape that were meaningful to a majority of a country's population. People could now identify themselves not by village or profession, clan or tribe, but by the institutions they shared with many thousands of other people they had never met— an abstraction. These institutions formed the foundation for ethnic identity. People in turn slowly began to identify with each other primarily on this basis—as German or French or English. Again, this was a relatively recent process in human history.

Growing ethnic identity was thus tightly connected to state development. Moreover, state leaders also saw this development as something that could serve their own interests. By encouraging the formation of a single ethnic identity, the state could in turn claim that it existed to defend and promote the unique interests and values of its people. The state came to be portrayed as the institution that embodied the people's collective identity.

Within this logic we can see the seeds of the next major step, the concept of national identity, which became a potent force in the eighteenth century. National identity, when added to ethnic identity, powerfully asserts that the state is legitimate because it maintains national values and that the people and the state are united in the quest to chart an independent political future. The development and fusion of ethnic and national identities radically transformed states. On the basis of the idea that the people and their state were bound together in common cause, states could mobilize the public in ways never before possible. Most important, countries with a strong sense of nation-alism could raise mass armies and generate tax revenue, as people would sac-rifice their resources and very lives for the glory and destiny of their nation.

The very thought that individuals would fight and die for some abstract polit-ical concept was a radical change in human history. In Europe, Napoleonic France became the first country able to use such nationalist sentiment to its own advantage, raising a huge volunteer army that would conquer much of Europe. Both threatened and inspired by such nationalist fervor, other European peo-ples and states in turn forged their own national identities and aspirations for independence and self-government. This transformation gave rise to the idea of a **nation-state**, a sovereign state encompassing one dominant nation that it claims to embody and represent. Within a hundred years, most of the multieth-nic empires that dominated Europe would be destroyed, replaced by nation-states that were dominated by distinct ethnic groups and political identities.

Finally, the development of ethnic and national identities paved the way for the concept of citizenship. As societies viewed themselves first in ethnic and then in national terms, their relationship to the state began to change. If the state was the instrument of national will, some extended this logic to con-clude that state and people must be bound by a set of mutual responsibilities and obligations in the form of a social contract, as we mentioned in Chapter 2. How far this citizenship should be extended and what rights it should entail have come to be central concerns for all societies and states.

As with states, with the rise of European imperial power the institutions of ethnic and national identity and citizenship began to spread around the world. Just as states now lay claim to almost all the earth, so too have nearly all human beings become identified by some ethnicity, some nationality, some form of citizenship. In some cases, this has been the foundation for political stability, economic development, and democracy; at the other extreme, where identities are weakly held or come into conflict, the result is civil strife. Why these conflicts emerge and how to prevent them from becoming violent can be a matter of life and death.

Ethnic and National Conflict

Why are some countries able to forge consensus between different identities whereas in other countries such differences lead to seemingly irreconcilable conflict? Why is it that different identities can coexist peacefully and then sud-denly clash? Political scientists have different and often contending explana-tions for such forms of conflict, a debate that grew rapidly over the past two decades as such conflict spread in numbers and intensity.[4] Before we discuss these debates to any degree, we should clarify our terms.

Two Views of Ethnic and National Conflict

Top-down view	Conflict is generated by elites.
	Conflict could be stopped by controlling political leaders responsible.
	Use of outside force can be effective.
Bottom-up view	Conflict is generated by long-standing friction between groups.
	Animosity must "burn itself out."
	Use of outside force will be ineffective.

Ethnic conflict can be defined as conflict between ethnic groups that struggle to achieve certain political or economic goals at each other's expense. Each may hope to increase its own position by gaining greater control over existing political institutions like the state or government. By contrast, in **national conflict** one or more groups have as their goal sovereignty, clashing with others in the quest to form an independent state. In both of these cases, violence is a common tool, using or bypassing the coercive powers of the state.

Around the world, we can find examples of both ethnic and national conflict as well as cases where both are present. Afghanistan, for example, has seen frequent ethnic conflict, but this is not national; different Afghan groups are seeking not independence but greater power over each other. Conflict in Kenya in 2007 similarly pitted rival ethnic groups over a contested presidential election. In contrast, the American Revolution can be seen as a national rather than an ethnic conflict. The American colonies broke away from Great Britain to form a separate country, but this separation was based on conflicts over political rights and the desire for sovereignty. And finally, conflicts can be both ethnic and national in nature, such as in Yugoslavia or the Soviet Union in the 1990s, where various ethnic groups seceded to create their own nation-states.

Why do such conflicts break out in the first place? There is no easy answer, as cultural, economic, political, and other factors can come into play, each one interacting with the others and differing from case to case That said, we can generalize that many of the factors that precipitate conflict can be divided into "bottom up" versus "top down" explanations. Bottom-up explanations tend to be institutional in nature, stressing economic, societal, or political institutions that generate conflict. Among these, a fundamental element is the nature of the state and territory itself. For example, some scholars have used the term *artificial states* to refer to those countries where territorial divisions do not coincide with ethnic or national groups. These are commonly the legacy of imperialism, where borders were drawn with little concern for ethnic or national differences on the ground (See Figure 3.1). For example, 80 percent of the borders in Africa were drawn according to longitude and latitude, not ethnic or geographic distinction. Even after empires collapsed or withdrew, these borders remained. In such cases, economic development and political stability tend to be lower, again perhaps due to the lack of solidarity across groups. This instability and lower development in turn contributes to grievances, animosity, and the potential for conflict—a vicious cycle.[5] In contrast, top-down explanations emphasize the roles of political leaders in mobilizing groups, "fanning the flames" of animosity to achieve their individual goals. In reality, both factors are common in cases of ethnic and nationalist conflict, often as a kind of feedback loop. A sense of grievance may long be present but become catalyzed by leaders who are striving for power. Or conflict may develop first, pushing political leaders into taking sides to preserve their political power. In either case, the result can be a cycle of conflict that is difficult to control and, at an extreme, can lead to state failure.[6]

How can such intractable problems be solved, especially when ethnic fragmentation is so widespread throughout the world? There are no clear answers, and what has been suggested is controversial and uncertain. In the past, conflicts were resolved either through integrating groups—assimilation—or physical separation, such as the exchange of populations between countries or the "peace walls" that divide groups in Northern Ireland, Palestine, or Iraq. These proposals clearly raise concerns. Assimilation is often forced, while physical separation can mean ethnic cleansing and segregation.

A more palatable alternative can be found in the greater decentralization of power. It is often suggested that greater decentralization (what is called devolution) can solve ethnic and national problems by giving aggrieved communities more power—such as a shift from a unitary to a federal state. Does this in fact work? Devolution in Spain in the 1980s and the United Kingdom in the 1990s contributed to the end of separatist violence; however, a high degree of federalism in Yugoslavia did not prevent its violent collapse, and many scholars have argued that decentralization can intensify animosity by undermining a sense of national unity. Thus, care must be taken to devolve power in a way that gives different groups autonomy but makes politics national as well. For example, an electoral system that encourages regional, ethnic-based parties as opposed to national ones is likely to reinforce differences, limit compromise, and make conflict worse. Not surprisingly, then, institutions matter, and how regions are constructed and electoral systems designed can make a huge difference.[7] We will speak more about this in Chapter 5, when we look at democratic institutions in detail.

Figure 3.1   **LEVELS OF ETHNIC FRAGMENTATION**

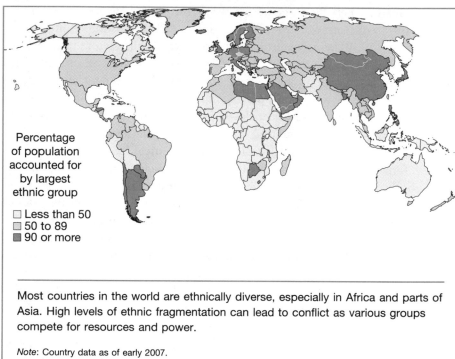

Percentage
of population
accounted for
by largest
ethnic group

☐ Less than 50
☐ 50 to 89
■ 90 or more

Most countries in the world are ethnically diverse, especially in Africa and parts of Asia. High levels of ethnic fragmentation can lead to conflict as various groups compete for resources and power.

Note: Country data as of early 2007.

Political Attitudes and Political Ideology

We have covered a great deal of ground so far in our discussion of the ways in which societies are organized and the identities they construct. In addition to these basic forms of group identity, people also hold individual views regarding the ideal relationship between freedom and equality. In the rest of this chapter, we will categorize these views into two different types: political attitudes and political ideology. Political attitudes are concerned with the speed of political change and the methods used to achieve it. Political ideology comprises the basic values held by an individual about the fundamental goals of politics regarding freedom and equality. Although political attitudes focus on the specific context of political change in a given country, political ideologies are more universal, as they assume that there is one ideal way to balance freedom and equality.

Where do attitudes and ideologies come from? These views are not defined by birth or by the state, although they may be influenced by either. Nor are the boundaries between such views as clear or evident as they are with eth-nicity, national identity, or citizenship. At the same time, they do not simply materialize out of thin air. Ideologies are built over time out of a set of ideas, and attitudes are articulated in response to the institutional conditions around us. More fundamentally, evolutionary biologists suggest that attitudes and ideologies—our individual or group preference for freedom, equality and the degree of change needed to get there—stem from basic survival strategies inherited from the past, balancing our need to establish order and embrace change. While our own political views may not be inherited, having such views in the first place is central to what makes us human.

Political Attitudes

Political attitudes describe views regarding the necessary pace and scope of change between freedom and equality. The attitudes are typically broken up into the categories of radical, liberal, conservative, and reactionary and are often arrayed on a spectrum, from left to right.

Radicals are placed on the extreme left. **Radicals** believe in dramatic, often revolutionary change of the existing political, social, or economic order. Radicals believe that the current system is broken and cannot simply be improved or repaired but must be scrapped in favor of a new order. As a result, most radicals do not believe in slow, evolutionary change. Politics will be improved, they believe, only when the entire political structure has been fundamentally transformed, remaking the political institutions of government, regime, and state. As a result, radicals may be more inclined to favor violence as a necessary or unavoidable part of politics. The institutions of the old order, in some radicals' view, will not change willingly; they will have to be destroyed. These views are not held by all radicals, however. Some may argue that radical change can be achieved through peaceful means, by raising public con-sciousness and mobilizing mass support for wide-ranging change.

Liberals, like radicals, believe that there is much that can be changed for the better in the current political, social, and economic institutions, and liberals, too, support widespread change. However,

IN FOCUS

Political Attitudes Are . . .

- Concerned with the speed and methods of political change.
- Generally classified as radical, liberal, conservative, or reactionary.
- *Particularistic*: relative to the specific context of a given country. A view that is "radical" in one country may be "conservative" in another.
- Distinct from political ideologies.

instead of revolutionary transformation, **liberals** favor evolutionary change. In the liberal view, progressive change can happen through changes within the system; it does not require an overthrow of the system itself. Moreover, liberals part from radicals in their belief that existing institutions can be an instrument of positive change. Liberals also believe that change can, and sometimes must, occur over a long period of time; they are skeptical that institutions can be replaced or transformed within a short period of time and believe that only constant effort can create fundamental change.

Conservatives break with both radicals and liberals in this view of the necessity of change. Whereas radicals and liberals both advocate change, disagreeing on the degree of change and the tactics to achieve it, **conservatives** question whether any significant or profound change in existing institutions is necessary. Conservatives are skeptical of the view that change is necessarily good in itself and instead view it as disruptive and leading to unforeseen outcomes. Conservatives see existing institutions as key to providing basic order and continuity; should too much change take place, conservatives argue, the very legitimacy of the system might be undermined. Conservatives also question the extent to which the problems that radicals and liberals point to can ever really be solved. At best, they believe, change will simply replace one set of problems with another, and at worst, it will actually create more problems than it solves.

Reactionaries are similar to conservatives in their opposition to further evolutionary or revolutionary change, yet unlike conservatives and like radicals, they view the current order as fundamentally unacceptable. Rather than a transformation of the system into something new, however, **reactionaries** seek to restore political, social, and economic institutions. Reactionaries advocate a restoration of values, a change back to a previous regime or state that they believe was superior to the current order. Some reactionaries do not even look back to a specific period in history, but instead seek to "return" to an envisioned past ideal that may never have existed. Reactionaries, like radicals, are more willing to use violence to advance their cause.

The left-right continuum on which these attitudes are typically illustrated gives the impression that the farther one travels from the center, the more polarized politics becomes. By this logic, then, radicals and reactionaries are miles apart from one another, with nothing in common (Figure 3.2). But our preceding discussion indicates that in many ways this is incorrect. Viewing left and right as a single continuum is misleading, for the closer one moves toward the extremes, the closer the attitudes become. In other words, the continuum of left and right is more aptly portrayed as a circle, bringing the two ends, radical and reactionary, close together (Figure 3.2). And in fact, radicals and reactionaries have much in common. Both believe in dramatic change, though in different directions, and both contemplate the use of violence to achieve this change. Although their ends may be quite different, the

Figure 3.2 TWO VIEWS OF POLITICAL ATTITUDES

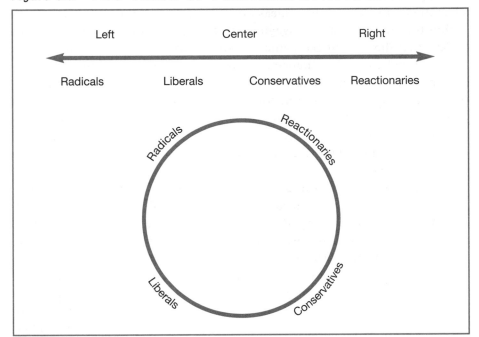

means of both groups can often be similar. In fact, just as liberals sometimes become conservatives and vice versa, radicals and reactionaries often cross over into each other's camps. For example, many reactionary fascists in Europe became supporters of radical communism after World War II. Some extreme forms of contemporary environmentalism exhibit both reactionary and radical elements.

One thing you may have noticed by this time is that our discussion of the political spectrum of attitudes has not provided any specific examples, such as welfare, civil liberties, or national defense—common sources of political division that separate right from left in most industrialized democracies. But these specific policy areas belong instead to the concept of political ideology, those basic beliefs about how politics should be constructed. It is important to emphasize again that ideology and political attitudes are not interchangeable. The attitudes of radicals, liberals, conservatives, and reactionaries often take on different ideological content in different societies, depending on the context. What might be considered radical in one country could be conservative in another.

Consider some examples. In the United States, Canada, or Western Europe, radicals are viewed as those who seek to fundamentally transform or overthrow the current capitalist democratic order, replacing it with a system of greater economic and social equality. Liberals in these countries are sympathetic to some of these ideas but believe in pursuing gradual changes within the current system, engaging democratic institutions. Conservatives believe that the current economic and social structures are as good as they are likely to be and that change is unlikely to improve the state of humanity, and indeed might make it worse. Reactionaries, meanwhile, not only would reject the radical and liberal critique of the status quo but would in fact favor a restoration of greater inequality or hierarchy between people through violence if necessary. The foregoing is a simplified but accurate description of how political attitudes are manifested in North America and much of the West.

These same political attitudes would manifest themselves quite differently in a country such as China, however. China has a nondemocratic regime dominated by a communist party, despite dramatic economic reforms. A Chinese radical, defined as someone who seeks the destruction of the current system, would advocate the overthrow of communist rule and its replacement, perhaps by a democracy like those found in the West. Students who were active in the Tiananmen Square protests for democracy in 1989 were frequently described or condemned by observers and the Chinese government as "radicals" because of their demands for sweeping political change. Chinese liberals are also likely to favor many of the changes that were advocated in Tiananmen Square, although they would approach these reforms much more slowly and in a less confrontational manner, favoring a process of gradual change within the existing political system. Chinese conservatives, those individuals suspicious of change, continue to resist calls for democratic reform. They may support or tolerate some market reforms, but they do not view these steps as leading down an inevitable path to democracy. Finally, Chinese reactionaries strongly oppose any reforms that might jeopardize communist rule. These hard-liners favor a return to earlier, "purer" communist values and policies, rolling back changes and restoring their communist ideal.

Clearly, American or Western European radicals would have little to say to Chinese radicals; they are united by their attitudes toward the scope and speed of political change, but in terms of their political values and goals—their ideologies—they are dramatically different. Indeed, Chinese radicals might have more in common with American or European conservatives in terms of their support for democracy and capitalism. Chinese reactionaries, on the other hand, might have more in common with American or European radicals: the former wish to return to communism as it existed before recent reforms, and many of the latter seek to achieve the same kind of outcome in their own countries—desiring to return to something that existed earlier. What gives any particular political attitude its position and power has everything to do with the context.

Political Ideology

The preceding discussion of the importance of context in understanding political attitudes might lead one to conclude that making any meaningful attitudinal comparisons between countries is difficult: what is radical in one country might be conservative in another. To move past these particularistic differences between countries, political scientists also speak about political ideologies. Like much of modern politics, the concept of ideology is relatively recent, with the term first coming into usage during the French Revolution to speak of a "science of ideas."[8] This meaning is important for it alludes to the fact that ideologies emerged with the construction of modern secular states to provide a means for guiding politics. Ideologies were thus viewed as alternatives to traditional sets of values such as religion; they were seen as based on rational thought rather than spiritual notions of good and evil. For our purposes, **political ideologies** are defined as sets of political values held by individuals regarding the fundamental goals of politics. Rather than being concerned with the pace and scope of change in a given context, as political attitudes are, ideologies are concerned with the ideal relationship between freedom and equality for all individuals and the proper role of political institutions in achieving or maintaining this relationship. Supporters of each ideology work to ensure that their values become institutionalized as the basic regime. In the modern world, there are five primary ideologies.

   Liberalism as an ideology (rather than as a political attitude) places a high priority on individual political and economic freedom. Adherents of a liberal ideology believe that politics should seek to create the maximum degree of liberty for all people, including free speech, the right of association, and other basic political rights. This goal requires a state with a low degree of autonomy and capacity so that it can be easily controlled or checked by the public should it begin encroaching on individual rights. For liberals, the lower the ability of the state to intervene in the public's affairs, the greater the scope and promise of human activity and prosperity.

As Thomas Jefferson said, "The legitimate powers of government extend to such acts only as are injurious to others. But it does me no injury for my neighbor to say there are twenty gods, or no God. It neither picks my pocket nor breaks my leg."[9]

   It is from these ideas of liberalism that we take our current definition of democracy, which is

IN FOCUS

Political Ideologies Are . . .

- Sets of political values regarding the fundamental goals of politics.
- Exemplified by five dominant modern ideologies: liberalism, communism, social democracy, fascism, and anarchism.
- *Universalistic*: not specific to one country or time.
- Distinct from political attitudes.

often defined as **liberal democracy**—a system of political, social, and economic liberties, supported by competition, participation, and contestation (such as voting). To be sure, liberals do recognize that not all individuals will succeed if left to their own devices and that there will inevitably be great economic inequality between the wealthiest and the poorest. In spite of this shortcoming, liberals argue that a high degree of freedom will produce the greatest amount of general prosperity for the majority. As a final point, we should note that liberalism as an ideology and liberalism as a political attitude are very different things (see box).

Communism differs greatly from liberalism in its view of freedom and equality. Whereas liberalism enshrines individual freedom over equality, communism rejects the idea that personal freedom will ensure prosperity for the majority. Rather, it holds that in the inevitable struggle over economic resources, a small group will eventually come to dominate both the market

---

INSTITUTIONS IN

ACTION

LIBERALISM, A CONFUSING TERM

The ideology and political-economic system of liberalism favors a high degree of individual freedom and a weak state in order to ensure the greatest prosperity, even if this means tolerating inequality. Yet this definition flies in the face of the term *liberal* as used in the United States and Canada, which typically implies a stronger state and greater state involvement in economic affairs. This confusion stems in large part from historical developments: over time, liberals who once placed their faith in the market to expand freedom and equality came to believe more and more that state intervention was necessary. Liberals in North America essentially became what many other countries would refer to as "social democrats."

This kind of ideological transformation did not occur in many other countries, however. Outside of North America, liberalism has retained its original meaning. Some political scientists therefore use the term classical liberalism to refer to the original tenets of the ideology. Others, particularly critics of the ideology, often use the term *neoliberalism* instead, indicating that the original ideas of liberalism (free markets and greater individualism along with a tolerance for inequality) are resurgent around the world.

So the term *liberal* can have many different meanings:

1. As a political attitude: favoring slow, evolutionary change
2. As a political ideology in North America: favoring a greater state role in limiting inequality, or what many outside of the region would call "social democracy"
3. As a political ideology outside of North America: favoring free markets and individualism, accepting greater inequality
4. As a political economy: favoring a limited state role in the economy

and the state, using its wealth to control and exploit society as a whole. Prosperity will not be spread throughout society but will be monopolized by a few for their own benefit. The gap between rich and poor will widen, and poverty will increase. For communists, liberal democracy is "bourgeois democracy"— of the rich, by the rich, and for the rich. Such institutions as free speech and voting are meaningless when a few control the wealth of society.

To eliminate exploitation, communism advocates that the state control all economic resources in order to produce true economic equality for the community as a whole. This goal requires a powerful state in terms of both autonomy and capacity, able to restrict those individual rights (such as owning property or opposing the current regime) that would hinder the pursuit of economic equality. Individual liberties must give way to the needs of society as a whole, creating what communists would see as a true democracy. The Soviet Union from 1917 to 1991 and China since 1949 are examples of countries where this communist ideology was installed as the political regime through revolution, creating what these countries call (or called) "people's democracies." Thus, democracy can be a slippery concept, defined differently, depending on a person's ideology. We will turn to this problem in greater detail in Chapter 5.

Social democracy (sometimes called **socialism**) shares some early influences with communism and liberalism to form its own distinct ideology. Social democracy accepts a strong role for private ownership and market forces while still maintaining an emphasis on economic equality. A state with strong capacity and autonomy is typically considered important to social democrats to ensure greater economic equality through specific policies, but this commitment to equality, while limiting freedom to a greater extent than under liberalism, recognizes the importance of individual liberty. In much of Europe, social democracy, rather than liberalism, is the guiding political regime. Many environmental parties, which seek to balance human and environmental needs, also have social democratic influences.

Fascism is hostile to the idea of individual freedom and also rejects the notion of equality. Instead, fascism rests on the idea that people and groups can be classified in terms of inferiority and superiority. Particular groups and people are superior to others, thus justifying a hierarchy among them. Whereas liberals, social democrats, and communists both see inherent potential in every person (although they disagree on the best means to unleash this potential), fascists do not. The metaphor of fascism is one of the society as an organic whole, a single living body, and the state as a vital instrument to express national will. State autonomy and capacity must therefore be high, and democracy, no matter how defined, is rejected as anathema, just as freedom and equality are rejected. No fascist regimes currently exist in the world, although fascism is well remembered from the Nazi system that ruled Germany from 1933 to 1945. Fascist political parties and movements still do exist, however, such as white supremacist groups in North America and Europe.

Anarchism departs from these other ideologies quite drastically. If liberalism, communism, and fascism differ over how powerful the state should be, anarchism rejects the notion of the state altogether. Anarchists share with communists the belief that private property leads to inequality, but they are opposed to the idea that the state can solve this problem; power in the hands of the state, in the anarchist view, would not necessarily eliminate inequality and would certainly eliminate freedom. As the Russian anarchist Mikhail Bakunin (1814–1876) once stated, "I am not a communist, because communism unites all the forces of society in the state and becomes absorbed in it . . . while I seek the complete elimination of the principles of authority and governmental guardianship, which under the pretence of making men moral and civilizing them, has up to now always enslaved, oppressed, exploited, and ruined them."[10]

Thus, like liberals, anarchists view the state as a threat to freedom and equality rather than as their champion, but they believe that both individual freedom and equality can be achieved only if the state is eliminated entirely. Without a state to reinforce inequality or limit personal freedom, argue anarchists, people would be able to cooperate freely as true equals. Moreover, without the state to reinforce private property and economic exploitation, people would be free to pursue their own lives and individual desires through cooperation.

Given that we live in a world of states, anarchism is the only one of the five primary ideologies that has never been realized. However, anarchist ideas played a role in the Russian Revolution (1917) and in the Spanish Civil War (1936–1939). In North America, some versions of libertarianism come close to an anarchist view in their hostility to the state, though libertarians differ from anarchists in their emphasis on private property.

Religion, Fundamentalism, and the Crisis of Ideology

Ideologies emerged alongside the modern secular state in many ways as an alternative or rival to religion. If religion had in the past helped describe and prescribe the world, including issues of freedom, equality, and power, then ideologies were seen as nonspiritual guides to that same end. Accordingly, ideologies and religions are in many ways similar, with their assertions about the fundamental nature of humans and society, the key to a good life and an ideal community, a host of core texts and prophets, and a promise of salvation.

IN FOCUS

Ideology and Political Attitudes

Ideology	Tenets	Corresponding Political Attitude in North America
Liberalism	Favors a limited state role in society and economic activity; emphasizes a high degree of personal freedom over social equality.	Conservative
Communism	Emphasizes limited personal freedom and a strong state in order to achieve social equality; property is wholly owned by the state and market forces are eliminated; state takes on task of production and other economic decisions.	Radical
Social democracy	Supports private property and markets but believes that state has a strong role to play in regulating the economy and providing benefits to the public; seeks to balance freedom and equality.	Liberal
Fascism	Stresses a low degree of both personal freedom and equality in order to achieve a powerful state.	Reactionary
Anarchism	Stresses the elimination of the state and private property as a way to achieve both freedom and equality for all; believes that a high degree of personal freedom and social equality is possible.	Radical

For the past two centuries, ideologies have increasingly replaced religion in public life. Whereas faith was central to public affairs, including politics, in the premodern world, the rise of ideology led to what has been termed "the privatization of religion," where faith was pushed out of the public sphere and relegated to private life. To be certain, this was never complete or uniform from country to country. But the emergence of modern states and ideology was central to the development of secularism and the retreat of religion. This process was described by Max Weber as "the disenchantment of the world," where faith in the mystical and spiritual was replaced by faith in the material world, in human-made institutions, and in the notion of progress.

In the past few decades, the claims and power of ideologies have themselves come under attack. In the past, the vibrancy of ideologies lay in the intensity of conflict between them. But slowly these battles have disappeared as many ideologies have fallen by the wayside. Fascism and communism have been largely discredited and defeated while anarchism has never been able to establish a lasting presence or a major following. This has left only social democracy and liberalism as the major ideological players, and even between these two, the differences have narrowed over time. To many people, politics now seems focused on the distribution of public benefits and the solution of technical issues rather than on any grand ideals.

Outside the West there has been a similar disenchantment, but for different reasons. Many individuals in less-developed countries who put their faith in Western ideology and institutions as a means of development and prosperity have been deeply disappointed. Communism, fascism, liberalism— none of these values has helped lift billions of people out of misery and tyranny. For all societies, rich or poor, the utopian claims associated with many ideologies—that modernity, science, and rationalism would usher in a golden age—have been discredited. It is in this vacuum of ideals that fundamentalism has appeared.

Before we proceed further, we should be clear about what we mean by the term *fundamentalism*. As with many politically charged words, fundamentalism is a term bandied about and used indiscriminately, often to describe someone holding strong views that repel us. Some scholars dislike the very use of the term beyond its original meaning, which described a particular kind of movement among Protestant Christians in the nineteenth century. But in spite of these problems or concerns, the term is useful and can describe a similar pattern across many religions.

The scholar Bruce Lawrence has defined fundamentalism as "the affirmation of religious authority as holistic and absolute, admitting of neither criticism nor reduction; it is expressed through the collective demand that specific creedal and ethical dictates derived from scripture be publicly recognized and legally enforced."[11] Following from this, **fundamentalism** can be viewed as an ideology that seeks to unite religion with the state, or rather, to make faith the sovereign authority—a kind of theocracy. This definition implies several things. First, fundamentalism is not the same as religiosity, puritanism, or religious conservatism. For example, Orthodox Jews or the

Amish are by definition not fundamentalists; any group that retreats from public life and politics hardly fits with our definition. Nor is merely a belief in a greater role for spirituality in politics or society, a movement seen in many places around the world, by definition fundamentalism. Second, fundamentalism is not a premodern view. As we mentioned earlier, in the premodern world, religion played a central role in public life. The rise of the modern state pushed faith into the private realm, replacing it in part with ideology. But fundamentalism seeks not to return to a premodern role for faith but rather to restructure religion as an ideology—to make faith the sole foundation for a modern regime, a concrete and inerrant guide for politics in the contemporary world.

To that end, fundamentalists base their beliefs on the failures of ideology. Through ideology, people sought to create heaven on earth, believing that they could deny the authority of God and seize control of their own destinies. The result has been, in the fundamentalists' view, not only greater human misery but spiritual malaise. Fundamentalists believe that even those who have benefited materially are still truly disenchanted, spiritually empty, and morally adrift, forced to fill their lives with mindless distractions—consumption, entertainment, sex—to avoid confronting this terrible truth. Fundamentalism, religion as a form of ideology, is thus a very modern phenomenon.[12]

As a political attitude, fundamentalism can often appear as a reactionary or radical view or a combination of the two. Fundamentalists will often make claims to return to some golden age of faith, but they also seek to solve the problems of the modern world, not simply turn back the clock. This mixture of reactionary and radical attitudes also explains why fundamentalism is often associated with violence. However, we should be clear that only a small number of fundamentalists embrace such an approach. We will delve into this issue in depth in Chapter 10 when we consider political violence. To reiterate, we should not confuse religiosity or piety with fundamentalism, or fundamentalism with violence.

How does fundamentalism fit the relationship between freedom and equality? Even within fundamentalist trends in a single religion, there is a great diversity of ideas. Some fundamentalist views emphasize collective equality but reject individual freedom in favor of submission to God; others posit an expression of individual freedom made possible through a political system based on faith and are less concerned with inequalities between people. There are also views that reject both freedom and equality in favor of hierarchy and the domination of believers over nonbelievers or the more faithful over the less so. Some forms of fundamentalism see the possibility of a religiously correct state; for others, that very notion of the state is incompatible with faith. It is thus a mistake to think of fundamentalism as a single ideology; rather, it is a pattern across many religions that has produced various ideological forms. In some cases, these remain nebulous and with few adherents. In other cases, the ideologies are well defined and exercise significant political power.

As the politics of fundamentalism continue to develop, this "return of God" may well prove to be one of the most important developments in future global politics, meaning not the end of history but its resumption in a new ideological form.[13]

Political ideologies differ according to where they see the proper balance between freedom and equality and what role the state should have in achieving that balance. Building on the preceding chapters' discussion of freedom and equality and state strength, Figure 3.3 shows how liberalism, social democracy, communism, fascism, and anarchism each try to reconcile freedom and equality with state power. These values are not particularistic, like

Figure 3.3 **POLITICAL IDEOLOGIES VARY ACCORDING TO THE BALANCE THEY STRIKE BETWEEN FREEDOM AND EQUALITY**

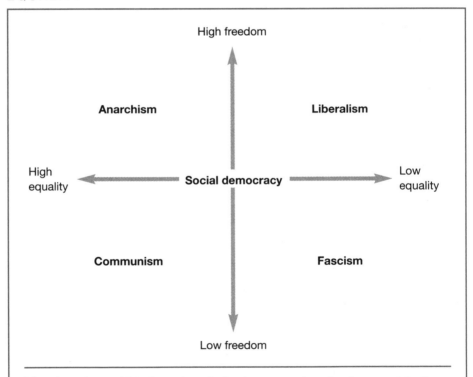

Liberals and anarchists favor decentralized power and weaker (or nonexistent) states, as well as high levels of individual freedom; communists and fascists favor the concentration of state power at the expense of individual freedom; social democrats prefer a balance between state power and individual freedom.

political attitudes, but are universal in their outlook. And although ethnic and national identities and citizenship may form the lines of conflict between groups, ideologies and attitudes shape the arena of political conflict within groups. How much change should there be? How fast? How peaceful or violent? And to what end? This is the essence of political life, as ideologies rise and fall in prominence, clash peacefully or violently, and pass from the scene as new ones take their place—as fundamentalism may now be doing. In 200 years, the ideas of liberalism or social democracy may make no more sense than monarchism does today.

Political Culture

So far, we have discussed how the ways in which societies identify themselves can have important implications for politics. Ethnicity, nationality, and citizenship provide collective identities with relatively clear boundaries, categorizing people and generating questions about the nature of freedom and equality between different groups. In contrast, political attitudes and ideologies shape debates over the pace and scope of political change and ultimately about the ideal relationship between freedom and equality for all groups. These differences in turn create political conflict, competition, and cooperation within societies and help us to understand how societal differences can profoundly shape politics within countries.

A final question remains. All of these forms of identification help set the arena for political struggles over freedom and equality, but what explains why countries differ so dramatically in their ideological outcomes? Why, for example, is the regime in the United States based on liberalism, with communist ideas considered radical by the public, whereas in China, communism forms the ideological core of the regime and liberalism is considered a radical notion? There are several possible explanations for these differences; some look to such factors as the level of economic development in society or the power of particular individuals or groups to spread or impose their political values. But a societal explanation also exists, embodied in a concept known as "political culture."

Before we discuss this concept any further, however, we need to understand what is meant by "culture" in general. If society is a complex collection of people bound by shared institutions, as it was defined at the start of this chapter, then **culture** comprises those basic institutions that help define a society. Culture acts as a kind of social road map, telling people what is and is not acceptable and providing guidelines and priorities for how people should organize their lives. In some societies, for example, alcohol may be viewed as a normal part of cultural activities whereas in other societies it may be frowned upon or taboo. Cultures can differ profoundly in their attitudes toward work, leisure, sex, privacy, and politics. Culture stands somewhere between the group identities of ethnicity, national identity, and citizenship on the one hand and individual political attitudes and ideologies on the other. Culture binds groups together, serving as part of the fundamental content of a society—of what makes the French different from the Peruvians or the Cambodians—yet at the same time it is a personal set of norms that people may choose to accept or reject to varying degrees.

In short, if ethnicity or nationality or citizenship is the definition of what group an individual belongs to, then culture is the activity that a group considers proper and normal for its members. **Political culture**, in turn, refers specifically to the basic norms for political activity in a society.[14]

Initially, it might be hard to believe that any society shares one specific set of political views that are somehow distinct from that of other countries. In fact, the discussion of political attitudes and ideologies so far in this chapter would seem to have taught us exactly the opposite—that people within countries differ widely in their views. Some political scientists in fact agree with this view, believing that political culture is not a useful concept. They see people everywhere as essentially rational, responding to politics in roughly similar and predictable ways. Others, however, argue that in each society fundamental political views and values are shaped by cultural institutions, and observers cannot accurately understand politics in a country if they do not grasp its political culture. In this view, ideologies and political attitudes rest on a foundation of political culture that gives meaning to political debates and defines what is rational.

Survey research done by the political scientist Ronald Inglehart and his colleagues indicates that across the globe, societies can be arrayed by the extent to which they are guided by values that fall along two axes: traditional versus secular-rational values and survival versus self-expression values (Figure 3.4). Traditional values emphasize such things as religion, family, and nation while secular-rational values are less deferential to authority in favor of individual autonomy. Survival values focus on economic and physical security and emphasize group conformity to that end whereas self-expression values emphasize greater diversity among people and tolerance for their behavior. As Inglehart's map of political culture shows, countries appear to

IN FOCUS

Political Culture Is . . .

- The basic norms for political activity in a society.
- A determining factor in what ideologies will dominate a country's political regime.
- Unique to a given country or group.
- Distinct from political attitudes and ideologies.

Figure 3.4   **CULTURAL VALUES AROUND THE WORLD**

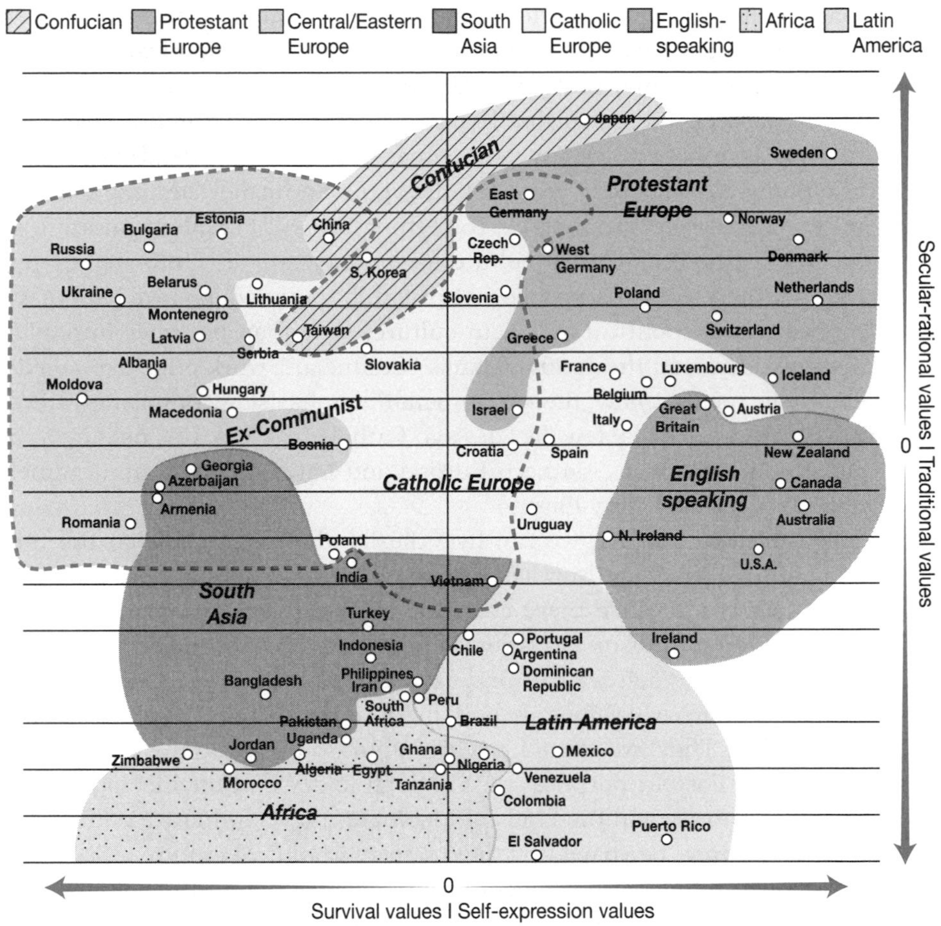

World values map. This figure charts cultural values of countries around the world. The figure shows not only that societies have distinct cultural differences, but that they tend to cluster based on religious, economic, geographical, or other shared experiences and institutions.

Source: http://margaux.grandvinum.se/SebTest/wvs/articles/folder_published/article_base_54.

group in certain cultural sets across these two axes, with African, Latin American, English-speaking, postcommunist, or historically Protestant countries falling in close proximity to one another. Interestingly, the United States shows a strong emphasis on self-expression values like much of

Europe but gives much greater emphasis to traditional values. Such differences can help explain why Europeans and Americans see eye to eye on many issues but seem worlds apart on others, such as abortion.[15]

At a broader level, some scholars have argued that political culture can be used to explain important political differences between countries For example, it has been suggested that levels of trust in government or levels of trust in other members of society (sometimes called social capital) are a function of cultural differences.[16] Some scholars go even further, arguing that there is in fact a culture of democracy, something we will talk about more in Chapter 5. Used badly, political culture arguments can veer into stereotyping or racism. There is also a problem of research methodology; we cannot simply attribute every political action to culture, as it then becomes impossible to disprove. Thus, in the 1980s, Japan's "Confucian" work ethic explained their economic success; now, their "Confucian" emphasis on conformity stifles economic change. Only a few decades ago Catholicism, too, was held up as a barrier to democracy in Southern Europe and Latin America, an argument no one takes seriously any longer.

With these caveats, we can hypothesize that countries that fall into the zone of traditional and survival values are going to have a more difficult time with democracy, since these cultural values may run up against individual freedom and pluralism. However, in all four corners of the world values map shown in Figure 3.4, we can find examples of democracies, even where traditional and survival values are both predominant, such as India, South Africa, and Turkey. Thus, we should be careful not to overstate the claims of political culture. For our purposes, it is enough to say that the ideological debates that take priority and the kinds of ideologies that dominate a country's political regime may be shaped by that country's political culture.

Assuming that this argument is correct, how resilient is political culture? Political culture, like culture in general, is subject to change over time. Some political scientists predict that as societies modernize, democratize, and interact as a result of economic globalization and technological innovation, their cultures will grow closer together, exchanging ideas, values, habits, and preferences, eventually leading to a fusion of cultures. They hypothesize that secular-rational and self-expression values, including environmentalism, individualism, human rights, and tolerance, will continue to spread around the globe. Others are more skeptical, arguing that as ideologies decline and globalization rises, people will in fact retreat back into culture as a source of identity in an uncertain world. Terrorist attacks in the developed world and wars in Afghanistan and Iraq, are often cited as horrible proof of this potential "clash of civilizations."[17] We will speak more of this in our chapter on globalization and the future of comparative politics.

In Sum: Society and Politics

Societies are complex and often difficult to unravel. In looking at how societal organization shapes politics, we have found that individuals have a number of identities that they hold simultaneously: ethnicity, national identity, citizenship, political attitude, ideology, and political culture. Ethnicity provides a group identity, binding individuals to a group, providing solidarity, and separating them from others. National identity provides a political aspiration for that group, a desire for freedom through self-government, while citizenship establishes a relationship between that group and a state. Although each of these identities is distinct, they are often strongly connected and in some cases blend into each other. Such identities may bind people together, but they can be the source of conflict when different groups see each other as threats to their freedom and equality.

Whereas group identities establish differences between groups, political attitudes, ideologies, and culture all help position an individual within a group. These three identities help clarify an individual's view of the ideal relationship between freedom and equality for society and of how fast and through what means change, if any, should be achieved.

Society's role in politics is clearly complicated, shaped by an array of factors that affect the ongoing debate over freedom and equality. Not long ago, many social scientists dismissed social identities such as nationalism and religion as outdated forms of identification that were giving way in the face of modernization and individualism. However, most now believe that collective identities are more resilient than was once thought and that they may in fact sharpen in the face of new societal challenges. More broadly, politics is not simply the sum of individual actions but the product of a rich array of institutions that overlap one another, providing meaning to our lives and informing the ideas, viewpoints, and values that we carry within us. We will consider this idea further in the next chapter as we turn to a new set of institutions and ideas that shape the struggle over freedom and equality: those concerned with economic life.

NOTES

1. Edward L. Glaeser, "Inequality," NBER Working Paper No. W11511, August 2005, available at SSRN: http://ssrn.com/abstract=776567.
2. For more on nationalism, see Benedict Anderson, *Imagined Communities* (London: Verso, 1983).

3. Charles Tilly, ed., *The Formation of National States in Western Europe* (Princeton, NJ: Princeton University Press, 1975). See also Reinhard Bendix, *Nation-Building and Citizenship* (Berkeley: University of California Press, 1964), and Douglass C. North and R. P. Thomas, *Rise of the Western World: A New Economic History* (New York: Cambridge University Press, 1976).

4. For an excellent overview, see David Horowitz, *Ethnic Groups in Conflict* (Berkeley: University of California Press, 2000).

5. Alberto Alesina, William Easterly, and Janina Matuszeski, "Artificial States," NBER Working Paper No. 12328, June 2006; see also M. Lim, R. Metzler, and Y. Bar-Yam, "Global Pattern Formation and Ethnic/Cultural Violence," *Science*, 317, no. 5844 (2007), pp. 1540–1544.

6. Michael Brown, ed. *The International Dimensions of Internal Conflict* (Cambridge, MA: Center for Science and International Affairs, 1996).

7. Dawn Brancati, *Peace by Design* (Oxford: Oxford University Press, 2009).

8. Destutt de Tracy, *A Treatise on Political Economy* (New York: Kelley, 1970).

9. Notes on the State of Virginia, chap. 17, available at www.xroads.virginia.edu.

10. Quoted in George Plechanoff, *Anarchism and Socialism* (Chicago: Kerr, 1909), p. 80.

11. Bruce Lawrence, *Defenders of God: The Fundamentalist Revolt against the Modern Age* (New York: Harper and Row, 1989), p. 78.

12. For an excellent discussion of fundamentalism in Christianity, Islam, and Judaism, see Karen Armstrong, *The Battle for God* (New York: Ballantine, 2001).

13. Gilles Kepel, *Revenge of God: The Resurgence of Islam, Christianity and Judaism in the Modern World*, Alan Brayley, trans. (University Park: Pennsylvania State University Press, 1994); Daniel Bell, *The End of Ideology: On the Exhaustion of Political Ideas in the Fifties*, with "The Resumption of History in the New Century" (Cambridge, MA: Harvard University Press, 2000).

14. Gabriel A. Almond, "The Study of Political Culture," in *A Discipline Divided: Schools and Sects in Political Science* (Newbury Park: Sage, 1990), pp. 138–156.

15. For more on the World Values Survey, see www.worldvaluessurvey.org.

16. See Francis Fukuyama, *Trust: The Social Virtues and the Creation of Prosperity* (New York: Free Press, 1996).

17. Samuel P. Huntington, *The Clash of Civilizations and the Remaking of World Order* (Simon and Schuster, 1996)

4 POLITICAL ECONOMY

KEY CONCEPTS

- All states are involved in the management of markets and property.

- States provide public goods, which are shared by society to some collective benefit.

- Different political economic systems reconcile freedom and equality through such things as social expenditures, taxation, regulation, and trade.

- Different states and political economic systems can be compared through levels of human development, wealth, and inequality.

- Political economic systems have become increasingly liberal over the past three decades.

Like politics, economies are made up of many different institutions—rules, norms, and values—that strongly influence how the economic system is constructed. People often think about economic systems as somehow "natural," with functions akin to the law of gravity. In reality, an economy relies on an array of institutions that enable individuals to exchange goods and resources with one another. Moreover, economic institutions, like political ones, are not easy to replace or change once they have been constructed. They become self-perpetuating, and people have a hard time imagining life without them.

Economic institutions directly influence politics, and vice versa. The economy is one of the major arenas in which the struggle over freedom and equality takes place. Some view the economy as the central means by which people can achieve individual freedom whereas others view the economy as the central means by which people can achieve collective equality. These values clash when different groups or ideologies have different expectations about how the economy should function and what kinds of societal goals should be pursued.

Inevitably, this struggle involves the government, the state, and the regime. How this balance between freedom and equality is struck directly influences such things as the distribution of wealth, the kinds of economic activity and trade that citizens may conduct, and the overall degree of security, insecurity, and prosperity that people enjoy. In short, the interactions between political institutions and economic institutions in any country will have a profound impact on the prosperity of every citizen. The study of how politics and economics are related and how their relationship shapes the balance of freedom and equality is commonly known as **political economy**.

In this chapter, we will address these issues through an investigation of the relationship between freedom and equality. We will start by asking what role states play in managing an economy. There are several different areas in which states commonly involve themselves in economic life; depending on such things as the dominant ideology and regime, the scope and impact of these actions can vary dramatically. Just as there are different ideologies concerning the ideal relationship between the state and society, as we saw in Chapter 3, there are different ideological views regarding the ideal relationship between the state and the market, each of which leads to a different political-economic system. Once we have compared these differing views, we will consider how we might measure and compare their relative outcomes. In the process, we will look at some of the most common standards by which to measure wealth and its distribution. Finally, with those concepts in hand, we will consider the future of the relationship between state and market and how their interaction shapes the balance between freedom and equality.

The Components of Political Economy

Before we compare the different types of relationships between states and economies around the world, we should first familiarize ourselves with the basic components of political economy. All modern states are strongly involved in the day-to-day affairs of their economies, at both the domestic and the global level. In shaping the economy to achieve their stated ideological goals, states and regimes use a variety of economic institutions.

Markets and Property

The most fundamental place to begin is with markets and property. When people speak of markets, one of the first things that may come to mind is a physical place where individuals buy and sell goods. For as long as human beings have lived in settled communities that were able to produce a surplus of goods, there have been markets. Markets are closely connected to the rise of cities; people would settle around markets, and markets would often spring up around fortifications, where commerce could be conducted with some sense of security. Such markets are still common in much of the world.

When social scientists speak of a market, they are speaking of these same forces at work, though without a specific location. **Markets** are the interactions between the forces of supply and demand, and they allocate resources through the process of that interaction. As these two forces interact, they create values for goods and services by arriving at specific prices. What is amazing about markets is that they can be so decentralized. Who decides how many cars should be built this year? Or what colors they should be? Or the cost of this textbook? These decisions are made not by any one person or government but by millions of individuals, each making decisions about what he will buy and what she will sell. If I produce a good and set its price at more than people are willing to pay, I will not be able to sell it and turn a profit. This will force me to either lower my price or go out of business. Similarly, if I produce a good that no one wants, I must change it or face economic ruin. Sellers seek to create products that people will desire or need, and buyers seek to buy the best or the most goods at the lowest price. Because more than one seller or producer typically exists for a product, this tends to generate competition and innovation. Sellers seek to dominate a market by offering their goods at the cheapest price or by offering a good that is innovative and therefore superior to any alternative.

In short, markets emerge as a community of buyers and sellers in constant interaction through the economic choices they make. At the same time, market forces typically require the state to enforce contracts, sanction activity, and regulate supply and demand where necessary. For example, by setting a minimum wage, a state is controlling to some extent the price of labor. By making certain drugs or prostitution illegal, the state is attempting to stamp out a certain part of the market altogether. Yet these goals are not always easily achieved. Minimum wages can be subverted by illegal immigrants, and "black" or underground markets appear where drugs and prostitution are illegal. While markets rely on states, they also have a life of their own, and each state must decide in what way and to what extent it will sustain and control the market.

Property is a second element critical to any economy.

IN FOCUS

Markets

- Sellers seek to create products that will be in demand.
- Buyers seek to buy the best or most goods at the lowest price.
- Markets are the medium through which buyers and sellers exchange goods.
- Markets emerge spontaneously and are not easily controlled by the state.

Just as markets are the medium through which goods and services are exchanged, **property** refers to the ownership of those goods and services. Property can refer to land, buildings, businesses, or personal items, to name some of the most common forms. In addition, a certain set of property rights can go along with ownership, such as the right to buy and sell property or the right not to have it taken away by the state or other citizens without a good reason (just cause) and compensation. As with market forces, property rights must be created and enforced by the state. Without state power functioning in a fair manner, property is insecure.

In many people's minds, property, unlike markets, has a physical presence. I can see a car, buy it, own it, and sell it when I want a new one. However, property is not always tangible. Intellectual property, for example, refers to ownership of a specific type of knowledge or content—a song, a piece of software code, or a treatment for diabetes. As economic developments center more and more on such intangible forms of information and knowledge, the concept of property and property rights becomes as fuzzy as that of markets, with no physical entity to speak of. Anyone who has downloaded a song, a movie, or software—often illegally—from the Web knows exactly what we are speaking of.

As with markets, states vary in how they construct and enforce property rights, both between people and between the state and society. States may fail to enforce the rights of individuals to protect their own property from other individuals—by failing, for example, to enact or enforce laws against counterfeiting or theft. States may also assume certain property rights for themselves, claiming ownership over property such as airwaves, oil, land, or businesses. Wherever these rights lie, it is important to understand that such rights do not automatically exist. In fact, many less-developed countries enjoy a wealth of property but a poverty of property rights, as these states are unable or unwilling to establish and enforce such rules. We will speak about this more in Chapter 9.

Public Goods

We have so far described property as goods that individuals acquire or utilize through the market for their own benefit, with the assistance of the state to sustain and secure those relationships. But there are limits. In some cases, the interaction of property and market do not produce certain benefits that society desires. Take, for example, transportation. Such infrastructure does exist in the private realm, such as toll roads or passenger ferries, and these private forms have a long history that predates the state. But most modern societies question the moral and practical implications of allowing these goods to belong only to a few. The privatization of such goods may limit economic development: a network of privately held roads might impede trade or fail to reach certain parts of the population. Because of such concerns, all states provide some level of **public goods**; indeed, the core definition of a state itself—a monopoly of violence—is the underlying public good on which all markets and property rest.

Public goods can be defined as those goods, provided or secured by the state, that are available for society and indivisible, meaning that no one private person or organization can own them. Unlike private goods, with their inherent link to individual freedom, public goods can generate greater equality, as the public is able to share broadly in their benefits.[1]

In many countries, roads, national defense, health care, and primary education are public goods, and everyone within the country may use them or benefit from their existence. But states do differ greatly in the extent to which they provide public goods, in large part because of the role of ideology in the relationship between states and markets. In the United States, health care is not a public good; it remains in private hands, and not everyone has equal access to it. In Canada, however, health care is a public good, provided by the state in the form of publicly owned hospitals and equal, universal benefits for all citizens. In Saudi Arabia and Iran, oil is a public good, owned by the state; revenue from its sale is spread (although not equally) among society. In Cuba, most businesses are owned by the state, making them public goods as well. The goods and profits of these firms belong not to a private owner, but to the state, to be distributed as the government sees fit.

Social Expenditures: Who Benefits?

This discussion of public goods leads us into the broader subject of **social expenditures**—the state's provision of public benefits, such as education, health care, and transportation, or what is commonly called "welfare" or the "welfare state." For many people, the very word *welfare*, like taxes, has an inherently negative connotation; it calls up images of "free riders" living off the hard work of others. To be certain, the redistribution of wealth in this manner can be controversial, with critics asserting that social expenditures lead to counterproductive behavior. High unemployment benefits, they argue, may discourage people from seeking work. Moreover, alternative forms of social security that people have relied on in the past, such as the family, the community, or churches, may be weakened by too broad a welfare system.[2]

Setting these arguments aside, one practical problem that does remain for many countries is that social expenditures can be very costly, especially where the population is aging and paying in less in taxes while drawing more social expenditures. In recent years, many countries have sought to control the growth of social expenditures, but this is easier said than done. We will explore this issue further in Chapter 7 as we consider the problem in the advanced democracies in particular.

Who benefits from social expenditures? If we use a strict definition, social expenditures are provided by the state to those who find themselves in circumstances where they require greater care: the unemployed, the elderly, the poor, and the disabled. Such expenditures include can health care, job training, income replacement, and housing. However, many forms of social expenditures are public goods that are more widely utilized. For example, a national health-care system treats employed and unemployed, wealthy and poor alike. Highways, public higher education, and cultural institutions such as museums may primarily benefit the well-off. In fact, if we look at social expenditures more broadly, we find that in many countries the majority of funds spent benefit the middle class, not the poor. In this sense, the modern welfare state is less a structure whereby the middle class and the rich are taxed to benefit the poor than one in which the middle class and the rich are taxed for services that benefit themselves.

Taxation

Over the past fifty years, public goods and social expenditures have become major and increasing responsibilities for states. How do states pay for these expenses? One of the major sources of funds is taxation. As with social expenditures, taxation generates passionate opinions: some view it as the means by which a greedy state takes the hard-earned revenues of its citizens, stunting economic growth, whereas others see it as a critical tool for generating a basic level of equality. Regardless of one's opinion of taxation, states are expected by societies to provide a number of public goods and services, and for most countries taxation is the key source of revenue.

How much tax is collected varies from country to country. Figure 4.1 illustrates this variation, showing that in some countries, taxes consume a large portion of the gross domestic product of the country (a term we will discuss in more detail shortly). Many European countries with large social expenditures tend to have high overall tax rates to fund those expenses. In addition, countries differ in where this revenue comes from. Some countries rely on high personal taxation while others rely on taxes on businesses or goods and services. All countries struggle with finding the right mix and level of taxation, aiming to extract needed funds without stunting economic growth by taking too much.[3]

Money, Inflation, and Unemployment

It should be getting clearer that many political-economic processes are tightly interlinked. States must form a relationship with markets and property, decid-

Figure 4.1 **TAXATION, 2005**

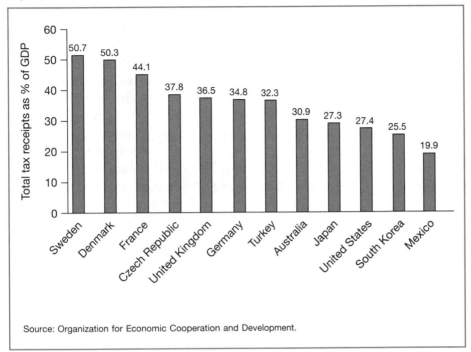

Source: Organization for Economic Cooperation and Development.

ing what goods and property should remain in private hands, what should be public, and what kinds of rights exist for each. They must also determine the level and forms of social expenditures needed to ensure a basic standard of living and security for all citizens. This distribution requires funds, and states must typically draw on the public's resources through taxation. But a successful and productive tax base needs a dynamic and growing economy, which is also necessary to meet the public's needs and demands. So while the state is charged with managing markets, property, and public benefits, it also has a hand in fostering economic growth.

One basic way the state does this is through the creation and management of money. Money is nothing more than a medium of exchange; unlike wealth, which consists of property that has value, money is an instrument through which people conduct economic transactions. Money represents only a tiny fraction of the wealth in the world, most of which is tied up in houses, factories, land, and other property. But without money, economic transactions are difficult. States thus play a critical role in providing money as a means to secure and stimulate economic transactions.

Long ago, money did not exist. As complex political systems began to take shape, however, they began to establish some basic monetary relationships through a monetary system, which typically rested on metals that held some intrinsic value (gold and silver). Within the past century, however, money has completely lost all its intrinsic worth. With these transformations, people have come to place their faith in a state's currency on the basis of their trust in that state. A person accepts payments in dollars or euros or yen because he or she knows that others will accept them in turn. The society functioning under that currency trusts that money only so long as it also trusts its state.

As a result of their control over money, states have a great deal of influence over their domestic economies. Part of this power comes through what is known as a **central bank**, an institution that controls how much money is flowing through the economy, as well as how much it costs to borrow money in that economy.[4] One of the main ways a central bank affects these two areas is by changing a national interest rate, that is, the rate charged to private banks when they need to borrow funds from the central bank or one another. When the central bank lowers the interest rate charged to banks, those banks in turn typically lower their own interest rates for businesses and individuals. Loans become less expensive and saving becomes less lucrative, prompting people to borrow more and spend more. This in turn increases the amount of money active in the economy and thereby stimulates economic growth. If the central bank raises interest rates, on the other hand, people are likely to borrow less and save more to take advantage of the higher interest their savings can earn. The money supply in the economy contracts as a result, and economic growth is likely to slow. Thus, during the first half of 2008 the U.S. Federal Reserve (the U.S. central bank) cut interest rates six times, lowering the national rate from over 4 percent to 2 percent in an effort stimulate the economy in the face of an economic downturn.

The actions of a central bank are also closely tied to two other important factors in any economy: inflation and unemployment. When the money supply is increased through inexpensive credit, an economy can wind up with too much money chasing after too few goods—an imbalance of supply and demand. In such circumstances, prices begin to rise and money loses its value, a problem known as **inflation**. Although small levels of inflation are not a problem, inflation can become problematic when it is too high. Savings rapidly lose their value, and workers and those on fixed incomes, such as the retired, find that their salaries or pensions buy less and less. People then press for higher wages or benefits to offset higher prices, and this in turn feeds inflation further.

In extreme cases, countries can experience **hyperinflation**, defined as inflation that is more than 50 percent a month for

IN FOCUS

A Central Bank . . .

- Controls the amount of money in the economy.
- Controls the cost of borrowing money.
- Lowers interest rates to stimulate the economy.
- Raises interest rates to check inflation.

more than two months in a row. (By comparison, the inflation rate in North America and Europe over the past decade ranged between 2 percent and 4 percent per year.) Hyperinflation usually occurs when governments find themselves lacking the tax revenues to cover basic expenditures. The government in question may therefore decide to simply print money to pay for its own expenditures. When large amounts of money are printed and dumped into the economy, however, its value quickly erodes, undermining the legitimacy of the currency itself. This in turn leads people to spend their money as quickly as possible, driving inflation even higher. As you can imagine, under such conditions, normal economic processes quickly collapse. For example, in 2008, Zimbabwe, suffering from economic and political turmoil as a result of the repressive and erratic leadership of its current government, faced an inflation rate of somewhere between 100,000 and 1,000,000 percent; one U.S. dollar could purchase approximately one billion Zimbabwean dollars.

The dangers of inflation might lead us to conclude that tight control over the money supply should be a government's first economic priority. Yet the trade-off of high interest rates can be higher rates of unemployment and low rates of economic growth. If money becomes too expensive to borrow, businesses may be unable to create new jobs because their supply of credit for additional investment is limited. Individuals may also avoid borrowing and spending, leaving their money in the bank to earn interest at attractive rates. This can lead to **deflation**, when too many goods are chasing too little money. Dropping prices might sound like a good thing, but they can be devastating for businesses if the businesses are unable to make a profit, leading to more unemployment, less spending as a result, and even more deflation. This has been a serious problem in Japan, where prices dropped each year between 1998 and 2007, hindering economic growth. Since 2008, deflation has been a growing concern in North America and Europe as well (even though interest rates are low). States thus walk a very fine line in managing the money supply, trying to create an economy with low inflation and low unemployment, yet knowing that these two factors may work against each other.

Given the difficulty of this balance and the temptation for governments to use the central bank for their own political ends (such as printing money to cover expenses or lowering interest rates around election time), many countries have insulated central banks from the government by making it difficult for elected leaders to dismiss the directors of the central bank. This is typically done by guaranteeing the head of the central bank a fixed term of office.

Regulation

So far, our discussion has dealt with the state's role in fostering the development of markets and property—what is to be provided, by whom, and at what cost. But states must concern themselves not only with economic output but also with the means by which that output is created. As with public goods, moral and technical issues often affect a state's approach in this area. Are some economic processes inherently counterproductive in creating goods and services? Are there processes that generate "public bads," problems that negatively affect society? Whose rights are primary in these cases? Those of citizens or those of business? These concerns draw states into the realm of economic regulation. **Regulations**—rules or orders that set the boundaries of a given procedure—may take a number of different forms. First, regulations may be fundamentally economic in nature. Such regulations may control prices for certain goods or services, such as food or energy. Economic regulations may also control what firms may operate in what markets. One example here are national telephone systems, which until recently functioned either as a private **monopoly** or a state monopoly in much of the world. A second set of regulations can be described as essentially social in nature. In contrast to economic regulations that focus on how business functions in the market, social regulations deal more with managing risk, such as safety and environmental standards.[5] Naturally there is an overlap between these regulations; for example, environmental regulations can strongly affect what firms may enter the market. Economic regulations may also affect international trade, to which we will turn next.

Trade

States must grapple with the challenge of regulating economic production not just within their country but between their citizens and the outside world. In most economies, markets are no longer only local; goods and services come from all over the world. States can influence the degree of competition and access to goods within their own country by determining what foreign goods and services may enter the domestic market.

The way in which a state structures its trade can have a profound impact on its own economic development. States have a number of tools to influence trade: **tariffs**, which are basically taxes on imported goods; **quotas**, which limit the

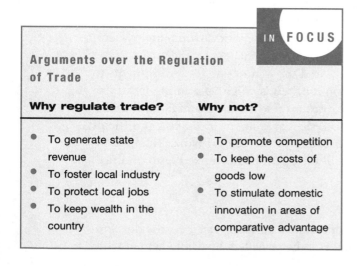

IN FOCUS

Arguments over the Regulation of Trade

Why regulate trade?	Why not?
• To generate state revenue	• To promote competition
• To foster local industry	• To keep the costs of goods low
• To protect local jobs	• To stimulate domestic innovation in areas of comparative advantage
• To keep wealth in the country	

quantity of a good coming into the country; and other **nontariff regulatory barriers**, which may create health, packaging, or other restrictions and whose ostensible purpose is to protect its citizens but which in reality make it difficult or expensive for foreign goods to be sold in the local market. For example, in Canada, 35 percent of all music on AM and FM radio must be of Canadian origin, and for television programs, 60 percent must be Canadian. Airlines that fly within the United States must be American owned.

Why regulate trade? States may favor tariffs as a way to generate revenue, and they and local manufacturers may see such barriers as a way to stimulate or protect local industries and firms. Those who oppose trade barriers argue that trade leads to more competition, innovation, and **comparative advantage**—the ability to produce a particular good or service more efficiently relative to other countries' efficiency in producing the same good or service.[6]

We've covered a great deal in this section, so let's quickly review what we have discussed. The most basic "building blocks" of political economy are markets and property, and states are involved in the creation and stability of both. States step into the market when the private sector cannot or should not provide or control certain products, creating public goods and other social expenditures. To fund such expenses, states must not only develop a system of taxation but also help stimulate and secure the economy. Expanding and contracting the money supply helps increase economic development and provide jobs, but states must be careful not to overstimulate or retard the economy, which can generate inflation or deflation. To prevent such mishaps, many states insulate their central banks from government interference. In addition to overseeing and drawing revenue from the creation of private and public goods, states must also concern themselves with regulating the means of the goods' production. Managing competition, both within the country and between countries, is a contentious task. All of these responsibilities are part of a complex web of cause and effect that can shape freedom, equality, and the generation of wealth. Which mixture of policies across these areas will result in economic prosperity and state power? States have taken radically different approaches to the ideal relationship between state and market, leading to a variety of distinct political-economic systems around the world—all of which are currently under challenge.

Political-Economic Systems

A **political-economic system** can be defined as the actual relationship between political and economic institutions in a particular country, as well as the policies and outcomes they create. Various types of political-economic systems view the ideal relationship between state and market, and between freedom and equality, in different ways. Political-economic systems are often classified as liberalism, social democracy, communism, or mercantilism. Three of these political-economic systems match the political ideologies we discussed in Chapter 3. This should not be too surprising: political-economic systems can be seen as the attempt to realize an abstract ideology in the form of real economic institutions and policies. There is always a disjuncture, however, between theory and practice. For example, some subscribers to a liberal ideology would say that existing "liberal" political-economic systems around the world do not live up to liberal ideals. Many communists similarly condemned the communist political-economic system that was practiced in the Soviet Union as a betrayal of "true" communist thought. In addition, the ideologies of fascism and anarchism do not have a political-economic counterpart to speak of. In the case of fascism, this is because the fascist political-economic systems that arose in the 1930s were destroyed by World War II. Anarchism, meanwhile, has never been effectively realized.

These basic typologies simplify the complexity of political economy. In reality, of course, there are many different variations within and among these categories. Each of these categories strikes a different balance between state power and the economy, thereby shaping markets and property, public goods and social expenditures, taxation, regulation, and trade.

Liberalism

Recall from Chapter 3 that as a political ideology, liberalism places a high priority on individual political and economic freedom; it advocates limiting state power in favor of greater freedoms for the individual and the market. Liberalism assumes that individuals are best suited to take responsibility for their own behavior and well-being. Liberal scholars such as Adam Smith put their faith in the market and in private property: If people are allowed to harness their own energies, sense of entrepreneurialism, and, yes, greed, they will generate more prosperity than any government could produce through "top-down" policy making and legislation.

For liberals, then, the best state is a weak one, constrained in its autonomy and capacity. Other than securing property rights, the state should have a limited involvement in the economy. Public goods should be located only in critical areas such as defense or education to limit "free riding" and to encourage individual responsibility. Unemployment should be accepted as an inevitable, even desirable, part of market flexibility. Taxation should be kept to a minimum so that wealth would remain in the hands of the public. Regulation should be light, and trade should be encouraged to stimulate competition and innovation. Overall, the state should act as a sort of night watchman, intervening to defend the public only when crises arise. These conditions describe the liberal tenet of **laissez-faire**, which holds that the economy should be "allowed to do" what it wishes. This is what we typically think of as **capitalism**—a system of private property and free markets.

Under these minimalist conditions, liberals believe, economic growth will be maximized. Moreover, under such conditions, people will enjoy the greatest amount of personal and political freedom. Liberals would in fact stress that democracy requires a free market. If too much economic and political power is concentrated in the hands of the state, they believe, this monopoly would endanger democracy. Thus, weak states are best; as Adam Smith, one of the fathers of liberal ideology, argued in 1755, "Little else is requisite to carry a state to the highest degree of opulence from the lowest barbarism but peace, easy taxes, and a tolerable administration of justice: all the rest being brought about by the natural course of things."[7]

Liberalism as a political-economic system, then, is defined by its emphasis on individual freedoms over collective equality and on the power of markets over the state. As you might imagine, the United States is typically touted as a paragon of liberal values. Regulations are often weaker and social expenditures and taxation lower than in other industrialized democracies, and the American public is largely skeptical of state power and embraces capitalism. But the United States is not the only country in the camp of liberalism. The United Kingdom, the intellectual wellspring for much of liberal thought, is also viewed as a liberal country, as are Canada, Australia, and New Zealand (all, like the United States, former British colonies). Many other countries around the world have over the past twenty years embraced the "neoliberal" economic model and are noted for their lower levels of government regulation, taxation, and social expenditures. However, even though these countries can all be classified as liberal systems, they too vary in a number of areas, such as the range of public goods such as higher education, unemployment, or retirement benefits. In addition, even though liberal ideology would argue that a free market and democracy are inseparable, we do find countries with liberal political-economic systems that nevertheless restrict democratic rights. Singapore, Oman, Bahrain, and the United Arab Emirates are regularly noted for having some of the freest economic systems in the world, and yet individual political and civil rights are restricted in each. Critics of liberalism often highlight this contradiction, pointing out that the free market can sit easily with political repression. We will discuss this contradiction further when we turn to authoritarianism in Chapter 6.

Social Democracy

In Chapter 3, we noted that social democracy draws from liberalism and communism in an attempt to temper the extremes of too much freedom or too much equality. Like liberalism, social democracy functions on a foundation of **capitalism**—private property and open markets—rejecting communists' call for revolution and state appropriation of private property and wealth. Most notable among early social democratic thinkers was Edward Bernstein (1850–1932). In his 1898 work *Evolutionary Socialism*, Bernstein rejected Karl Marx's belief in inevitable revolution, concluding instead that democracy could evolve into socialism through the ballot box rather than through the gun.[8]

Based on this rejection of revolution and embrace of democracy, social democracy accepts a role for private property and market forces, but it remains ambivalent about their ultimate benefits to society. Unchecked economic development produces great inequality, social democrats argue, by concentrating wealth in the hands of a very few. This in turn can polarize society, pitting owners against laborers, rich against poor, city against countryside. In this way of thinking, the state is seen not as a threat to society or economy but as a creator of social rights, otherwise lost in the vicissitudes of the market.

State power can thus manifest itself in a number of ways. A wide array of public goods, such as health care, pensions, and higher education, should be made available by the state. The need for competition should not stand in the way of strong state regulation or even ownership of certain sectors of the economy, and trade should similarly be managed in such a way that it does not endanger domestic businesses and jobs. Finally, the goal of equality requires a higher level of social expenditures to ensure basic benefits for all. Taxes make these social expenditures possible while also redistributing wealth from the rich to the poor. Thus, taxes tend to be higher in a social democratic system, and capitalism more constrained.

As with the case of liberalism, social democracies are not all of one type. Social democratic systems can vary in labor flexibility. Jobs may be highly regulated in hours worked, benefits paid, and conditions of termination, or firms may be able fire workers more easily and hire at full or part time. Unemployment benefits may be generous, contingent on retraining or government work schemes, or rather limited. Tax rates and the redistribution of income can also be quite varied; taxes as a percentage of GDP are not significantly different in the liberal United Kingdom and the social democratic Germany, though in general social democratic systems rely on higher taxes.[9]

IN **FOCUS**

How Do Social Democracies Seek to Achieve Greater Equality?

- Through taxes, which make high levels of social expenditure possible while redistributing wealth from rich to poor.
- Through trade, which is promoted but balanced with preserving domestic industry and jobs.
- Through government regulation and even ownership of important sectors of the economy.

In addition to these policies, another element found in some social democratic systems is the use of **neocorporatism**, a system of policy making involving the state, labor, and businesses. In the liberal model, economic decisions are made through the competitive interaction of business and labor; workers demand higher wages or better safety conditions, striking or quitting their jobs when necessary, and employers hire, fire, and negotiate with workers as they see fit. The state plays a limited role in these relations. In contrast, a neocorporatist system relies on a limited number of associations that represent a large segment of business and labor. These associations, such as trade unions and business associations, are in turn recognized by the state as legitimate representatives of their members, and together these associations and the state forge agreements on such important economic policy issues as wages, unemployment compensation, and taxation. The result, supporters argue, is

---

IN FOCUS

Contributors to the Theories of Political Economy

System	Thinker	Contribution
Liberalism	Adam Smith	*The Wealth of Nations* (1776), considered one of the first texts on modern economics. Articulated the idea that economic development requires limited government interference.
Mercantilism	Friedrich List	*National System of Political Economy* (1841). Rejected free-trade theories of liberalism, arguing that states must play a strong role in protecting and developing the national economy against foreign competitors.
Communism	Karl Marx	*Das Kapital* (1867). Asserted that human history is driven by economic relations and inequality and that revolution will eventually replace capitalism with a system of total equality among people.
Social Democracy	Edward Bernstein	*Evolutionary Socialism* (1898). Rejected Marx's belief in the inevitability of revolution, arguing that economic equality can be achieved through democratic participation.

a system that is much less prone to conflict and that provides a greater role for both business and labor in state economic policies.

Finally, social democratic systems often involve themselves in the economic system through partial or total state ownership of firms, which they consider to be public goods. Until 2002, the French state owned more than 40 percent of the auto manufacturer Renault (it is now around 15 percent); and in Sweden, all iron mines are owned by the state, having been purchased from private businesses decades ago.

Social democratic systems are most common in Europe, with states that have more autonomy and capacity in order to actively manage the economy.[10] Liberals criticize such systems as costly and a drag on innovation and competition; social democrats respond that their system avoids the excesses of liberalism while still encouraging entrepreneurial activity.

Communism

Whereas social democracy departs from liberalism in its attempt to balance individual freedom and collective equality, the political-economic system of communism chooses effectively to eliminate individual freedom to achieve equality. We will discuss communism in much greater detail in Chapter 8, when we look at communist and postcommunist countries; for now we will focus on its basic political economic institutions. Communist thinkers such as Karl Marx began with the premise that capitalism, with its private property and free markets, cannot truly serve the needs of society as a whole. Communists view private property and markets as a form of power that inevitably leads to control over others. Economic competition between people creates exploitation and the development of social classes in which a small group of the wealthy dominate and benefit from the labor of the poor majority. Both domestically and internationally, this exploitation opens an ever-wider gap between those who control the economy and those who merely labor in it. Such inequalities, Marx argued, will inevitably lead to a revolution, during which a single communist party will take control of the state on behalf of all people.

Given this interpretation of markets and property, communist systems use the state to transform both. Private property is fully nationalized, placed in the hands of the state on behalf of the people. Through nationalization, communism seeks to eliminate the economic differences between people and the instruments of exploitation. In other words, the entire economy becomes a public good, existing for the benefit of all. In addition, market forces are eliminated by the state; almost all private transactions are considered black markets (illegal transactions). In stark contrast to the "invisible hand" of liberalism's market and the guided economies of social democracy, communism's economic decision making is entrusted entirely to the state, which is assumed to be the only institution that can rationally allocate resources to the greatest benefit for all of society. This requires a large planning bureaucracy to determine what needs to be made and how it should be distributed.

Because all economic decision making and ownership are centralized under state control, many of the essential tasks of states in other political-economic systems are fundamentally different under communism. As we noted, in the absence of markets and property, there are no property rights to speak of; other than personal effects, individuals do not own businesses, land, or their homes. Taxation takes an indirect form through fixed prices and wages; any profit produced by a worker or a firm goes to the state for public expenditures. Unemployment is eliminated, and labor allocated by the state—

IN FOCUS

Political-Economic Systems

	Liberalism	Social Democracy	Communism	Mercantilism
Role of the state in the economy	Little; minimal welfare state	Some state ownership, regulation; large welfare state	Total state ownership; extensive welfare state	Much state ownership or direction; small welfare state
Role of the market	Paramount	Important but not sacrosanct	None	Limited
State capacity and autonomy	Low	Moderate	Very high	High
Importance of equality	Low	High	High	Low
How is policy made?	Pluralism	Corporatism	State/party	State
Possible flaws	Inequality, monopolies	Expense of welfare state, inefficiency	Authoritarianism and inefficiency	Can tend toward authoritarianism; can distort market
Examples	U.S., UK, former British colonies	Europe (Germany, Sweden)	Cuba, Soviet Union, China	Japan, South Korea, Russia

in other words, the state decides who will work where. Because all firms are owned by the state, competition is also eliminated, and regulations, although present, may be much weaker—since the state winds up regulating itself. Social expenditures are extensive, with all basic services, including health care, education, retirement, even leisure activities, owned and provided by the state. Finally, trade is highly restricted; the only imports are those the state deems necessary that cannot be produced domestically. State capacity and autonomy are extremely high; the state can operate without the interference of either the public or private economic actors.[11]

As you would expect, supporters of private property and market forces argue that states with communist political-economic systems lack the ability to make the kinds of economic decisions that are the normal product of a decentralized market. Moreover, placing all economic power in the hands of the state would essentially make democracy impossible. If there are no property rights left with the people and if all economic decisions are made by the state, there is no separation between public and private. States wind up controlling the fates of people—where they live and work, what they earn, what they may buy. In response, communists would say that what they offer is total equality for all; their system emphasizes equality over individual freedom, just as liberalism does the opposite. And even if such a system is inefficient, its supporters might argue, better that economic resources are wasted in the attempt to provide for all than squandered on luxuries for a wealthy few, as is common in market economies.

Mercantilism

The final political-economic system, **mercantilism**, stands quite apart in the debate over freedom and equality that separates liberalism, social democracy, and communism. Whereas all three systems we have studied so far theoretically emphasize the needs of society, albeit in different ways, mercantilism focuses on the needs of the state; it is much less concerned with either individual freedom or collective equality. Instead, national economic power is paramount. As a result, mercantilism views the domestic economy as an instrument that exists to serve the needs of the state by generating wealth that can be used for national power. Mercantilist states focus in particular on their position in the international system, for they believe that economic weakness undermines national sovereignty. Political power must be backed by wealth, in the mercantilist view, and that wealth should be directed toward national ends.[12]

Although this system may seem a strange outlier in the debate between freedom and equality, as it seems to emphasize neither, as a political-economic system mercantilism is the oldest of the four we have covered. At the advent of modern economies in Europe centuries ago, most countries engaged in mercantilist practices. The building of empires, in particular, was an outgrowth of mercantilism, a way in which a state could use its political power to gain control over resources and markets, shutting out its rivals. The creation of British colonies in North America and elsewhere and the requirement that they trade only with the home country are good examples of mercantilist practices at work. And in spite of the challenges posed by other political-economic alternatives, mercantilism has been used to great effect, particularly in Asia.

One way that mercantilist states attempt to achieve state economic power is through an active industrial policy. Economic ministries seek to direct the economy toward certain industries and away from others through such policies as taxation and subsidies. In some cases, mercantilist states, like social democracies, may rely on partial or full state ownership of specific industries (sometimes called **parastatals**), attempting to create certain businesses that are viewed as critical for international competitiveness. Capitalism is guided by the state toward goals set by the government.

Another complementary method to boost the domestic economy under mercantilism is the strong use of tariffs, nontariff barriers, and other trade regulations. Here the rationale is that goods that are not locally produced lead to a loss of national profits and an increased dependence on foreign economies. High tariff barriers are a common way to shield and promote domestic industry. For example, after World War II, the Japanese government relied on its Ministry of International Trade and Industry to steer the economy toward exports such as electronics and automobiles. High tariff barriers kept foreign competition at bay, and subsidies were provided to certain industrial sectors, such as producers of semiconductors. South Korea subsequently followed a similar set of policies.

In its emphasis on state power, mercantilism does not typically focus on social expenditures in the way that social democracy does. Welfare benefits tend to be much lower. Indeed, there is a logic to this policy: a low level of benefits can encourage higher public sav-

IN FOCUS

How Do Mercantilist States Seek to Achieve Economic Power?

- By directing the economy toward certain industries and away from others through the use of subsidies and taxation.
- Through partial or full state ownership of industries that are considered critical (parastatals).
- With the strong use of tariffs, nontariff barriers, and other regulations.
- By limiting social expenditures and thereby keeping taxation to a minimum.
- With low interest rates set by the central bank to encourage borrowing and investment.

ings, which can in turn be borrowed by the state or businesses. Lower levels of expenditure are also likely to translate into lower taxes. State capacity and autonomy tend to be higher in mercantilist political economic systems, though markets and private property remain.

Supporters of mercantilism cite its ability to direct an economy toward areas of industrial development and international competitiveness that the market, left on its own, might not pursue. For developing countries such direction is particularly attractive, and Japan and South Korea are cited as exemplars of mercantilism's strengths.[13] Some cite contemporary China as now more mercantilist than communist and ascribe its rapid growth to this shift. Critics of mercantilism observe that as with communism, states are ill-suited to decide an industrial path for the country, and the result is often inefficient industries that survive only because they are protected from outside competition. In addition, the tight relationship between private property and the state is a recipe for corruption, further dragging down development. In the past, mercantilism was often associated with nondemocratic and even fascist regimes, creating a certain stigma around this political economic system. However, postwar Japan and India are examples of democratic countries that long relied on mercantilism. Overall, though, mercantilism is more commonly correlated with authoritarian systems than with democracies.

Political-Economic Systems and the State: Comparing Outcomes

Having gained an understanding of the different political-economic systems used around the world and the different ways they approach their tasks, we next should consider how to compare them. Since each system is founded on a different ideological approach and set of institutions to reconcile freedom and equality, it might seem that trying to compare them would be meaningless. However, there are indicators we can use to compare these systems. These indicators are by no means the only ways to make comparisons and draw conclusions, but they are useful tools for our purposes.

Measuring Wealth

One basic criterion for comparison that we can use is the level of economic development. The most common tool that economists use to measure economic development is **gross domestic product (GDP)**, defined as the total market value of all goods and services produced within a country over a period of one year. GDP provides a basic benchmark for the average per capita income in a country. However, GDP statistics can be quite misleading. For one thing, a given amount of money will buy more in certain parts of a country than in others. A salary of $30,000 a year will go a lot further in Boise, Idaho, than it will in New York City, where the cost of living is much higher. The same problem arises when one compares countries: people may earn far more in some countries than they do in others, but those raw figures do not take into account the relative costs of living in those countries, especially when trying to convert different economies into a single currency, such as the U.S. dollar. As exchange rates rise or fall between countries, this can make countries look richer or poorer in comparison, which is misleading. To address these difficulties, economists often calculate national GDP data on the basis of what is known as purchasing-power parity. **Purchasing-power parity (PPP)** attempts to estimate the buying power of income in each country by comparing similar costs, such as food and housing, using prices in the United States as a benchmark. When these data are factored in, comparative incomes

Table 4.1 Measuring the Size of Economies, 2007		
	GDP Per Capita (in U.S. $)	**GDP Per Capita (PPP, in U.S. $)**
Sweden	48,584	36,500
United States	45,800	45,800
United Kingdom	44,693	35,100
France	41,523	33,200
Canada	40,222	38,400
Germany	40,079	34,200
Japan	34,254	33,600
South Korea	19,983	24,800
Russia	9,115	14,700
Mexico	8,486	12,800
Brazil	6,859	9,700
South Africa	5,833	9,800
Iran	3,815	10,600
China	2,485	5,300
India	964	2,900
Nigeria	1,120	2,000

Sources: Central Intelligence Agency, World Bank.

change rather dramatically, as shown in Table 4.1. For example, without PPP, Sweden's national income is higher than that of Canada, but when the cost of living in each country is factored in through PPP, the reverse is true. Incomes in poorer countries such as China and India also rise quite dramatically when PPP is taken into account.

Although GDP can be a useful way to measure wealth, it has its limitations. For example, since these figures capture economic transactions, a country that suffers a natural disaster may see its GDP go up as a result of increased activity to rebuild the damage. High crime might also increase GDP if more police are hired and prisons built. Nor does GDP take into consideration the costs of eco-

Table 4.2 Distribution of Wealth					
	Percentage of Total National Income Held by Segment of Population				
Country	Poorest 10% of Population	Richest 10% of Population	Year of Data for Poorest, Richest %	Gini Index	Year for Gini Index
Sweden	3.6	22.2	2000	23	2005
France	2.8	25.1	1995	28	2005
Germany	3.2	22.1	2000	28	2005
Canada	2.6	24.8	2000	32.1	2005
United Kingdom	2.1	28.5	1999	34	2005
South Korea	2.9	22.5	1998	35.1	2006
India	3.6	31.1	2004	36.8	2004
Japan	4.8	21.7	1993	38.1	2002
Iran	2.5	29.6	2005	43	1998
Russia	2.4	30.6	2002	43.1	2007
Nigeria	1.9	33.2	2003	43.7	2003
United States	1.9	29.9	2000	45	2007
China	1.6	34.9	2004	47	2007
Mexico	1.6	39.4	2004	50.9	2005
Brazil	0.9	44.9	2005	56.7	2005
South Africa	1.4	44.7	2000	65	2005

Source: World Bank.

nomic growth, such as pollution, or other indicators of social development, such as life expectancy—though these, too, can be measured, as we will see shortly.

Measuring Inequality and Poverty

Perhaps more problematic is the fact that GDP does not tell us how wealth is distributed among a population (the issue of inequality). A more sophisticated approach that does so is the **Gini index**, a mathematical formula that measures the amount of economic inequality in a society. Perfect equality is given a Gini ranking of zero, and perfect inequality gets a ranking of 100. Thus, the greater the Gini index, the greater the inequality within a given economy. As Table 4.2 reveals, there is a correlation between the amount of wealth held by the poorest 10 percent of the population and the concentration of wealth in the hands of the richest 10 percent. In countries where those at the bottom hold less wealth, those at the top (as opposed to those in the middle) tend to hold more. These greater inequalities in turn lead to a higher Gini rating. To look over time, in 1985, China's Gini index was 29, similar to Germany today. But as a result of economic reforms that dismantled much of the communist political economic system, their index rating has risen to 47, in line with the United States.

What conclusions can we draw from the Gini index? One is that social democratic countries tend to have the lowest Gini ratings, which is not surprising given their emphasis on equality. Denmark and Sweden have the lowest Gini ratings in the world. Liberal political economic systems are more unequal, but these vary widely, from Canada or Ireland at one end to the United States on the other. Mercantilist and (post-) communist countries show a similar range. Latin America and Africa have the highest levels of inequality overall, irrespective of the political economic system.

IN **FOCUS**

Measuring Wealth

Gross domestic product (GDP)	Total production within a country, regardless of who owns the products.
Purchasing-power parity (PPP)	Takes cost of living and buying power into account.
Gini index	Assesses inequality.
Human development index (HDI)	Assesses health, education, and wealth of population.

Having looked at inequality in a comparative format, it is important to stress that this is not the same thing as poverty.[14] While poverty tends to be measured by some fixed material standard, inequality can be measured in a number of different ways. We should therefore be careful about confusing the two. If, for example, those making $10,000 a year and those making $100,000 a year find that their incomes are rising at the same rate (say, 10 percent), overall poverty may drop while relative inequality stays the same—the latter group will still be making ten times more than the former. However, in absolute terms, a 10 percent increase in a $10,000 income is only $1,000, whereas a 10 percent increase in a $100,000 income is $10,000; thus, in absolute terms, the difference in inequality has grown.

That having been said, what is the trend around the world? Global data indicate that worldwide poverty has fallen since the 1980s, from a third of the world's population to less than 20 percent. Most of this reduction has occurred in Asia, particularly China and India, while in much of Africa, poverty has in fact risen. At the same time, within many countries inequality has increased, as we saw in the case of China, while inequality *between* countries overall has declined. The picture is therefore complicated: One of declining world poverty, but not in Africa; increasing inequality inside countries, but not between them. The conclusions you draw about poverty and inequality depend on what data you examine.[15]

Human Development Index (HDI)

Poverty, inequality within countries, inequality between countries—how can we make sense of any of this if we want to simply determine whether people are better off? There is another measurement that might help. The **human development index (HDI)**, developed by the United Nations Development Program, looks not only at the total amount of wealth in a society, as GDP does, nor even at its distribution, as with the Gini index, but at the overall outcome of that wealth—the well-being of a country's people. The HDI takes into consideration such factors as adult literacy, life expectancy, and educational enrollment, as well as GDP. By looking at such data, we can consider whether the wealth generated in a country is actually used in a way that provides a basic standard of living for all, whether through public or private means. Nearly all countries in the world are ranked on the HDI; in 2008, Iceland was ranked at number one, and Sierra Leone, wracked by civil war, came in at the very bottom.[16]

The HDI does show a strong correlation between standard of living and a country's GDP, as shown in Table 4.3. Those countries with the highest national incomes also show the highest levels of education and life

	GDP Per Capita (PPP, in U.S. $)	HDI Rank
Table 4.3 Measuring Wealth and Prosperity		
Canada	38,400	3
Sweden	36,500	7
Japan	33,600	8
France	33,200	11
United States	45,800	15
United Kingdom	35,100	21
Germany	34,200	23
South Korea	24,800	25
Mexico	12,800	51
Russia	14,700	70
Brazil	9,700	73
China	5,300	84
Iran	10,600	94
South African	9,800	125
India	2,900	132
Nigeria	2,000	154

Note: HDI rank is out of a total of 179 countries in 2006; GDP data are for 2007.
Sources: Central Intelligence Agency, United Nations Development Program.

expectancy in the world. Interestingly, the HDI lists social democratic systems such as Sweden (number 6) right alongside more liberal countries such as Australia and Canada (numbers 3 and 4) and more mercantilist ones such as Japan (number 8). Across these countries, HDI scores have consistently increased over the past thirty years, while many postcommunist countries showed an initial decline after their political transitions before rising again in the last few years. Worldwide, HDI scores have improved consistently since 1980, and many African states have shown an upturn after a decade of decline.

Happiness

Given the rather technical nature of our discussions so far, it may seem strange to speak of happiness as an indicator that we can use to compare political-economic systems. But when we think about it, happiness is at the core of human activity, the result of the interaction between freedom and equality. From philosophers to evolutionary psychologists, there is a common argument that the pursuit of personal happiness is one of the central motivations that drives human behavior. If that is the case, happiness can be a useful indicator of political economic development.

One caveat that we should start with is whether we are speaking about absolute or relative happiness. Psychologists note that a great deal of human happiness is relative; that is, once a particular goal is reached, the happiness that follows soon wears off. This makes sense; if individuals had a fixed sense of what made them happy, it would stand to reason that there would not be much economic development over time. In a related argument, for many years

INSTITUTIONS IN ACTION

WEALTH AND PROSPERITY IN THE UNITED STATES AND EUROPE

One of the major debates between the United States and Europe has been over their rival visions of prosperity and economic development. At first glance, the issue appears rather simple. Although Europe's per capita gross domestic product (GDP) might at first appear higher than that of the United States, when converted into purchasing-power parity, it drops below the U.S. GDP by about a third. Similarly, many observers in both the United States and Europe have noted Europe's lower growth rate. Europe would seem to be falling behind the United States in wealth and prosperity. But is this correct? It depends on how one measures wealth. According to some research, when one looks more closely at the numbers, the major differences between Europe and the United States in terms of productivity or growth are in fact not as significant as they first appear. This, however, would make the differences in GDP even more puzzling. The answer may lie in how Europeans and Americans choose to take that wealth. In the United States, the rise in GDP has been accompanied by an increase in working hours, to the extent that Americans work five or six weeks more a year than workers in Europe. More hours worked, of course, means a higher GDP. In Europe, the trend has been toward greater leisure, longer vacations, and earlier retirement. Such leisure is typically supported by social expenditures and state regulations. While this does not count toward GDP, it can certainly be seen as an important component of prosperity. Thus, while Americans on average may be wealthier, they work longer and harder for it. The remaining puzzle is why there is this difference in the first place. Is it due to cultural values? The power of trade unions? The specific effects of particular political-economic systems? There is more research to be done before we can answer these questions.

Source: Alberto Alesina, Edward Glaeser, and Bruce Sacerdote, "Work and Leisure in the US and Europe: Why So Different?" NBER Working Series 1128 April 2005, www.nber.org.

social scientists have pointed to what is known as the "Easterlin paradox," which found that when standards of living rise past a certain level of moderate human development (perhaps $15,000 per capita GDP), happiness stagnates. Relative income—your wealth relative to those around you—is more important than your overall standard of living. Some have gone even further to argue that increased wealth leads not just to a stagnation in happiness, but to a decline, as material goods come at the cost of social connections.[17]

Of late, much of this argument has come into question. More recent research reinforces the view that poorer societies are indeed much less happy than wealthier ones (See Figure 4.2). At the same time, the long-standing assumption that there is some ceiling after which happiness stagnates or declines is not borne out by the data. For example, in Europe, general indi-

Figure 4.2 **MEASURING SATISFACTION**

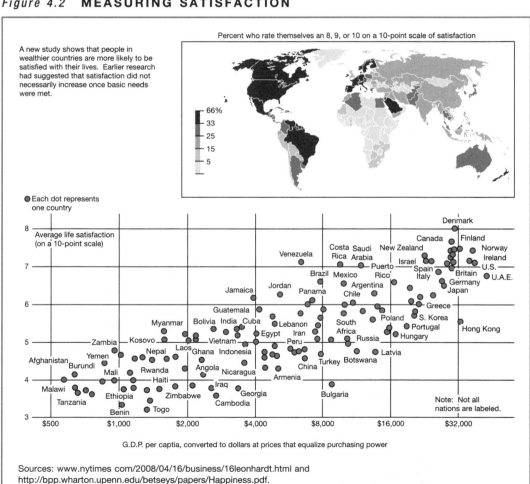

Sources: www.nytimes com/2008/04/16/business/16leonhardt.html and
http://bpp.wharton.upenn.edu/betseys/papers/Happiness.pdf.

cators of happiness have continued to rise alongside the standard of living over the last thirty years, with no evidence of some threshold after which happiness does not increase. Similarly, where there has been economic stagnation or decline, happiness has moved downward as well, as in Japan. However, the distribution of income within a country does seem to make a difference. Wealthy countries with a lower Gini index (that is to say, lower inequality) show higher levels of happiness than those that are more unequal. Denmark, with the lowest Gini index of any country, also ranks highest in happiness. In contrast, growing inequality in the United States over the past decade, for example, appears to explain why levels of happiness have stagnated there, in spite of high and rising overall GDP.[18] In short, economic growth does appear to matter in absolute and relative terms, and the relationship between freedom and equality may have much to do with the level of happiness within and between countries.

The Rise and Fall of Liberalism?

We've covered a lot of ground in this chapter, laying out variations in the relationship between property, markets, the state, and political economic systems. From there, we laid out some different tools to make comparisons of these arrangements, such as GDP, the Gini index, the Human Development Index, and measurements of happiness. In this discussion we've had glimpses of change in the international system, but have not addressed this head-on. Where do we seem to be heading?

For at least a century, our four major models of political economy have rivaled one another as they have sought to strike the ideal relationship between freedom and equality. At the dawn of modern capitalism, mercantilism was a dominant force, central to the establishment of empires and industries. At the same time, liberalism began to emerge as a challenge to mercantilism, particularly in the United Kingdom and its former colonies. But by the early twentieth century, liberalism was in turn challenged by fascism and communism and their alternative forms of political and economic organization. For many observers in that period, the strong role given to the state in Germany and the Soviet Union were attractive alternatives to a liberalism that was faltering under a global depression. After World War II when fascism was defeated, communism continued to spread worldwide, social democracy came to define much of Europe, and mercantilism drew adherents in Asia and beyond.

Yet as we stand at the beginning of the twenty-first century, the world is a quite different place. As with fascism before it, communism has effectively vanished. Even in places like China, where a communist party still controls the state, private property and market forces drive the economy. Mercantilism, too, not long ago seen as the path to development for poorer countries like India, has retreated, leaving only social democracy and liberalism as major political economic alternatives.

Until recently, many argued that even between these two rivals the contest is over, and that liberalism has won, something supported by the evidence. Table 4.4 from the Fraser Institute in Canada compares the overall level of economic changes around the world consistent with liberalism, taking into account such factors as government expenditures, price controls, taxes, individual property rights, and trade. Changes in these areas that limit the power of the state over that of private property and market forces are what we call economic liberalization. The ratings in the table are given on a 10-point scale, with 10 being the most liberal and 1 being the least. The study concludes that from 1980 to 2005, there was a steady move toward greater

Table 4.4 Increasing Levels of Economic Liberalization, 1980–2005			
Country	1980	2005	Change
Canada	7	8.1	1.1
United Kingdom	6.1	8.1	2
United States	7.4	8.1	0.7
Germany	7.1	7.6	0.5
Japan	6.4	7.5	1.1
Sweden	5.6	7.5	1.9
South Korea	5.7	7.3	1.6
Mexico	5.1	7.1	2
France	5.7	7	1.3
South Africa	5.4	6.8	1.4
India	4.9	6.6	1.7
Iran	3.4	6.4	3
China	3.8	6.3	2.5
Brazil	3.7	6	2.3
Russia	N/A	5.8	N/A
Nigeria	3.5	5.7	2.2

Note: 10 = most liberal.

Source: Fraser Institute.

economic liberalization, from an average global score of 5.4 in 1980 to 6.6 in 2005.[19] Economic liberalization grew, in some cases dramatically, around the world.

So is this the century of liberalism? Some serious qualifications are in order. First is that in spite of the increasing liberalization of many economic systems, to a large extent most industrialized democracies remain quite social democratic.[20] The United States is very much an outlier in this regard in such areas as health care, retirement, or education; indeed, we could argue that in looking back at our Gini index and HDI, the reasons many liberal countries rank alongside social democratic ones is because they are more like them than the United States. Since the 1930s, liberal political-economic systems dramatically expanded their social expenditures in ways that look much like social democracies. Even in the United States, by some measures social expenditures are similar to those of social democracies but take a different form, such as tax breaks.[21] Second, in spite of increased liberalization, many countries that have traditionally relied on the social democratic model continue to manage social expenditures and good economic growth.

Third and most important, since 2008 the global economy has seen one of the worst downturns since the Great Depression of the 1930s, battering liberalism and its adherents. To many, the economic crisis has been a direct result of growing and excessive global liberalization, where states relinquished their regulatory responsibilities and contributed to an irrational economic frenzy that eventually collapsed. The deep economic decline that has followed has undermined many of the arguments of liberalism, specifically that the economic pursuits of each individual will contribute to overall prosperity. As long as economic difficulties continue, it will be difficult for supporters of liberalism to argue that the state is an obstacle to development.

The ideological battering that liberalism has taken is compounded by actions on the ground. In response to economic crisis, states around the globe have actively intervened in their economies, nationalizing banks, supporting declining industries, and creating new policies to regulate the economy. State power in the economy has grown suddenly and dramatically, and one can expect it to grow further in the immediate future. This might lead to a reinvigoration of social democratic or mercantilist institutions, or new forms of political-economic relations. Whatever the outcome, liberalism may spend many years on the margins of political economy, as was once the case.

In Sum: The End of Economic History?

As we have seen, states play a large role in the domestic and international economy. They must deal with and manage markets and property, with an eye toward generating societal wealth and revenue so that basic political tasks can be funded. This is no small task, as it goes to the heart of freedom and equality: How should freedom and equality be reconciled through economic policy, and what mixture of the two will create the greatest degree of wealth? Different political-economic systems give very different answers to those questions. Economic liberalism has weathered various challenges to emerge as the dominant system in much of the world. As we shall see in the coming chapters, this "triumph" of liberalism has occurred alongside political liberalization as well, as many authoritarian regimes around the globe have given way to democracy.

But in spite of these dramatic changes, it would be foolish to assume that political economy has reached its endgame. We cannot know what other economic challenges, opportunities, and ideas lie on the horizon. The modern industrial economy and the various political-economic systems that describe and manage it are all relatively new, having formed only in the past few centuries—the blink of an eye in terms of human history. Can we be so certain that in a world of rapid economic change our current assumptions about markets and property, freedom, and equality will remain valid for long? Dramatic transformations are certain to come.

NOTES

1. For a discussion of the difficulties inherent in providing public goods, see Mancur Olson, *The Logic of Collective Action: Public Goods and the Theory of Groups* (Cambridge, MA: Harvard University Press, 1965).
2. For a discussion of this problem as it relates to the United States, see Charles Murray, *Losing Ground: American Social Policy, 1950–1980* (New York: Basic Books, 1984).
3. See Sven Steinmo, *Taxation and Democracy: Swedish, British, and American Approaches to Financing the Modern State* (New Haven: Yale University Press, 1993).
4. A good comparative discussion of central banking can be found in Majorie Deane and Robert Pringle, *The Central Banks* (New York: Viking, 1995).
5. For a discussion of environmental regulation, see Christopher Klyza and David Sousa, *American Environmental Policy, 1990–2006: Beyond Gridlock* (Cambridge, MA: MIT Press, 2008).
6. The arguments in favor of free trade can be found in Jagdish Bhagwati, *Free Trade Today* (Princeton: Princeton University Press, 2003); a more critical discussion can be found in Joseph E. Stiglitz and David Charlton, *Fair Trade for All: How Trade Can Promote Development* (Oxford: Oxford University Press, 2007).
7. Clyde E. Dankert, ed., *Adam Smith, Man of Letters and Economist* (Hicksville, NY: Exposition Press, 1974), p. 218.
8. Edward Bernstein, *Evolutionary Socialism: A Criticism and Affirmation* (New York: Schocken, 1961).

9. OECD tax Database, http://oberon.sourceoecd.org/vl=2607849/cl=16/nw=1/rpsv/factbook/100401-gl.htm.

10. For more on the variation within social democratic systems, see Gosta Esping-Anderson, *The Three Worlds of Welfare Capitalism* (Princeton: Princeton University Press, 1990).

11. For a discussion of communist political economies, see Robert W. Campbell, *The Socialist Economies in Transition: A Primer on Semi-Reformed Systems* (Bloomington: Indiana University Press, 1991).

12. The classic work on mercantilism is Friedrich List, *The National System of Political Economy* (New York: Kelley, 1966).

13. For a recent defense of mercantilism, see Ha-Joon Chang, *Bad Samaritans: The Myth of Free Trade and the Secret History of Capitalism* (New York: Bloomsbury, 2007).

14. For more on poverty, see the World Bank's Povertynet: http://povlibrary.worldbank.org/library/.

15. Xavier Salai-i-Martin, "The World Distribution of Income: Falling Poverty and Convergence . . . Period," draft paper, October 2005.

16. See the *United Nations Human Development Report 2008*, available at undp.hdr.org.

17. Richard A. Easterlin, "Does Economic Growth Improve the Human Lot?" in Paul A. David and Melvin W. Reder, eds., *Nations and Households in Economic Growth: Essays in Honor of Moses Abramovitz* (New York: Academic Press, 1974). See also Robert E. Lane, *The Loss of Happiness in Market Democracies* (New Haven: Yale University Press, 2000).

18. Betsey Stevenson and Justin Wolfers, "Economic Growth and Subjective Well-Being: Reassessing the Easterlin Paradox," Brookings Papers on Economic Activity, May 2008.

19. Fraser Institute, *Economic Freedom of the World Annual Report 2007*, available at www.fraserinstitute.ca/; also Heritage Foundation, *Index of Economic Freedom 2008*, www.heritage.org.

20. Sheri Berman, *The Primacy of Politics: Social Democracy and the Making of Europe's Twenty-First Century* (Cambridge, MA: Cambridge University Press, 2006).

21. Christopher Howard, *The Hidden Welfare State* (Princeton: Princeton University Press, 1997).

5 DEMOCRATIC REGIMES

KEY CONCEPTS

- Democracy is political power exercised either directly or indirectly through participation, competition, and liberty.

- There are various, and competing, explanations for why democracy has emerged in some cases and not in others.

- Executive, legislative, and judicial institutions can vary dramatically across democracies in their construction and degree of power.

- Democracies are often divided among parliamentary, presidential, and semi-presidential systems.

- Electoral systems are often divided among plurality, majority, and proportional systems.

For most of human history, people have not been organized in a way that we would consider democratic. Only a few people have been able to exercise power. But in recent centuries, revolution, war, and the destruction of rival ideologies such as fascism and communism have paved the way for democracy around the globe. Political leaders and publics have sought and gained greater democratic rights, from Eastern Europe to Asia and from Africa to Latin America, pushing aside other ideologies and regimes—sometimes peacefully, sometimes not. From the perspective of those already living in a democratic society, the spread of this political system may appear natural or inevitable: Who wouldn't want to live in a democracy? But we must ask ourselves why this should be the case. Why would democracy be an attractive or effective form of government? How does democracy actually work? Does democracy by definition reconcile freedom and equality in a single way, or does democracy allow for different mixtures of the two?

This chapter will speak to these questions in some detail as we consider the origins, structures, strengths, and weaknesses of democracy. We will begin by defining democracy itself, and then democracy's origins in modern politics. Next we will consider the various institutions that represent the core "goods" of democracy: participation, competition, and liberty. As we shall see, there is no one relationship among these three. Various democracies construct them differently, shaping freedom, equality, and the locus of power. Democracies are more diverse than one might expect, with different advantages and disadvantages. Finally, we will consider some of the challenges to democracy around the world as we move into the next set of chapters in the text.

Defining Democracy

Before we proceed, we must nail down our terminology. The word *democracy* has, for many people, an inherently positive connotation: things that are "democratic" are good; things that are "undemocratic" are inherently bad. Of course, in reality, this is far from the truth: a university is not a democratic institution, but that does not mean that it is bad or somehow deficient. But because of the word's symbolism many individuals and organizations describe themselves as democratic but then define the term in very different ways. For example, in Chapter 3, we noted that for communists, democracy means collective equality and not individual freedom. Countries such as the Soviet Union thus saw themselves as "true" democracies, which they defined as featuring, among other things, full employment, universal education, and the elimination of economic classes. These societies saw democracy in the United States or Europe as little more than the struggle among a small elite. Naturally, capitalist countries viewed communist systems, with their single-party control and lack of civil liberties, as anything but democratic. As you can see, each side is using different criteria to define democracy.

How can we make any comparisons if democracy is in the eye of the beholder? One way to begin is to go back to the origins of the word itself. The word *democracy* comes from the Greek words *demos*, meaning "the common people," and *kratia*, meaning "power" or "rule." Democracy at its most fundamental is a system in which power resides with the people. Based on this origin, we can begin by defining democracy as a system in which political power resides with the people. The people, in turn, may exercise that power either directly or indirectly, and the exercise of power typically takes three forms: participation, such as through voting and elections; competition, such as that between political parties; and liberty, such as freedom of speech or of assembly. **Democracy**, then, can be fully defined as political power exercised either directly or indirectly through participation, competition, and liberty. Some scholars have spoken of these as "veto points," by which they mean those players in the democratic process who must assent for any change in status quo.

This definition is subjective; it clearly emphasizes individual freedom and is in keeping with the ideology of liberalism. Indeed, many political scientists use the more specific term **liberal democracy** to indicate that they are referring specifically to a political system that promotes participation, competition, and liberty. Liberal democracies are rooted in the ideology of liberalism, with its emphasis on individual rights and freedoms.[1] But liberal democracy is not found only where a liberal ideology and a liberal political-economic system are predominant. Many liberal democracies have social democratic regimes, which place a much higher emphasis on collective welfare over individual rights, tempering individual freedoms in favor of greater equality. But social democracies nevertheless continue to respect the basic liberal democratic tenets of participation, competition, and liberty. Mercantilism, too, emphasizes a strong role for the state and lower personal freedoms as a result, but this has not prevented countries such as India, Japan, Taiwan, and South Korea from developing liberal democratic institutions. In each case, we find the basic rights of participation, competition, and liberty, though to different degrees. This in turn affects the degree of state autonomy and capacity.

Finally, it is important to remember what is not being said here about democracy. This book is not saying that a particular kind of democracy, or even democracy itself, is the only or even the best way to organize politics. All it is saying is that democracy is a particular system of institutions that have developed over time and out of liberal thought. Each person must decide for himself or herself whether the particular goals enshrined in liberal democracy are those that are most important and whether society is best served by being organized in this manner. We will speak more about this at the end of the chapter.

Origins and Sources of Democracy

We now have an understanding of the most basic elements of democracy, but this still does not explain why it has come about and where it comes from. First, history: Where did democracy come from? Some elements of democratic participation can be found in many societies around the world, dating back thousands of years. But liberal democratic institutions and practices have their roots in ancient Greece and Rome, each contributing to modern democracy in different ways.

Athenian and other early Greek democracies are important because they provide the foundation for the concept of public participation. Typically found in small communities, ancient Greek democracy allowed the public (excluding women, children, and slaves) to participate directly in the affairs of government, choosing policies and making governing decisions. In this sense, the people were the state.[2] In contrast, the Roman Empire laid out the concept of **republicanism**, which emphasized the **separation of powers** within a state and the representation of the public through elected officials (as opposed to the unaccountable powers of a monarchy or the direct participation of the people). Thus, while Greece gives us the idea of popular sovereignty, it is from Rome that we derive the notion of legislative bodies like a senate. In their earliest forms, neither Greek democracy nor Roman republicanism would be defined as liberal democracies by today's standards. Both emphasized certain democratic elements but restricted them in fundamental ways. As political rights and institutions have expanded over the centuries, republicanism and democracy—Roman and Greek thought and practices—have become intertwined to produce the modern liberal democratic regime we know today.

The discussion above may lead us to conclude that the development of democracy was thus a long unbroken line from Greece to today. But that was not the case. Roman republicanism was quite different from Greek participatory democracy, and in time both collapsed. Yet democratic institutions and practices slowly reemerged, most notably in thirteenth-century England. At that time, English nobles forced King John to sign the Magna Carta, a document that curbed the rights of the king and laid the foundation for an early form of legislature, a key element of republicanism. In addition, the Magna Carta asserted that all freemen (at the time, only the aristocracy) should enjoy due process before the law; this assertion set the stage for the idea of liberty. The Magna Carta states:

> No freeman shall be taken, imprisoned, . . . or in any other way destroyed
> . . . except by the lawful judgment of his peers, or by the law of the land.
> To no one will we sell, to none will we deny or delay, right or justice.

IN FOCUS

Two Forms of Democracy

Direct democracy	Public participates directly in governance and policy making; historically found in small communities such as ancient Athens.
Indirect democracy	Public participates indirectly through its elected representatives; the prevalent form of democracy in the modern age.

Although the Magna Carta was limited in its goals and application, it presented the idea that no individual, not even the king, was above the law. This concept thrived in England over the centuries as democratic practices expanded and an ever-greater proportion of the public was given political rights. Periodic attempts by the monarchy to expand its power led to violent resistance, most notably in the 1642 English Civil War between King Charles I and Parliament, in which the king eventually lost (and lost his head). The emergence of democracy in England was thus incremental, developing across centuries.

Was there something special about England that allowed democracy to flourish there in the first place? As noted in Chapter 2, European states emerged out of centuries of conflict as rival warlords slowly concentrated their holdings and extended their power. In this regard, England enjoyed both relatively early unification and the defensive benefits of being an island; the need to maintain a large army to unify and defend the country was much lower for isolated England than for the many other European states. Ocean trade, too, provided revenue through port duties, which meant less of a need for a strong state to squeeze taxes from the public. The end result was a relative decentralization of power that facilitated individual freedom. This in turn would eventually give shape to the ideology of liberalism. It is no accident that an ideology that emphasized individual freedom and private property emerged in a country where the state was historically weak. The public, able to gain the upper hand against the state early on in England's political development, could check attempts by the state to increase its power. This public power paved the way for an expansion of rights over time, culminating in modern liberal democracy.[3]

Contemporary Democratization

This historical background helps us understand the emergence of democracy, but for scholars of contemporary politics, it does not provide much guidance. We can understand what happened in the United Kingdom, but why has democracy since spread to most of Europe but not China? Why is South Africa a democracy when neighboring Zimbabwe is not? Why did Russia not institutionalize democracy after the collapse of communism? There are competing explanations for democratization and democratic institutionalization, which have fallen in and out of favor over time. Some of this is the result of changes in contemporary politics that force scholars to reevaluate their theories, but it may also be that explanations that were accurate at one point in time lose their explanatory power as the world changes.

TIME LINE / MILESTONES IN THE RISE OF DEMOCRACY

18th century B.C.E.	Babylonian ruler Hammurabi establishes the earliest known legal code
6th century B.C.E.	Autocratic rule overthrown and first democracy established in Athens
5th century B.C.E.	Democracy collapses in Athens as it is undermined by war and economic crisis
1st century B.C.E.	Roman philosopher Cicero writes of *res publica,* or "affairs of the people," viewing the public as an important source of political power
5th–10th century C.E.	European dark ages: power in Europe is fragmented, fostering intense competition among rulers and setting the stage for the emergence of the nation-state
1215	Writing of the English Magna Carta, an early precedent for establishment of the rule of law
1646	Treaty of Westphalia asserts the right of European states to choose their own religion, enforcing the notion of state sovereignty
1689	Bill of Rights is passed in England, establishing parliamentary supremacy
1690	English philosopher John Locke writes *Two Treatises of Government,* arguing that government's job is to protect "the right to life, liberty, and the ownership of property"
1762	Jean-Jacques Rousseau writes *The Social Contract*, arguing that if a government fails to serve its subjects, the populace has the right to overthrow it
1787	U.S. Constitution and Bill of Rights codify the separation of powers and civil rights
1832–84	Reform Acts in the United Kingdom expand voting rights to much of the male population
1893	New Zealand grants women the right to vote
1945	Defeat of the Axis powers eliminates fascism as a threat to democracy in Europe and Japan
1948	United Nations approves the Universal Declaration of Human Rights, setting the stage for the internationalization of civil rights
1989–91	Soviet Union disintegrates, leading to democratization in Russia and Eastern Europe
1994	First democratic elections in South Africa, ending racial restrictions on voting

Modernization and Democratization

One of the most prominent theories of democratization argues that democratization is correlated with, if not caused by, modernization. As we recall from Chapter 1, the behavioral revolution in political science was strongly connected to modernization theory, which believed that as societies became more modern, they would inevitably become more democratic. Why? Several factors have been suggested. Modernization is associated with greater education, weakening of older traditional institutions that stressed authority and hierarchy, greater gender equality and the rise of a middle class. To sum up, modernization theory suggests that as societies become more economically and societally sophisticated, they would need and desire greater control over the state in order to achieve and defend their own interests. In this view, democracy is an almost inevitable process that comes with modernization.

In the 1970s this theory fell out of favor as democracy failed in many countries in Latin America while development in Asia leapt forward alongside nondemocratic regimes. Modernization seemed not only irrelevant but could in fact destabilize existing institutions and lead to political violence (see Chapter 10) and democratic failure. More recently, however, modernization has regained currency with the wave of democratic change in places like Eastern Europe. Scholars no longer make sweeping claims that modernization inevitably causes democracy. However, some note that economic development alongside low inequality does appear to correlate with democratization, the reasons for which we will discuss below.

Elites and Democratization

We noted above that modernization theory has risen, fallen, and risen again in prominence over time. In the past, modernization theory implied that democratization was almost automatic once a country developed a strong middle class and reached a certain standard of living. One problem with the argument, however, is that it did not explain how this change would come about—democratization was taken as somewhat automatic. This did not explain countries where standards of living did rise, such as in the oil states of the Middle East, but democracy did not result. What explains this puzzle?

One answer may lie in the role of those in power, or political elites. For the past several decades many scholars who had turned away from modernization theory concentrated instead on the strategic motivations of those in power, and what would lead them to hang on to or surrender power. Much of this work tended to describe, rather than explain, political change, but of late these arguments have been given new life drawing on some of the earlier ideas of modernization theory. Central to modernization theory is the idea that a middle class is essential for democratization—a significant segment of the population with both the resources and the sophistication to want to advance and demand their own rights. Modernization theory has long noted that in contrast, poverty is an obstacle to democracy—where people have little, they have little to fight for. But it is not simply poverty but also inequality that may be a central factor. Where economic wealth is concentrated in the hands of those in power, political change is much less likely, as change would mean those in power are likely to lose not just control over the state but over their assets as well. Think, for example, of countries where there are significant natural resources, such as oil, held in the hands of the state. Should those in power step down, they would also lose control over this tremendous source of wealth. However, where resources are more equally distributed among the population, political change may be more likely, since those in power have less to lose. This was the case in early Britain, and also much more recently in Communist Europe. In short, development is important, but how those resources are distributed also can make a big difference in the likelihood for change. We will speak of this in much greater detail in the next chapter on nondemocratic regimes.

Society and Democratization

A somewhat different view of democratization emphasizes not the importance of political elites but the political power of society itself. Elite-based theories can give us a sense of why leaders may be more or less willing to surrender power to the public but not why the public would demand power in the first place. Modernization theory, too, explains how societies might change in a direction more in tune with democratic institutions but also doesn't provide a clear sense of what would give these preferences form. Scholars more interested in the role of society have in the past stressed the importance of public organization, or specifically what is called **civil society**. Basically, civil society can be defined as organized life outside the state, or what the French scholar Tocqueville called the "art of association."[4] These are not necessarily political organizations but rather a fabric of organizations created by people to help define their own interests, whatever they may be: clubs, environmental groups, churches, sports teams, and the like. What is important here is that although such groups may be inherently apolitical, they serve as a vehicle for democratization and democracy by allowing people to articulate, promote, and defend what is important to them. Where civil society has been able to take root, it is argued, democratization is more likely, as it provides both the ideas and the tools of political action and mobilization—the tools of small-scale democratic practice that soon begin to spread. Indeed, the very term *civil society* gained currency in reference to movements in Eastern Europe in the 1970s that organized independent of communist rule.[5] Where civic association can emerge, it may create a powerful incentive for democratic change, even if that is not the original intent. As with our arguments above, this is not necessarily in opposition to modernization or elite theories. Modernization may help foster civil society, and civil society in turn may pressure elites for change—and these elites may or may not acquiesce, depending on their incentives to do so.

International Relations and Democratization

So far, our discussion of democratization has focused on variables inside the country in question. Can international factors also play a role? We can think of extreme cases, such as the occupation of Japan and Germany after World War II, where democracy was installed by the Allied occupiers. A similar effort is under way in Iraq. But scholars also believe that the international community plays a role in less obvious ways. Modernization can be the result of foreign investment, globalization, and trade, which may push democratization forward. Elites, too, may favor democracy as a result of international pressure or incentives. For example, some have suggested that the institutionalization of democracy in Eastern Europe came partly because democracy was a prerequisite for eventual membership in the European Union. Where such outcomes were less likely, as among many of the states of the former Soviet Union, authoritarianism and conflict were greater. Civil society, too, can be strengthened by the transmission of ideas across borders by education, media, and nongovernmental organizations. How influential the international community may be probably depends on a number of factors, including the degree to which that society is open to and dependent on the outside world. North Korea's isolation means that there is little contact between that society and the outside. The vast size of China's economic resources means that the international community has far fewer tools it can use to press for change.

Culture and Democratization

Our last argument is a familiar one. In Chapter 3 we spoke of the idea of political culture, which is essentially the argument that there are differences in societal institutions—norms and values—that shape the landscape of political activity. Political culture may influence the preference for certain kinds of policies as well as the particular relationship between freedom and equality. Some scholars take this idea much further, arguing that there is in essence a culture of democracy. This may be a result of modernization, as older institutions give way to modern conceptions of individual freedom and citizenship. It may be much older, however, emerging from historical, religious, and philosophical foundations. In this view, for example, it is not modernization that leads to individualism and democracy; it is a Western democratic and individualist culture that gave rise to modernity. In contrast, other societies' cultures may disfavor individual autonomy, making liberal democracy hard to construct. By this logic, then, democracy is not a final product of a series of historical processes but a cultural value that develops and is institutionalized over a long period, shaping the views of society and those in power. If this argument is true, then democratization is less likely to be found the farther one travels from the West, and countries like China and Russia or Iran, even as they continue to modernize, organize their societies, and deepen their international ties, will remain resistant to democratic change. As we have discussed earlier, such arguments make many scholars uncomfortable, both because they are difficult to test and they smack of stereotyping or racism. They also have a questionable track record; not long ago, it was cultures dominated by Roman Catholicism, such as Spain, Portugal, and Latin America, that were seen as unlikely to democratize—until they did. But this has not kept such arguments from finding currency, even among supporters of nondemocratic regimes who argue that "Western" democracy has no place in their society. We will talk more of this in the next chapter on nondemocratic regimes.

To summarize, there are numerous explanations for why democratization may take place in some cases and not others. While scholars each tend to favor one of these explanations over the others, we see that most if not all of these can be integrated together. Modernization can set the stage for political activity and awareness, which can find its organizational expression in civil society. Elites may be influenced by economic conditions at home and international inducements or sanctions. Even culture may encourage certain kinds of ideas that may serve to catalyze democracy or act as an obstacle to it. In the end, changing domestic and international conditions may mean that what leads to democracy now is different from its origins in the past and what will spark it in the future. Politics is not the law of gravity, unchanging over time and space.

Institutions of the Democratic State

We now have an understanding of the basic definition of liberal democracy and some of the explanations for how it emerged in the past and present. Next we should spend some time looking at how liberal democracies are actually constructed. As we shall see, liberal democratic institutions vary dramatically. Legislatures and executives differ greatly from country to country, both in comparison to each other and in terms of legislative-executive relationships. Judiciaries, too, are each quite distinct in their role in the democratic process. There is tremendous variation in the range and number of political parties, and this in part is shaped by the myriad of electoral systems used around the world. Even what we consider basic civil rights and civil liberties differ so much that what is considered a basic democratic right in one liberal democracy is constrained in another. There is no one way, no right way, to build a liberal democracy. Once the basic elements of participation, competition, and liberty are in place, there is tremendous diversity. Comparing these institutions helps us not only to understand politics outside our own system but also to evaluate the benefits and limitations of our own democratic order. Let's look at some of the major differences in these institutions before we consider several of the most common combinations of liberal democratic institutions.

Executives: Head of State and Head of Government

We begin with what is the most prominent office in any country, the **executive**, the branch that carries out the laws and policies of a state. When we think of this office, what often comes to mind is a single person in charge of leading the country and setting a national agenda, as well as leading foreign policy and serving as commander in chief in times of war. But in fact, the executive comprises two distinct roles. The first is **head of state**, a role that symbolizes and represents the people, both nationally and internationally, embodying and articulating the goals of the regime. The role of foreign policy or war making is also sometimes considered part of the head of state's duties. In contrast, the role of the **head of government** is to deal with the everyday tasks of running the state, such as formulating and executing policy, alongside a cabinet of other ministers who are charged with specific policy areas (such as a minister of foreign affairs or agriculture). The distinction, then, runs along issues of direct management of policy and international and symbolic functions. This distinction is an old one that goes back to the days when monarchs reigned over their subjects, leaving others in charge of ruling the country.

Countries differ in the extent to which they combine or separate these two roles. Heads of government are usually referred to as prime ministers: they serve as the main executive over the other ministers in their cabinet. They may serve alongside a head of state, who may be a monarch or a president. A country may also combine the two roles, as in the United States. The balance of power between the head of state and that of government differs from country to country, as we will learn shortly.

Legislatures: Unicameral and Bicameral

The **legislature** is typically viewed as the body in which national politics is considered and debated; it is charged with making or at least passing legislation. As with executives, legislatures vary in their political powers and construction, with a major distinction being bicameral and unicameral systems. As you might guess from their names, **bicameral systems** have two houses in the legislature whereas **unicameral systems** have only one. Small countries are more likely to be unicameral systems, though the majority of liberal democracies are bicameral. Bicameral systems can be traced back to pre-democratic England and other European states, where two or more chambers were created to serve the interests of different economic classes. Even as feudalism gave way to liberal democracy, the idea of bicameralism remained, for two major reasons. First, in some countries an upper chamber was retained as a check over the lower house, often reflecting a fear that a popularly elected lower house, too close to the people's current mood, would make rash decisions. Thus, upper houses often can amend or veto legislation originating in the lower house. One can also see this concern in tenure: members of upper houses often serve for longer terms than members of lower houses. A related element is federalism; federal states typically rely on an upper house to represent local interests, with members able to oversee legislation particularly relevant to local policies. In some cases, local legislatures may even appoint or elect the members of

---

IN **FOCUS**

Branches of Government

Branch	Functions, Attributes, and Powers
Executive	Head of state / head of government
	Parliamentary, presidential, and semipresidential systems
	Term length may be fixed (president) or not (prime minister)
Legislative	Lawmaking
	Unicameral or bicameral
Constitutional court	Determines the relative constitutionality of laws and acts
	Judicial Review (abstract and concrete)

that upper chamber, again reflecting a desire to check a directly elected lower house. In the United States, the Senate was indirectly elected by local legislatures until 1913. However, there are many unitary liberal democratic systems that also have bicameral legislatures. Legislatures may wield a great deal of power over the executive, serving as the prime engine of policy or legislation, or take a back seat to executive authority. Moreover, the relative power between upper and lower houses differs from country to country and issue to issue, though generally speaking upper houses tend to be weaker than the lower house.

Judiciary: Concrete and Abstract Review

The judiciary is the last major institution central to liberal democracies. All states rely on laws as a means to prescribe behavior and lay out the rules of the political game. At the core of this body of laws lies a constitution, which is the fundamental expression of the regime and the justification for subsequent legislation and the powers of executives, legislatures, and other political actors. In nondemocratic systems, constitutions may count for little, with the state acting as it sees fit. In liberal democracies, however, constitutional power is central to maintaining what we refer to as the *rule of law*—the sovereignty of law over the people *and* elected officials. As a result, judicial institutions are important components in upholding law and maintaining its adherence to the constitution.

But as with executives and legislatures, there is a great deal of variation across liberal democracies—not simply in the scope of law but also in how laws are interpreted and reviewed. Most (but not all) liberal democracies have some form of **constitutional court** charged with the task of ensuring that legislation is compatible with the constitution. But the powers of the courts vary dramatically. In some cases, they serve as an appellate court, meaning that rulings by lower courts may be appealed to this higher court. Trials may thus become an important source of constitutional interpretation. In other countries, constitutional courts have no such power and function independently of the court system. Related to this is that constitutional courts differ in their powers of **judicial review**, and whether those powers are concrete, abstract, or both. In the case of **concrete review**, courts can consider the constitutionality of legislation only when this question has been triggered by a court case. In **abstract review**, a constitutional court may rule on legislation without a court case and even before that law has been exercised. Courts may exercise only one or both of these powers, to varying degrees of authority. Courts may also differ in the appointment and tenure of their judges, which may affect their degree of independence and politicization.

Models of Democracy: Parliamentary, Presidential, and Semipresidential Systems

With our overview of state institutions in hand, let's look at the main differences in how some of these institutions can be constructed in relation to one another.

Parliamentary Systems

Parliamentary systems can be found in a majority of democracies around the world. Two basic elements comprise parliamentary systems: first, prime ministers and their cabinets (the other ministers that make up the government) come out of the legislature, and second, the legislature is also the instrument that elects and removes the prime minister from office. In these cases, we have a division of power between a head of government and a head of state, with the overwhelming majority of power residing with the head of government (the prime minister). In contrast, the head of state may be a monarch or a president who is directly elected, chosen by the legislature, or has inherited the office. Their powers are typically little more than ceremonial, particularly in the case of monarchs. They may hold some reserve powers such as the ability to reject legislation if it is seen as running counter to the constitution. Even in these cases, however, the powers of the president or monarch are rarely exercised.

The prime minister is elected from the legislature and therefore reflects the balance of power between parties in the legislature. Typically, he or she is the head of the party in the lower house that holds the largest number of seats. Indeed, in most parliamentary systems the prime minister simultaneously holds a seat in the lower house of the legislature, as do other members of her or his cabinet. This tight connection between the prime minister and the legislature means that while there is a separation of power or responsibility, executives and legislatures serve less of a "checks and balances" function, since prime ministers draw their strength from their own members in the legislature. However, under conditions when the largest party in the legislature does not hold a majority, it is commonly necessary to forge a coalition government with one or more other parties. As a result, the prime minister will come from the largest party, while other members of the cabinet may come from the coalition parties. It is also possible that a coalition of smaller parties could form a government and select the prime minister, in fact shutting out the largest party, as long as that party lacked a majority. Here we should remind ourselves of the important difference between majority and plurality. A party with a majority in the legislature can choose its own prime minister and cabinet with little concern for other parties. However, if the largest party holds only a plurality (the largest share, as opposed to more than 50 percent), getting support for their prime minister and keeping her or him in power will require the cooperation of other parties.

Returning to our two essential elements of parliamentary systems, it is important to note that in these systems the public does not directly elect their country's leader. That task is left to the parties. Equally important and related to this, since prime ministers are not directly elected, the length of time they serve in office is uncertain. Legislatures will hold regular elections, but prime ministers serve in office usually for as long as they can command the support of their party and its allies. As a result, prime ministers can sometimes serve in office for many years—in the United Kingdom, Tony Blair was prime minister for a decade. On the flip side, they often can be removed relatively easily through what is known as a **vote of no confidence**. Parliaments typically retain the right to dismiss a prime minister at any time simply by taking a vote of confidence; in such a vote the absence of majority support for the prime minister will bring down the government. Depending on the constitution, this may trigger a new national parliamentary election, or simply a search for a new prime minister from among the ranks. Even when there is not a vote of no confidence, prime ministers typically will hold the right to call for elections, which can give them the power to schedule elections when they imagine it will serve their party best.

In parliamentary systems, legislatures and judiciaries also often take a back seat to the prime minister, who along with the cabinet is the main driver

---

IN FOCUS

Parliamentary, Presidential and Semipresidential Systems

Type	Executive powers and relationships
Parliamentary	Indirectly elected prime minister holds executive power as head of government; directs cabinet, formulates legislation and domestic and international policies. Serves for an unfixed term, and may be removed by a vote of no confidence. Head of state (president or monarch) is largely ceremonial.
Presidential	Directly elected president holds majority of executive power as head of state and government. Directs cabinet, formulates legislation and international and domestic policies. Serves for a fixed term and cannot be easily removed from office.
Semipresidential	Directly elected president and indirectly elected prime minister share power. President helps set policy while prime minister executes it. President also manages foreign policy. Which office holds more power depends on the country.

of legislation and policy. Especially when the prime minister enjoys a majority in the parliament, the house's role is often limited to debating policy that comes down from the cabinet. Upper houses, too, typically have little say in the selection or removal of the prime minister, and what powers they may have in rejecting legislation can often be overturned by the lower house. Judicial systems are frequently much weaker under these conditions as well. In parliamentary systems there is a norm against the idea of checks and balances, favoring a concentration of power as a means of greater political autonomy. In addition, the fusion of power between prime ministers and the lower house, and the weakness of upper houses, means that there are fewer opportunities for real constitutional conflicts to arise that would empower constitutional courts. Finally, in some cases heads of state and upper houses have certain powers of constitutional review, further limiting the opportunity for judicial power. That said, there has been a trend toward more powerful constitutional courts in parliamentary systems over the past two decades. This may be a response to the growing power of prime ministers themselves, who have become more dominant figures as states have grown more complex. It may also be the result of a growing body of international law, such as treaties that necessitate judicial interpretation.

Presidential Systems

Presidentialism represents the minority of democratic systems around the world. In this case, the president is directly elected by the public for a fixed term and has control over the cabinet and the legislative process. The positions of head of state and head of government are typically fused in the presidency. Here we see a significant difference between parliamentary and **presidential systems**. In the former, the prime minister and her cabinet come from the legislature and must command a majority of support to stay in office. One's term in office derives from this tenuous relationship, and while elections are specified by a constitution, they could be triggered through a vote of no confidence or by the decision of a prime minister. In presidential systems, however, the president and legislature serve for fixed terms, typically between four and seven years. Election dates may not be altered easily. Nor can presidents or legislatures be removed by anything resembling a vote of no confidence. Only in the case of malfeasance can elected officials lose their seats.

The way in which this institutional relationship affects government is profound. First, as directly elected individuals, the president is able to draw on a body of popular support in a way in which no member of a legislature, or even a prime minister, can. Only a president can say that she or he has been elected by the whole of the people in a single national vote (even if the reality is more complicated than that). Second, as a fusion between head of state and government, the president serves as the official who both rules and reigns, an important national symbol as well as overseer of policy. Third, the president is able to choose a cabinet, many or perhaps all of whom are not members of the legislature. Unlike prime ministers, a president need not be concerned that the composition of the cabinet reflect the top leadership in his party. Nor need a president be concerned with coalition government. Since the president is directly elected, minority parties have no effective control over the government. Fourth, and related to this, the president's power is not directly beholden to the legislature, and vice versa. Neither one has the ability to easily remove the other, creating a much stronger separation of powers between executive and legislature. This separation of powers is also more likely to lead to checks and balances and divided government. Presidents and legislative majorities can be from different parties, and even when they are the same, the separation of these institutions means greater independence from one another. President and legislature can easily clash over legislation and check one another in a way unlikely in a parliamentary system. Presidentialism can in fact weaken political parties, since their leaders are concerned with winning a single national office as opposed to working their way up through the ranks of the party in order to finally take the top leadership position in the hopes of becoming prime minister. Finally, the conflict between an independent legislature and president in turn may pave the way for a more active judiciary, as it is drawn into disputes between the president and legislature, as has been the case in the United States. There are relatively few presidential democracies around the world, with the United States being the most commonly cited example. This form is also common in Latin America.

Semipresidential Systems

Our final variant is an interesting hybrid between parliamentary and presidential systems that has become more widespread over the past fifty years (though it still remains far less common than presidential and parliamentary systems). In this model, power is divided between the head of state and the head of government, with a prime minister and a directly elected president both exercising power. Presidents enjoy fixed terms while prime ministers remain subject to the confidence of the legislature and, in some cases, the confidence of the president as well. How much power is divided between these two offices depends on the country. In some cases, the prime minister remains relatively separate from the president; while the president exercises important powers, her control over the prime minister is limited. In other cases, the prime minister is beholden to both the legislature and the president, giving the president greater authority over the selection, removal, and activity of the prime minister. In either case, the president holds power independent of the legislature yet at the same time shares powers with a prime minister. **Semi-**

presidential systems often reflect the old distinction between "reign" and "rule" that existed under monarchies. Presidents will often set forth policy but expect the prime minister to translate those policy ideas into legislation and to ensure that it is passed. Presidents will also take the lead in foreign policy and serve as commander in chief, representing the country in international relations. The most prominent semipresidential systems, such as in France, place the preponderance of power in the hands of the president, with the prime minister playing a supporting role. In semipresidential systems the role of the judiciary varies. The independence of constitutional courts is often limited by the fact that they are appointed by the president. At the same time, however, conflicts between presidents and prime ministers, and a lack of clarity over which executive has what power, has on a few occasions created opportunities for more judicial scope—and in some cases effectively prevented the emergence of semipresidentialism by confirming that power resided with the head of government, not state. Since the collapse of communism, semipresidentialism has spread into several former Soviet republics, most notably Russia, and is also used in a few cases in Asia (such as South Korea and Taiwan).

Parliamentary, Presidential, and Semipresidential Systems: Benefits and Drawbacks

Having reviewed these three systems, it makes sense to ask which is the best system of governance. As you might imagine, the first answer is that it depends on how one defines "best"; each system has certain advantages and drawbacks. That said, scholars have made some arguments about how effective, democratic, or stable these systems may be.

Advocates of parliamentary systems point to the fusion of power between the executive and legislature as a system that promotes greater efficiency by reducing the chances of divided government and deadlock. The prime minister's office, even when beholden to several parties in a coalition government, has a good degree of confidence that it can promulgate and pass legislation in a relatively expeditious manner, without having to take into consideration the narrow interests of individual legislators or smaller parties. In fact, prime ministers can use the vote of no confidence to their own advantage, threatening, for example, to make passage of individual pieces of legislation an effective vote of no confidence—should the legislature vote against the prime minister, the legislature will be dissolved and new elections called. The potential for efficacy—that prime ministers have greater ability to generate and quickly pass legislation—comes, critics say, at the cost of the separation of powers. Legislatures may have far fewer opportunities to influence the passage of legislation or effectively express the more specific interests of voters. Legislation can be much less of a bottom-up process, giving the public a more distant relationship to the process. This distance can apply to the executive as well, since that indi-

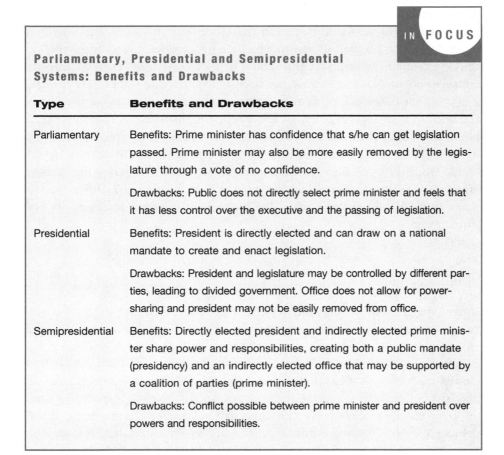

Parliamentary, Presidential and Semipresidential Systems: Benefits and Drawbacks

Type	Benefits and Drawbacks
Parliamentary	Benefits: Prime minister has confidence that s/he can get legislation passed. Prime minister may also be more easily removed by the legislature through a vote of no confidence.
	Drawbacks: Public does not directly select prime minister and feels that it has less control over the executive and the passing of legislation.
Presidential	Benefits: President is directly elected and can draw on a national mandate to create and enact legislation.
	Drawbacks: President and legislature may be controlled by different parties, leading to divided government. Office does not allow for power-sharing and president may not be easily removed from office.
Semipresidential	Benefits: Directly elected president and indirectly elected prime minister share power and responsibilities, creating both a public mandate (presidency) and an indirectly elected office that may be supported by a coalition of parties (prime minister).
	Drawbacks: Conflict possible between prime minister and president over powers and responsibilities.

vidual is directly accountable only to the legislature. Efficacy may thus come at the cost of public oversight and control over elected officials.

Presidentialism has its own problems. The benefits of this system can be seen first and foremost in the public's direct selection of its leader, who will serve for a predictable term. But this can generate difficulties. Unlike prime ministers, who must keep the confidence of their party (or parties, as in the case of coalition government), presidencies are "zero-sum" offices. Power is not shared, and even if a president loses the confidence of the public, he or she cannot be replaced except through new elections. Presidents also enjoy (or suffer from) the separation of power with the legislature, which can lead to divided government. Whether "checks and balances" are a benefit or a hindrance to democracy is open to debate. Several prominent scholars have asserted that presidentialism is a more unstable system, since it limits power sharing and also lacks the mechanism through which legislatures and executives can easily be changed. The result can be more polarized, and therefore unstable, politics. We might conclude then, that semipresidentialism would be the best of both worlds, but the track record is limited and mixed. In many cases, power still becomes concentrated in the presidential office, and in some cases, like Russia, it has become a platform from which democracy has been dismantled.

One problem with investigating any of these questions goes back to the concerns about the comparative method we discussed in Chapter 1. We have relatively few cases to look at and compare, and in many cases we are unable to control variables effectively. While presidentialism may look more unstable, is this due to the nature of the institution or because it is more commonly found in Latin America, whose political and economic conditions are far different from those of Europe? Has semipresidentialism's performance been affected by postcommunist legacies in many of these cases? Differences in party and electoral systems may also make a difference, something we will turn to next.

Political Parties

Among the many actors engaged in politics, political parties are the most organized, the most powerful, and seemingly inevitable. As James Madison once wrote, "In every political society, parties are unavoidable."[6] He did not say that political parties are desirable; since the early days of democracy, many people have viewed them as little more than a necessary evil. Why must we have parties at all? Isn't political choice, rather than parties per se, the most important thing?

Observers have offered several reasons that political parties are vital to liberal democracy.[7] For one thing, parties are important organizations that bring together diverse groups of people and ideas under the umbrella of some ideological mandate. These organizations serve two functions. By bringing together different people and ideas into a single group, they help establish the means by which the majority can rule. In other words, without political parties that provide candidates and agendas for politics, the political process would be too fragmented and it would be impossible to enact policy or get much else done. But although political parties bring individuals and ideas together, they remain relatively loose, with differences and factions within them. This relative heterogeneity also prevents a "tyranny of the majority" where minority views are marginalized, since competitive parties still lack the kind of internal unity to impose their will. Parties in liberal democracies are thus homoge-

---

IN FOCUS

Competition

- Political parties encourage democratic competition by articulating broader coalitions while simultaneously preventing domination by any one group.
- The separation of powers between different branches of government prevents abuses of power by any one branch.

neous enough to create majority rule but too weak to facilitate a tyranny of the majority, so long as open and regular elections create the opportunity to turn the ruling party out of power. Accordingly, in nondemocratic systems a single dominant party is the norm, with other parties banned or effectively marginalized by corrupt voting practices.

Political parties also create the means by which politicians can be held accountable by the electorate and fellow political elites. By articulating an ideology and a set of goals, parties hold their members responsible for achieving those goals. Voters are able to evaluate a group of politicians on the basis of these goals and promises: Did they do what they promised? Lacking parties, the public would have a difficult time evaluating the goals and achievements or failures of each candidate. Parties can thus serve as a political symbol, a shorthand for a set of ideas and objectives, and voters can distill complex decisions into questions of whether to vote for party A or party B. Political parties thus play a key role in encouraging democratic competition. They help articulate broader coalitions while preventing domination by any one group, provide a means to hold elected officials accountable, and thereby encourage democratic debate and the evolution of ideas.

That said, countries can exhibit a variety of party systems, shaped by a number of different factors. Some countries have seen the virtual dominance of two or even one party over a long period of time—Sweden's Social Democratic Party and Japan's Liberal Democratic Party were able to control government for much of the postwar era. Other countries, such as Italy, have experienced much greater instability among a handful of parties, with power moving back and forth between parties on a regular (sometimes yearly) basis. Coalition governments are the norm in some parliamentary systems while in others coalition governments are rare. Some legislatures are dominated by a few well-institutionalized parties; in other countries, the party spectrum is much more diverse, with numerous parties in the legislature and parties much less institutionalized.

What explains this diversity? There are so many reasons for this, specific to each case, that we can't make easy generalizations. Compact ethnic groups may lead to the rise of ethnic parties; a high degree of socioeconomic division may promote parties that speak for workers or farmers. Religious divisions or specific historical events may also influence party creation. One general factor that does affect parties everywhere, however, is how those parties are elected into office. **Electoral systems** can have a huge impact on the diversity and content of party politics, so it is important that we turn to this next.

Electoral Systems

We have discussed why there are political parties, but we still must look more closely at why certain countries may have more or fewer parties, or why they exhibit the ideological content that they do. There might be no single answer to this—the fortunes of political parties rise and fall over time. But as we look around the world, we see a tremendous diversity in the way the public casts their votes, how those votes are applied, and as a result, how many and what kinds of parties enter the legislature.

A liberal democracy is such only if there are free and fair elections. This means that the right to vote (**suffrage**) is open to all citizens and that votes are counted fairly. This having been said, there are clearly variations here. Women and many indigenous people around the world were given the right to vote only in the past century, and the age at which individuals should be allowed to vote is also open to debate. In some countries, suffrage is more than a right; it is a formal responsibility. In Australia, Belgium, Brazil, and a number of other democratic countries, voting is actually compulsory, and those who fail to vote can be fined.

Beyond the basic right to vote is the more complicated question of electoral rules, which decide how votes are cast, counted, and translated into seats in a legislature; these systems vary widely and make a huge difference in the distribution of political power.

All democracies divide their populations into a number of electoral boundaries or constituencies (a **constituency** is a geographical area that an elected official represents) that are allocated a certain number of legislative seats. The total number of constituencies may vary widely: Norway is broken up into nineteen constituencies that correspond to the country's nineteen counties, whereas in Nigeria there are 360 constituencies for elections to their lower house. How these boundaries are drawn matters, too. For example, if an ethnic or religious minority is concentrated in one area and is reflected in the constituency boundaries, this benefits their political power more than if they were divided across a number of constituencies. In another variation, different districts may have very different population sizes but the same number of legislative seats; these circumstances give those in less populated districts more power. How governments draw electoral boundaries thus can have a huge impact on who gets elected and are often a source of great contention in new democracies.

A second distinction is how votes are cast and counted.[8] There are essentially two broad

---

IN FOCUS

Participation

- One of the most basic ways in which the public participates in politics is through voting and elections.
- The two main types of electoral systems are the single-member district (SMD) and proportional representation (PR). The majority of democratic countries today use PR. Many use a mix of SMD and PR.
- Voters may also participate in political decision making through referenda and initiatives.

forms of electoral systems in use in liberal democracies today. The first are plurality and majority systems, often called **single-member district (SMD) systems** for reasons that will become clear in a moment, and **proportional representation (PR)** systems. Let us consider each one in turn.

A minority of democratic countries around the world, including the United Kingdom, Canada, the United States, India, Nigeria, and other former British colonies, rely on plurality-based single-member district systems, or what is often (confusingly) called **first past the post**. In these systems, electoral constituencies are structured as single-member districts, by which we mean that there is only one representative for that constituency. In elections, the candidate with the largest number of votes wins the seat. This need not be a majority of votes; a plurality of votes (the largest share of the total) is sufficient. Those votes cast for other candidates are "wasted"; that is, if the candidate for whom a vote is cast does not win, that vote does not count toward anyone getting into office. Plurality SMD is thus "winner take all" and can therefore amplify the political power of some parties while weakening the political power of others.

By way of illustration, let's look at the outcome of the 2005 elections for the House of Commons (the lower legislative house) in the United Kingdom. As Table 5.1 shows, the Labour Party won 35 percent of the vote but 55 percent of the seats. Meanwhile, the Conservatives, who came just 2 percent behind Labour, won only 30 percent of the seats. Why this disparity? The answer is because Labour came in first place in a larger number of districts than the Conservatives, and thus many of the votes cast for the Conservatives were effectively wasted.

Single-member district systems are seen by political scientists as having a profound impact on the number of parties in the legislature. The French political scientist Maurice Duverger argued that under SMD systems most people are unwilling to vote for smaller parties. Since such parties are unlikely to win first place, voters feel that a vote cast for a small party will be wasted and that they would be better off giving their vote to a stronger party that has a chance of coming in first.[9] The example of the United Kingdom's Liberal Democrats, who won 22 percent of the vote but less than 10 percent of the seats, bears this concern out. As a result, an SMD system is much more likely to produce a legislature dominated by two parties, as in the United States and the United Kingdom. This is not to say that smaller parties cannot win seats, however; in the United Kingdom, ethnic parties, such as the Scottish Nationalist Party, are able to win seats in districts in Scotland. Perhaps more surprising are fortunes of the Liberal Democrats, who have been able to gain seats as a third party in spite of SMD. Across all parties, SMDs may weaken party discipline, since voters are choosing between individual candidates who are representing parties, making elections as much a personal contest as one

Table 5.1 Electoral Systems and Outcomes: The United Kingdom and South Africa

Party	Plurality Single-Member District: United Kingdom, House of Commons, 2005		Party	Proportional Representation: South Africa, National Assembly, 2004	
	Percentage of Votes Won Nationally	Percentage of Seats Won in Legislature		Percentage of Votes Won Nationally	Percentage of Seats Won in Legislature
Labour Party	35	55	African National Congress	70	70
Conservative Party	32	30	Democratic Alliance	12	13
Liberal Democrats	22	10	Inkatha Freedom Party	7	7
Scottish National Party	2	1	United Democratic Movement	2	2
Democratic Unionist Party	1	1	Independent Democrats	2	2
Sinn Fein	1	1	New National Party	2	2
United Kingdom Independence Party	2	0	African Christian Democratic Party	2	2
Green Party	1	0	Freedom Front	1	1
			United Christian Democratic Party	1	1
			Pan-African Congress	1	1

Source: Electionworld.org.

between competing ideologies. This can especially be the case when an **SMD** system is combined with presidentialism, since voters need not worry about voting for their particular party for the legislature in order to win a majority to elect the executive. Under these conditions, candidates competing for a single-member district may function quite independently of their party (weakening party discipline as a result).

It is possible to alter the impact of single-member districts with a small modification in the electoral rules. Majority SMD systems function largely the same as plurality systems, with the exception that certain mechanisms ensure that the winner is elected by a majority of the voters in the district. The simplest way to do this is by having two electoral rounds, where the top two or more vote getters go on to a runoff. This is used in France and in several mixed electoral systems (discussed shortly). In a more complicated variation, a majority can be generated by having voters rank candidates by preference. If no candidate wins an outright majority, the candidate with the lowest number of first preferences is eliminated, and her or his ballots are then reassigned on the basis of their second preferences. This elimination of the lowest ranking candidates continues until one candidate has a majority. This system, called alternative, preferential, or instant runoff vote, is currently used in Australia, Fiji, and Papua New Guinea, as well as in local elections in several other countries. Advocates have supported its adoption for national elections in the United Kingdom, United States, Canada, and elsewhere.[10] Supporters believe that this system would increase the chances for smaller parties to gain office, since voters would worry less about wasting their vote. However, in France and Australia, in spite of majority SMDs, politics remains dominated by two large parties.

Quite different from plurality and majority single-member districts is proportional representation (PR), which is used in some form by a majority of democracies around the world. Proportional representation generally attempts to decrease the number of votes that are wasted, thus increasing the number of parties in the legislature. Rather than relying on single-member districts, PR relies on **multimember districts (MMDs)**; in other words, more than one legislative seat is contested in each district. In PR systems, voters cast their ballots for a party rather than for a candidate, and the percentage of votes a party receives in a district determines how many of that district's seats the party will gain. In a simple theoretical version, a party that won 17 percent of the vote in a district would receive 17 percent of that district's seats; if it wins 100 percent of the vote in a district, it would receive all of the seats. In reality the ways in which votes are counted and applied are rather complex and can have profound effects on how seats are distributed between competing parties. That said, in comparison to plurality and majority SMDs, in PR even a small percentage of the vote can result in winning seats. The 2004 elections in South Africa, also detailed in Table 5.1, show how votes under pro-

portional representation can correspond much more closely to the percentage of seats won in the legislature. Small parties that would not have won a
single seat under plurality or majority systems are in fact represented in the
South African National Assembly.

Because proportional representation is based on multimember districts,
elections are not centered on competitions between individuals, as in single-
member district systems. Instead, political parties draw up in advance a list of
their candidates for each electoral district, often proposing as many candidates
as there are seats. If a district has ten seats and a party wins 50 percent of the
vote in that district, the party will send the first five candidates on its party list
to the legislature. As you can imagine, one result of this system is that political
parties have tremendous power over who will get on the list and at what rank.
A candidate would want to be listed as high on the list as possible in order to
gain a seat even if the party gets a small share of the district vote.

Proportional representation can have several effects. Most important—and
in contrast to plurality or majority systems, in which voters tend to support
only those parties with a chance of winning a large share of votes in a
district—PR voters are more willing to vote for small parties, since they stand
a better chance of winning at least some seats in the legislature. Even if a
party wins less than 10 percent of the vote, it may well gain seats, as the 2004
South African elections showed. As a result, countries with PR are likely to
have many more parties in the legislature. Israel's legislature, for example,
has 12 parties, some of which are coalitions of several smaller parties. Some
PR systems try to limit the number of small parties by establishing a threshold or minimum percentage needed by any party to gain seats in the legislature; in Germany, it is 5 percent, in Turkey, 10 percent. Of course, this also
leads to wasted votes, since voters choosing parties that do not make it over
the threshold will not have their vote count (in Turkey's elections in 2007, this
counted for nearly 20 percent of the vote). Still, the degree of wasted votes
tends to be much smaller than in single-member district systems.

Finally, party discipline and ideology may be more pronounced in a PR
system, for two reasons. First, the diversity of parties is related to the need
for parties to carve out their particular ideological space relative to their competitors. This is opposed to SMD systems where parties want to reach as many
people as possible in order to win a plurality or majority. Second, PR may
lead to more internally disciplined parties, since those who do not follow the
party rules can be dropped from the party lists in the next election. Where
PR is combined with a parliamentary system, party discipline may be even
greater since it can make the difference between stable government and a vote
of no confidence.

Which system better serves participation: single-member districts or proportional representation? Supporters of PR note that it wastes votes to a much
smaller degree and in so doing allows for a greater range of political interests

to be expressed.[11] For example, if PR were used in the United States or Canada, would either country see the emergence of parties that represented Native Americans (U.S.) or First Nations (Canada)? Proportional representation can encourage the sharpening and expansion of different ideological views, increasing the competition of ideas and providing a means by which new issues can enter into the system. Environmental parties, for example, were able to form and make an impact in many PR systems already in the 1970s, while they remain marginal forces in SMD systems. In addition, when combined with the parliamentary form of government, PR often makes it necessary for parties to form coalitions to muster a majority of votes, thus building consensus across a range of views. Finally, PR's use of party lists can also make it easier for the parties themselves to expand the representation of underrepresented groups, such as women or minorities, by placing them on their party lists.

Those who favor SMDs emphasize the benefits of single-member districts and winner-take-all elections. Such a system can make it easier for individuals to connect with their elected representatives than under PR, since voters express their support or rejection of particular candidates, who form ties that are as close to their constituents as to their party, if not more so. Single-member-district supporters would note that as Russia has moved away from democracy in recent years, it has moved from a mixed system of SMD and PR (which we will discuss next) to pure PR in order to eliminate the means by which independent candidates who were critical of the growing centralization of power could be elected. Supporters also note that an SMD system

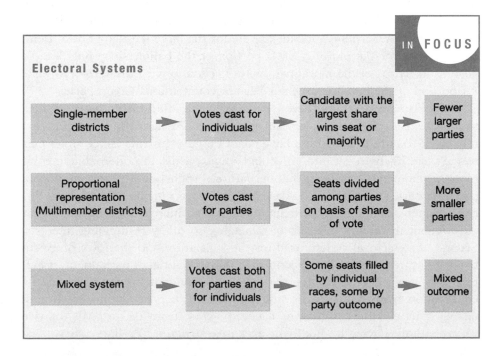

(especially plurality SMDs) allows for the creation of large parties that are able to muster the majorities needed to govern without being held hostage by smaller, often fringe parties. The flip side of party diversity under PR, critics argue, may be fragmentation and political instability.

For single-member districts, then, representative accountability and majority control over the legislature are the major strengths; for proportional representation, a greater diversity of representation and coalition building are key. Clearly, there is no correct side to this debate because it turns on different perceptions of what makes a system more or less democratic or effective, and again we lack an easy way to evaluate the merits of either system. Advanced democracies have thrived under variants of both SMD and PR.

Given the trade-offs between SMD and PR, some countries have combined the two. For example, Germany, Hungary, Japan, and Mexico use what is known as a **mixed electoral system** that combines plurality or majority SMDs with PR. Voters are given two votes—one for a candidate and the other for a party (this can be divided on the ballot itself, or there can be two separate elections). Candidates in the single-member districts are elected on the basis of plurality or majority, while in the proportional representation portion of the election, votes are allocated proportionally. The actual percentage of the seats allotted for each electoral method varies from country to country. For example, in Germany, the seats in the lower house of the legislature are divided evenly between SMDs and PR, whereas in Japan, the breakdown is 60 percent SMD and 40 percent PR. Under this system, voters not only get two votes but also have the option to split their choice, voting for a candidate from one party for their SMD vote while choosing a different party for their PR vote. For example, in Germany, one might vote for the large left-wing Social Democratic Party for the plurality SMD portion of the ballot (since only a large party is likely to get the plurality of votes needed to win) while reserving the PR portion of the ballot for the smaller environmentalist Green Party.

A final important point here is to look at the relationship between electoral systems and executive-legislative relations. Parliamentary systems that rely on SMDs are less likely to have coalition governments, since small parties are less likely to get into office and single parties are often able to command a majority of seats in the legislature. Proportional representation in parliamentary systems may make coalition governments more likely; this can broaden the range of participation but also increase the likelihood for government instability inherent in managing so many contending interests. Second, the electoral system used for the legislature and the form of executive-legislature relations are unconnected. A presidential or parliamentary system may use PR or SMD for the legislature. A country could change its constitution from having a president to having a prime minister without changing its electoral system, or it could switch from PR to SMD (or vice versa) without having to modify its executive structure. Parliamentary, presidential, and semipresidential systems are independent of whether a country uses SMD, PR, or a mixed system for its legislature.

Referendum and Initiative

In addition to shaping how one's participation is counted, electoral systems can also affect policy. Although voting is typically used to choose parties or candidates for office, many countries also have the option of allowing a public vote on a particular policy issue. Such a national ballot is commonly known as a **referendum**. In contrast to the more indirect impact that elections have on politics, referenda allow the public to make direct decisions about policy itself by putting certain issues before the public and allowing them to decide. There is no constitutional provision for referenda in the United States and Canada (although they exist in some local and state governments), but they are used in many other democracies. Recently, Italy and New Zealand used national referenda to dramatically restructure their electoral and legislative systems, and in Switzerland, where the political system comes closest to the idea of direct democracy than in any other country, many of the most important national decisions are regularly decided by referenda. Some European countries have used referenda to approve changes in their relationship with the European Union, with unpredictable results (see Chapter 7). These referenda may be called by the government, with the formal power often resting with the head of state. In addition, in some countries citizens may collect signatures to put a question to a national vote in what is known as an **initiative**. Such direct participation can help legitimize the democratic process, but others are concerned that national votes place too much power in the hands of an uninformed public, weakening representative democracy.[12]

As you can see, democratic participation is rather complex. When we speak about the right to vote, we must also consider how that vote is cast and counted. How elections are structured and votes cast and counted shape the power of one's vote, the number of parties in government, and the kinds of interests they may represent. Referenda and initiatives also widen the scope for public participation by giving the people a direct say in policy. Using these institutions, liberal democracies can secure the participation of their citizens.

Civil Rights and Civil Liberties

The last component of liberal democracy is liberty itself. To speak of liberty, we must go beyond democratic process and speak about the substance of democracy: civil rights and civil liberties. **Civil rights** typically refers to the promotion of equality, whereas **civil liberties** refers to the promotion of freedom, though there is clearly an overlap between the two. Civil rights and liberties include free speech and movement, the right to religious belief, the right of public assembly and organization, equal treatment under the law, the prevention of inhumane punishment, the right to a fair trial, the right to privacy, and the right to choose one's own government. These go back to our earlier discussion of the **rule of law**—that legal institutions exist that everyone is subject to, rulers and ruled, and that these rules contain and support liberty.

Some liberal democracies include civil rights in the area of social or economic outcomes, such as universal education, health care, or retirement benefits. Such rights are particularly strong in social democratic regimes. For

INSTITUTIONS IN

ACTION

NEW ZEALAND CHANGES ITS ELECTORAL SYSTEM

New Zealand is a good example of the differences between a single-member district system and proportional representation because it is one of the few examples where a country has shifted from the former toward the latter. In the late 1970s and early 1980s, national elections in New Zealand produced a result in which one party gained an outright majority of seats in the legislature even though it had won fewer votes than the other major party. As a result, in the mid-1980s, the government commissioned a study on electoral reform that proposed that the country shift from plurality SMDs to a mixed electoral system similar to that of Germany, with a 5 percent threshold. Two referenda on this electoral change received majority public support, and the first election under this mixed system was held in 1996.

What has been the effect? One important change is something we should have expected: since 1996, no one party has been able to gain a majority of seats in the legislature, in contrast to the previous fifty years. Instead, the two major parties now find themselves having to contend with additional parties in the legislature. In the 2002 elections, some seven parties gained seats. A second related effect is coalition government. With no one party able to muster a majority, parties have been forced to form coalitions (both stable and unstable) to elect a prime minister. Finally, representation has become more diverse. Under the mixed system, new parties were able to form and win seats representing the indigenous Maori people, environmentalism, libertarianism, and anti-immigration views. The share of women and minorities in the legislature also increased. One might conclude that New Zealand's electoral change has thus been an unqualified success. Yet the public has complained that the reform has made politics more confusing, given too much power to small parties, and made members of Parliament less accountable to the public.

example, the Swedish constitution states that "it shall be incumbent upon the public administration to secure the right to work, housing and education, and to promote social care and social security and a good living environment." In addition to differences in how far civil rights should be collectively expanded, liberal democracies also differ in the range of individual liberties they ensure. For example, all liberal democracies uphold the rights of free speech and association. Yet in some countries, such as Germany, the democratic constitution outlaws antidemocratic activity, meaning that the state can ban political parties that are seen as hostile to democracy. The South African constitution limits freedom of expression by forbidding "advocacy of hatred that is based on race, ethnicity, gender, or religion, and that constitutes incitement to cause harm."[13] Similar issues are at work regarding the right to possess firearms, abortion, smoking, or euthanasia. What are the limits to rights or liberties, and the acceptable balance between individual rights and society's norms or needs? These vary across country, case, and time, meaning that the concept of liberty allows for its practice to evolve.

In the above discussion, we see that liberty is not simply the absence of controls over our scope of action—a negative freedom. Rather, liberty is something that must be created, institutionalized, and defended—a positive freedom. The state, government, and regime are thus central to fostering and furthering liberty. But it would be a mistake to conclude that liberty flows only from the state, a gift to the people. Recall our opening discussion of democratization. Domestic and international institutions, culture, civil society, modernization, committed leaders, and other factors can open the space for democratic change. The challenge becomes vesting that space with liberty—the institutionalization of norms for civil rights and civil liberties that fuels democratic participation and competition. Where liberty is weak or absent, even the trappings of democracy may be in place but repression will remain the norm. This will be the focus of our next chapter, as we turn to nondemocratic regimes.

In Sum: Future Challenges to Democracy

As we have seen, democracy is one way to manage the dilemma of individual freedom and collective equality, one that this chapter has traced back centuries if not millennia. In its modern liberal form, democracy emphasizes individual freedom through participation, competition, and liberty. Participation, such as elections, helps provide the public a means of control over the state and the government; competition ensures an open arena of ideas and prevents too great a centralization of power; and liberty creates norms for human freedom and equality. When these elements are institutionalized—valued for their own sake, considered legitimate by the public—democracy is institutional-ized, and we can speak of the existence of a rule of law. No one stands above the democratic regime.

In the next chapter, we shall consider politics when this is not the case. In nondemocratic regimes, all those things we have taken for granted are unin-stitutionalized or absent. Participation, competition, liberty, and the rule of law are circumscribed, with the preponderance of power in the hands of a few elites who are not accountable to the public. How do these systems come about? How do they differ? Are their days numbered, or will democracy con-tinue to struggle against nondemocratic actors and institutions for the fore-seeable future? We will discuss these questions in the coming chapters.

NOTES

1. C. B. MacPherson, *The Life and Times of Liberal Democracy* (New York: Oxford University Press, 1977).
2. Christopher Blackwell, ed., *Demos: Classical Athenian Democracy*, www.stoa.org/projects/demos/home.
3. For details, see Charles Tilly, "War Making and State Making as Organized Crime," in Peter B. Evans, Dietrich Rueschemeyer, and Theda Skocpol, eds., *Bringing the State Back In* (New York: Cambridge University Press, 1985), pp. 165–191.
4. Alexis de Tocqueville, *Democracy in America* (1840), available at http://xroads .virginia.edu/.
5. Vladimir Tismaneanu, *In Search of Civil Society: Independent Peace Movements in the Soviet Bloc* (London: Routledge, 1990).
6. William T. Hutchinson et al., eds., *The Papers of James Madison* (Chicago: Univer-sity of Chicago Press, 1985), vol. 14, pp. 197–198.
7. John Aldrich, *Why Parties? The Origin and Transformation of Political Parties in America* (Chicago: University of Chicago Press, 1995).
8. An exhaustive discussion of the different forms of electoral systems and other facets of voting and elections can be found at the Administration and Cost of Elections website at www.aceproject.org.
9. Maurice Duverger, *Political Parties: Their Organization and Activity in the Modern State* (New York: Wiley, 1964).
10. Advocates for majority single-member districts in the United States can be found at www.fairvote.org/irv/.
11. An extensive argument in favor of adopting proportional representation in the United States can be found at the website of Professor Douglas Amy of Mount Holyoke College: www.mtholyoke.edu/acad/polit/damy/prlib.htm.
12. For a critique of the use of direct democracy, see Fareed Zakaria, *The Future of Freedom: Illiberal Democracy at Home and Abroad* (New York: Norton, 2003).
13. The South African and other constitutions of the world can be found online at www.uni-wuerzburg.de/law/home.html.

6 NONDEMOCRATIC REGIMES

KEY CONCEPTS

- Nondemocratic regimes are often divided between authoritarianism and totalitarianism.

- As with democracy, there are various and competing theories for the emergence and perseverance of nondemocratic regimes.

- Coercion, co-optation, and personality cults are common means through which nondemocratic regimes maintain their power.

- Nondemocratic regime types include personal and monarchical, military, one-party, theocratic, and illiberal/hybrid.

- The general trend worldwide has been away from nondemocratic regimes, though illiberal regimes seem to be growing in importance.

"Man is born free but everywhere he is in chains," wrote Jean-Jacques Rousseau in 1762. Since his time, democracy has emerged and flourished in many places throughout the world. However, according to Freedom House, an American nongovernmental organization that monitors and promotes open markets and democratic institutions around the world, over half the world's population still lives in societies defined as either "partly free," where significant personal liberties and democratic rights are limited, or "not free," where the public has little political freedom.[1] In neither case can these regimes be described as democratic.

In this chapter, we will look at the internal dynamics and origins of nondemocratic regimes. After defining these regimes and their relationship to freedom and equality, we will look at their sources, addressing the puzzle of why nondemocratic regimes are the norm in some countries but not in others. Behind this lies the broader question of the origins of nondemocratic rule, which will mirror our discussion in the previous chapter on competing explanations for democratization. What variables are associated with nondemocratic rule? This discussion of the possible sources of nondemocratic regimes will lead us into an examination of how nondemocratic rulers maintain their hold on power. Nondemocratic regimes display a great diversity; nevertheless, we can identify and contrast a number of common features. Finally, we will consider the future of nondemocratic rule. At the end of the Cold War, many assumed that liberal democracy was the wave of the future. In recent years, however, nondemocratic rule has shown an ability to adapt and thrive. The "wave of democracy" may be facing a reverse tide. Whether this is true, and with what implications, will be the final consideration of our chapter.

Defining Nondemocratic Rule

One of the challenges in studying nondemocratic regimes is that it represents what we could call a "residual category." Unlike democracy, which can be defined and identified, nondemocratic regimes represent a wide array of different kinds of systems, many of which bear little resemblance to one another. This in turn leads to a proliferation of terms that are often used interchangeably and indiscriminately: autocracy, oligarchy, dictatorship, tyranny. Even more confusing, in some cases, nondemocratic regimes may have more resemblance to democracies than to other nondemocratic regimes. As a result, we tend to speak of nondemocratic regimes in terms of what they deny their citizens, using democracy as the benchmark: restricted participation, restricted competition, restricted liberty. In many cases we will use the term **authoritarianism** to cover many of these different forms of nondemocratic rule.

If we want to speak of nondemocratic regimes as having more than simply the absence of democracy, however, we need some kind of definition to work with. Scholars define **nondemocratic regimes** as those in which a political regime is controlled by a small group of individuals who exercise power over the state without being constitutionally responsible to the public. In nondemocratic regimes, the public does not play a significant role in selecting or removing leaders from office; thus, political leaders in nondemocratic regimes have much greater leeway to develop policies that they "dictate" to the people (hence the term *dictator*). As one can imagine, nondemocratic regimes by their nature are built around the restriction of individual freedom. At a minimum, they eliminate people's right to choose their own leaders, and they also restrict to varying degrees other liberties, such as freedom of speech or of assembly. Nondemocratic regimes' relationship to equality is less clear. Some nondemocratic regimes, such as those under communism, limit individual freedom in order to produce greater social equality. Others seek to provide neither freedom nor equality, existing only to enhance the power of those in control.[2]

There are various kinds of nondemocratic regimes. Non-democratic leaders do not nec-essarily rule in a capricious or arbitrary manner; indeed, non-democratic regimes can have a strong institutional underpin-ning of ideology. As ideologies, fascism and communism, for instance, explicitly reject liberal democracy as an inferior form

IN FOCUS

Nondemocratic Regimes

- A small group of individuals exercises power over the state.
- Government is not constitutionally responsible to the public.
- Public has little or no role in selecting leaders.
- Individual freedom is restricted.
- Nondemocratic regimes may be institutionalized and legitimate.

of social organization, favoring instead a powerful state and restricted indi-vidual freedoms. This ideology provided the norms that fascist and commu-nist nondemocratic leaders followed in places like Nazi Germany or the Soviet Union. But other nondemocratic regimes are not ideological and may even be anti-ideological in nature, asserting that the leadership speaks for "the peo-ple." In other cases, few if any substantial political ideas are evident among those in power, whose rule is predicated simply on power for power's sake and the benefits that come with it. In these cases, it becomes difficult even to speak of a regime, and the term *regime* is often used pejoratively by critics, coupled with a leader's name (such as the "Saddam Hussein regime" in Iraq). This terminology reflects the critics' view that all decisions flow from the ruler, unfettered by political institutions of any sort. The leader, in essence, is the regime.

Totalitarianism and Nondemocratic Rule

Before we go any further in our discussion, we should take some time to exam-ine one particular concept that falls within the category of nondemocratic rule: **totalitarianism**. Totalitarianism is a tricky and often misused term, though quite distinct from authoritarianism. Totalitarianism connotes vio-lence and terror, and so the word is often used in a partisan way to label a political system that we particularly dislike. This problem of definition goes back the earlier part of the last century. Many scholars used the term *totali-tarianism* to describe Nazi Germany and the Soviet Union and its satellite states; others countered that the term was being applied as much for politi-cal reasons as for any objective means of classification, equating fascism and communism. Some thus called for abandoning the term altogether, claiming that it had no real scholarly utility. However, totalitarianism remains a valuable concept, especially if used consistently and judiciously.

What then is the difference between totalitarianism and other forms of nondemocratic rule? There are several important elements. Totalitarianism is a form of nondemocratic rule with a highly centralized state and a regime with a well-defined ideology that seeks to transform and fuse the institutions of state, society, and the economy. Unlike other nondemocratic regimes, the main objective of totalitarianism is to use power to transform the total institutional fabric of a country according to some ideological goal. Finally, because of the ambitious goals of totalitarianism, violence often becomes a necessary tool to destroy any obstacle to change.[3] The use of terror not only destroys enemies of the totalitarian ideology but, as the political philosopher Hannah Arendt pointed out, also shatters human will, destroying the ability of individuals to create, much less aspire to, freedom.[4] Under these conditions, the use of terror and violence is common in order to break down existing institutions and remake them in the leadership's own image. This is not to say that any violent regime is totalitarian. The central issue is to what end that violence is used. Totalitarianism often emerges when those who have come to power profess a radical or reactionary political attitude, both of which reject the status quo and see dramatic, often revolutionary change as indispensable and violence as a necessary or even a positive force toward that goal.

Many countries in history have been controlled by leaders with totalitarian aspirations, but few of these leaders have been able to put their theories to practice. The Soviet Union under the rule of Josef Stalin from the 1930s to the 1950s is commonly viewed as totalitarian, with most domestic institutions radically restructured, most aspects of private life controlled by the state and the Communist Party, and millions imprisoned and executed toward those ends. Nazi Germany is also commonly viewed as a totalitarian regime, although in some areas, such as the economy, changes were relatively few. Other fascist regimes, such as Italy during World War II, lacked the capacity and power to be totalitarian, even though they openly aspired to be so. Similarly, while China during the Cultural Revolution of the 1960s experienced widespread violence against people and institutions, the fragmentation of the Communist Party and the state was quite different from totalitarianism. As we see, in spite of a more precise definition, we find *totalitarian* a difficult word to apply, making it liable to subjective, rather than objective, use.

IN FOCUS

Totalitarian Regimes . . .

- Seek to control and transform all aspects of the state, society, and economy.
- Use violence as a tool for remaking institutions.
- Have a strong ideological goal.
- Have arisen relatively rarely.

In the modern world, only communist North Korea can still properly be described as totalitarian, dominated by an elaborate ideology that covers all aspects of life and is backed by violence, widespread fear, and the absence of even small personal freedoms. By way of comparison, a country such as Iraq under Saddam Hussein, although highly oppressive, could not be described as totalitarian because it lacked a strong ideology and in many ways was less centralized than outsiders imagined. Saddam Hussein's primary goal as Iraq's leader was to maintain and expand his own political power as an end in itself. In spite of this, critics often described Iraq as a totalitarian society. Similarly, Iran is frequently described as a totalitarian system, but though one might describe the current regime as embodying a "totalist" ideology, large swaths of the state, society, and economy function with varying degrees of independence.

To sum up, nondemocratic rule is a political regime in which power is exercised by a few, unbound by public or constitutional control. The public lacks not only the right to choose its own leaders but also other personal liberties that those in power may see as a threat, such as freedom of speech or assembly. Totalitarianism, as a particular form of nondemocratic rule, is distinguished from other forms of nondemocratic rule by its totalist ideology that seeks the fundamental transformation of most domestic institutions and the potential use of violence toward that end.

Origins and Sources of Nondemocratic Rule

Now that we have defined nondemocratic regimes, we might consider their emergence and perseverance. Recall that in the last chapter we spoke about some of the competing explanations for why democracy comes about. In a number of these explanations, the survival or elimination of nondemocratic regimes was implicit. So let's return to these arguments, with an emphasis on nondemocratic perseverance rather than decline. As always, there is no single or dominant explanation for nondemocratic regimes, and the explanatory power of any theory may be limited by space or time.

Modernization and Nondemocratic Rule

Recall that one of the central assertions of the behavioral revolution was that with modernization, societies would become more urban, educated, and politically sophisticated, creating the basic conditions that would catalyze democracy. And indeed, there is a strong correlation between societies that lack modern institutions and nondemocratic rule. Societies that are poor and poorly developed are less likely to have democracy for a number of reasons, which we noted in Chapter 5. First, such societies are more likely to be highly unequal—what little wealth there is in society is likely to be concentrated in the hands of a few individuals. As a result, there is a strong incentive for those with economic power to also want to monopolize political power in order to fend off any challenges from the public to redistribute that wealth. In the common political science dictum "no middle class, no democracy," the absence of a middle class will likely result in nondemocratic rule. There are notable exceptions, such as India, but in most cases a combination of poverty and inequality are strongly correlated with nondemocratic rule.

Even where modernization has taken place, nondemocratic rule may be the outcome—and even replace existing democratic regimes. In contrast to our previous expectations, modernization can be a disruptive and uneven process. Urban areas may experience the sudden transformation of institutions and norms while rural areas lag behind; technological benefits, from telephones and Internet access to roads and schools, may be enjoyed by some and unavailable to others. Similar disruptions and shifts in economic institutions (such as from agricultural to industrial) and social institutions (such as changes in gender relations or increased secularism) can generate instability. Modernization can also trend backward, with increased inflation or unemployment, destabilizing the political order. Where a sufficient number of individuals feel disoriented by change, this can pave the way for political movements and leaders who promise to restore "order" and reconcile the tensions between old institutions and new. This can bring down a democratic regime if it is seen as incapable of reconciling the tensions or pitfalls of modernity. In fact, one important observation to make is that these nondemocratic movements are often driven by the direct beneficiaries of modernization, such as students and urban intellectuals, who have gained the organizational and ideological tools to articulate an alternative political vision to the status quo.

We should be clear, however, in what we are not arguing. First, while nondemocratic rule may be correlated with poverty and inequality, this is not to say that the former necessarily leads to the latter. We have ample examples of nondemocratic regimes that have been highly equal societies, particularly communist ones like the Soviet Union or Cuba, whose ideology was predicated on eliminating differences between rich and poor. Similarly, we can find cases where the standard of living is high, like Singapore or Kuwait, but which lack democracy. Regime type and poverty or inequality do not correlate neatly, though in general, nondemocratic countries tend to be found among those countries whose per capita GDP at purchasing-power parity is below $7,000.

Elites and Nondemocratic Rule

Modernization theory has taken a beating over time as an overly optimistic and deterministic vision of political and economic change. In the previous chapter, however, we noted that modernization theory has found new life in the idea that democratization may be more likely under conditions where there is not simply economic development but also a relatively equitable distribution of those resources. Elites may be more willing to share power when they have fewer fears of losing economic opportunities in the process. Accordingly, highly unequal societies will reinforce nondemocratic rule, and in fact, the longevity of nondemocracy may be precisely due to the fact that rivals for power seek control specifically so that they can enrich themselves. The state under these conditions becomes a tool to siphon off resources and maintain control. Given these higher levels of inequality, those in power may be particularly loath to surrender power, not only because they may be forced to give up their assets but because they may lose their lives as well. The threat of revolution may make these systems particularly unlikely to provide much in the way of participation, competition, or liberty.

One particular variant of this argument that has gained currency of late is what is referred to as the "resource trap" theory of development. The resource being referred to here is natural resources, such as oil, gas, or minerals. While these might be a source of great wealth, the puzzle is why so many resource rich countries are development or democracy poor. According to this theory, the existence of natural resources acts as a barrier to modernization and democracy, for several related reasons. First, resources in the ground give leaders the wealth necessary to run the state without taxation. This means those in power need not bother themselves with the taxation and representation trade-off; since they do not need to tax the people, they can also effectively ignore their political demands. Even worse, natural resources tend to stunt the development of a modern economy and middle class, since neither is of concern to those in power (and in fact may represent a threat). The result is that wealth is highly concentrated in the hands of those in power. Under these conditions, nondemocratic rule can effectively subsidize itself, so long as the resources last and have a market. Oil is clearly the most obvious example of a resource trap, but diamonds, gold, or timber could also serve this function.

Society and Nondemocratic Rule

This discussion returns us to the idea of civil society. Recall that we defined civil society as a fabric of organizations created by people to help define their own interests. These are not necessarily political, and in fact, the vast majority of them have no specific political content. Sports groups, collectors and enthusiasts, religious and other organizations all form civil society. It is commonly argued that civil society is crucial to democratic life because it allows individuals to organize, articulate their preferences, and form networks that cross normal economic, social, or political divides. Civil society is thus commonly viewed as a crucible for democratic action, laying the groundwork for democratic institutions.

Conversely, many authoritarian systems are characterized by the absence of civil society. This can be the specific result of those in power, who have taken steps to harass, absorb, monitor, or destroy any form of independent action outside of the state and those in power. Civil society may also have little precedent in society or be hindered by significant ethnic or other societal divisions that dissuade people from forming organizations across these institutional barriers. The result can be a society that is more familiar with viewing the state as a primary arena for social organization, or that thinks of association more in terms of mass movements and protest. Sometimes both of these go hand in hand in what is known as **populism**. Populism is not a specific ideology and in fact draws much of its power from an anti-institutional approach. But generally, populism carries within it the view that elites and established institutions do not fully represent the will of the people and that a new movement, free from ideology and often led by a charismatic leader, can usher in a new order. Where civil society is weak, populism may find more fertile ground.

Finally, it is also possible that civil society may emerge alongside a nondemocratic regime but may itself take on nondemocratic tendencies, especially where more democratic forms have been repressed by the state. Across parts of the Middle East there are strong civil society movements rooted in Islamic fundamentalism, but these organizations, while opposed to current nondemocratic regimes, wish to take their place, not democratize them.

International Relations and Nondemocratic Rule

International influences can support and contribute to nondemocratic rule. The most obvious way can be through occupation. While the occupation of Japan and Germany led to democratization, in Eastern Europe, Soviet control after World War II brought an end to democratic movements and eliminated much of civil society. Some countries, like Czechoslovakia, saw their vibrant prewar democracies quickly dismantled and replaced with communist rule. In more indirect situations, imperialism has contributed to nondemocratic rule in various ways. Borders badly drawn by imperial powers, as we discussed in Chapter 2, have created many countries with ethnic and religious divisions that make consensus building difficult and authoritarianism an effective way to monopolize power over other groups. Imperial institutions, from infrastructure and education to state institutions, have similarly fostered authoritarianism by contributing to such things as uneven modernization and weak state autonomy and capacity. Finally, other states and international organizations may also support or sustain authoritarian control. During the

Cold War, both the Soviet Union and the United States backed authoritarian rulers against democratic forces in order to maintain or expand their influence. The United States played a significant role in overthrowing the democratically elected government in Iran in 1953, fearing that the prime minister was tilting toward the Soviet Union. The Soviet Union crushed revolts in Hungary in 1956 and Czechoslovakia in 1968. With the rise of China and the move away from democracy in Russia, these two countries have become important supporters of nondemocratic regimes in Africa and the Middle East through investment and diplomatic support in the international community. Iran and Venezuela, too, have sought to use their oil wealth to support like-minded regimes.

Culture and Nondemocratic Rule

Let us return to the idea of political culture, which argues that there are differences in societal institutions—norms and values—that shape the landscape of political activity. In the previous chapter we discussed the controversial idea that there may be a culture of democracy or liberty that must be a precondition for institutionalized democracy, and that certain cultures may, for whatever reason, hold these values while others do not. By way of extension, it could be argued that there are nondemocratic political values as well. If we return to our map of political culture in Chapter 3, we can see an array of countries whose cultural values tend more toward authority over individual freedom. This may be a function of modernization or something more fixed in the cultural landscape of these societies, raising the controversial question of modernization versus Westernization. In contrast to modernization theory, which essentially views "Western" and "modern" concepts as the same, culture is much more fixed, according to some scholars; they believe that modernization will not necessarily lead to Westernization, meaning the adoption of such values as secularism, individualism, and liberal democracy. Nondemocratic rule in this view is not the absence of democracy—it is its own set of values.

Let's look at some specific examples. A common argument is that democracy is a unique product of interconnected historical experiences in Europe, such as Christianity (particularly Protestantism), the emphasis on individualism and secularism, the development of the nation-state, ideology, early industrialization, and the development of capitalism, among others. These factors, the argument goes, allowed for the creation of democracy as a regime built on liberal values that emphasize freedom—what we typically call "Western" societies. In contrast, some have asserted that under Islam, political power and religious power are one and the same: laws are seen not as societal institutions to protect or advance individual rights, but as codes handed down by

Figure 6.1   **REGIONS AND POLITICAL SYSTEMS, 2008**

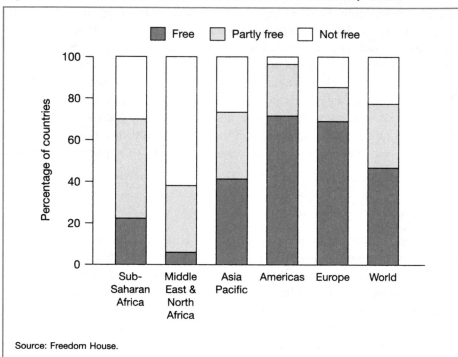

Source: Freedom House.

Allah that are to be observed and defended, and democracy is essentially anathema to the will of God. Cultural arguments can also be found in what has been called the "Asian values" debate. Proponents of the idea of Asian values argue that Asia's cultural and religious traditions stress conformity, hierarchy, and obedience, which are more conducive to a political regime that limits freedom in order to defend social harmony and consensus. The philosophy of Confucianism is frequently cited in this regard, with its emphasis on obedience to hierarchy and its notion of a ruler's "mandate from heaven." The ruling elite stands as a parental figure over the people, acting in the public's best interest but not under its control. As the former Malaysian prime minister Mahathir Mohamad, one of the major proponents of "Asian values," has put it, "When citizens understand that their right to choose also involves limits and responsibilities, democracy doesn't deteriorate into an excess of freedom. . . . These are the dangers of democracy gone wrong, and in our view it is precisely the sad direction in which the West is heading."[5]

As you might imagine, there are many both inside and outside societies with Islamic or Confucian traditions who reject the idea that these or any other cultures create a culture of nondemocratic rule. These countries and the peoples within them are far too diverse to speak of one set of values. Differences in history, religion, social structure, and other institutions have led to an array of different and overlapping ideas that are in a continuous process of interaction and reinterpretation. Confucian thought, just like the Bible in the West or the Koran in Islamic countries, can be interpreted in very different ways. Recall that in the previous chapter we noted that not long ago, it was asserted that certain forms of Christianity created cultures more amenable to authoritarian rule. Roman Catholicism emphasized hierarchy and the power of organized religion over the state, while Orthodox Christianity in Eastern and Southern Europe fused religious and political authority in a single head. Yet nondemocratic rule in societies with these religious traditions has also given way since the 1970s. Cultural arguments may inform the content of nondemocratic or democratic institutions, but we should be wary of making sweeping arguments about culture and regime type.

Let's sum up. There are numerous explanations for nondemocratic rule, and these arguments are contingent on time and space—what might be the explanation for one country at one point in time may be irrelevant in another. The lack of modernization or its disruptive nature may reinforce nondemocratic rule. Elite strategies and the fear of sharing power can also help support nondemocratic rule, especially when natural resources are in play. A weak civil society at home and support abroad can also play an important role. Finally, culture can be a factor in shaping the contours of nondemocratic institutions, but whether this can explain authoritarianism itself is much more questionable and contentious. The intersection of these forces can explain how and why nondemocratic rule comes to power.

Nondemocratic Regimes and Political Control

We have so far covered some of the main explanations for the establishment of nondemocratic regimes. In addition, we should consider how these systems stay in power. In liberal democracies, we take the system of government for granted; so long as participation, competition, and liberty are provided and defended, democracy can continue, often even in the face of inequality, economic crisis, and civil or international conflict. We assume that for nondemocratic regimes, however, their existence is much more precarious, held in place only by fear and vulnerable to revolution at any moment. This is a misleading image. Nondemocratic regimes vary in their mechanisms of political control, some of which can generate legitimacy like that found in democratic systems. A consideration of the means of nondemocratic rule will give us a sense of this complexity.

Coercion and Surveillance

One feature that we initially, and perhaps primarily, associate with nonde-mocratic regimes and especially with totalitarianism is the use of **coercion**. Coercion can be defined as compelling individuals by threatening harm to their lives or livelihoods. Compliance and obedience with regime goals are often enforced through the threat or use of force against the population, send-ing a clear signal that those who oppose the regime or government will be dealt with harshly: loss of job or access to certain resources, arrest, detention without trial, torture, death. In an extreme example, in the 1970s several non-democratic regimes in Latin America used "death squads" made up of police or military troops to target individuals suspected of harboring political views opposed to the regime. These individuals were abducted by the death squads and murdered, frequently after torture. In some cases, their bodies were dumped in the open as a warning to others who dared to question the regime; in other cases, the victims simply joined the thousands of the "disappeared," individuals abducted and never seen again.

In other regimes, violence has been used even more indiscriminately. When Stalin consolidated his totalitarian rule in the Soviet Union in the 1930s he car-ried out what are known as "purges," widespread arrests that decimated the ranks of the Communist Party and the state bureaucracy. Former leaders of the 1917 revolution, city mayors and local party bosses, high-ranking officers in the army and navy, university professors, scientists, diplomats, and many others were detained, tortured, coerced into confessing during "show trials," forced to impli-cate others in their supposed crimes, and either sent to forced labor camps or executed. The targets of the purges were not limited to the party or the state; writers, artists, students, farmers, and workers were also among those accused of political sabotage and anti-Soviet views. It is not known how many died in these purges; estimates range from 5 million to 20 million. Undoubtedly, in the vast majority of these cases, the victims were innocent; yet this was unimportant to Stalin's regime. By making everyone fear that he or she, too, can be arrested, the public can be controlled and even turned against itself, with all fearing that they will be denounced by someone else. The use of arbitrary arrests, torture, disap-pearances, and murder continues to be common in many nondemocratic regimes.

IN FOCUS

Nondemocratic Means of Control

- *Coercion*: public obedience is enforced through violence and surveillance.
- *Co-optation*: members of the public are brought into a beneficial relationship with the state and government, often through corporatism or clientelism.
- *Personality cult*: the public is encouraged to obey the leader based on his or her extraordinary qualities and compelling ideas.

Another important means of control is the ability to maintain a close watch over the population. Surveillance allows the government to prevent opposition from organizing and also instills uncertainty among the population—who is being watched? Surveillance may be conducted through the use of an internal security force, or "secret police," charged with monitoring public activity, spying on individuals, and interrogating members of the public suspected of political activity hostile to the regime. In some countries, surveillance has included widespread telephone tapping and the creation of a huge network of public informers, where nearly anyone may be the eyes and ears of those in power. With the rise of the Internet and cellular technology, surveillance has become more sophisticated, including the ability to monitor certain forms of communication, such as e-mail or text messages.

Co-optation: Corporatism and Clientelism

The prevalence of coercion and surveillance in some nondemocratic regimes may again give the impression that those in power must be ever vigilant against the public to prevent opposition or revolution that might spring up at any time. But not all regimes need or choose to rely on punishment or surveillance as a central means of control. Another method they may use is **co-optation**, the process by which individuals outside of an organization are brought into a beneficial relationship with it, making them dependent on the regime for certain rewards. Although co-optation is not unique to nondemocratic regimes, it tends to be much more widespread under such regimes than under democracy, which is usually more suspicious of such favoritism as contrary to the democratic process.

CORPORATISM Co-optation can take many forms. The most structured form is corporatism. Recall from Chapter 4 the term *neocorporatism*, in which business, labor, and the state engage in bargaining over economic policy. In its earliest form, however, modern **corporatism** emerged as a method by which nondemocratic regimes attempted to solidify their control over the public by creating or sanctioning a limited number of organizations to represent the interests of the public and restricting those not set up or approved by the state. These organizations are meant to replace independent organizations with a handful that alone have the right to speak for various sectors of society. For example, under a corporatist regime, churches, labor unions, agricultural associations, student groups, neighborhood committees, and the like are all approved and funded by the state. Nonsanctioned, alternative organizations are not allowed.

Unlike the overlapping memberships, competition, and ever-changing nature of civil society and political parties in a pluralistic society, corporatism arranges society such that each organization is empowered by the state to have a monopoly of representation over a given issue or segment of society (meaning that no other organization may act in that area or speak on that issue). State, society, and the market under corporatism are viewed as a single organic body, with each element cooperating and performing its own specific and limited role and subordinate to the state and regime.

Corporatism can be an effective form of control, as it gives the public a limited influence (or at least the pretense of influence) in the policy-making process. Farmers or students have an official organization with elected officers and resources that are meant to serve their interests. In return, the regime is able to better control the public through these institutions, which are funded and managed by the state, and civil society is marginalized or eliminated. For the average individual, a state-sanctioned organization is better than none at all, and many willingly participate in the hope that their needs will be met.

Many nondemocratic regimes have used variants of corporatism as a means of control. It is an integral part of totalitarianism, but it also existed in nontotalitarian Spain and Portugal up to the 1970s. In Spain, for example, a single political party organized most business and labor interests together into a limited number of "syndicates" that represented both owners and workers in different sectors of the economy. Communist regimes are similarly corporatist. In Cuba, for example, all labor is organized under a single union directly controlled by the state, and independent unions are illegal. Although different in form and degree, in all corporatist regimes we see the presence of a limited number of organizations used to represent and direct societal interests, bringing the public under organized state control.

CLIENTELISM A less structured means by which states may co-opt the public is through **clientelism**, whereby the state co-opts members of the public by providing specific benefits or favors to a single person or small group in return for public support (such as voting in elections). Unlike corporatism, clientelism relies on individual patronage rather than organizations that serve a large group of people, and it is more ad hoc than corporatism. Clientelism does not require a set of sanctioned and licensed organizations but can target and respond to individuals and groups as those in power see fit, trading benefits for particular forms of support.

In both corporatism and clientelism, the state has a number of perquisites it can use in co-opting individuals. Jobs within the state or in state-run sectors of the economy, business contracts or licenses, public goods such as roads or schools, kickbacks and bribes are a few of the tools in its arsenal. Such largesse often leads to **rent seeking**, a process in which political leaders essentially rent out parts of the state to their supporters, who as a result control public goods that would otherwise be distributed in a nonpolitical manner. For example, leaders might turn over control of a nationalized industry, providing supporters with jobs and the ability to siphon off public funds from that branch of the state.

In general, co-optation may be much more successful than coercion at maintaining nondemocratic regimes, since many in the public may actively support the regime in return for the benefits they derive. Political opposition is dealt with not through repression and violence but by incorporating one's opponents into the system and making them dependent on it, or withholding such largesse. Such a regime, however, faces limitations. Corporatist and clientelist institutions can run out of benefits with which to pacify the public; national industries or resources can drag on the economy, run out, or decline in value. In addition, in a regime where economic resources are doled out for political reasons, problems may emerge as productive resources are siphoned off to secure the acquiescence of the public. At its worst, such a regime can decline into a kleptocracy (literally, "rule by theft"), where those in power seek only to drain the state of assets and resources. As these resources dry up, co-optation can quickly unravel.

Personality Cults

Nondemocratic regimes may also reinforce their rule through emphasis on veneration of the leadership—essentially an emotional appeal to legitimize rule. The most extreme example is what is known as a **personality cult**. First used to describe Stalin's rule in the Soviet Union, a personality cult refers to the promotion of the image of a leader not merely as a political figure but as someone who embodies the spirit of the nation, possesses endowments of wisdom and strength far beyond those of the average individual, and is thus portrayed in a quasi-religious manner as all-wise, all-seeing, all-knowing. In other words, personality cults attempt to generate a charismatic form of authority for the political leader from the top down by convincing the public of the leader's admirable qualities. In one recent example, in Turkmenistan, Saparmurat Niyazov, president from 1990 until his death in 2006, dubbed himself "Turkmenbashi," or "Father of the Turkmen," and built his personality cult around such trappings as changing the months of the year (renaming April after his mother and January after himself) and constructing a large, gold-leaf statue of himself that rotated during the day to follow the sun.

The media and culture play a vital role in a personality cult, promoting it through all aspects of daily life—news reports, public rallies, art, music, films, and other imagery of the leader. Successes in the country are attributed to the power of the leader, and mistakes are blamed on the mortal flaws of the public or on external enemies. Cults of personality may also be coupled to coercion; the public may not believe the praise, but no one is willing to say so. This is especially the case where charismatic power has faded over time to become little more than a facade, held up only by force. Under these conditions, there is always the chance that the cult will crack, leading to a rapid political decompression. This occurred in Romania in 1989, when Nicolae Ceauşescu, the self-styled "conductor" of his country, was shown on national television reacting in a stunned and confused manner when attendees at a public rally he was addressing suddenly grew hostile. Within hours, revolution had swept the country, and within three days, Ceauşescu and his wife had been executed by firing squad.

Personality cults may also take a weaker but still powerful form. In Iran, the image of Supreme Leader Ayatollah Khamenei adorns shops and billboards around the country, and he is viewed as a conduit to God. Yet in spite of his power, few Iranians would view him as a kind of deity in his own right or believe that has superhuman powers. In recent years, Latin America has produced a number of populist leaders whose personal charisma and symbolic power are significant. Most notable of these is Hugo Chávez in Venezuela, known for his regular presence in the media, including unscripted speeches on national television that can last for several hours. His personal popularity is strong and amplified by the state-run media, but it would be a stretch to call this a personality cult. Chávez remains, in the eyes of the public and in his own political communication, an exceptional, but still flawed, human being.

Looking back over what we have discussed so far, we find that nondemocratic regimes come to power and stay in power in various ways: some of these ways are "carrots" (reward for compliance and support), others "sticks" (threatened or actual punishments). It also follows that some people, perhaps even a majority, may therefore view the regime as legitimate. They may agree with the regime's ideology, be direct beneficiaries of its rule, venerate its leaders, or simply fear political change. The idea of nondemocratic legitimacy may be hard for us to accept. Particularly in Western democracies, there is the assumption that in every nondemocratic regime, the people are simply waiting for the chance to install democracy. This belief is an exaggeration. Nondemocratic regimes can be just as institutionalized and stable and legitimate as any democratic regime, enjoying some, or even a great deal of, public support, especially if benefits are widespread enough, coercion limited, and political change viewed as fraught with risk. Many, for example, would suggest that the current Chinese regime enjoys widespread public support and that the public has little interest in democratization, which it views as potentially undoing the economic progress of the last twenty years.

Models of Nondemocratic Rule

By now it should be clear that nondemocratic regimes may emerge for different reasons and may persist in different ways by using, to different degrees, tools of coercion and support. Based on these characteristics, political scientists often classify these regimes into a number of specific forms of rule. The most commonly seen forms are personal and monarchical, military, one-party, theocratic, and illiberal/hybrid regimes. Personal rule is based on the power of a single strong leader who typically relies on charismatic or traditional authority to maintain power. Under military rule, in contrast, the monopoly of violence that characterizes militaries tends to be the strongest means of control. One-party rule is often more corporatist in nature, creating a broad membership as a source of support and oversight. Theocracies, though limited in number, derive their power from their claim to rule on behalf of God. Finally, in illiberal or hybrid regimes, the basic structures of democracy exist but are not fully institutionalized and often not respected. In many if not most of these cases, we find the institutions we are familiar with in liberal democracies: heads of state and government, legislatures and judiciaries, and various forms of elections. But these institutions do not rest on the rule of law, in which the public and those in power are subject to the legal order. In the absence of the rule of law, these institutions reflect the preferences of those in power.

Personal and Monarchical Rule

Personal and monarchical rule is what usually comes to mind when people think of nondemocratic rule, perhaps because long before modern politics, states, or economies came into being, people were ruled by powerful figures—kings and Caesars, emperors and sultans, chiefs and caudillos. Drawing from charismatic or traditional legitimacy, **personal** and **monarchical rule** often rests on the claim that one person alone is fit to run the country, with no clear regime or roles to constrain that person's rule. Under this form of rule, the state and society are commonly taken to be possessions of the leader, to be dispensed with as he (or, occasionally, she) sees fit. The ruler is not a subject of the state; rather, the state and society are subjects of the ruler. Ideology may be weak or absent, as the ruler justifies his control through the logic that he alone is the embodiment of the people and therefore uniquely qualified to act on the people's behalf. This claim may be coupled with a strong personality cult or a reliance on the traditional authority of bloodlines.

In some cases, personal or monarchical rule relies less on charismatic or traditional authority than on a specific form of co-optation known as **patrimonialism**. Patrimonialism can be seen as a form of clientelism, in that those in power trade benefits for political support—a patron-client relationship. However, under patrimonialism, the benefits are not distributed among society but instead are limited to a small group of regime supporters inside the state itself. This ruling group gains direct benefits in return for enforcing the ruler's will. The state elite swear allegiance to the leadership in return for personal profit (that is, a kleptocracy). This is a form of co-optation, although under patrimonialism, it is only the ruler's own personal followers who benefit. All others in society tend to be held in check by force.

An example of **personal rule** based on patrimonialism was found in Zaire (now the Democratic Republic of Congo) under the rule of Mobutu Sese Seko from 1965 until 1997. Although he once commanded a great deal of charismatic legitimacy, over time Mobutu increasingly used patrimonialism as a way to maintain his power. In particular, Mobutu built his patrimonial regime around Zaire's abundant natural resources, such as diamonds, gold, copper, and cobalt. These resources were used by the regime not to benefit the country as a whole but as Mobutu's personal treasury; he siphoned off the profits from these resources to enrich himself and his followers. The result was a coterie of supporters who were willing to defend Mobutu in order to maintain their economic privileges.[6] This system of dependence and economic reward helps explain how Mobutu maintained power for more than three decades while Zaire's per capita GDP dropped two-thirds from the 1970s to the 1990s.

While monarchies have waned, they remain powerful in parts of the Middle East, such as Saudi Arabia. Personal rule remains common in Africa and typically coupled to patrimonial regimes that are enriched through control over natural resources or trade.

Military Rule

A second form of nondemocratic regime is **military rule**. Once considered relatively unusual, military rule became much more common over the past half century, particularly in Latin America, Africa, and parts of Asia. Where governments and states are struggling with legitimacy and stability, often as a result of modernization, and where there are high levels of public unrest or violence, the military has sometimes chosen to intervene directly in politics, seeing itself as the only organized force able to ensure stability. This view is often combined with a sense among military leaders that the current government or regime threatens the military's or the country's interests and should be removed. Military rule may even have widespread public support, especially if people believe that the strong arm of the military can bring an end to corruption or political violence, prevent revolution, and restore stability.

Military rule typically emerges through a **coup d'état**, in which military forces take control of the government by force. In some cases, military actors may claim that they have seized control only reluctantly, promising to return the state and government to civilian rule once stability has been restored. This was the case in Thailand in 2006 when the military deposed the prime minister, but then returned the country to democratic rule in 2007. In recent years, the Turkish military has similarly threatened military action against the ruling Islamist party, claiming that its religious orientation conflicts with the country's secular constitution. Often, under military rule, political parties and most civil liberties are restricted; civilian political leaders or opponents of military rule are arrested and may be killed or disappear. The use of coercion is a common aspect of military rule, since by their nature, militaries hold an overwhelming capacity for violence.

Military rule typically lacks a specific ideology, although some military leaders espouse radical or reactionary political attitudes. Military rule also tends to lack any charismatic or traditional source of authority, meaning that if the military seek legitimacy in the eyes of the people, they often must fall back on rational authority. One particular variant of military rule that reflects this logic is known as **bureaucratic authoritarianism**, a regime in which the state bureaucracy and the military share a belief that a technocratic leadership, focused on rational, objective, and technical expertise, can solve the problems of the country—as opposed to "emotional" or "irrational" ideologically based party politics. Public participation, in other words, is seen as an obstacle to effective and objective policy making and so is done away with. In the 1960s and 1970s, bureaucratic authoritarian regimes emerged in a number of less-developed countries as rapid modernization and industrialization generated a high degree of political conflict. State and industry, with their plans for rapid economic growth, clashed with the interests of the working class and peasantry, who sought greater political power and a larger share of the wealth. This increasing polarization in politics often led business leaders and the state bureaucracy to advocate military rule as a way to prevent the working class and the peasantry from gaining power over the government.[7]

Over the past thirty years, many bureaucratic authoritarian regimes have transitioned to democracy. However, there remain some noteworthy examples. Russia now might be viewed as a bureaucratic authoritarian regime, where those in power have tended to come from within the secret service or military, including Vladimir Putin. Supporters of military rule believe that dispensing with democracy can help facilitate modernization and development; they point to cases like South Korea, Taiwan, and Chile as success stories. But this is a problem of selection bias, where we have only looked for cases of economic success. If we concentrate instead on military rule, we can find many more cases that led to instability, the loss of life, and poor economic development, such as much of Central America.

One-Party Rule

Commonly associated with totalitarianism, **one-party rule** is a regime in which a single political party monopolizes politics, with other parties banned or excluded from power. The ruling party serves several functions. It helps to incorporate the people into the political regime through membership and participation. Typically, the party incorporates only a small minority of the population—in most communist countries, for instance, party membership was less than 10 percent—but this still means that hundreds of thousands or millions of people are party members. One-party rule is often also combined with a larger corporatist regime of public control.

Through membership, the party can rely on a large segment of the public that is willing to help develop and support the policies of nondemocratic rule as well as to transmit information back to the leadership on developments in all aspects of society. Single-party regimes are often broken down into smaller units or "cells" that operate at the university, workplace, or neighborhood level. These units report back to higher levels of the party, help deal with local problems and concerns, and keep tabs on society as a whole. No area is untouched by the presence of the party, and this helps to maintain control over the public.

In return for their support, members of the party often are granted privileges that are otherwise denied to the public at large. They may have access to certain resources (better health care or housing, for instance) that nonmembers do not; positions in government and other important areas of the economy or society may also be restricted to party members. One important result of such membership is that a large group of individuals in society directly benefits from the regime and is therefore willing to defend it. This pragmatic membership, however, can backfire: those who embrace party membership only for the personal benefits and not out of any ideological conviction may quickly desert the leadership in a time of crisis.

Finally, the party serves as a mechanism of mobilization. The leadership uses the party as an instrument to deliver propaganda that extols the virtues of the current regime and government; it relies on its rank-and-file members, through demonstrations and mass rallies, to give the appearance of widespread public support and enthusiasm for the leadership. If necessary, it also uses party members to control and harass those who do not support the regime. However, co-optation is the primary mechanism that ensures compliance and support.

One-party regimes are often associated with communism and fascism and were present in all cases of totalitarianism. However, they also can be found around the world as part of a variety of nondemocratic regimes. Other parties may exist, but they typically are highly restricted by the government so that they cannot challenge the current regime. For many years, this was the case in Mexico, which was dominated by the Institutional Revolutionary Party, or PRI. Cuba, North Korea, China, Vietnam, and Laos are other examples of one-party regimes, each controlled by a single communist party.

Theocracy

Theocratic rule is probably the hardest form of nondemocratic rule to describe and analyze, though it probably is one of the oldest forms of rule. Although **theocracy** can be defined as, literally, "rule by God," where the faith is the foundation for the political regime, such a regime can be founded on any number of faiths and variations within them. Thus, in theory, a Christian theocracy might look completely unlike a Jewish one, drawing on very different texts, traditions, and interpretations of the faith. Another problem with a definition of theocracy is that there are currently very few examples of theocracies around the world. In fact, some scholars would say there is none. However, we can observe some commonalities and elements of theocratic rule, even if such a system does not exist in pure form. In Chapter 3, we noted that one of the recent challenges to ideology has been the rise of fundamentalism, which we defined as the fusion of religion and politics into an ideology that seeks to merge religion and the state. Such a merger, where faith is the sole source of the regime, would render democratic institutions as subordinate or in contradiction to the perceived will of God. In the vast majority of cases, such a goal remains hypothetical. Yet we can note cases where theocratic institutions are present and powerful.

Iran is the best example of a country that could be described as a theocracy. In 1979, revolution overthrew the existing secular monarchy, ushering in a new government headed by the cleric Ayatollah Khomeini. For many years, Khomeini had the idea of an Islamic government, which was put in practice in Iran. Most important, in the Iranian system, the traditional forms of secular government (executive, legislature, judiciary) are mirrored by unique institutions that are controlled by religious leaders. Thus, the Supreme Leader, a religious figure, holds power over the president, while a Guardian Council can reject legislation and candidates for office for being insufficiently Islamic. Afghanistan, too, could be described as a theocracy between 1996 and 2001, lacking any constitution and relying on local clerics to rule on judicial matters based on their interpretation of Islamic law.

In a more mixed form, Saudi Arabia combines both monarchical and theocratic forms of rule. Politics is monopolized by the ruling family, and the king also acts as the supreme religious leader. Judicial and other matters must conform to Islamic law and are enforced by the Mutawwai'in, or morality police. Conversion from Islam in Saudi Arabia and Iran is punishable by death, and

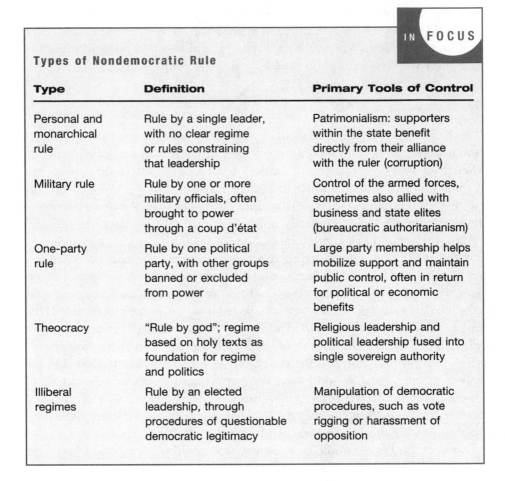

IN FOCUS

Types of Nondemocratic Rule

Type	Definition	Primary Tools of Control
Personal and monarchical rule	Rule by a single leader, with no clear regime or rules constraining that leadership	Patrimonialism: supporters within the state benefit directly from their alliance with the ruler (corruption)
Military rule	Rule by one or more military officials, often brought to power through a coup d'état	Control of the armed forces, sometimes also allied with business and state elites (bureaucratic authoritarianism)
One-party rule	Rule by one political party, with other groups banned or excluded from power	Large party membership helps mobilize support and maintain public control, often in return for political or economic benefits
Theocracy	"Rule by god"; regime based on holy texts as foundation for regime and politics	Religious leadership and political leadership fused into single sovereign authority
Illiberal regimes	Rule by an elected leadership, through procedures of questionable democratic legitimacy	Manipulation of democratic procedures, such as vote rigging or harassment of opposition

other faiths or sects within Islam are brought under strict control or banned outright. Many have suggested that other countries in the Middle East, such as Iraq or Egypt, could eventually move toward a theocracy; surveys, however, provide a more mixed picture of the public's desire to fuse religion and state.[8] As with fundamentalism, we should not confuse religiosity, or even greater religion in politics, with a desire for theocracy. In fact, many of the strongest critics of Iran's theocracy are some of its most prominent religious leaders.

Illiberal/Hybrid Regimes

Our last example is perhaps the most important for us to consider, since it seems to be growing in prominence around the world. In fact, Figure 6.1, shown earlier, includes a large group of countries that are categorized as neither "free" nor "not free," but as "partially free," falling somewhere between democratic and nondemocratic regimes. Examples would include Venezuela, Turkey, and Thailand. These regimes go by a number of names, such as semidemocratic regimes, quasi-democratic regimes, or electoral democracies. They are what we will term **illiberal or hybrid regimes**; scholars use both of these terms to mean the same regime type, though each term captures a different aspect of this particular form. By illiberal, we mean that they do not fully institutionalize liberty, while the idea of a hybrid speaks to a combination of democratic and nondemocratic institutions and practices. We will use the terms *illiberal* and *hybrid* interchangeably.

What do illiberal or hybrid regimes have in common? These regimes feature many of the familiar aspects of democracy, though with important qualifications. As a starting point, while the rule of law may be in place, it is weak. As a result, all the democratic institutions that rest upon the rule of law are weakly institutionalized and respected. Thus, executives, legislatures, and judiciaries have their respective arenas of authority; the public enjoys the right to vote; elections take place on a regular basis; and political parties compete. But these institutions and processes are circumscribed or unpredictable in ways inconsistent with democracy. Executives typically hold an overwhelming degree of power. This power is often concentrated in a presidency of a semipresidential system that limits the ability for removal. Moreover, presidents in illiberal systems often rely on referenda to bypass the state and confirm executive power. Legislatures in turn are less able to check the power of the executive, and judicial institutions such as constitutional courts are often packed with the supporters of those in power. In addition, while political competition may exist on paper, parties and groups are restricted or harassed. Government monopolies over print and electronic media are used to deny the opposition a public platform while the judicial system is used to harass them. The military or state-run industries can also be used by those in power to compel their members to vote and act as instructed. Elections are manipulated through changing electoral rules, barring candidates from running, vote-buying, or intimidation.

Illiberal regimes in many ways represent a gray area between nondemocratic and democratic rule. Although these regimes look much like democracies on paper, they are much less so in practice. The big question here is whether illiberal regimes are transitional, in the process of moving from nondemocratic to democratic rule (or vice versa), or a new form of nondemocracy that uses the trappings of democracy to perpetuate its control. Increasingly we are seeing more of the latter: the spread of democratic institutions but with circumscribed participation, competition, and liberty.[9]

INSTITUTIONS IN

ACTION

POPULISM IN AN ILLIBERAL REGIME: HUGO CHÁVEZ AND VENEZUELA

The rise to power of Hugo Chávez in Venezuela has been an interesting example for political scientists who study the intersection among populism, illiberalism, and natural resources. A former army officer jailed for a failed coup in 1992, he was elected president in 1998 by a strong majority of the vote. Since then, Chávez has sought to carry out dramatic change in the country through means that have polarized the international and domestic community. Many of these changes are rooted in socialist or at least populist ideas, concentrating on the needs of the poor over the wishes of the elites; they have included increased education and health care in what is a highly unequal society. At the same time, the president has asserted greater control over the country's oil industry, which provided the means by which the president can influence domestic and international affairs. The media, once strongly critical of Chávez, has been stifled by laws that prohibit slandering elected officials and the refusal to relicense one of the largest private television stations known for its hostility to Chávez. Chávez has also been given the power to rule by decree in certain areas, effectively bypassing the legislature, and he has sought to ban members of the opposition from running in local elections. In the international arena, Chávez has combined his political platform and oil revenues to forge ties with such countries as Cuba and Iran, and with other populist leaders in Latin America.

But to illustrate the complexity of illiberal regimes, Chávez does not enjoy unchecked political power. His presidency has been hindered by term limits, which require that he step down in 2013. In 2007, Chávez called for a national referendum to eliminate term limits but it was defeated in the polls; a decree to increase the powers of the intelligence services was rescinded after a public outcry, and members of the military have criticized what they see as the politicization of the military. At the same time, a second referendum to eliminate term limits passed in 2009, which may pave the way for more nondemocratic actions by the president. A clear transition to a fully democratic or authoritarian regime is probably the least likely result.

In Sum: Retreat or Retrenchment for Nondemocratic Regimes?

Although nondemocratic regimes exhibit an amazing diversity and flexibility in maintaining political control, the global trend over the past half century has been away from this form of rule. In the early part of the last century, democratic countries were few and beleaguered, wracked by economic recession, whereas nondemocratic regimes and totalitarianism in particular, backed by communist and fascist ideologies, seemed to promise radically new ways to restructure state, economic, and societal institutions. The German philosopher Oswald Spengler summarized these views in his 1922 work *The Decline of the West*: "The era of individualism, liberalism and democracy, of humanitarianism and freedom, is nearing its end. The masses will accept with resignation the victory of the Caesars, the strong men, and will obey them. Life will descend to a level of general uniformity, a new kind of primitivism, and the world will be better for it.[10]

Yet the exact opposite has taken place. In spite of the rise of illiberal and hybrid regimes, Figure 6.2 shows that the number of countries classified as "not free" and "partly free" has declined dramatically over just the past thirty years. In 1992, only a quarter of the global population lived in free societies; but in 2008, this had risen to nearly half. Why this decline in nondemocratic regimes? We have advanced economic, political, and societal arguments regarding the sources of nondemocratic rule and democratization. One final explanation may be that nondemocratic rule has lost much of its mobilizing power. Fifty years ago, ideologies predicated on nondemocratic regimes could

Figure 6.2 **AUTHORITARIANISM IN DECLINE, 1977–2007**

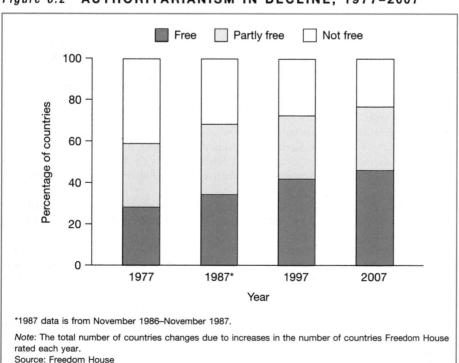

*1987 data is from November 1986–November 1987.

Note: The total number of countries changes due to increases in the number of countries Freedom House rated each year.
Source: Freedom House

mobilize people with visions of a world to be transformed. However, in the aftermath of World War II and the Cold War, there is no longer any strong ideology that combines the absence of individual freedom with some broader goal. Leaders may claim that limitations on political rights are necessary for political stability or economic development, but they no longer offer any real alternative vision for politics. It is increasingly difficult to justify nondemocratic regimes through any universal set of ideas.

Does this mean that the days of nondemocratic regimes are numbered? Perhaps. There may in fact come a time when all societies are democratic, and nondemocratic rule, like slavery, is an aspect of human behavior consigned to history and the margins of global society. However, we cannot know what new or perennial issues may again give power and purpose to nondemocratic rule. Will inequality clash with freedom? Will people someday come to see the absence of freedom as a benefit rather than a form of bondage? Might a new religious or secular vision of human life reject democracy as antiquated or profane? Perhaps what we now enjoy is simply a brief aberration in the long human history of nondemocratic rule.

NOTES

1. See the Freedom House website at www.freedomhouse.org.
2. For an excellent discussion of the bewildering varieties of nondemocratic rule, see Juan Linz, *Totalitarian and Nondemocratic Regimes* (Boulder: Lynne Rienner, 2000). This work was originally published in Fred I. Greenstein and Nelson W. Polsby, eds., *Handbook of Political Science* (Reading, MA: Addison-Wesley, 1975).
3. Linz, *Totalitarian and Nondemocratic Regimes*.
4. Hannah Arendt, *Totalitarianism* (New York: Harcourt, Brace and World, 1951).
5. Mahathir Mohamad and Shintaro Ishihara, *Voice of Asia: Two Leaders Discuss the Coming Century* (Tokyo: Kodansha International, 1996), p. 82.
6. For details, see Michael Bratton and Nicholas Van de Walle, "Neopatrimonial Regimes and Political Transitions in Africa," *World Politics*, 46, no. 4 (1994), pp. 453–489.
7. Guillermo O'Donnell, *Modernization and Bureaucratic Non-democratic Regimes: Studies in South American Politics* (Berkeley: Institute of International Studies, 1973).
8. See "Iraqi Public Rejects Iranian Model but Wants Major Role for Islam in Government," Program on International Policy Institute, 14 June 2005, www.pipa.org; also "Iranians Egyptians, Turks: Contrasting Views on Sharia," Gallup, 10 July 2008, www.gallup.com.
9. Marina Ottaway, *Democracy Challenged: The Rise of Semi-Authoritarianism* (Washington, DC: Carnegie Endowment for International Peace, 2003); Arch Puddington, "Findings of Freedom in the World 2008—Is the Tide Turning?" *Freedom in the World Report 2008*, www.freedomhouse.org
10. Oswald Spengler, *The Decline of the West* (New York: Knopf, 1928), p. 347.

7 ADVANCED DEMOCRACIES

KEY CONCEPTS

- Advanced democracies are characterized by institutionalized liberal democracy and capitalism.

- Despite a set of shared core institutions, advanced democracies differ greatly in how their political, economic, and social institutions are constructed.

- All advanced democracies have faced changes in and challenges to sovereignty, in the forms of supranational integration and devolution.

- Many advanced democracies have seen a rise in postmodern values, though these may come into conflict with increased ethnic and religious diversity.

- Economic institutions in the advanced democracies have become increasingly postindustrial and tied to large welfare states, which present demographic challenges as their populations grow older.

In the text so far we have moved through various concepts that help us compare politics. With these tools now in hand, we can begin to investigate some specific parts of the world. The areas we will study are not themselves geographical locations but rather groups of countries that are in some way similar in their political institutions. Recall the discussion in Chapter 1 about the comparative method: by looking at similar countries, we can hope to control our variables so as to better pose questions and test possible answers. Our first group of countries is commonly known as the **advanced democracies**. This term is problematic since it is value laden and also teleological—that is, it sounds as if advanced democracies represent some "end stage" that other countries are heading toward. Recalling the hubris and disappointment of the behavioral movement and modernization theory, we should emphasize the following: For many, advanced democracy does represent a goal to strive toward, but that term can cover a diverse set of countries that may get only more diverse in the future. With that said, we use the term here to refer to countries that have institutionalized democracy and a high level of economic development and prosperity.

In this chapter, we will look at the basic institutions and dynamics that characterize advanced democracies, applying the concepts we have studied so far. We will start by categorizing advanced democracies: What do they have in common? What differences exist between them? This comparison will lead us to a discussion of the role of individual freedom and collective equality in the advanced democracies. How do these countries reconcile the two? Once we have a grasp of these ideas, we will move on to consider political, economic, and societal institutions in advanced democracies, particularly the challenges those institutions face in contemporary politics. The forces of integration and devolution—transferring power to international institutions or down to local ones—challenge the notion of state sovereignty that has been at the core of modern politics. Whether this is the trend of the future is something worth investigating. In economics, too, the emergence of postindustrial societies is transforming the very nature of wealth and labor, providing new opportunities to some countries, groups, and individuals while bypassing or marginalizing others. Similar changes can be seen in societal institutions: new social values may be emerging as a reflection of political and economic change, reshaping ideology in the advanced democracies and the debate over freedom and equality. All of these issues are further compounded by demographic issues as the populations of the advanced democracies become older and more diverse.

Are the advanced democracies on the brink of transformation or are they approaching stagnation and decline? And what are the implications of either for comparative and international politics? This chapter will lay out some of the evidence so that we can consider the possibilities.

Defining Advanced Democracy

What, exactly, are advanced democracies? In the past, scholars typically spoke of these countries as belonging to the "First World," meaning that they were economically developed and democratic. They were contrasted with the countries of the "Second World," or communist states, and those of the "Third World," meaning the vast body of less-developed countries. Categorizing countries into these three "worlds" was always somewhat problematic, since various factors in various combinations around the world often confounded the categories. The rise of oil-based economies in the Middle East, for example, created countries with a great degree of wealth, but this wealth was based on natural resources controlled by the state rather than on private property and free markets. The rise in wealth in these countries also did not coincide with a move toward liberal democracy. With the end of the Cold War and the collapse of communism, the three-worlds approach became even more confusing, as many industrialized, formerly communist countries successfully embraced capitalism and liberal democracy while others experienced economic decline and continued authoritarianism. Over time, they had little left in common except history (something we will consider in the next chapter).

Instead of using this problematic three-worlds approach, this book will refer to advanced democracies, communist and postcommunist countries, and developing and less-developed countries. These categories, too, have their limitations, and critics might say they differ from past approaches only in name. One difference, however, is that our groupings imply that movement is possible between the categories—that countries can industrialize or democratize, can move to or from communism, can develop or remain less developed. In fact, we will place some countries in more than one category, especially those that lie in a transitional area from one category to the next.

So, how do we determine which countries belong to the category of advanced democracies? In the area of democracy, we can rely on the factors discussed in Chapter 5, looking at the degree and institutionalization of participation, competition, and liberty in each. In the area of economic development and prosperity, we can consider those issues raised in Chapter 4: the presence of private property, open markets, and the level of gross domestic product (GDP) at purchasing-power parity (PPP). We might also consider the kind of economic output that countries produce. In general, advanced democracies tend to have a relatively small portion of their GDP arising from agriculture and industrial production. During the Industrial Revolution and after, industry displaced agriculture in many of today's advanced democracies; but today, industry itself is increasingly being displaced by the service sector, which includes such things as retail sales, information technology, and education. Finally, we should also consider the output of wealth in terms of prosperity by looking at the overall well-being of society (as measured by the Human Development Index, HDI).

Table 7.2 lists several countries that can be classified as advanced democracies, with a few other countries listed for comparison. The advanced democracies share in common not only liberal democratic regimes but also capitalist economic systems (liberal, social democratic, or mercantilist) in which the service sector dominates; additionally, they have a high HDI ranking. They contrast with countries that are poorer, have low HDI rankings, and lack a strong industrial and service sector, institutionalized liberal democracy, or both.

Table 7.1 Advanced Democracies, 2008

North and South America	Europe	Asia	Middle East and Africa
Argentina	*European Union members:*	Australia	Israel
Canada		Japan	
Chile	Austria	New Zealand	
Costa Rica	Belgium	South Korea	
Bahamas	Bulgaria	Taiwan	
Barbados	Cyprus		
Bermuda	Czech Republic		
Mexico	Denmark		
United States	Estonia		
Uruguay	Finland		
	France		
	Germany		
	Greece		
	Hungary		
	Ireland		
	Italy		
	Latvia		
	Lithuania		
	Luxembourg		
	Malta		
	Netherlands		
	Poland		
	Portugal		
	Romania		
	Slovakia		
	Slovenia		
	Spain		
	Sweden		
	United Kingdom		
	EU nonmembers:		
	Croatia		
	Iceland		
	Norway		
	Switzerland		

Given our definition of advanced democracies, the countries that we place in this category are rather diverse—a diversity that has grown particularly strong over the past decade. For example, countries such as Poland and South Korea were historically categorized as part of the Second and Third Worlds,

Table 7.2   Economic Portraits, 2008

Country	Percentage of GDP Contributed by			GDP (PPP, in U.S. $)	Institutionalized Democracy?	HDI Ranking
	Agriculture	Industry	Services			
United States	0.9	20.5	78.5	45,800	Y	12
Canada	2.1	28.8	69.1	38,400	Y	4
Sweden	1.4	28.9	69.8	36,500	Y	6
United Kingdom	0.9	23.4	75.7	35,100	Y	16
Germany	0.8	29	70.1	34,200	Y	22
Japan	1.4	26.5	72	33,600	Y	8
France	2.2	21	76.7	33,200	Y	10
South Korea	3	39.4	57.6	24,800	Y	26
Saudi Arabia	3	65.9	31.1	23,200	N	61
Poland	4.1	31.6	64.4	16,300	Y	37
Mexico	4	26.6	69.5	12,800	Y	52
Iran	10.7	42.9	46.4	10,600	N	94
South Africa	3.2	31.3	65.5	9,800	Y	121
Brazil	5.5	28.7	65.8	9,700	Y	70
China	11.3	48.6	40.1	5,300	N	81
India	17.6	29.4	52.9	2,700	Y	128
Nigeria	17.6	52.7	29.7	2,000	N	158

Note: Countries in italics are NOT advanced democracies.

Source: CIA, United Nations Development Program.

respectively. But with economic and political changes in both countries, it makes less and less sense to think of them in these terms. Postcommunist Poland now has much more in common economically and politically with Western European countries such as Germany and France than with neighboring countries that also were once part of the communist world; South Korea has more in common with Japan and the United States than it does with other, less-developed countries in Asia.

The countries listed as advanced democracies in Tables 7.1 and 7.2 have high levels of economic development (GDP at PPP of over $7,000) and small agricultural sectors. They are also democratic regimes and are among the top fifty-five countries on the HDI, or what the United Nations classifies as having "high human development." Note that within this category are several recent democratizers and postcommunist countries that also exhibit the hallmarks of economic development and democracy. This group is not meant to be exhaustive, certain, or definitive. Indeed, a number of these countries will be discussed again in the chapters on postcommunist and developing and less-developed countries. This overlap indicates that as a result of recent global economic and political changes, the camp of advanced democracies appears to be expanding well beyond its traditional provinces of Western Europe and North America—though as we saw in the last chapter on nondemocratic regimes, whether this will continue is uncertain.

One result of using a broad definition for advanced democracies is the inclusion of countries that have come to this category by very different means—countries that were early industrializers and early democratizers as well as countries that have moved into both categories more recently. Indeed, the paths to advanced democracy have been varied. Some countries experienced democratic and economic development early and simultaneously, as did the United States and the United Kingdom in the late eighteenth and early nineteenth centuries. In other cases, economic development did not lead directly to democratization. For example, in Germany, capitalist industrialization in the nineteenth century occurred under the guidance of a non-democratic and mercantilist regime. This was also the case somewhat later in Japan and subsequently in countries such as South Korea and Taiwan. In these cases, democracy came only in the latter half of the twentieth century. Finally, countries in Eastern Europe saw their industrialization carried out primarily by communist regimes; their transitions to capitalism and democracy have occurred since the 1990s.

Freedom and Equality in Advanced Democracies

How do advanced democracies reconcile the dilemma of freedom and equality? All countries that fall into this category share in common an institutionalized liberal democracy, private property, free markets, and a high level of economic development based on industry and services. However, this similarity does not mean that these countries' approaches to reconciling freedom and equality are identical. Advanced democracies differ in how they reconcile freedom and equality, particularly in the area of political economy. Countries with liberal economic systems are focused more on individual freedoms than on collective equality, limiting the role of the state in regulating the market and providing public goods, whereas social democratic systems tend to do the opposite. Mercantilist systems, meanwhile, have relied on policies that tend to be more development oriented, with freedom and equality issues of less direct concern to the state. In spite of this wide variation, however, these countries are united by common democratic and economic institutions.

First, consider the role of freedom: all advanced democracies are institutionalized liberal democracies, sharing in common a belief in participation, competition, and liberty. Yet there are real differences in how countries define each of these categories. For example, civil rights and/or liberties may be expanded or restricted without calling into question the democratic nature of a country. Take the case of abortion. Some advanced democracies, such as Sweden, the United States, Hungary, Canada, France, and Austria, allow abortions during a pregnancy's first trimester with relatively few restrictions. In other countries, such as South Korea, Argentina, and Poland, abortions are more restricted. And some advanced democracies ban abortions altogether or allow them only in exceptional circumstances (in Chile, Mexico, and Ireland, for example). We can find similar distinctions in the regulation of prostitution, drugs, or hate speech or in the degree to which privacy is protected from state or economic actors. The advanced democracies vary widely in how the judicial system interprets or defends these rights. Some rely on vigorous constitutional courts with a wide array of powers to overturn legislation; other courts take a more conservative role, while in a few cases (the United Kingdom, Israel), there is no formal constitution.

Advanced democracies also vary in their levels of political participation. The different electoral systems discussed in Chapter 5 can all be found among these countries, alone and in combination. The use of referenda and initiatives differs greatly across these countries; most advanced democracies use them to some degree, although a few countries allow for such votes only at the local level (the United States, Canada, Germany, and Japan), and still others make no provision for such ballots at any level of government (Israel). Another difference can be found in voter registration; in most advanced democracies, it is the responsibility of the state to ensure that all eligible voters are automatically registered to vote; yet in a few (the United States and France), it is contingent on the individual voter to register. Voting rights and obligations may also differ. In Norway, Sweden, the Netherlands, and Denmark, any foreigner who has taken up permanent residence may vote in local elections. In Australia, Argentina, Uruguay, and Belgium, voting is mandatory, though with varying degrees of enforcement and sanction.

Nor is competition uniform across the advanced democracies. Its variations include the ways in which political parties and campaigns are funded: Some countries impose specific limits on the amount of money that can be contributed by private actors to any political party or candidate and require the disclosure of the source of private political contributions. These are in turn shaped by the electoral systems in use. The majority of advanced democracies rely on some form of proportional representation to elect their legislatures, with a minority (such as the United States, the United Kingdom, Australia, and Canada) relying on single-member district plurality or majority. Another group (such as Germany, Hungary, and Japan) uses mixed electoral systems that combine proportional representation and single-member districts. Executives, too, differ; as we read in Chapter 5, prime ministers tend to be the dominant executive in most advanced democracies, though we find purely presidential systems in the United States, Chile, Mexico, and Taiwan, and semipresidentialism in France and South Korea. We also find federal and unitary, bicameral and unicameral institutions, all managing liberal democracy in different ways.

In short, the advanced democracies are politically diverse. All advanced democracies guarantee participation, competition, and liberty, but they differ in where the boundaries of these freedoms are defined or how these freedoms are exercised. Freedom is a basic guarantee, but the form and content of freedom varies from case to case.

In addition to a commitment to freedom, advanced democracies also share a similar approach to equality that emphasizes capitalism—that is, private property and free markets. This approach appears to have generated a great deal of economic prosperity—overall basic standards of living are higher across the advanced democracies than in other countries, and life expectancy is over seventy years (among the upper tier, closer to eighty). But this prosperity coexists with varying degrees of inequality, with the wealth sometimes concentrated disproportionately among certain ethnic groups. Recall from Chapter 4 that the Gini index, a measurement of inequality around the world, found a surprising degree of difference among countries even when their levels of economic development were roughly the same. For example, Germany and the United States have comparable levels of economic development as measured by GDP but very different levels of inequality as measured by the Gini index.

This difference in equality is in part a function of the role of the state. Across advanced democracies, states differ greatly in their economic functions, including their role in the distribution of wealth. In the United States,

Mexico, and Japan, the state provides relatively low levels of social expenditure. Individuals or families have a greater responsibility for funding basic needs, and the total tax burden on the public in these countries is typically lower as a result. This is not to say, however, that inequality is necessarily the end result; in Japan, Estonia, and South Korea, a small welfare state coexists alongside a higher level of economic equality than in the United States. In social democratic systems, such as those in much of Europe, taxation is often higher, and these resources are used for income redistribution through a strong system of social expenditures. Here too, we should recall that social democratic systems are not uniform; some have more job protection, unemployment insurance, taxation rates, or neocorporatist institutions. All of these variations do not change the fact that in each of these countries, private property and free markets are fundamental institutions (Table 7.3).

In short, the advanced democracies hold in common a basic set of institutions through which to reconcile freedom and equality. These institutions include liberal democracy, with its emphasis on participation, competition, and liberty, and capitalism, with its emphasis on free markets and private property. Yet each of the advanced democracies has constructed these institutions in different ways, resulting in quite significant variations among them.

IN FOCUS

Political Diversity in Advanced Democracies

Participation

- Standards of voter eligibility differ.
- Referenda and initiatives are used in varying degrees.
- Some, but not all, states automatically register all eligible voters.
- Voting is compulsory in some nations, but voluntary in most.

Competition

- Different methods and levels of funding are used for political parties and campaigns.
- Separation of powers varies greatly and is based primarily on the relative strength of different branches of government.

Liberties

- Distinctions exist in the regulation, allowance, or prohibition of activities such as abortion, prostitution, and hate speech.
- Different degrees of individual privacy are protected from state and corporate intrusion.

Table 7.3 Income Redistribution in Advanced Democracies, 2008			
Country	Political-Economic System	Taxes as a Percentage of GDP, 2005	Gini Index
Sweden	Social democratic	50.7	23
Denmark	Social democratic	50.3	24
France	Social democratic	44.1	28
United Kingdom	Liberal	36.5	34
Germany	Social democratic	34.8	28
Canada	Liberal	33.4	32.1
United States	Liberal	27.3	45
Japan	Mercantilist	27.4	38.1

Sources: CIA, Organization for Economic Cooperation and Development.

Advanced Democracies Today

The institutions that the advanced democracies share are part of what makes these countries **modern**—that is, secular, rational, materialistic, technological, bureaucratic, and placing a greater emphasis on individual freedom than on collective equality. But like any other set of countries, the advanced democracies are not only diverse but also dynamic; their institutions are subject to change under the influence of domestic and international forces. Indeed, many argue that the advanced democracies are currently undergoing significant social, political, and economic changes. If true, this would mean that existing modern institutions may also give way to new ones as these countries make a transition from modernity to something else. Expressing this confusion, those writing on this topic lack even a proper word to describe this change, using instead the awkward term *postmodern*. Clearly, this word says more about what isn't than what is. We'll spend the remainder of this chapter considering the challenges to modernity in the advanced democracies and whether these challenges are indicative of dramatic change. If so, are the advanced democracies making a transition to postmodernity, and what would that mean? Or is change overstated or perhaps not in the direction we imagine? These are big questions that lie in the realm of speculation and rely on fragmentary evidence. We will sort this information by breaking it down along the lines of our discussion to this point: political, societal, and economic institutions.

Political Institutions: Sovereignty Transformed?

In Chapter 2, we discussed a number of ways in which states can be analyzed and compared. In particular we spoke about state sovereignty and noted that state power can be viewed in terms of autonomy and capacity. Although advanced democracies differ in their levels of autonomy and capacity, they are all distinguished by the ability to formulate and carry out the basic tasks expected of them by society. In other words, advanced democracies are notable for their sovereignty, or their ability to act independent of outside actors, which ever since the rise of the modern state has been a hallmark of power.

Yet in recent decades, these concepts have come under challenge. In particular, within the advanced democracies we have seen a movement toward greater integration between countries and greater devolution within countries. **Integration** is a process by which states pool their sovereignty, surrendering some individual powers in order to gain political, economic, or societal benefits in return. Integration blurs the line between countries by forging tight connections, common policies, and shared rules that bind them together. In contrast, **devolution** is a process by which political power is devolved, or "sent down," to lower levels of government. This process is intended to increase local participation, efficiency, and flexibility, as tasks once handled at the national level are managed by local authorities. These two processes differ in the direction in which power is flowing—either "above" the state in the case of integration or "below" the state in the case of devolution. But in both cases, state capacity, autonomy, and sovereignty are affected, influencing the relationship between freedom and equality. Although both integration and devolution can be found to varying degrees around the world, it is among the advanced democracies that such processes are the most advanced and profound. While many have expected this twin process of integration and devolution to effectively transform the modern state and sovereignty as we know it, there are also countervailing processes that may limit, or even end, these movements. A consideration of one of most ambitious examples of this process, the European Union, will illustrate these points well.

The European Union: Integration, Expansion, and Resistance

The most important example of integration is the European Union (EU), a project without precedent and whose possible long-term implications are huge, uncertain, and a source of contention. Recall that while European unification may seem rather "normal" today, it came on the heels of a devastating war between these countries that left millions dead. It was in fact the divisions in Europe that served as the catalyst for integration. In the aftermath of World War II, a number of European leaders argued that the repeated conflicts in the region were caused by a lack of interconnection between the countries themselves—which in turn fostered insecurity, inequality, and nationalism. These leaders believed that if their countries could be bound together through economic, societal, and political institutions, they would reject war against each other as an irrational act. Moreover, they argued, a common political agenda would give European states greater international authority in a postwar environment that had become dominated by the Soviet Union and the United States. With these motivations, a core of Western European countries began the process of integration in the early 1950s. As you can imagine, this was a radical step away from sovereignty and not an easy one for any state or society to swallow. As a result, integration moved forward slowly and in a piecemeal fashion.[1]

As the time line on page 179 shows, the EU developed incrementally over time. This was intentional; from the start it was an ambitious project, but one that its supporters realized could be achieved only by moving slowly and cautiously. Starting with a constitutional or federal project would have been unthinkable and unacceptable to political leaders and their citizens. Thus, the EU began its life as a small agreement among a handful of countries that dealt primarily with the production of steel and coal, only to expand over time to become a body that included many more members and vastly greater responsibilities. Out of these changes a basic set of institutions has developed, with increasingly sovereign power in many areas over the member states themselves. Now there is a huge number of EU bodies and subgroups, but four institutions are central. The European Commission, made up of representatives appointed by the member states' governments, develops legislation. The Council of Ministers, made up of cabinet ministers from the countries' respective national governments, approves or rejects this legislation (with each minister voting in accordance with his or her country's concerns). A third body, the European Parliament, is directly elected by the member states' citizens. In other words, EU citizens vote in elections both for their national legislatures and for the European Parliament. The European Parliament is able to modify or reject most legislation that comes from the Commission, as well as approve the addition of new members to the EU. Finally, the European Court of Justice plays an important role in resolving disputes over legislation once it has been adopted; it also decides matters of EU law. As these statelike institutions have gained power over time, many people no longer speak of the EU as an **intergovernmental system** like the United Nations, where countries cooperate on issues but are not bound to them, but as a **supranational system**, with its sovereign powers shared among the members and held by EU institutions over the member states themselves. As a result, for most Europeans the reconciliation of freedom and equality has become as much an international task as a domestic one.

TIME LINE / EUROPEAN INTEGRATION	
1951	European Coal and Steel Community founded by Belgium, France, Germany, Italy, Luxembourg, and the Netherlands
1957	European Economic Community created
1967	European Community (EC) created
1973	Denmark, Ireland, and the United Kingdom join EC
1979	Direct elections to the European Parliament
1981	Greece joins EC
1986	Spain and Portugal join EC
1993	European Union (EU) created
1995	Sweden, Finland, and Austria join EU
1999	Monetary union created among most EU member states
2002	Euro currency enters circulation; most EU national currencies eliminated
2004	EU accepts ten new members
2005	EU constitution rejected by France and the Netherlands in referenda
2008	Lisbon treaty rejected by Ireland

Each of the individual states of the EU has had to weigh the benefits of integration against the loss of sovereignty. For example, Sweden is a relative latecomer to the EU, having joined only in 1995. Its long resistance toward membership stemmed in part from its tradition of political neutrality (Sweden did not take sides during World War II) and from the fear that membership would require it to change domestic institutions and policies to conform to EU standards. Of greatest concern were Sweden's large social expenditures, created to ensure greater collective equality. However, the end of the Cold War changed Swedish thinking about neutrality, and in the 1990s, the government moved toward EU membership. A few European countries, such as Norway and Switzerland, have chosen to stay out of the body altogether, their publics having rejected membership in referenda.

The growing breadth and depth of the EU have been further underscored by three recent projects, each of which changed (or hoped to change) the EU in fundamental ways. The first was monetary union. On January 1, 1999, the majority of EU member states linked their currencies to the euro, a single currency eventually meant to replace those of the member states as a means to promote further economic integration and growth. The logic of monetary union was that member states would benefit through a single currency, as it would allow for one measure of prices and values across the EU, increasing competition (and thus lowering prices) by stimulating trade and cross-border investment within the EU. More generally, proponents hoped the euro would help foster a true European identity, with a single currency to bind these countries together. Finally, a single currency backed by some of the world's wealthiest countries would increase the EU's power in the international system by creating what could become a "reserve currency" for other countries—that is, a currency with global legitimacy that central banks would use as part of their monetary holdings. Reserve currencies are also the main monetary standard for businesses and individuals around the world. The U.S. dollar has been the global reserve currency for decades, giving the United States certain benefits as a result, so the euro represented a real challenge to its global authority. In short, monetary union was promised to have both domestic (intra-EU) and international benefits.

On January 1, 2002, all EU member states that joined the monetary union withdrew their own currencies from circulation and replaced them with the euro. In Chapter 4, we noted that one important facet of a state's power is its ability to print money and set interest rates; in the European monetary union, this power has been surrendered to the European Central Bank. This monetary union represents the largest single transfer of power to date within the EU; it has also been extremely contentious. Some EU members, such as Sweden, Denmark, and the United Kingdom, have declined to join the monetary union. These countries, while quite different in their domestic political and economic systems, share a similar fear that the single currency would force their state to align its political economic systems more with the other EU member states. More generally, each sees monetary union as an important loss of sovereignty that is unacceptable to their publics. In Denmark and Sweden, referenda on euro membership have failed, while in the United Kingdom, a promised referendum failed to materialize altogether.

Has monetary union been a success? That depends on how we define it. The hope to make the euro a reserve currency appears to have been borne out, as the currency has become a serious rival to the U.S. dollar. Many international investors who once held only dollars as a foreign reserve are increasingly relying on the euro. Newer members of the EU, too, have also recently adopted the euro or plan to do so in the near future. This acceptance stands in sharp contrast to those skeptics who believed that the euro could never take the place of national currencies. But this success has not been complete. Citizens of the European Union, while perceiving the euro as a currency with prestige akin to the U.S. dollar, have not felt as though it strengthened their identification to the EU or necessarily brought the economic benefits promised.[2] Economists, meanwhile, continue to be concerned that the economic diversity of EU member states works against the idea of a single currency, since it forces all members into a single set of monetary policies such as interest rates that may be unsuitable for different kinds of economies with different rates of growth or unemployment. Therefore, even as use of the euro expands, there are concerns that a significant economic downturn in one or more members could force some member states to reassert monetary sovereignty and restore their own currencies.[3]

A second important development has been the ongoing expansion of the EU (Figure 7.1). From 1951 to 2004, the EU grew from six member states to fifteen, and with the collapse of communism in Eastern Europe, a new wave of mostly postcommunist countries sought membership. After a long period of negotiation, between 2004 and 2007, twelve new countries were accepted, adding over 100 million people to the EU. This brought the total population

Figure 7.1 **EUROPEAN UNION MEMBERSHIP, 2009**

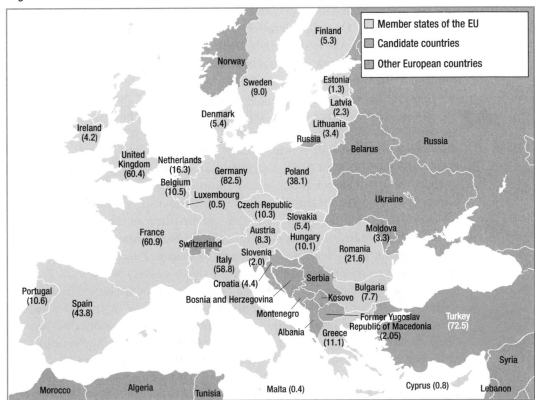

Note: Numbers in parentheses indicate population size, in millions.

Source: http://europa.eu/abc/european_countries/index_en.htm.

of the EU to nearly a half-billion people (compare this to the United States which has just over 300 million), and made the EU's total GDP larger than that of the United States.

As enlargement has made the EU a much bigger body, it has also created new issues and concerns. One is economic. The majority of the new member states are far poorer than the older EU member states. For example, while the current EU per capita GDP at PPP stands at around $32,300, most new members stand at only a third or less of that amount. Because of this, the EU has spent a large sum of money trying to improve the economic and social conditions of these nations before and after membership. Older members of the EU have resented this redirection of support toward the new members, and this has increased conflict between and within old and new members— over how much support the EU should provide to member states, where these funds should come from, and who should receive them. Related to this, lower costs in the new member states created an opportunity for firms inside the EU to relocate eastward, shutting down high-wage and high-cost industries in places like Germany in favor of Slovakia or Romania. At the same time, liberalization of movement allowed many East Europeans to seek work elsewhere in the EU. Overall, migration of neither jobs or workers has been as dramatic as some expected, though it has affected some countries more than others.[4] These economic changes have fed into broader European concerns about globalization and the loss of jobs to other countries or migrants, and in turn shaped how EU citizens consider the future of the organization.

Alongside economic changes, politics inside the EU has also become more contentious as the organization has grown. The majority of the new member states spent the last half century under communist rule, several of them as part of the Soviet Union itself. As a result, among many of them there is great support for EU membership as a foundation for capitalism and democracy, but there is also skepticism toward large bureaucratic institutions that seek to direct economic, societal, and political institutions and policies at the national level. Many of the new members also have pursued much more liberal economic politics than is the norm in Europe, and they favor further enlargement to other countries that meet the necessary standards. This last point is not hypothetical; a number of other countries are either in the negotiation process or interested in beginning negotiations in the next decade. Most important and problematic among these is Turkey, which after years of delays finally began negotiations in 2005 to join the EU. Turkey is unlike any other candidate country to date: With a population of over 70 million people, it is second in size only to Germany among EU member states, while having a per capita GDP that is only a third of the EU average. It is also the only country with a Muslim majority and a strong ruling party with a religious orientation. The possibility of Turkish membership has brought into focus a number of questions, old and new, about the meaning of the EU. If the EU is a "European" organization, where exactly does Europe end? What would it mean to have a Muslim state alongside a community of Christian ones and have the borders of the EU stretch as far as Iraq and Iran? More generally, is it possible to sustain integration when the membership of the EU is increasingly differentiated along economic, historical, cultural, and religious lines? EU membership and enlargement was easier when the members had relatively similar institutions and experiences. This is no longer so. In the meantime, negotiations have stalled while some member states such as France have openly expressed their opposition to Turkish membership.

This brings us to a third issue, alongside monetary union and enlargement: constitutional reform. As a statelike body, the EU has created a number of documents over time to deal with its structure, powers, and scope, dating back to the Treaty of Rome in 1957. However, there has never been a single document that codified the functions and role of the EU. With monetary union and enlargement, it was clear that the old institutions, originally created to serve a half-dozen countries, could no longer effectively function in a body of more than twenty members. In 2002, the EU held a special convention with the goal of creating a true single constitution for the EU that would reform the existing structure and set forth its future tasks and responsibilities. As one can imagine, this was a difficult and acrimonious process. Member states had different notions about the degree and kind of reform necessary, as well as the extent to which additional sovereign powers should be vested with the EU. The final draft attempted to balance these competing views and desires, producing a document that ran over 250 pages and moved the EU in a more federal direction. Expectations were that the new constitution, in spite of various national concerns, would pass, but this was not the case. In June 2005, referenda in France and the Netherlands led to a defeat of the constitution—especially surprising given that France and the Netherlands were founding members and had been traditionally strong supporters of the EU.

What happened? Observers have given several reasons for why the constitution failed to gain public support. For some, the constitution became a symbol of the rapid changes going on inside and outside the EU that we have discussed so far, such as economic reform, enlargement, and the loss of sovereignty. The sheer opacity and length of the constitution did not help matters. Finally, for many the rejection was evidence of the long-discussed "democratic deficit" in the EU, meaning that the citizens are largely disconnected from direct control over the European Union. Opposition to the constitution represented a way to give direct voice to these concerns.

Chastened by this setback, the member states attempted to revive the process with a less dramatic undertaking. The Lisbon Treaty, as it was called, essentially repackaged the constitution, presenting it as an add-on to existing EU legislation rather than an entirely new document that replaced all earlier treaties. This may seem a matter of semantics, especially since the proposed institutional changes were largely the same. However, by presenting the Lisbon Treaty as merely an addition to existing EU law, this meant that most national legislatures could ratify the treaty without direct public input. Only in Ireland was a referendum required by the constitution, and in June 2008 the Irish voted no, again throwing EU reform into disarray. As in France and the Netherlands in 2005, many Irish who voted "no" viewed the Lisbon Treaty as a threat to national identity and sovereignty—this in spite of the fact that Ireland is one of the greatest supporters (and financial beneficiaries) of the EU.[5]

How all these challenges will shape the EU in the future is uncertain. The EU may work around Ireland's referendum, as it has with similar setbacks in past. There is also the possibility that over time such conflicts will lead to a more multitiered organization, with different levels of integration for different members. Enlargement, too, may become differentiated, with future applicants offered some of the benefits, but not the rights, of membership. This shift away from a federal vision could foster an EU that is more flexible and able to deal with a diversity of members and issues. Less optimistically, it may lead to a period of drift that only compounds uncertainty and rancor among its citizens, members, and countries in waiting.

The lessons here extend beyond Europe. The attempt of the United States and Canada to expand their free-trade agreements to Central and South America has faced similar resistance at home from those who see such integration as a loss of sovereignty and economic prosperity, with little gained in return. The current economic difficulties faced in many countries may only further compound these anxieties and opposition to integration.

Devolution and Democracy

Integration continues to exert a strong pull on many advanced democracies in spite of resistance. At the same time, many advanced democracies also face the tug of devolution from below. As mentioned above and in Chapter 3, devolution is a process by which powers and resources are transferred away from central state institutions and vested at a lower level. What is interesting about this process is that it is a reversal of the historical development of the state, which is noteworthy for its centralization of power over time. Over the decades, ever greater power has moved from the local level to the national level on issues such as social welfare. Yet across the advanced democracies, there have been moves of late to redirect power in the opposite direction.

Why this apparent reversal? Many political leaders in advanced democracies are concerned that the public mistrusts the state, viewing it as too large, too distant, and too inflexible. Devolution is viewed as a way to counteract this distrust by bringing government closer to the public, thereby increasing local control and participation. Devolution can also help give voice to more diverse communities, such as ethnic minorities, by giving them greater control over their local affairs. By increasing the public voice and the public's capacity to shape politics, it is hoped, democracy can be reinvigorated.[6]

How does devolution take shape in reality? One way is through the transfer of responsibility and funds to local authorities, giving them greater say in how policies are crafted and executed. When local institutions have more control and responsibility, they can craft policy to meet their own particular conditions. One example of such devolution occurred in the United States in the 1990s, when welfare reform created bulk transfers of funds to the states, which could then use this money to design and implement their own particular social welfare policies. Another is through the creation of wholly new political institutions to provide a new level of public participation. An example of such innovation was seen in Canada in 1999, when an entirely new province, Nunavut, was created out of a portion of the Northwest Territories. The creation of this new province was intended to give the native Inuit people self-government and control over the natural resources in the region where they live. Similarly, in 1999, the United Kingdom created new, directly elected assemblies for the regions of Scotland, Wales, and Northern Ireland. The EU itself, as part of its integration process, has encouraged devolution as a way to give local and regional interests a greater voice in government even as more powers were transferred upward from the member states. Across many of the advanced democracies, powers have been devolved to varying degrees.

As with integration, it is not certain whether devolution is a trend among the advanced democracies that will continue to spread and deepen in the future, nor is it clear what the long-term implications of such a process would be. Devolution may be a means to rebuild democratic participation by making people more directly responsible for policy making. However, it may also undermine the capacity and autonomy of the central state, especially if coupled with integration. As we discussed in Chapter 3, when devolution is a response to eth-

IN FOCUS

Means of Devolution

- Transfer of policy-making responsibility to lower levels of government.
- Transfer of funds and powers to tax to lower levels of government, affording them more control over how resources are distributed.
- Creation of new political institutions at lower levels of government.

nic conflict, it may help resolve these issues or it may only increase demands for sovereignty, depending on how the institutional reforms are structured. In the United Kingdom, devolution has gone a long way toward bringing religious conflict between Catholics and Protestants in Northern Ireland to an end; but devolution in Belgium has not resolved conflicts between the French- and Flemish-speaking populations, and the country has grown only more polarized over time. Finally, the trend toward devolution in the advanced democracies has perhaps reached its limits. In the aftermath of September 11 and terrorist attacks in Europe, a number of advanced democracies have moved away from devolution in important ways, centralizing and increasing capacity and autonomy as a way to fight the threat of terrorism and deal with immigration (which are often conflated, as we shall discuss below). The EU's goal to create a strong "Europe of Regions" has similarly waned. As with integration, external and internal conditions can influence devolution's pace and strength. Not long ago, observers saw integration and devolution as inexorable processes that states and citizens could not stop. That may not be the case.

Societal Institutions: New Identities in Formation?

Just as advanced democratic states are undergoing a number of challenges and changes in the new millennium, societies confront change and also seem to be pulled from two directions. Some political scientists point to a new set of shared norms and values emerging across the advanced democracies that are not bound to traditional identities of nation and state; others emphasize the strengthening of local identities that are turning these same societies inward. These processes are strongly connected to the struggle over integration and devolution. Whether these social forces are complementary or contradictory, and whether such developments are a sign of greater cooperation or conflict, is still a matter of debate.

Postmodern Values and Organization

In recent years, a number of political scientists have begun to track the emergence of what they see as the development of postmodern values in the advanced democracies.[7] As we have noted, in premodern societies, people were focused to a greater extent on traditional forms of authority and on basic survival; this focus often led to authoritarian systems with clear standards of obedience and collectivism. Starting in the eighteenth century, those countries that would become the advanced democracies began to embrace the notions of rationality and science, individualism, and autonomy. The modern state, society, and economy promised a world of progress, development, and limitless possibilities, and it did enable unprecedented economic growth, material abundance, and improved standards of living for hundreds of millions of people.

Yet by the 1960s, modern values came under attack, just as they themselves had challenged premodern ones more than two centuries earlier. These challenges took several forms. Economic development came into question due to the environmental cost. Modern values stressed the environment as an instrument for achieving material goals, but critics argued that the environment should be valued for its own sake—a public good to be shared by all. Science, too, was similarly viewed with greater skepticism. Technological innovation did not lead to unmitigated benefits but rather carried with it risks and uncertainty. Fears over nuclear power or chemical contamination led to a belief among many that the very notion of "progress" was a questionable goal. In politics, too, postmodern values challenged nationalism and patriotism, questioning authority, hierarchy, and deference to the state. In general, these criticisms indicated the possible emergence of a new set of social norms and values.

Postmodern values differ from modern ones in a number of ways. As already indicated, **postmodern** values are much less focused on the idea of progress as embodied by material goods, technological change, or scientific innovation. Instead, postmodern values center on what have been called "quality of life" or "postmaterialist" issues, which give primary attention to concerns other than material gain. These include concerns over the environment, health, and leisure as well as a greater focus on personal equality and diversity. At the same time, postmodern values are skeptical of state power while supportive of democracy, especially in the form of direct participation and action. These values in many ways reflect both integrationist and devolutionary tendencies, with their concern for greater tolerance among people (integration) and their greater hostility toward centralized power (devolution). Turn back to our map of political culture in Chapter 3 (Figure 3.4 on page 73). Postmodern values can be located in the upper right-hand corner, a combination of secular-rational and self-expression values.

We must be careful not to overstate these findings, however. As Figure 3.4 shows, many countries grouped as part of the advanced democracies have much more traditional values, which cannot be explained away by economic development. These include the United States, Canada, Chile, Ireland, and Australia. These differences indicate that domestic factors in each country remain important in shaping the value systems of societies, even as they undergo a general process of development and consequent change. The central question then becomes whether there is a shared set of postmodern values that all advanced democracies are converging toward, and if so, whether these values will inexorably spread to new members of this community.[8] At one time, scholars answered both questions in the affirmative; more recently, however, doubts regarding the inevitability of postmodern values have surfaced.

Diversity, Identity, and the Challenge to Postmodern Values

There are reasons why scholars have become more tentative about the institutionalization of postmodern values. Perhaps the most important factor influencing this debate is the almost unprecedented wave of immigration that has impacted most of the advanced democracies. In 1960, the foreign-born population of the United States stood at around 4 percent; today, that number is 12 percent. In Canada the number is much higher, at around 20 percent, while in the larger countries of the European Union (Germany, France, and the United Kingdom) it is around 10 percent. This rapid increase in immigration is changing the ethnic, religious, and racial compositions of these countries; for example, forecasters have concluded that by the middle of this century, whites of European origin will make up half of the U.S. population, compared to nearly 90 percent in 1960.[9] Moreover, the makeup of the immigrant population is quite different across the advanced democratic countries. In the United States, the largest proportion of these immigrants come from Latin America; in Canada, Australia, and New Zealand, from Asia; and in Europe, from North Africa and Turkey. Thus, while many advanced democracies are experiencing immigration, the nature of that immigration and the challenges or opportunities it brings are very different.

In many countries, increasing numbers of immigrants have increased xenophobic tendencies in the existing population—that is, fear of foreigners. This takes on economic, societal, and political dimensions. The economic dimension is perhaps most familiar to us. Although supporters of immigration note the benefits of new sources of labor and skills that can come from immigrants, critics view immigrants as a threat to existing workers, competing for scarce jobs and depressing wages. The debate in Europe over the EU constitution in 2005 and 2007 turned in part on fears of immigration, that a stronger European Union would facilitate greater immigration into and within Europe. Immigration has been a similar sticking point in U.S.-Mexican relations, and Australians, Canadians, and New Zealanders express concern over an influx from Asia. Some countries, like Japan, have avoided this issue by limiting immigration, though this brings with it its own problems, as we shall discuss shortly.

A more complicated issue is that of societal institutions. As more and more diverse groups of immigrants enter the advanced democracies, they raise questions about what it means to be American, Canadian, French, or European, as advanced democracies struggle with questions of assimilation and multiculturalism. How much should new groups be accommodated in their relationship with national institutions and identities? At one end, arguments for multiculturalism assert that societies should help support these new groups, preserving what is distinct about them as a positive contribution to a diverse society. At the other end, arguments for assimilation hold that immigration implies an agreement to accept and adapt to the existing culture, values, and norms of that society. For countries like the United States, Canada, or Australia, multiculturalism may be somewhat easier to embrace because the vast majority of people have come from somewhere else within the last two or three generations, creating a norm of a society where each person brings a new contribution to society that can be incorporated. Yet even in these countries there are strong tendencies toward assimilation and fears that the sheer numbers of immigrants mean that assimilation, even if desired, is simply not possible.[10]

If multiculturalism is a source of controversy in traditionally immigrant countries, it is an even more explosive subject in countries where ethnic and national identity are much more tightly fused, as in much of Europe. There, the influx of non-Europeans, especially Muslim North Africans and Turks, has raised even greater fears. Racial, religious, and ethnic homogeneity in Europe must now confront people whose geographical, cultural, religious, and historical traditions are quite different. Indeed, the paradox that has emerged is one of postmodernism itself. In the past, many European states prided themselves on their high degree of secularism and tolerance for different lifestyles. But how do they tolerate immigrant groups that may be much more religious and socially conservative—immigrants coming from societies that are quite removed from postmodern values?

In Europe, this has been most sharply defined by several events. In the Netherlands, the controversial writer and filmmaker Theo Van Gogh was murdered in 2004 after making a film critical of the role of women in Islam; his killer, born in Amsterdam to Moroccan parents, claimed that anyone who insulted God needed to be killed.[11] In 2005, a Danish paper sparked a global controversy when it published editorial cartoons lampooning Mohammed and Islam. In these and other cases, the questions that arose turned on issues of tolerance. Postmodern societies emphasize individual tolerance and a skepticism of institutions; one problem that follows, however, is a resulting incomprehension of (and often intolerance for) others who hold strong religious, ethnic, or cultural identities. Some argue that the greatest virtue of a democracy is the ability to criticize and even offend others, and that limiting this is an attack on liberty. Reconciling such views with those who hold some values and beliefs sacred is not easy.

Needless to say, such economic and social concerns translate into politics. In many advanced democracies, growing ethnic and religious diversity has fueled the rise of anti-immigration, nationalist, and xenophobic movements that seek to restrict immigration, increase assimilation, and assert ethnic and national primacy. More generally, there are calls to limit the use of second languages or regulate religion, especially Islam in Europe. This in turn causes immigrant groups to feel marginalized or humiliated. Europeans, in particular, fear that incorporating Muslim immigrants will lead to domestic terrorism, making Europe in future a more likely target than the United States. Such critics point to Spain, where in 2004 a terrorist attack on a commuter train, carried out in part by immigrants from Morocco, left nearly 200 dead. Similarly, in 2005 four suicide bombings in London killed over fifty people; particularly worrisome was the fact that three of the four suicide bombers had been born in the UK and raised there by Pakistani parents. We will speak more about this in Chapter 10.

A final issue is how these changes will affect relations between the advanced democracies. Although most of these countries face similar questions regarding immigration and its effects, as we already noted, the source of migration differs from country to country or region to region. This diversity can become a source of growing difference between the advanced democracies, pulling the West apart by shaping different cultural values and external orientations. In North America, migration from Latin America and East Asia may reorient these countries south and east, away from Europe, while in Europe, larger Muslim communities will draw these countries closer to the Middle East and South Asia. Faith may also come into play, with Hispanic immigrants into the United States bringing with them more conservative Roman Catholic, Evangelical, or Pentecostal religious values, while Islam will grow more central to European life. Advanced democracies may see less and less of themselves in each other. This need not be a source of conflict; democratic values and a commitment to prosperity have linked very different countries together in the past (think of Japan, South Korea, and Eastern Europe, which not long ago were not considered part of the West). But some speculate that a growing divergence of the advanced democracies may eventually create cultural barriers that a shared commitment to democracy cannot overcome. It may also mean an end to the idea of a single set of postmodern values that defines the advanced democracies.

Economic Institutions: A New Market?

Our discussion so far has asked to what extent postmodernity is changing state and societial institutions. Our last area of interest is that of economic development, the area that is perhaps most obvious. Dramatic changes have taken place in the economic structures of the industrialized democracies over the past generation, to such an extent that it is no longer logical to refer to them as "industrial" at all. At the same time, long-standing assumptions about the role of the state in such areas as the redistribution of income and social expenditures have come under question, challenging the traditional functions of the welfare state.

This may lead to an overturning of existing ideas and policies regarding the proper balance of freedom and equality in the advanced democracies.

Postindustrialism

So far, we have considered postmodernity and how it may affect advanced democratic states and societies. In both of these arenas, what is going on is open to interpretation. But in the economic realm the data are clearer: the advanced democracies have experienced a dramatic shift during the last half century, from economies based primarily on industry and manufacturing to postindustrial economies. In **postindustrialism**, the majority of people are employed and the bulk of profits are made in the **service sector**—work that involves not the creation of tangible or physical goods, such as cars or computers, but industries such as finance, insurance, real estate, education, retail sales, transportation, communication, high technology, utilities, health care, and business and legal services. Just as modern economies made the transition from agriculture to industry, they are now moving away from their industrial orientation. As Table 7.4 indicates, this shift has been occurring across the advanced democracies over the past several decades. In these countries,

Table 7.4 Employment by Economic Sector, 1960–2006/2007

| | Percentage of Total National Employment in | | | |
	Agriculture	Industry	Manufacturing	Services
United States				
1960	8.4	33.4	26.1	58.1
2007	1.4	19.8	11.2	78.5
Canada				
1960	13.3	32.0	24.7	54.7
2007	2.5	20.4	12.1	77.1
Japan				
1960	29.5	28.5	21.7	41.9
2007	4.1	27.0	18.3	68.9
France				
1960	22.5	36.9	27.3	40.7
2006	3.4	22.0	15.0	74.6
Germany				
1960	13.8	46.0	34.4	40.2
2006	2.3	29.0	22.0	68.8

Source: U.S. Bureau of Labor.

around three-quarters of the working population are now employed in the service sector. This shift has occurred for a number of reasons. Much industrial production has migrated outside of the advanced democracies in search of lower labor and other costs. Globalization is accelerating these tendencies. Furthermore, technological innovation in the advanced democracies is changing the requirements of labor. Employees are expected to have higher levels of education than in past; in the United States, 40 percent of those between twenty-five and thirty-four have a college degree; in Canada, the number is over 50 percent.[12]

Postindustrialism in some ways reflects and may reinforce the political and social trends discussed earlier. The emergence of an information-based economy, for example, may contribute to a greater devolution of power within the economy as firms become less hierarchical and more decentralized, less physical and more "virtual," less national and more international (something we will speak about more later), and with much greater individual autonomy and flexibility. This shift, in turn, may well reinforce postmodern values that question hierarchical structures and authority. However, for those without specialized training and education, postindustrialism may mean less freedom and equality; the growing importance of knowledge may well marginalize these workers, creating an educational underclass whose prospects for upward mobility are limited.

As always, we should be careful not to overestimate postindustrialism's impact. Although it is clear that the advanced democracies are moving toward economies centered more on information and less on industry, this does not automatically mean that the old economic system will disappear. The rise of the Internet does not mean that "bricks and mortar" businesses are doomed. Nor does it mean that hierarchical forms of organization have outlived their usefulness. Finally, the elimination of industrial jobs does not automatically mean that those without education will no longer find work—only that the nature of unskilled labor will change, bringing different advantages and problems. As these transformations proceed, states will be called on to manage the marketplace in new ways, reconciling freedom and equality in the face of social and economic change.

Maintaining the Welfare State

This leads us to the final aspect of economic transformation in the advanced democracies: the future of the welfare state. As we discussed in Chapter 4, for the past half century, a defining element of the advanced democracies has been the development of social expenditures as a way to reduce inequality and provide public goods through such programs as national pension plans, public health care, education, and unemployment benefits—social expenditures collectively known as the welfare state. There can be no doubt that the welfare state has provided a wide array of benefits among the advanced democracies: extreme poverty, especially among the elderly, has been reduced; infant mortality has declined and life expectancy has increased; and literacy and education have improved dramatically. Social expenditures have played an important role in socializing risk—that is, making the uncertainties that come with work, health, and age a community, rather than an individual, concern.

The welfare state has also brought costs and controversies. First, although social expenditures have been lauded as an essential part of a humane society, they are increasingly expensive. During the early part of the twentieth century, social expenditures typically amounted to around 10 percent to 15 percent of advanced democracies' GDPs. Currently, however, in most of these countries social expenditures consume a quarter or more of GDP. This increased spending has required higher taxes, which among advanced democracies averages close to 40 percent of GDP. Even in more liberal or mercantilist countries, such as the United States and Japan, public expenditures have risen dramatically over the past half century, requiring new taxes or government borrowing.

This trend will be magnified by important demographic changes within the advanced democracies. One contributing factor is increased health. In 1900, residents of these countries had an average life expectancy of around forty to fifty years; by 2050, they can expect to live to over eighty. A second factor is lower birthrates. In most of the advanced democracies, the birthrate is below the replacement level, leading to fewer children, with the United States an interesting exception.[13] There are two results from these demographic changes. First is that for many advanced democracies, their populations will eventually begin to fall. For example, projections indicate that in the EU deaths will begin to exceed births as early as 2010, and that in spite of immigration, the population will peak around 2025 and then begin to decline. By 2050 the current members of the EU would have a population of around 450 million (down 20 million from 2025). Second, as a result of increased longevity and fewer births, all advanced democracies will see a growing elderly population. According to some estimates, by 2050, a quarter to over a third of the population in the advanced democracies will be over sixty-five years old, compared with around 15 percent in 2000. As an ever-larger proportion of the population, this older segment of society will seek more welfare benefits, but as a result of declining birthrates there will be fewer working-age individuals to fill needed jobs and pay into these systems.[14]

The solutions are not easy. Increased immigration is one obvious solution, though we've already noted the problems that lie therein. Immigration becomes even more contentious when social expenditures are involved, for while young immigrants may be needed to support the welfare of those who are older, there is often much less desire among the public to extend those same benefits to immigrants.[15] A second course is to cut back on benefits. However, politicians face well-organized opposition to welfare reform, and in many countries benefits have continued to increase even as revenues shrink. A third solution would be to expand the labor market. This could be done by raising the retirement age or by making job markets more flexible, encouraging more part-time work among parents, younger, or older workers. But in many countries, retirement remains akin to a constitutional right, and labor markets are highly protected, making these suggestions unwelcome.

To give an example of the complexities involved in these demographic changes and policy responses, let's consider Japan. By current estimates, the population of Japan, at around 127 million, has already peaked and is beginning to decline. By 2050, it is expected to have dropped to around 100 million, a loss of over 20 percent. Moreover, a third of the population will be over sixty-five. To prevent population decline, the country would need to accept nearly 400,000 immigrants a year until 2050. By that time, nearly 20

INSTITUTIONS IN ACTION

DIVERSITY AND THE WELFARE STATE

We have considered the ways that many advanced democracies face the issues of increased immigration, demographic shifts, and costs of maintaining the welfare state. It may turn out that these are tightly connected, making the problem that much more complicated. A puzzle we mentioned in Chapter 4 is why the United States is such a small welfare state compared with Europe, lacking, for example, national health care, which is a norm in the advanced democracies. Many arguments have been put forth to explain this, but one explanation may have to do with ethnic and racial diversity. The argument is that societies that are more diverse have a more difficult time building social institutions to redistribute income and distribute public goods for the simple reason that people are less comfortable giving up some of their money if they perceive the benefits going disproportionately to people unlike them. Equality and solidarity are in part a function of homogeneity. Racial divides in the United States thus limit the extent to which the majority is willing to accept redistribution. Contrast this with strong social democratic countries in Europe, such as Scandinavia, that are highly homogeneous. If true, the question then becomes what will happen to the welfare state in countries where the immigrant population is growing? If more individuals come from places that are racially, culturally, or religiously quite different, will this engender resentment and conflict over those social expenditures that have been a cornerstone of society? Is there a trade-off between diversity and social solidarity? The issue will become more contentious in the coming years.

percent of the Japanese population would be made up of immigrants and their descendants—a huge demographic shift in a country noted for its ethnic homogeneity. As can be imagined, there is little desire in Japan to follow such a course, though the alternative is for the country to shrink significantly in population and wealth. If solutions are not found for Japan and the other advanced democracies, many will find themselves unable to sustain some of the most basic elements of prosperity and risk management they have constructed over the past century, and they may face societal conflict that pits young against old and immigrant against native.[16]

In Sum: The Advanced Democracies in Transition

Advanced democracies are in many ways unique, both in their institutions and in the challenges they face. Although there is variation among them, these countries are characterized by liberal democracy and high levels of economic development. They represent, in many ways, what we consider modern social, economic, and political life. Yet none of these institutions is set in stone. State sovereignty is confronted by the twin dynamics of devolution and integration. Social norms are similarly in flux, as postmodern values challenge the status quo and are in turn being challenged. Modern industrial structures have given way to a new, information-based economy that empowers some and dislocates others, and demographic changes will affect how countries provide public goods to their people. All of these factors can shape the existing balance of freedom and equality.

In the coming chapters, we will turn to these same issues as they exist outside the advanced democracies. Communist and postcommunist, less-developed and newly industrializing countries all confront issues of state sovereignty, social values, industrialization, and social welfare. What unique challenges each group faces in these areas will be the focus of the next two chapters. Will these countries eventually join the ranks of the advanced democracies in a convergence of political, economic, and social institutions around the globe? This question will remain with us through our remaining discussion.

NOTES

1. For details on the historical development of the EU, see Derek Irwin, *The Community of Europe: A History of European Integration since 1945* (New York: Addison-Wesley, 1995).

2. See Eurobarometer 175, *The Euro, 4 Years after the Introduction of Banknotes and Coins,* http://ec.europa.eu.

3. For a skeptical view of this danger, see Barry Eichengren, "The Breakup of the Euro Area," unpublished paper, May 2007, www.econ.berkeley.edu/~eichengr/.

4. European Foundation for the Improvement of Living and Working Conditions, *Global Competition and European Companies' Location Decisions,* June 2008, www.eurofound.europa.eu/.

5. See Post-Referendum Survey in Ireland, Flash Eurobarometer 245, 13–15 June 2008, http://ec.europa.eu/public_opinion/index_en.htm.

6. For a broader discussion of devolution, see Larry Diamond with Svetlana Tsalik, "Size and Democracy: The Case for Decentralization," in Larry Diamond, ed., *Developing Democracy: Toward Consolidation* (Baltimore: Johns Hopkins University Press, 1999).

7. Robert Cooper, *The Postmodern State and the World Order* (London: Demos, 1996).

8. For further discussion, see Ronald Inglehart and Marita Carballo, "Does Latin America Exist? (And Is There a Confucian Culture?): A Global Analysis of Cross-Cultural Differences," *PS: Political Science and Politics,* 30, no. 1 (March 1997), pp. 34–46.

9. U.S. Census Department, *Projected Population by Race and Hispanic Origin, 2000–2050,* www.census.gov.

10. For two controversial works on this topic, see Samuel Huntington, *Who Are We? The Challenges to America's National Identity* (New York: Simon and Schuster, 2004), and Victor David Hanson, *Mexifornia: A State of Becoming* (San Francisco: Encounter, 2004).

11. See Ian Buruma, *Murder in Amsterdam: The Death of Theo Van Gogh and the Limits of Tolerance* (New York: Penguin, 2006).

12. Travis Reindl, "Hitting Home: Quality, Cost and Access Challenges Confronting Higher Education Today," in *Making Opportunity Affordable,* March 2007, www.makingopportunityaffordable.org/.

13. For data on population trends worldwide, see Population Reference Bureau, *World Population Data Sheet,* www.prb.org.

14. See *OECD Factbook 2008,* www.oecd.org.

15. Markus Crepaz, *Trust Beyond Borders: Immigration, the Welfare State, and Identity in Modern Societies* (Ann Arbor: University of Michigan Press, 2007).

16. For an interesting discussion of how this may affect social welfare in the United States, see Jacob Hacker, *The Great Risk Shift: The New Economic Insecurity and the Decline of the American Dream* (Oxford: Oxford University Press, 2008).

8 COMMUNISM AND POSTCOMMUNISM

KEY CONCEPTS

- Communist ideology is founded on the understanding that politics stems from economic inequality.

- Communist systems sought to eliminate inequality by eliminating private property and market forces, under the direction of a one-party state.

- State control over markets and property proved too complex, and these systems eventually collapsed or radically reformed their institutions.

- Postcommunist states have had to transform their economic institutions to restore markets and private property, with mixed results.

- Post-communist states have had to transform their political institutions, with some becoming liberal democracies while others remain authoritarian.

The advanced democracies we studied in Chapter 7 have become the wealthiest and most powerful countries in the world. In spite of this success, however, these countries continue to struggle with a number of issues, among them economic inequality—both within their societies and between themselves and the rest of the world. Their dilemma is no small matter: Must freedom always come at the expense of equality? Particularly with the rise of economic and political liberalism and the challenges to the welfare state, it would seem that the answer is yes. But throughout history humans have struggled to find a way in which equality might be secured, providing benefits for all. This concern goes to the heart of communism in both theory and practice, for communism has sought to create a system that limits individual freedoms in order to divide wealth in an equitable manner. This vision of a world without economic distinctions drove the formation of communist regimes around the world, eventually bringing hundreds of millions of people under its banner.

Yet in spite of the lofty ideals of communist thought, and in spite of its dramatic emergence as a political regime in the early part of the twentieth century, within less than a century the majority of the world's communist regimes began to unravel. Why? What brought the quest for collective equality to a dead end? Was there a mistranslation of theory into practice, or were the theories themselves inherently suspect, unable to be realized in any practical manner?

In this chapter, we will look at how communism attempted to reconcile freedom and equality and why communist systems have largely failed at that endeavor. We will begin by looking at the original theories of modern communism, particularly the ideas of Karl Marx. From there we will investigate how communism was changed from theory into practice as communist regimes were built around the world, most notably in the Soviet Union, Eastern Europe, and China (See Table 8.1). How did these systems seek to create equality and bring Marx's ideas to life? Our answer will discuss the nature of government, regime, and state under communism.

After examining the dynamics of communism in practice, we will study its demise. What were its shortcomings, and why could these limitations not be corrected? Why did attempts at reform in the Soviet Union and Eastern Europe turn into a rout, and what does this mean for those countries that remain communist—at least in name—like China? Our look at the downfall of communism will take us to our last issues: What comes after communism, and is communism dead? In addressing each of these questions, we will uncover the enormous scope and vision of communist thought, the tremendous challenges of putting it into practice, the serious flaws and limitations that this implementation entailed, and the daunting work of building new political, social, and economic institutions from the rubble of communism's demise.

Communism, Equality, and the Nature of Human Relations

Communism is a set of ideas that view political, social, and economic institutions in a fundamentally different manner from most political thought, essentially challenging much of what we have studied so far. At its most basic level, we can define it as an ideology that seeks to create human equality by eliminating private property and market forces.

In modern politics, communism as a political theory and ideology can be traced primarily to the German philosopher Karl Marx (1818–1883).[1] Marx began with a rather straightforward observation: Human beings are able to

Table 8.1 Communist Regimes in the 1980s

Europe	Asia	Africa and the Middle East	Latin America
Albania	Afghanistan	Angola	*Cuba*
Bulgaria	Cambodia	Benin	
Czechoslovakia	*China*	Ethiopia	
East Germany	*Laos*	Mozambique	
Hungary	Mongolia	South Yemen	
Poland	*North Korea*		
Romania	*Vietnam*		
Soviet Union			
Yugoslavia			

Note: Communist countries as of 2008 are shown in italics.

create objects of value by investing their own time and labor in their creation. That "surplus value of labor" stays with the object, making it useful to anyone, not just the maker. It is this ability to create objects with their own innate value that sets people apart from other animals, but it also inevitably leads to economic injustice, Marx concluded. He argued that as human beings develop their knowledge and technological skills, an opportunity is created for those with political power to essentially extract the surplus value from others, enriching themselves while impoverishing others. In other words, once human beings learned how to produce things of value, others found that they could gain these things at little cost to themselves simply by using coercion to acquire them.

For Marx, then, the world was properly understood in economic terms; all human action flowed from the relations between the haves and the have-nots. Marx believed that structures, rather than people or ideas, made history. Specifically, Marx spoke of human history and human relations as being based on what he termed the base and the superstructure. The base is the system of economic production, including the level of technology (what he called the "means of production") and the kind of class relations that exist as a result (the "relations of production"). Resting on the base is the superstructure, which represents all human institutions—politics and the state, national identity and culture, religion and gender, and so on. Marx viewed this superstructure as a system of institutions created essentially to justify and perpetuate the existing order. People consequently suffer from

Terms in Marxist Theory

Surplus value of labor: the value invested in any human-made good that can be used by another individual. Exploitation results when one person or group extracts the surplus value from another.

Base: the economic system of a society, made up of technology (the means of production) and class relations between people (the relations of production).

Superstructure: All noneconomic relations in a society (for example, religion, culture, national identity). These ideas and values derive from the base and serve to legitimize the current system of exploitation.

False consciousness: Failure to understand the nature of one's exploitation; essentially "buying into" the superstructure.

Dialectical materialism: Process of historical change that is not evolutionary but revolutionary. The existing base and superstructure (thesis) would come into conflict with new technological innovations, generating growing tensions between the exploiters and the exploited (antithesis). This would culminate in revolution, overthrowing the old base and superstructure.

Dictatorship of the proletariat: Temporary period after capitalism has been overthrown during which vestiges of the old base and superstructure are eradicated.

Proletariat: The working class.

Bourgeoisie: The property-owning class.

Communism: According to Marxists, the final stage of history once capitalism is overthrown and the dictatorship of the proletariat destroys its remaining vestiges. In communism, state and politics would disappear, and society and the economy would be based on equality and cooperation.

Vanguard of the proletariat: Lenin's argument that an elite communist party would have to carry out revolution, because as a result of false consciousness, historical conditions would not automatically lead to capitalism's demise.

"false consciousness," meaning that they believe they understand the true nature of the world around them, but in reality they are deluded by the superstructure imposed by capitalism. Thus, liberal democracy was rejected by Marx and most other communists as a system created to delude the exploited into thinking they have a say in their political destiny, when in fact those with wealth actually control politics.

Revolution and the "Triumph" of Communism

Having dissected what he saw as the nature of politics, economics, and society, Marx used this framework to understand historical development and to anticipate the future of capitalism. Marx concluded that human history developed in specific phases, each driven by the particular nature of exploitation at that point in time. In each historical case, he argued, the specific form of exploitation was built around the existing level of technology. For example, in early agrarian societies, feudalism was the dominant political and economic order; the rudimentary technology available tied individuals to the land so that their labor could be exploited by the aristocracy. But although such relations may appear stable, technology itself is always dynamic. Marx recognized this and asserted that the inevitable changes in technology would increase tensions between rulers and ruled as new forms of technological development empowered new groups who clashed with the base and the superstructure. Again, in the case of feudalism, emerging technology empowered an early capitalist, property-owning middle class or bourgeoisie, whose members sought political power for themselves and the remaking of the economic and social order in a way that better fit capitalist ambitions.

Eventually, this tension would lead to revolution; those in power would be overthrown, and a new ruling class would come to power. In each case, change would be sudden and violent and would pave the way for a new eco-

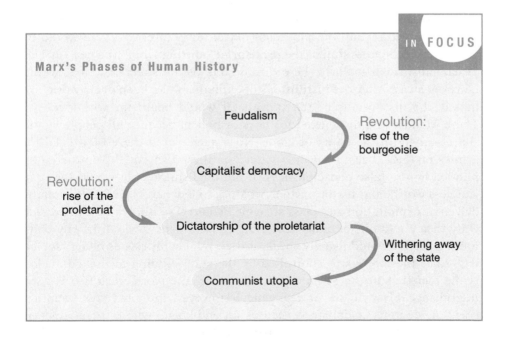

IN FOCUS

Marx's Phases of Human History

Feudalism

Revolution: rise of the bourgeoisie

Capitalist democracy

Revolution: rise of the proletariat

Dictatorship of the proletariat

Withering away of the state

Communist utopia

nomic base and superstructure. This entire process is termed dialectical materialism. The dialectic portrays history as a struggle between the existing order (the thesis) and the challenge to that order (the antithesis), resulting in historical change (the synthesis). Revolutions inevitably come about as a result of this tension between economic classes.

On the basis of these ideas, Marx concluded that capitalist democracy, which had displaced feudalism, would itself eventually be overthrown by its own internal flaws. As capitalism developed, competition between firms would intensify. The working class, or proletariat, would find itself on the losing end of this process as firms introduced more and more technology to reduce the number of workers and as unprofitable businesses began to go bankrupt in the face of intense competition. The bourgeoisie would grow smaller and smaller as the wealth of society became concentrated in fewer and fewer hands, and large monopolies would come to dominate the economy. The wages of the working class would decline in the face of increased competition (an oversupply of labor as technology reduces the number of workers needed), and the ranks of the unemployed would swell.

Alienated and driven to desperation by these conditions, eventually the proletariat would "gain consciousness" by realizing the true source of their poverty and rise up in rebellion. They would carry out a revolution, seizing control of the state and the economy. Marx saw this process not simply as a national phenomenon but as an international one. When the conditions were right, he hypothesized, revolution would spread among all the capitalist countries, sweeping away this unjust order in a relatively short period of time.

Once world revolution had taken place, Marx foresaw, there would be a temporary "dictatorship of the proletariat," during which the last vestiges of capitalism, particularly the old remnants of the superstructure, would be swept away. After the institutions of capitalism had been decisively eliminated, the institutions of the state itself would begin to "wither away." There would be no more need for laws or police, because all people would share equally in the fruits of labor. No longer would there be a need for armies or flags, because people would be united in equality rather than blinded by the false consciousness of nationalism. People would live in a stateless world, and history, which in Marx's view had been fundamentally driven by exploitation and class struggle, would essentially come to an end. Only then could one actually speak of "communism"—which is why communist parties would usually speak of their own countries as being "socialist," since they were still controlled by the state. Adding to this confusion is the fact that in the advanced democracies, the word *socialism* is used interchangeably with *social democracy*. However, for most contemporary social democrats, socialism is seen as an end stage, where the state exercises significant but not total control over the economy. For communists, however, socialism is a transitional phase toward an outcome where private property and the state no longer exist.

Putting Communism into Practice

Communism thus provides an entire worldview, explaining the course of human history and the inevitable ascent into utopia as the product of economic interaction. As we know, such a sweeping theory has proved compelling for many people, especially those who sought to put Marx's ideas into practice. Two of the most notable followers of Marx's ideas were Vladimir Ulyanov, more commonly known as Lenin, and Mao Zedong, who came to lead communist revolutions in Russia (1917) and China (1949), respectively. Yet, although both Mao and Lenin were inspired by Marx, they departed from his ideas by seeking to carry out revolution in two countries that were weakly industrialized and far from being capitalist. Marx had argued that revolution would occur only where and when capitalism was most advanced and thus most prone to collapse; however, at the end of his life, he did hold out the possibility that revolution could occur in less-developed Russia, in contradiction to his own theories.[2] Lenin and Mao had believed that revolution could be carried out in less advanced countries if leaders constructed a "vanguard of the proletariat"—Lenin's term for a small revolutionary movement that could seize power on behalf of the people.[3]

This approach meant that in reality, communism spread where the level of economic development was relatively low—exactly the opposite of what Marx had originally theorized. Whereas communism made no headway in more developed countries, it continued to spread in much of the less-developed world, often with the backing of the Soviet Union and China. By the 1980s, communist regimes accounted for approximately one-third of the world's population.

Yet even as it expanded, communist countries faced a common dilemma: How exactly did one go about building communism? Marx had left no blueprint for that task—for what to do once the revolution had succeeded. In many ways, communists assumed that the revolution was the difficult part, and what should occur afterward would unfold as a matter of course.

In part because Marx provided no specific outline for how communism would be built, the institutions that were created varied widely, shaped by domestic economic and political conditions, historical context, cultural factors, and the ideas and authority of those in power. But beyond these differences, they shared a common form, first developed in the Soviet Union after 1917. Because of the desire to so fundamentally reshape human relations, communist states accrued a high level of autonomy and capacity; their regimes

IN FOCUS

Important Figures in Communism

Karl Marx (1818–1883) First philosopher to systematically construct a theory explaining why capitalism would fail and be replaced by communism; father of modern communist thought.

Lenin (Vladimir Ulyanov) (1870–1924) Applied Marxist thought to Russia, leading successful revolution in 1917; modified Marxist ideas by arguing that revolution would occur not in most developed societies, but rather in struggling countries such as Russia.

Stalin (Josef Dzhugashvili) (1879–1953) Succeeded Lenin as leader of the Soviet Union; embarked on rapid industrialization of the country, modifying Marxism to argue that socialism could be built in a single country; extended communism to Eastern Europe after World War II; denounced by Nikita Khrushchev in 1956 for his use of a personality cult and terror.

Mao Zedong (1883–1976) Led Chinese Communist Party and fought against Chinese rivals and Japanese occupiers during World War II; modified communism to focus on peasantry instead of working class, given the primarily agrarian nature of China; unleashed Cultural Revolution in 1966 to weaken party and increase his own power.

Fidel Castro (1926–) Led Cuban revolution in 1959 and defended the communist system against anticommunist forces and U.S. opposition; continues to defend Cuban socialism in spite of the collapse of the Soviet Union and other communist regimes in Eastern Europe.

Deng Xiaoping (1905–1997) Fought with Mao Zedong against Chinese nationalists and Japanese invaders during World War II; named general secretary of the Chinese Communist Party in 1956; stripped of all posts during the Cultural Revolution, but emerged as country's leader after death of Mao; pursued economic liberalization in 1980s and supported repression of Tiananmen Square protests.

Mikhail Gorbachev (1931–) Made general secretary of the Communist Party of the Soviet Union in 1985; initiated twin policies of perestroika (economic restructuring) and glasnost (political liberalization), which eventually led to increasing discord within the country and a failed coup attempt by hard-line communists who opposed further reform; the resulting dissolution of the Soviet Union left Gorbachev without a country to lead.

have at times become totalitarian in their desire to transform virtually all basic human institutions, from work to prayer to gender to art.

The task of this transformation was entrusted to the communist elite who came to direct and staff the state.[4] At its apex, political power rested within the Communist Party, a relatively small "vanguard" organization (typically comprising less than 10 percent of the population) whose leading role in the country was typically written directly into the constitution—meaning that there was no constitutional way to remove the party from power. Because the Communist Party embodied what it saw as the "correct" view of human history and future relations, alternative organizations and ideologies making up civil society were seen as hostile to communism and were repressed.

But as we discussed in our chapter on nondemocratic regimes, no system of rule can survive through the threat of force alone. Communist parties maintained control over society not only through repression but also by carefully allocating power throughout the country's various political, social, and economic institutions—a thorough form of co-optation. This can be seen clearly in the *nomenklatura*, politically sensitive or influential jobs in the state, society, or economy that were staffed by people chosen or approved by the Communist Party. The *nomenklatura* encompassed a wide range of important positions: the head of a university, the editor of a newspaper, a military officer, a film director. Not surprisingly, party approval often required party membership, making joining the party the easiest way to prove one's loyalty and rise up the career ladder. Party membership could also bring other benefits: better housing, the ability to travel abroad, or access to scarce consumer goods. As a result, party membership was often driven more by opportunism than by idealism; many joined so that they could pursue certain careers or simply gain the benefits that party membership could buy.[5]

The dominant role played by the Communist Party and the *nomenklatura* created a power relationship different from those in democratic and many other nondemocratic systems. Power, rather than being centered within the state and government, rested within the party. For example, when observers referred to the "leader" of a communist country, they were usually referring not to a government official but to the general secretary of the Communist Party. Indeed, top party leaders often did not hold any important position within the state. Communist countries by and large resembled political systems we see elsewhere in the world, typically with a prime minister or president, a parliament, a judiciary, and local government—all encompassing positions that were part of the *nomenklatura* and thus staffed by party members. Although trappings of democracy, such as parliamentary elections, typically existed, electoral candidates were almost exclusively Communist Party members with no real competition. Moreover, parliaments and other organs of power were little more than "rubber-stamp" institutions, approving of decisions sent down the party hierarchy.

As for the party itself, in many ways it intentionally mirrored the state, with a general secretary serving as chief executive, and a **Politburo** (short for "Political Bureau") and **Central Committee** acting as a kind of cabinet and legislature, respectively, shaping national policy and confirming the decisions of the party leadership. Below the Central Committee, various other bodies extended all the way down to individual places of work or residence, where party members were organized into basic party organizations called "cells." These cells were ostensibly intended to represent the interests of the people, but they were primarily mechanisms by which the party could closely monitor the population. Traditionally, the party held a congress every few years, at which its leadership was elected by delegates sent from the party cells, but these elections were little more than confirmations of those already in power.

Outside of the party and state, a limited number of organizations, such as unions, were allowed to function; these were in turn linked to the state and party, completing this highly corporatist structure, with sanctioned organizations for all facets of society.

While the party and its *nomenklatura* controlled key organizations, communist ideology shaped policy and sought to legitimize authoritarian control. Based fundamentally on the theories of Marx as adapted by Lenin and Mao, communist ideology focused on the elimination of inequality and the promotion of economic development. Because of the expansive nature of communist ideology and its promise of a future utopia, it was, perhaps more than the other ideologies we discussed in Chapter 3, a secular "religion," requiring unquestioning faith in a set of beliefs and sacrifice for a future reward and boasting its own collection of holy texts, shrines, saints, martyrs, and devils. In this view, adherents venerated charismatic leaders who served as prophets of communism, such as Lenin, Mao, Josef Stalin, and Fidel Castro. Many charismatic communist leaders reinforced their position through elaborate personality cults, as we discussed earlier.

The quest for and exercise of this monopoly on power, as expressed through the *nomenklatura* and the deep penetration of the state and society by the party, down to the most basic level of home and work, proved to be dangerous and even lethal. In the first decades of communist rule in the Soviet Union, China, and Eastern Europe, terror was used to eliminate opposition and to maintain control. Tens of millions perished in such campaigns, especially in the Soviet Union under Stalin and in China under Mao. Under the rule of Stalin, many people were purged from within the Soviet Communist Party itself and executed for imaginary crimes. These were not cases of mistaken punishment: Stalin used terror and victimized symbolic "criminals" as a way to cow the Communist Party and the population as a whole.[6] Similarly, in China, Mao unleashed the Cultural Revolution in the late 1960s, encouraging the public (students, in particular) to attack any institution or individual that was either a remnant of precommunist China or lacked revolutionary zeal. Mao's targets included the **party-state**, which he believed had grown conservative over time and was restricting his power—indeed, his notable slo-gan was "bombard the party headquarters." During the next decade, not only did countless Chinese die (estimates are over 1 million), but books were burned, art destroyed, and cultural relics demolished—all for the crime of being "reactionary."[7]

Communist Political Economy

If the Communist Party's singular quest for power led in the cases of Stalin and Mao to its gross abuse, the centralization of economic power similarly created problems that Marxist theory did not anticipate. Communist political-economic systems shared a set of institutions fundamentally different from liberal, mer-cantilist, or social democratic alternatives, as both markets and property were essentially absorbed by the state.[8] With the means of production held by the state, many of the typical aspects of capitalism that we take for granted—individual profit, unemployment, competition between firms, bankruptcy—were eliminated. Individuals lost their right to control property, including their own labor; the party-state made the decisions about how these resources should be used. In turn, communist leaders redirected national wealth toward the goal of collective equality through such mechanisms as industrialization and social expenditures. But none of this was painless. Several million died in the Soviet Union in the 1930s during the forced collectivization of agriculture, while an attempt at rapid industrialization and the collectivization of agri-culture under the Great Leap Forward in China (1959–1961) led to some 30 million famine deaths.[9]

Alongside the elimination of private property, communist systems also eliminated the market mechanism, believing that it was incapable of equitably distributing wealth. Communist countries by and large chose to replace the market with the state bureaucracy, which explicitly allocated resources by planning what should be produced and in what amounts, setting the final prices of these goods, and deciding where they should be sold. This system is known as **central planning**.

As one might imagine, planning an entire economy is an extremely diffi-cult task. A market economy responds to the relationship of supply and demand in a spontaneous and decentralized manner. If there is a market for something, a producer will often come along to fill that need in the hope of making a profit. In a centrally planned economy, however, bureaucrats must centralize these decisions. How much steel should be produced this year? How many women's size eight shoes? How many apartments? Determining needs for each and every good produced in a country requires huge amounts of infor-mation and an ability to account for future changes.

Communist Political Economy

- Markets and property are wholly absorbed by the state.
- Central planning replaces the market mechanism.
- Individual property rights, individual profit, unemployment, competition between firms, and bankruptcy are all virtually eliminated.
- Most of the nation's means of production are nationalized.
- The economy functions in essence as a single large firm, with the public as its sole employees.
- The state provides extensive public goods and social services, including universal systems of public education, health care, and retirement.

As communist planners found, matching up all these inputs and outputs is overwhelming. There are simply too many things to plan—in the Soviet Union, for instance, there were some 40,000 to 50,000 physical items—and too many unforeseen outcomes, such as a factory failing to deliver its full output, or a change in demand. Because most entities in an economy are interdependent, small problems can have a huge effect on the entire plan. A miscalculation resulting in the underproduction of steel, for

example, would have disastrous effects on all those goods dependent on steel, some of which would themselves be components in other finished goods, such as nails or bolts. Any mistakes or changes in the central plan, and production begins to go out of balance.

Another problem encountered in centrally planned economies was the lack of worker incentives. Factories and farms were unconcerned about the quality of their goods, since central planners simply indicated a numerical quota they had to fulfill. Workers did not have to fear losing their jobs or factories going out of business as a result of shoddy work, because under communism, employment was guaranteed, and firms, being owned by the state, could not go bankrupt. This explains in part why all communist countries eventually fell behind economically. In the absence of competition and incentives, innovation and efficiency disappeared, leaving these systems to stagnate.

Societal Institutions under Communism

In addition to reengineering politics and economics to eliminate the inequality and exploitation associated with capitalist systems, communist parties also sought to reorder human relations, hoping to sweep away the old superstructure held responsible for generating false consciousness. Individual freedoms were also repressed, since they were viewed as an expression of false consciousness and therefore a threat to communist goals.

One example of this hostility can be seen in communism's view of religion. Marx is known for his oft-cited statement that "religion is the opiate of the masses," meaning that it is part of the superstructure that serves to perpetuate inequality and legitimize suffering in return for rewards in some afterlife. As a result, in most communist countries, religion was strongly suppressed. In the Soviet Union, most places of worship were closed, converted to other uses, or torn down. In China during the Cultural Revolution, temples and other religious shrines were destroyed. Even where religion was tolerated to a greater extent, it was still harassed or directly controlled by the Communist Party.

Traditional gender relations were also seen by Marxists as a function of capitalism; specifically, gender relations were seen to be class relations in microcosm. Men exploit women through the family structure, just as the bourgeoisie exploit the proletariat, and sexual morality serves as a means to perpetuate this gender inequality. Communism envisioned complete economic, social, and political equality between men and women. Even the repressive institution of marriage, like the state, would fade away, replaced by what Marx called "an openly legalized community of free love."[10] This was quite a radical view of gender relations for its time; after all, Marx was writing in the late nineteenth century, when women did not even have the right to vote anywhere in the world.

In spite of Marxist ideals, gender relations only partially changed under communist rule. In most communist countries, women were given much greater opportunities than they had experienced previously. To promote industrialization, communist parties encouraged women to enter the workforce and to increase their education. Most countries also enacted liberal divorce and abortion laws and provided social benefits such as state-run child care. In spite of these changes, however, women's traditional roles as housekeepers and mothers did not change. The "new socialist woman" was not complemented by a "new socialist man"; traditional patterns of sexism persisted, and women found themselves burdened by the double duty of work inside and outside the home. In addition, while many women worked in important occupations, few rose to positions of any significant political or economic power. The top ranks of the party membership, the state, and the economy remained dominated by men.[11]

A final aspect of society that communist countries sought to change was national and ethnic identity. As part of the superstructure, nationalism and ethnicity were seen as mechanisms by which the ruling elite pit the working classes of different countries against one another in a tactic of divide and rule. With the advent of the world communist revolution, such divisions were expected to disappear, to be replaced by equality and harmony among all peoples. As a result, communist parties tended to reject any overt expressions of

Societal Institutions under Communism

Ideal	Reality
Religion, the "opiate of the masses," will disappear.	Religion was suppressed but not eliminated.
Men and women will be economically, socially, and politically equal.	Opportunities for women increased, but women were still expected to fulfill traditional duties in the home.
Repressive institutions such as marriage will be replaced by "an openly legalized system of free love."	Many communist countries remained sexually very conservative.
Nationalism, exposed as part of the elite's "divide and conquer" strategy, will be eliminated.	Though discouraged from doing so, people clung to old national and ethnic identities.

nationalism, though such identities often lurked beneath the surface. For example, encompassed within the vast Soviet Union were many ethnic groups, although the Communist Party tended to be dominated by Russians, who made up the single largest ethnic group. Many non-Russians resented this Russian domination. Many Eastern Europeans also viewed communist rule as little more than Russian imperialism; their national identity was therefore sharpened, not erased. This simmering nationalism played an important role in the fall of communism in Eastern Europe and the Soviet Union.

The Collapse of Communism

In retrospect, it may seem obvious that communism was bound to fail, and yet on the eve of its collapse in Europe few expected that it would happen anytime soon. Two factors played an important role in bringing about its sudden decline.

The first was the reemergence of Cold War struggles between the Soviet Union and the United States. After the tense decades of the 1950s and 1960s, which were marked by international competition, arms races, and harrowing events such as the Cuban missile crisis, the United States and the Soviet

Union settled into a period of détente in which peaceful coexistence became the main goal. But détente lasted less than a decade. The Soviet Union's invasion of Afghanistan in 1979 to prop up a failing communist regime there and the election of Ronald Reagan as U.S. president in 1980 soured relations between the two countries. Reagan, who viewed the Soviet Union as an "evil empire," embarked on a new policy of military buildup. Growing economic stagnation made it difficult for the Soviet Union to meet this expensive challenge.

At the same time as the United States and the Soviet Union entered a new and costly stage of the Cold War, a new generation of political leaders rose to power in the Soviet Union, among them Mikhail Gorbachev, who was chosen as general secretary of the Communist Party in 1985. Unlike his predecessors, Gorbachev recognized the stagnation of the Soviet system and understood the cost of a new arms race. He thus proposed reforming international and domestic relations, revitalizing both the Soviet Union and communist thought.

At the domestic level, Gorbachev initiated the twin policies of glasnost (openness) and perestroika (restructuring), intended to liberalize and reform communism. **Glasnost** encouraged public debate, with the hope that a frank discussion of the shortcomings of the system would help foster change and increase the legitimacy of the regime. **Perestroika**, or actual institutional reforms in the economy and political system, would flow from these critiques. These reforms were expected to include some limited forms of democratic participation and market-based incentives in the economy. Moderate reform, not wholesale transformation, was Gorbachev's goal.[12]

In the international arena, Gorbachev similarly proposed widespread, if moderate, changes. To reduce the Soviet Union's military burdens and improve relations with Western countries, he began to loosen his country's control over Eastern Europe, which had been under the thumb of the Soviet Union since the end of World War II. Gorbachev hoped that some limited liberalization in the region would ease tensions with Europe and the United States, enabling expanded trade and other economic ties.

But as Alexis de Tocqueville famously wrote with regard to the French monarchy, the most dangerous moment for a bad government is usually when it begins to reform itself. Highly institutionalized and rigid, the communist system was incapable of reform. Glasnost encouraged public debate, but rather than simply criticize corruption or the quality of consumer goods (which is what Gorbachev expected), the public began to challenge the very nature of the political system. Ethnic groups within the Soviet Union and citizens of Eastern European states used glasnost to agitate for greater freedom from Russian domination.

TIME LINE / **COMMUNIST HISTORY**	
1848	Karl Marx and Freidrich Engels write *The Communist Manifesto*, a central document in communist thought.
1917	Lenin leads the Russian Revolution, creating the Soviet Union as the world's first communist country.
1930s	Stalin begins to arrest and execute Soviet Communist Party members and others to consolidate power and terrorize the population.
1945	Soviet Army occupies Eastern Europe, imposing communist regimes; tensions between the United States and the Soviet Union lead to Cold War.
1949	Chinese Communist Party, led by Mao Zedong, gains control over mainland China after a long struggle against local opposition and Japanese occupiers.
1953	Stalin dies.
1956	Nikita Khrushchev denounces Stalin's use of terror and allows limited open debate; debate turns to unrest in parts of Eastern Europe; protests in Hungary lead to open revolution against communism; Hungarian revolution put down by Soviet army.
1966–76	Mao unleashes Cultural Revolution in China; student "Red Guard" attacks symbols of precommunism and party leaders accused of having grown too conservative; Cultural Revolution used to eliminate Mao's political rivals.
1976	Mao Zedong dies; China and the U.S. begin to improve relations; rise to power of Deng Xiaopeng, who enacts widespread economic reforms.
1979	Soviet Union invades Afghanistan, worsening relations between U.S. and Soviet Union; reintensification of the Cold War.
1985	Gorbachev becomes general secretary of the Soviet Communist Party and begins to carry out economic and political liberalization.
1989	Student protests for political reform in China's Tiananmen Square crushed by the military.
1989–90	East Europeans seize on reforms in the Soviet Union to press for dramatic political change; largely peaceful political protests lead to free elections and the elimination of communist rule in Eastern Europe.
1991	Increasing turmoil in the Soviet Union leads communist conservatives to oust Gorbachev and seize power; coup fails due to weak military support and public demonstrations; Soviet Union breaks into fifteen separate states.

Perestroika had similarly unexpected effects. By seeking political and economic reform, Gorbachev threatened those within the party who had long benefited from the status quo. Political leaders, administrators, factory bosses, and many other members of the *nomenklatura* resisted reform, leading to infighting and instability. This problem was compounded by Gorbachev's actual policies, which were largely halfhearted measures. Confusion deepened within the party, the state, and society as to where communism and the Soviet Union were heading.

Meanwhile, among the Soviet Union's satellite states, change was proceeding faster than anyone expected. In 1989, civil society rapidly reasserted itself across Eastern Europe and used Gorbachev's new hands-off policy to oppose their countries' communist regimes, demanding open elections and an end to one-party rule. Eastern European Communist Party leaders, realizing that the Soviet Union would no longer intervene militarily to support them, had little choice but to acquiesce. As a result, by 1990, communists had been swept from their monopolies on power across the region. In most cases, this regime change was largely peaceful.

The Soviet Union would not be far behind. By 1991, the country was in deep turmoil: limited reforms had increased the public's appetite for greater change; the end of communism in Eastern Europe further emboldened opposition within the Soviet Union; and ethnic conflict and nationalism were on the rise as various groups sought political power.[13] Communist hard-liners eventually tried to stop the reform process through a coup d'état, seizing power and detaining Gorbachev. However, these leaders lacked the support of important actors such as the military and other segments of the state, and public demonstrations helped bring the poorly planned coup to an end.[14]

In the aftermath of the 1991 coup and in response to their own ethnic constituents, the individual republics that made up the Soviet Union broke up, forming fifteen new independent countries, of which Russia is one. But communism did not collapse everywhere. Although 1989 marked liberalization and the first moves toward democracy in Eastern Europe and the Soviet Union, similar protests in China that year, led by students and encouraged by Gorbachev's example, were met with deadly military force in Tiananmen Square. Communist leaders in China did not heed public demands for reform and political liberalization and showed themselves both willing and able to use the army to violently quell peaceful protests.

Here lies an important puzzle: Why sudden political change in the Soviet Union and not China? Let's return to our discussion in Chapter 5 on the sources of political change and democratization. In that chapter we noted some different explanations for why political transition may occur, among them modernization, society, elites, international relations, and culture. All of these may have played some role. The Soviet Union and Eastern Europe in the 1980s were certainly more modernized than China, which contributed to a stronger civil society or potential for political organization. Leadership, too, differed; while Gorbachev pressed for political change, leaders in China explicitly opposed political reforms in favor of economic development. The international conditions were also different, with the Soviet Union promoting change in order to end the Cold War and better integrate with Europe, issues that were not a concern for China. Perhaps culture, too, played a role, in linking communist Europe to the ideal of a democratic west in a way not familiar to China. All of these factors may have figured into the events that occurred.

The Transformation of Political Institutions

So far, we have discussed the communist theory regarding the origins of and solutions to inequality, the difficulties in translating theory into reality, and how eventually these institutions unraveled across most of the communist world. Yet although the downfall of communism was dramatic, what followed was no less awesome. Postcommunist countries faced, and continue to face, the challenge of building new political, social, and economic institutions to strike a new balance between freedom and equality. No country had ever made such a dramatic change in all three areas at once, and this task has met with varying degrees of success.

Reorganizing the State and Constructing a Democratic Regime

An underlying task in the transition from communism is to reorganize the state in terms of its autonomy and capacity. Under communism, the party-state was able to dominate virtually all aspects of human relations without any effective check. State autonomy and capacity were extremely high. But with the collapse of communism, the party was ejected from its leading role in political life, and new leaders had to change the very role and scope of the state. But reducing state power was not easy, as dramatic political change occurs alongside a substantial weakening of the state precisely when state power is most needed. Many postcommunist countries thus sought to narrow their states' capacity and autonomy without incapacitating them in the process.

Another important aspect of postcommunist reform is the establishment of the rule of law. In Chapter 5 and elsewhere, we have seen that laws and regulations are essential institutions in political life; they are the basic "rules of the game" that the majority of people obey because it is in their best interest. Under communist systems, the rule of law was weak. The Communist Party could make, break, or change laws as it saw fit, and as a result, people came to view laws rather cynically. This attitude encouraged evasion and corruption, problems that expanded dramatically once the repressive power of the state was retracted or weakened. Postcommunist countries must now institutionalize regulations and legal structures, so that leaders do not act in a capricious manner or take advantage of their authority. In society, too, the rule of law must be instilled in such a way that people willingly obey the system even when it is not in their personal interest to do so.

Along with reconstructing state power and the rule of law, postcommunist countries have faced the prospect of building a democratic regime where authoritarianism has long been the norm. This project requires numerous

INSTITUTIONS IN

ACTION

PRESIDENTIALISM, PARLIAMENTARIANISM, AND POSTCOMMUNISM

Among the various issues that confronted postcommunist countries was that of executive-legislative relations. Recall that under communism, real executive authority rested with the general secretary of the Communist Party; the positions of head of state and government had little power. However, with the end of the Communist Party's monopoly of power, the executive became a major source of conflict. As we have noted, most of Western Europe follows the parliamentary model, where power is vested in a prime minister who comes from the legislature and is beholden to them. However, in many postcommunist countries, there were strong pressures for presidentialism. For communist elites, a strong presidency was seen as a way to reinvest their power in a new institution that would be independent of the legislature. For opposition forces, too, a presidency promised the ability for the people to elect their leader directly and use the office to sweep away the vestiges of communist rule. In short, the concerns often raised about presidentialism—its insulation, lack of power sharing, and the difficulty in removing presidents from office—were precisely what made this office attractive. In the end, countries chose a variety of solutions. Most of postcommunist Europe opted for parliamentary government, with presidents that hold relatively little power (even in those cases where they are directly elected). In Russia and central Asia, however, more powerful semi- or purely presidential offices were created, giving these offices an extraordinary amount of power. Interestingly, presidentialism can be correlated with the absence of democracy in postcommunist countries; where democracy is weaker, presidencies are stronger, and in Russia in particular, the presidency was used by Vladimir Putin as a way to dismantle democratic institutions. Cause and effect is not clear in these cases, however. Is it the creation of strong presidencies that have undermined democracy? Or is it weakness of democratic preconditions that helped create more authoritarian presidencies?

tasks: revising or rewriting the constitution to establish civil rights and free-doms, creating a separation of powers between branches of government, revamping judicial bodies and high courts, generating electoral laws and reg-ulating political parties, and doing all of this in such a way as to generate sup-port among the majority of actors in society.

Creating all of these institutions requires many decisions as to their final shape and form. For example, should these countries follow the European parliamentary model or opt for a presidential system like that of the United States? Most postcommunist countries in Eastern Europe opted for the prime ministerial model, while across the former Soviet Union, many adopted a semipresidential system or a purely presidential system. Another issue is that of electoral rules. Supporters of proportional representation (PR) favored that system as a way to include many different political ideologies and actors in the government, thus increasing legitimacy; opponents favored the use of single-member district (SMD) systems to create two large parties that they believed would be more effective in passing legislation. Many postcommunist countries opted for pure PR, but several opted for mixed PR and SMD.

Civil rights are a final area of concern. Under communism, constitutions typically established an elaborate set of civil liberties, though in reality such liberties were largely ignored by those in power. With the collapse of com-munism, leaders were faced with deciding how civil liberties should be con-stitutionally protected. This meant not only strengthening the rule of law so that those once-hollow rights could be enforced, but also deciding what kinds of rights should be enshrined in the constitution and who should be the final arbiter of disputes over these rights. The role of constitutional courts became a major issue in countries where traditionally the judiciary had been neither powerful nor independent.

Evaluating Political Transitions

Twenty years have passed since communism began to collapse in Eastern Europe and the former Soviet Union. How have their political transitions fared? The picture is mixed. Freedom House, a liberal nongovernmental organ-ization that studies democracy around the world, ranks countries on a 1 to 7 freedom scale, with countries given a 1 the most free and those given a 7 the least free. This ranking is based on such considerations as electoral competi-tion, freedoms of speech and assembly, rule of law, levels of corruption, and protection of human and economic rights.

As Table 8.2 shows, a number of postcommunist countries have made dra-matic strides toward democracy and the rule of law, to such an extent that Freedom House now considers them consolidated democracies—meaning that their democratic regimes have been ranked highly on the Freedom House scale

Table 8.2 Freedom in Selected Communist and Postcommunist Systems, 2007

	Political Rights	Civil Liberties	Regime Type
	(1 = most free, 7 = not free)		
Poland	1	1	Liberal democracy
Hungary	1	1	Liberal democracy
Estonia	1	1	Liberal democracy
Czech Republic	1	1	Liberal democracy
Latvia	2	1	Liberal democracy
Bulgaria	1	2	Liberal democracy
Croatia	2	2	Liberal democracy
Romania	2	2	Liberal democracy
Albania	3	3	Illiberal democracy
Moldova	3	4	Illiberal democracy
Georgia	4	4	Illiberal democracy
Ukraine	3	2	Illiberal democracy
Russia	6	5	Authoritarian
Tajikistan	6	5	Authoritarian
Kyrgyzstan	5	4	Authoritarian
Belarus	7	6	Authoritarian
China	7	6	Authoritarian
Uzbekistan	7	6	Authoritarian

Source: Freedom House.

for a decade or so and are therefore stable and fully institutionalized. The majority of these consolidated democracies can be found in central Europe (such as Hungary, Poland, and the Czech Republic) and the Baltics, areas that share a precommunist history of greater economic development, civil society, democratic institutions, and the rule of law; they also enjoyed more contact with Western Europe and a shorter period of communist rule. All of these factors may help explain why democratic transition in these regions has been more successful and culminated in EU membership. Even the Balkans, which experienced widespread violence and civil conflict only a decade ago, have seen their democratic practices improve over this decade, and the EU continues to expand into this region. Many of these countries were listed in our previous chapter, having made the transition to advanced democracies.

As we move eastward, however, the situation is less promising (Table 8.3). In many of the former Soviet states, democracy is illiberal and weakly institutionalized or completely absent. These countries tend to be poorer, with little historical experience of democracy and a long period of Soviet control. In many of these countries, authoritarian leaders have consolidated power, many of them former members of the communist *nomenklatura*. Democratic rights and freedoms are still restricted, civil society is weak, and those in power have frequently enriched themselves through corrupt practices. In many cases, it is difficult to speak of the rule of law. Equally disturbing, many of these countries have become less democratic and less lawful over time. There are a few hopeful signs; in recent years, mass movements have swept away entrenched leaders in a few of these countries in Europe and the Caucasus. Yet at the same time, Russia itself has become steadily less democratic.

Outside of Eastern Europe and the former Soviet Union, democracy has been slow to spread; in fact, several communist regimes continue to hold on to power: China, Laos, Vietnam, North Korea, and Cuba. Elsewhere in Asia and Africa, communist regimes have given way, but this has often only resulted in state collapse and civil war. Most notable is Afghanistan; upon the Soviet Union's withdrawal from that country in 1989, civil war raged until 1996, when the Taliban gained power over most of the country, thus paving the way for the eventual establishment of Al Qaeda. Thus, not everywhere has the end of communism been peaceful or democratic, and in some ways, it created a path for the current global battle against terrorism.

Table 8.3 Varying Support for A Return to Communism or Authoritarianism, 2004

Percentage Who Strongly or Somewhat Endorse Alternative Government

Country	Return to Communist Rule	Dictator Better
Czech Republic	14	16
Slovak Republic	28	21
Poland	24	48
Ukraine	25	42
Bulgaria	31	38
Russia	42	37

Source: Richard Rose, "Insiders and Outsiders: New Europe Barometer 2004," *Studies in Public Policy*, no. 404, Centre for the Study of Public Policy, University of Strathclyde.

The Transformation of Economic Institutions

In addition to transforming the state and the regime, transitions from communism have also confronted the task of reestablishing some separation between the state and the economy. This involves two processes: marketization, or the re-creation of market forces of supply and demand, and privatization, the transfer of state-held property into private hands. In both cases, decisions about how to carry out these changes and to what end were influenced by different political-economic alternatives. Let's consider the ways in which privatization and marketization can be approached before we investigate the different paths postcommunist countries have taken in each area.

Privatization and Marketization

The transition from communism to capitalism requires a redefinition of property. To generate economic growth and limit the power of the state, the state must reentrust economic resources to the public, placing them back into private hands. But the task of privatization is neither easy nor clear. In fact, prior to 1989, no country had ever gone from a communist economy to a capitalist one, so no model existed.

Among the many questions and concerns facing the postcommunist countries was how to place a price on the various elements of the economy—factories, shops, land, apartments. To privatize these assets, the state first must figure out their values, something difficult in a system where no market has existed. And who should get these assets? Should they be given away? Sold to the highest bidder? Made available to foreign investors? Each option has its own advantages in developing a thriving economy but also dangers in increasing inequality and generating public resentment.

Privatization was eventually carried out in a number of different ways, depending on the country and the kinds of economic assets. In many cases, small businesses were sold directly to their employees. Some countries did sell many large businesses to the highest bidder, often to foreign investors. Other countries essentially distributed shares in firms to the public as a whole. Scholars debated the benefits of each model, but in the

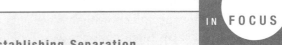

IN FOCUS

Reestablishing Separation of State and Economy

- *Privatization:* the transfer of state-held property into private hands.
- *Marketization:* the re-creation of the market forces of supply and demand.

end, there were examples where each one of these forms, whether alone or in combination, worked well (or badly).

No matter what the privatization process, in the end there were many firms in postcommunist countries that were overstaffed, outdated, and unable to turn a profit in a market economy. Most problematic were very large industrial firms, such as coal mines and steel plants built in the early years of industrialization; these antiquated behemoths are uncompetitive in the international market. Such firms often must be sold or radically downsized, leading to unemployment in a society where previously employment had been guaranteed. In some cases, such firms employed thousands of people and represented the main source of work in a city or region. To close down such firms is not an easy task for any politician, especially in a newly democratic system in which people are likely to vote with their pocketbooks and turn such leaders out of office. As a result, in some countries, privatization proceeded slowly for fear of widespread unemployment and resulting social unrest.

In addition to re-creating private property, states must re-create a market in which property, labor, goods, and services can all function in a competitive environment to determine their value. On the surface, marketization appears easier than privatization—a simple matter of eliminating central planning and allowing the market to naturally resurface. But marketization, too, is a complicated process. One issue of debate concerned how rapidly marketization should take place. Some argued that given the profound nature of the economic transformation in postcommunist states, changes should be gradual to minimize any social disruptions that might undermine these fledgling economies and democracies. In particular, supporters of this "gradualism" feared that sudden marketization would lead to a wild jump in prices as sellers became able to charge whatever they wanted for their goods. Inflation and even hyperinflation could result, undermining confidence in the transition process and generating widespread poverty. Others rejected these arguments, advocating rapid market reforms that would free prices and bring an end to central planning and state subsidies for businesses virtually overnight—a policy known as **shock therapy**. Such changes would be painful and might initially involve a high degree of inflation, but the pain would be shorter than that accompanying gradualism.

In choosing particular forms of privatization and marketization, postcommunist countries adopted new political economic models—some gravitating toward the social democratic models of Western Europe, others to the liberalism of the United States and the United Kingdom, and still others to more mercantilist policies.

Evaluating Economic Transitions

How successful have all of these reforms been? The answer again depends on what country you are looking at. Table 8.4 shows some of the results of ten years of transition. In Eastern Europe and the Baltics economic reforms have borne fruit—in some cases, dramatically. Estonia is now as wealthy as Greece; Slovakia and Hungary are comparable to Portugal. In contrast, many of the former Soviet republics have done less well. Why this variation? Those countries that have done particularly well benefited from many of the factors we discussed earlier: shorter periods of Soviet control; more precommunist experience with industrialization, markets, and private property; closer ties with Western Europe; and strong support from the European Union, including membership. Those countries that have done more poorly have experienced

Table 8.4 Economic Indicators in the Communist and Postcommunist World, 2007–2008

Country	Per capita GDP, 2007–08 (PPP, in U.S. $)	2008 GDP as a Percentage of 1989 GDP	Amount of Foreign Direct Investment, 1989–2007 (Per Capita in U.S. $)
Czech Republic*	24,200	136	6,128
Estonia[†]	21,100	155	5,756
Hungary*	19,000	135	4,915
Latvia[†]	17,400	125	3,447
Poland*	16,300	169	2,572
Croatia*	15,500	111	3,932
Russia[†]	14,700	102	199
Romania*	11,400	120	1,984
Bulgaria*	11,300	107	3,824
Belarus[†]	10,900	146	470
Ukraine[†]	6,900	68	660
Albania*	6,300	152	834
China	5,300	1,053	569
Georgia[†]	4,700	60	1,090
Moldova[†]	2,900	51	502
Uzbekistan[†]	2,300	150	62
Kyrgyzstan[†]	2,000	95	190
Tajikistan[†]	1,800	56	102

*Former communist country, Eastern Europe.
[†]Former republic of the Soviet Union.

Sources: CIA, World Bank, European Bank for Reconstruction and Development.

just the opposite. In these countries, freeing up markets often led to uncontrollable inflation and a rapid decline in the standard of living. These problems were compounded by the way privatization was carried out, with many of the most valuable assets falling into the hands of the old *nomenklatura* and/or a handful of private individuals, typically supported by corrupt political leaders. One theme that runs through all these cases is the correlation between economic growth and the rule of law. Where the rule of law is weak, economic transition is much less successful. Entrepreneurs (both domestic and international) lack a predictable environment in which to invest, while political leaders and state officials use their positions to siphon off resources for themselves.

Overall, postcommunist countries have seen an increase in inequality, relative poverty, and unemployment, which is to be expected as markets and private property become central economic forces. Where this has been balanced by economic prosperity for the majority of the population, support for change has been stronger. When the majority of the population feels worse off, as in much of the former Soviet Union, economic change has bred resentment, nostalgia for the old order, and obstacles to democratization. Russia is a particularly notable example, where during the last decade there has been a renationalization of many large industries and more mercantilist policies toward the economy.

Outside of Eastern Europe and the former Soviet Union, economic transition is equally varied. Much attention has been focused on China, which, as we noted, historically had a much more weakly institutionalized system of central planning and control over property. Since the 1970s, China's reforms have included a dramatic expansion of private business and agriculture, all with the support of the Chinese Communist Party. The slogan of this economic reform—"To get rich is glorious"—sounds anything but Marxist, but it is rooted in the practical realization that earlier drives for rapid economic growth led to disaster. Some observers argue that these reforms have succeeded where reforms in many other communist countries have failed because the Chinese introduced economic transition while restricting political change so as to better manage the course of reform. Indeed, since 1989, the Chinese economy has grown by leaps and bounds, lifting hundreds of millions out of poverty and dramatically transforming the country, not to mention world trade.

Yet the Chinese model has its problems. Along with economic growth and the development of a free market and private property, problems such as inflation, rampant corruption, unemployment, and growing inequality have also surfaced, often exacerbated by the still-powerful presence of the state in the Chinese economy. The lack of the rule of law only compounds these problems. China's rapid development has been profound; the question is to what extent this will continue into the future. Some see in China a growing economic superpower that will eclipse much of Asia and perhaps the world. This development could, in turn, foster a middle class that would pave the way for the democratization of one-fifth of the world's population. Others believe that the Chinese "miracle" covers up serious problems, such as conflict between urban and rural, rich and poor, alongside significant environmental problems. China could see a future of greater development, greater liberty, and greater conflict, all at the same time.[15]

The Transformation of Societal Institutions

Like political systems and economies, societies, too, have been fundamentally transformed in postcommunist countries. Where once communist control asserted one interpretation of human relations, people now face a future much more uncertain and unclear. Postcommunist societies have the potential for greater individual action, but with this potential comes greater risk. The elimination of an all-encompassing ideology from people's lives has created a social vacuum that must be filled. In all of these countries, the transition from communism has been a wrenching process as people adjust to new realities and seek new individual and collective identities.

Re-creating Identities

This transformation of society has manifested itself in a number of different ways. Religion, once suppressed by Communist parties, has resurfaced in many countries. In Eastern Europe and parts of the former Soviet Union, Western evangelical movements have made many new converts; in other parts of the former Soviet Union, such as central Asia, Islam has reemerged as a powerful force, with thousands of mosques and religious schools built in part with funds from other Muslim countries, such as Saudi Arabia. In many countries, this return to religion has helped rebuild social norms and values and has also led to the emergence of fundamentalism and increased conflict between politics and religion. In China, too, new and old religious movements are gaining strength. For example, the spiritual group Falun Gong, which attracted somewhere between 70 million and 100 million followers in the 1990s, was the target of a harsh crackdown by government authorities, who feared any organization that could command greater loyalty than the regime.[16] Underground Christian churches in China may claim a similar number of members. In the face of economic hardship, corruption, and often still-oppressive regimes, this religious resurgence should not be surprising: religion can play an important role in providing people with a sense of community and purpose.

Like religion, ethnic and national identities have reemerged as potent forms of group identification. In many postcommunist countries, both leaders and publics have sought to reinstill national pride and resurrect the values, symbols, and ideas that bind people together. The scope of this task varies among the postcommunist countries. In much of Eastern Europe, a clear sense of ethnic and national identity has existed for many generations, and in spite of communist rule, many of these social structures not only remained intact but were reinforced as a form of resistance. In contrast, across the diverse ethnic groups of the former Soviet Union, national identity has historically been much weaker. Many of these peoples have few ethnic or national institutions to draw on, and their identities are not so much being resurrected as they are being created from scratch, with new words, anthems, symbols, and myths. All such identities can be a double-edged sword, of course. Although they can help mobilize the public and provide stability in a time of great transition, religious, ethnic, and national identities can also generate division and conflict, particularly when several identities coexist in one country or in opposition to the state or regime.

The changes under way in social identities cannot help but affect gender relations as well. Recall our earlier discussion of how communist theory advances the radical notion of gender equality. Although equality was not truly realized in practice, women were incorporated into the workforce and provided with social benefits that generated new opportunities for them. With the end of communism, however, many of these policies and institutions have been weakened or challenged. Critics have attacked many communist-era practices such as easy access to abortions, while economic reforms have cut back much of the elaborate social safety net that once benefited women and families. The reemergence of religion has also challenged women's roles in society in some cases.

Evaluating Societal Transitions

New societies in postcommunist countries have developed in very different ways. In some, the emergence of new religious and national identities has contributed to violence and civil war. In Eastern Europe, the dissolution of Yugoslavia pitted ethnic and religious groups against one another, claiming more than 200,000 lives. Parts of the former Soviet Union, such as Tajikistan, Chechnya (part of Russia), Uzbekistan, Moldova, Azerbaijan, and Armenia, also have seen violent conflicts with thousands killed. Finally, the almost endless wars in Afghanistan since the 1970s are yet another tragedy whose consequences have rippled throughout the domestic and international communities. In Afghanistan during the 1980s, volunteers from numerous Muslim countries, such as Osama bin Laden, fought alongside Afghan guerrillas against Soviet occupation in what they saw as a need to defend Muslims from atheist communism. At the end of that conflict and the dissolution of the Soviet Union, some of these fighters turned their attention toward the postcommunist world, taking up the cause of Muslim populations in central Asia, the Caucasus, and the Balkans. What were regional and ethnic conflicts quickly became international and religious ones, feeding into the idea of a global war to defend Islam.[17] Other fighters would later regroup in Afghanistan, forming Al Qaeda—"the base"—under bin Laden's leadership as a launching pad for this international jihad. Thus, the current struggle against Al Qaeda and related groups has its origins in the collapse of communism.

However, we should recall that much of the postcommunist world has been largely peaceful over the past decade, with ethnic and religious conflicts resolved or averted. Nationalism also has not been a significant force in most of these countries. This is consistent with data from the World Values Survey and the Pew Research Center, which indicate that national pride among postcommunist countries has not changed significantly since 1990 and that few of them show a level of national pride commensurate with that of the United States or Canada (where 60 to 70 percent of those surveyed said they were "very proud" of their nationality). In the area of religion, too, the surveys show that in many postcommunist countries people do not believe that faith is an important precondition for political leadership or that religion is a necessary foundation for morality. (An important distinction appears to be Central Asia, where religion has become an important force since 1991.)

Two important exceptions are Russia and China. In both countries there has been a growing nationalism—in part, generated by the government as a way to shore up legitimacy in the absence of communist ideology. This nationalism emphasizes mistreatment by the West and emphasizes the unique nature of Chinese or Russian identity. Such values may be part of the difficult transitions these countries are making. They may fade in time, but they have complicated relations with the rest of the world over such things as NATO and the European Union, Tibet, and Taiwan.[18] Given the size and relative power of these two countries, the future of their national identities has the potential to strongly affect the rest of the world.

Gender relations in postcommunist countries are similarly complex to evaluate and measure. The United Nations tracks data across several indicators that measure the standard of living and differences in that standard between genders, and the results are mixed. The UN's Gender Empowerment Measure (GEM) ranks countries on the extent to which women and men are able to actively participate in economic and political life and take part in decision making in those arenas. The Gender Development Index (GDI), meanwhile, draws from the Human Development Index (see Chapter 4) to investigate life expectancy, education, and income, with an emphasis on inequalities between women and men. When we consider these rankings, we find that in the wealthier postcommunist countries, such as Slovenia, GEM and GDI rankings fall at the outer range of the advanced democracies' rankings (see Table 8.5). However, many others lag further

Table 8.5 Gender Development Index and Gender Empowerment Rankings 1995–2008

	GDI, 1995	GDI, 2005	GEM, 2008
Iceland	4	1	5
Canada	1	4	10
France	7	7	18
United Kingdom	11	10	14
Japan	13	13	54
United States	6	16	15
Germany	17	20	9
Slovenia	24	25	41
Czech Republic	25	29	34
Hungary	34	34	50
Poland	35	35	39
Lithuania	62	38	25
Slovakia	26	39	33
Estonia	59	41	31
Latvia	71	44	38
Croatia	61	46	40
Cuba	69	49	26
Bulgaria	47	50	42
Mexico	49	51	46
Romania	57	53	68
Belarus	51	56	n/a
Russian Federation	53	58	71
Brazil	56	59	70
Albania	91	60	n/a
Kazakhstan	73	64	74
Ukraine	83	68	75
China	93	72	57
Armenia	75	74	n/a
Iran	92	83	87
Azerbaijan	100	86	n/a
Vietnam	108	90	52
Moldova	101	96	55
Uzbekistan	86	97	n/a
Mongolia	84	99	77
Kyrgyzstan	97	101	89
Tajikistan	106	105	n/a
South Africa	74	106	n/a
India	128	112	n/a
Cambodia	129	113	83
Lao People's Democratic Republic	125	114	n/a
Nigeria	133	138	n/a

Note: Countries are ranked from highest to lowest among 177 countries surveyed. Countries in italics are non-Communist examples used for comparison.

behind, particularly in Central Asia, China, and Russia. More worrisome, in Russia and Central Asia, the GDI rankings have stagnated or declined over the past decade even as the majority of other postcommunist states have trended in the opposite direction. This reinforces the idea that as we move further away from communism, a number of these states are moving into the category of the advanced democracies while others may more closely resemble less-developed countries. As with national identity, Russia and China are cases where the direction of change remains open to question.

In Sum: The Legacy of Communism

According to Marxist thought, capitalism inevitably led to great industrialization but also to great injustice, a contradiction that would result in its downfall. Communism would build on capitalism's ruins to generate a society of total equality. But constructing communism proved to be a daunting task. People within communist systems found almost no incentive for hard work and innovation and had little freedom to express themselves individually.

For the Soviet Union and Eastern Europe, attempts to solve these problems led to outright collapse. One might use the analogy of renovating a dilapidated house only to find that the whole structure is unsound and that renovations are only making the situation worse. At that point, one has to either demolish the whole structure or be demolished by it. In 1989, people in a number of Eastern European countries chose to demolish the institutions of communism. Communist structures in the Soviet Union eventually collapsed on the Communist Party and Soviet society. China seems to be in a process of endless (and perhaps precarious) remodeling, while other communist countries, such as Cuba, have yet to carry out any major reforms.

It is not clear what the coming decades will bring to the postcommunist world. All of these societies are attempting to grapple again with the dilemma of freedom and equality. New political, economic, and social institutions are needed, but in many cases they must be forged out of the rubble of the old order, a situation that is creating unique difficulties and contradictions. Over the past decade, both individual freedom and collective inequality have grown in many countries. Increased civil liberties have arisen alongside poverty, and the rebirth of society alongside conflict and hostility.

The results of this diverse process have been dramatically different across the communist and postcommunist world. In some countries, we see the institutionalization of democracy and capitalism; in others, authoritarianism and state-controlled economies remain in place. Moreover, it is apparent that over time, these countries will grow increasingly dissimilar. Democratic consolidation and economic growth in Eastern Europe appear to have placed many of these countries on the path to becoming advanced democracies. Within parts of the former Soviet Union, however, economic stagnation or decline, political instability, and nondemocratic rule are more common; those countries more resemble the less-developed world. China and Russia remain question marks.

Communism as a set of political institutions may now be finished. Yet even if this is the case, the motivations that drove these institutions—the desire to eliminate inequality—remains. And in fact, these concerns have fed into a recent wave of populist ideas in Latin America, inspired in part by Marxist and Leninist thought. As long as inequality or poverty remains, there will be room for ideologies that seek to use politics and the state to create economic justice.

NOTES

1. For a good overview of communist theory see Alfred Meyer, *Communism* (New York: Random House, 1984).
2. See Marx's 1882 preface to the Russian translation of the *Communist Manifesto*; www.marxists.org.
3. See V. I. Lenin, *What Is to Be Done? Burning Questions of Our Movement*, Joe Fineberg and George Hanna, trans. (New York: International, 1969).
4. For a comparative discussion of different communist systems, see Stephen White, John Gardner, George Schopflin, and Tony Saich, *Communist and Post-Communist Political Systems* (New York: St. Martin's, 1990).
5. See Michael Voslensky, *Nomenklatura: Anatomy of the Soviet Ruling Class* (Garden City, NY: Doubleday, 1984).
6. See Robert Conquest, *The Great Terror: A Reassessment* (New York: Oxford University Press, 1990).
7. See Lowell Dittmer, *China's Continuous Revolution: The Post-Liberation Epoch, 1949–1981* (Berkeley: University of California Press, 1987).
8. Robert W. Campbell, *The Socialist Economies in Transition: A Primer on Semi-Reformed Systems* (Bloomington: Indiana University Press, 1991).
9. Dali Yang, *Calamity and Reform in China: Rural Society and Institutional Change since the Great Leap Famine* (Stanford, CA: Stanford University Press, 1996).
10. Karl Marx and Friedrich Engels, *Manifesto of the Communist Party*, available online at www.marxists.org/archive/marx/works/1848/communist-manifesto/.
11. Joni Lovenduski and Jean Woodall, *Politics and Society in Eastern Europe* (Bloomington: Indiana University Press, 1987), p. s158.
12. Marcy McAuley, *Soviet Politics 1917–1991* (New York: Oxford University Press, 1992).
13. The best retrospective studies of the collapse of communism in Eastern Europe and its effects in the Soviet Union can be found in Mark Kramer, "The Collapse of East European Communism and the Repercussions within the Soviet Union," Parts 1–3, *Journal of Cold War Studies* (Fall 2003, Fall 2004, and Spring 2005.)

14. On the collapse of communism in Eastern Europe, see Timothy Garton Ash, *The Magic Lantern: The Revolution of 1989 Witnessed in Warsaw, Budapest, Berlin and Prague* (New York: Random House, 1990); on the Soviet Union, see David Remnick, *Lenin's Tomb: The Last Days of the Soviet Empire* (New York: Random House, 1993).

15. See Minxin Pei, *China's Trapped Transition: The Limits of Developmental Autocracy* (Cambridge, MA: Harvard University Press, 2006).

16. See the website of Falun Gong at www.faluninfo.net/.

17. This idea is articulated in Abdullah Azzam, *Join the Caravan* (London: Azzam, 2001).

18. See, for example, Xu Wu *Chinese Cybernationalism: Evolution, Characteristics, and Implications* (Lanham, MD: Lexington, 2007), and Marlene Laurelle, *Russian Nationalism in Putin's Russia* (New York: Routledge, 2009).

LESS-DEVELOPED AND NEWLY INDUSTRIALIZING COUNTRIES

KEY CONCEPTS

- Less-developed and newly industrializing countries have both struggled with economic and political development.

- Imperialism and colonialism strongly affected less-developed and newly industrializing countries' state, societal, and economic institutions.

- Many postimperial countries have suffered from ethnic and national division, limited economic growth, and weak states.

- Scholars and policy makers are increasingly turning to civil society, small-scale economic development, and political decentralization as pathways to development and democracy.

So far, we have investigated two major parts of the world—the advanced democracies, often described as the First World, and communist and postcommunist countries, or what has been known as the Second World. But these two categories leave out much of Latin America, Asia, and Africa. These regions are populated with countries that historically have had neither liberal democratic nor communist regimes. Moreover, the vast majority of these countries have levels of economic industrialization far below those in the advanced democracies or the communist and postcommunist world. The traditional labeling of these countries as belonging to the Third World unhelpfully grouped together a diverse range of people and political systems according to what they were not, rather than what they were—what we call a residual category.

How, then, should we understand these countries? Whereas the advanced democracies are noted for their early modernization and capitalist development, and the communist states for their later rapid modernization and industrialization directed by the state, the countries that are the subject of this

chapter are characterized by their mixture of premodern and modern institutions and a hybrid of economic, societal, and political institutions, both foreign and indigenous.

In this chapter, we will attempt to develop some ideas and categories to
investigate and understand this part of the world. We will begin by distinguishing between newly industrializing and less-developed countries and
examine the relationship between freedom and equality. From there we will
look at some of the fundamental experiences and institutions that these countries share, particularly those associated with imperialism and colonialism.
Although imperialism had different effects in different parts of the world, there
are generalizations we can make about its legacies. Next we will consider what
challenges and obstacles these countries have faced after gaining independence. How does a country reconcile freedom and equality when the conditions may favor neither? And how is it that some countries have managed to
enjoy economic and political development while others have stagnated or
declined? These topics will lead us into a final discussion of the prospects for
political, economic, and societal development in this part of the world. What
policies might help generate greater democracy, political stability, and economic prosperity in these countries? The difficulties they face are great and
the tasks daunting. But out of such dilemmas can emerge new ideas and innovations with the potential for positive change.

Freedom and Equality in the Newly Industrializing and Less-Developed Countries

The countries of what was traditionally referred to as the Third World are
in fact often divided into two groups that indicate important differences in
their levels of development. Over the past fifty years, some countries, particularly in Asia and parts of Latin America, have experienced dramatic rates
of economic growth and democratization, to the point that they now resemble the advanced democracies in many ways. These are typically known as
newly industrializing countries (NICs). Although this name emphasizes
their rapid economic growth, in recent years many newly industrializing
countries have also shown a marked tendency toward democratization and
political and social stability, such that many such countries are also listed
in Chapter 7 as moving into the category of advanced democracies. South
Korea is one such country. A relatively poor agricultural country in the early
1960s, divided and damaged by the Korean War, over the next fifty years
South Korea became one of the world's largest economies and slowly developed a set of democratic institutions alongside its growing wealth. In coun-

tries such as South Korea, one finds an effective state, a web of non-governmental institutions and civil society, and a robust economy. Such countries, however, tend to be in the minority. In many other cases, economic and political structures have remained weak or grown weaker over the past decades; these countries are marked by economic stagnation or even decline, with some sliding into poverty, violence, and civil conflict. These countries are often referred to as the **less-developed countries (LDCs)**, a term that implies a lack of significant economic development or political institutionalization (Table 9.1). An example here might be the country of Ghana in Africa. Despite expectations in the 1960s that this newly independent country was on the road to rapid political and economic development, Ghana sank into economic stagnation, political instability, and authoritarian rule. Paradoxically, in the early 1960s Ghana had a higher per capita gross domestic product (GDP) than did South Korea. What happened? We will return to this puzzle later in the chapter.

Thus, as with postcommunist countries, newly industrializing and less-developed countries have grown increasingly dissimilar, making it difficult to place them in a single category. However, comparisons remain valuable in trying to understand why these variations have taken place. Why have some countries broken out of the trap of underdevelopment and others not? Is it a question of how states are constructed? Regimes? Political economic systems? Democracy or the lack thereof? Ethnic, national, or religious institutions? Culture? Are there lessons that could be drawn from the NICs that could be adapted and applied elsewhere? Does South Korea, for example, provide "lessons" for a country like Ghana, or is Eastern Europe's experience after communism useful in improving conditions in Latin America? These are big questions and in recent years have generated some very heated debates.

Before we address the problems of the present, we should return to our history. Irrespective of current conditions, what less-developed and newly industrialized countries share in common is that they have a legacy of colonialism and imperialism and they were formerly part of much larger empires, possessions of more powerful states. This imperial rule, which lasted for decades or even centuries, dramatically and often rapidly transformed economic, political, and societal institutions in these countries. Although resistance eventually brought down imperial rule, the changes wrought by this system could not be easily unmade. To better understand these institutional legacies, it is worth looking at them in some detail, though we should also keep in mind that history is not destiny—imperialism matters, but it is only one factor in explaining the problems of the postimperial world.

Table 9.1 Less-Developed and Newly Industrializing Countries, 2009

Central and South America	Asia	North Africa and Middle East	Sub-Saharan Africa (continued)
Antigua & Barbuda	Afghanistan	Algeria	Equatorial Guinea
Argentina	Bahrain	Egypt	Gabon
Belize	Bangladesh	Eritrea	Gambia
Bolivia	Bhutan	Ethiopia	Ghana
Brazil	Brunei	Iran	Guinea
Chile	Burma (Myanmar)	Iraq	Guinea-Bissau
Colombia	Cambodia	Jordan	Ivory Coast
Costa Rica	Cyprus	Lebanon	Kenya
Dominica	Fiji	Libya	Lesotho
Dominican Republic	India	Morocco	Liberia
Ecuador	Indonesia	Oman	Madagascar
El Salvador	Kiribati	Qatar	Malawi
Grenada	Korea (South)	Saudi Arabia	Mali
Guatemala	Kuwait	Syria	Mauritania
Guyana	Laos	United Arab Emirates	Mauritius
Haiti	Malaysia	Yemen	Mozambique
Honduras	Maldives		Namibia
Jamaica	Marshall Islands	**Sub-Saharan Africa**	Niger
Mexico	Micronesia		Nigeria
Nicaragua	Nauru	Angola	Rwanda
Panama	Nepal	Benin	São Tomé and Príncipe
Paraguay	Palau	Botswana	Senegal
Peru	Pakistan	Burkina Faso	Seychelles
St. Kitts & Nevis	Papua New Guinea	Burundi	Sierra Leone
St. Lucia	Philippines	Cameroon	Somalia
St. Vincent & the Grenadines	Samoa	Cape Verde	South Africa
Suriname	Singapore	Central African Republic	Sudan
Trinidad & Tobago	Solomon Islands	Chad	Swaziland
Uruguay	Sri Lanka	Comoros	Tanzania
Venezuela	Taiwan	Congo (Republic of)	Togo
	Thailand	Congo (Democratic Republic of)	Tunisia
Europe	Tonga	Djibouti	Uganda
Turkey	Turkey		Zambia
	Tuvalu		Zimbabwe
	Vanuatu		
	Vietnam		

Imperialism and Colonialism

In the first three chapters of this book, we saw that over the past millennium, Europe, the Middle East, and Asia embarked on a series of dramatic societal, economic, and political changes that formed the outlines of what are now recognized as the hallmarks of modern society: ethnic and national identity, technological innovation, and political centralization. This growing power was soon projected outward to conquer and incorporate new lands and peoples that could contribute to this rapid development. The result was the emergence of **empires**, which are defined as single political authorities that have under their sovereignty a large number of external regions or territories and different peoples. Although this definition might lead one to conclude that any large, diverse country is an empire, central to the definition is the idea that lands and peoples that are not seen as an integral part of the country itself are nonetheless under its direct control. The term **imperialism** describes the system whereby a state extends its power to directly control territory, resources, and people beyond its borders. The term *imperialism* is often used interchangeably with the term **colonialism**, though they are different. Colonialism indicates to a greater degree the physical occupation of a foreign territory through military force, businesses, or settlers. Colonialism, then, is often a means to consolidate one's empire.

Although imperialist practices date back many thousands of years, modern imperialism can be dated from the 1500s, when technological development in Europe, the Middle East, and Asia—advanced seafaring and military technology in particular—had advanced to such an extent that these countries were able to project their military might far overseas. In Asia, the powerful Chinese Empire turned away from this path. Having consolidated power hundreds of years before the states of Europe did, the Chinese state had grown conservative and inflexible, interested more in maintaining the status quo than in striking out to acquire new lands. Indeed, at the same time that Europeans were setting out for the Americas, the Chinese were actually retreating from overseas voyages; by 1500, it had become illegal for Chinese subjects to build oceangoing vessels. Similarly, in the Middle East, the powerful Ottoman Empire expanded its power over much of the Arab world and into Asia, North Africa, and

IN FOCUS

Imperialism Is . . .

- A system in which a state extends its power beyond its borders to control other territories and peoples.
- Propagated by European powers from the sixteenth to the twenty-first centuries.
- Driven by economic, strategic, and religious motives.
- Often led to *colonialism*, the physical occupation of foreign territories.

parts of Europe, nearly conquering Vienna in 1683. But the Ottoman Empire also turned inward and lost interest in technological innovation and in expanding power beyond the Islamic world, for reasons that are open to debate and will be discussed later. In contrast, the Europeans saw imperialism as a means to expand their resources, markets, subjects, and territory in order to gain the upper hand in their frequent battles with one another.

What should be clear is that those peoples who became subject to modern imperialism were not a blank slate, without any of their own institutions. On the contrary, many of the regions that were so dominated already possessed their own highly developed economic, political, and societal systems, in some cases as sophisticated as those found in Europe, or even more advanced. Nevertheless, they lacked the military power to withstand European imperial pressure.

TIME LINE / MODERN IMPERIALISM

1494	Following European discovery, Spain and Portugal partition the Americas between their two empires.
1519–1536	Indigenous groups (Aztecs, Incas) are defeated by imperial powers in South America.
1602–1652	Dutch begin to establish control over parts of Indonesian archipelago and southern Africa. English settlement begins in North America.
1810–1825	Wars of independence in Latin America; Spanish and Portuguese rule is brought to an end.
1839–1858	United Kingdom expands control into Asia, notably Hong Kong and India.
1884	The Berlin Conference: Africa is rapidly divided among European powers, notably France, Portugal, and Belgium.
1939–1945	World War II catalyzes the eventual decolonization of Asia and Africa.
1947	Independence of India; first major decolonization of twentieth century.
1956–1968	Independence of most British, French, and Belgian colonies in Africa after local rebellions against imperial rule.
1975	Independence of most former Portuguese colonies in Africa and Asia.
1997–1999	Hong Kong (United Kingdom) and Macau (Portugal) returned to China.

Thus, starting in the sixteenth century, Europe began a process of imperialism that would not end for nearly five centuries. Driven by economic and strategic motives as well as by a belief that Christianity and Western culture needed to be brought to the rest of the world, European empires stretched their power around the globe. First, Spain and Portugal gained control over South and Central America. By the seventeenth century, British, French, and other settlers began to arrive in North America, displacing the local population. In the eighteenth century, Europeans began to assert control over parts of North Africa and the Middle East, shocking Ottoman elites who had long viewed Europeans as technologically and culturally backward. This shock was shared by the Chinese in the nineteenth and early twentieth centuries as European imperialism rapidly expanded into Asia. Nearly all of Africa, too, was eventually divided up by the European states. This European imperialist expansion was joined briefly by Japan, which in the early twentieth century established its own empire across parts of Asia. In each of these cases, imperial powers possessed well-organized political systems, military structures, technological advances, and economic resources; these advantages were combined with a belief that imperial control was not only possible, but necessary, just, and willed by God.[1]

Institutions of Imperialism

The effect that imperialism had on those societies that came under foreign rule differs across time and place, but some common elements resulted from the imposition of modern political, societal, and economic systems onto largely premodern societies. As we shall see, the imposition of modern institutions onto premodern peoples had a dramatic (and often traumatic) effect that continues to the present.[2]

Exporting the State

One of the first major effects of imperialism was the transfer of the state to the rest of the world. Recall from Chapter 2 how the modern state that we take for granted today emerged as a result of a long historical process in Europe; prior to that time, political units tended to have much weaker control over land and their subjects, and territorial sovereignty was rather tenuous. States, however, eventually succeeded in consolidating power over other forms of political organization, eliminating their rivals, clearly delineating their borders, and establishing sovereignty.

When European empires began to expand around the world, new territories were incorporated into these state structures, territories carved up by rival states in the quest for economic resources and strategic advantages. The borders drawn by imperial states were often reflections of their own power or cartography rather than existing geographical, religious, or linguistic realities. Recall that in Chapter 2 we noted that the borders of 80 percent of African states are drawn according to longitude and latitude, not local geography or the boundaries of populations on the ground. Many of these externally imposed and arbitrary boundaries later became the demarcations for independent countries once imperial rule ended. Even those countries that were able to resist direct imperial rule, such as Iran or Ethiopia, nevertheless found themselves under the continuous influence and pressure of these empires.

Having conquered these territories, imperial powers went about establishing state power and authority. In many empires, this meant establishing bureaucratic structures similar to those found in the home country in an attempt to "civilize"—to modernize and Westernize—the local population. These institutions commonly included the establishment of a national language (typically that of the imperial power), police and military, taxation and legal systems, and basic public goods such as roads, schools, and hospitals. How this process was carried out and enforced differed. Some empires relied on local leaders to enforce their will whereas others bypassed indigenous elites in favor of their own centralized forms of authority. (These differences tended to reflect the degree of state capacity and autonomy found in the imperial country itself.) In both cases, few if any democratic practices were introduced, even if they were the norm in the home country. Individuals under colonial rule were considered subjects, not citizens, and thus had few political rights.

This imposition of the state had mixed effects. Many subject peoples experienced increased education and the benefits of a basic infrastructure that improved communication and transportation. Life expectancies rose and infant mortality rates declined, although when those trends were combined with traditional family practices, they produced a population explosion that in many poor countries continues today. Traditional institutions such as local religions and customs were eroded and replaced by or fused with modern practices and institutions. This transition was incomplete and uneven. Imperial territories remained economically and politically underdeveloped, placing many subject peoples in a kind of limbo—no longer part of a premodern system but not fully incorporated into the modern one. The frustration that grew out of this conflict over identity helped fan the flames of anti-imperialism, the desire for freedom from foreign control.

Social Identities

The imposition of organizational forms from outside included various new identities that often displaced or were incorporated into existing social institutions. Among these were ethnic and national identities. In much of the world that came under imperial control, people identified themselves by tribe or religion, by economic position, or by vocation rather than by some ethnic or national identity (which were essentially modern institutions). But just as empires brought their own political institutions with them, the concepts of ethnicity and nation were also introduced by the new ruling powers. Imperial elites, themselves shaped and defined by national and ethnic identities, took great interest in identifying and classifying different ethnic groups in the regions they came to occupy and structuring their political and economic control around these classifications. The irony here is that even as groups were subject to Western classification, they were often divided across imperial borders that had been drawn with little regard for their ethnicity, religion, or any other characteristic.

Suddenly, people who had never thought of themselves as being part of an ethnic group found that their basic rights were tied to how they were ethnically defined by the empire. In some cases, this ethnic classification was determined by early pseudo-scientific notions of race, which held that certain ethnic groups were naturally superior to others. The European and Japanese empires were influenced by the assumption that the colonizing race was superior to the colonized and thus destined to rule them. Different peoples within the empire, too, were subject to hierarchical classification. Certain ethnic groups were promoted to positions of power and economic advantage while other groups were marginalized. Colonialism often further exacerbated these hierarchies as non-indigenous peoples migrated into colonies. Sometimes these migrants were settlers from the home country; in other cases, they were peoples from other parts of the empire or beyond it (for example, Indians migrating into Africa or African slaves brought to Brazil). These foreign presences further sharpened ethnic and racial divisions, especially when such groups were accorded specific economic or political privileges. In short, inequality and ethnicity, or race, became tightly interconnected and rigid.

In addition to ethnicity, imperial powers also introduced the idea of national identity. During the late nineteenth and early twentieth centuries, in particular, national identity grew to be a powerful force in the industrializing world, helping give shape to the imperialist cause. But the peoples brought under imperial control had little familiarity with

---

IN FOCUS

Political and Social Institutions of Imperialism

- The state, as a form of political organization, was imposed on much of the world outside of Europe.
- Ethnic and national identities were created where none had existed prior to colonization.
- Gender roles from the imperial country were often imposed on colonies.

national identity, little notion of any right to a sovereign state. This combination of nationalism and imperialism proved dangerous. Empires viewed the peoples living in their overseas possessions as inferior subjects and gave them only a limited ability to improve their standing within the empire. Yet the imperial powers' own concept of nationalism provided these subject peoples with the very means to challenge foreign rule. If nationalism meant the right for a people—any people—to live under their own sovereign state, did this not mean that subject peoples had a right to rule themselves? Empires would thus provide the ideological ammunition that their subjects would eventually use to overturn imperialism.

Colonialism also affected gender roles within the colonies. It is hard to make generalizations in this area, since in each region existing gender roles differed greatly and each imperial power viewed gender in a somewhat different way. Some scholars argue that on balance, imperialism brought a number of benefits to women, increasing their freedom and equality by improving their access to health care and education. Others reject this argument, asserting that quite the reverse occurred in many cases. In many premodern societies, gender roles may have been much less fixed than those found in the modern world, allowing women particular areas of individual freedom and relative equality with men. For example, in precolonial Nigeria, the women of the Igbo people wielded substantial political power. Under British imperialism, however, gender roles in Nigeria became much more rigid and hierarchical. Imperial powers brought with them their own assumptions regarding the subordinate status of women, views that were shaped in part by their religious values. These views were imposed through such policies as education and the legal system. The economic systems imposed by the colonizers marginalized women in many ways. On balance, although imperialism may have provided new avenues for women, this progress may have come at the cost of other freedoms or areas of equality that women once enjoyed in their premodern societies.[3]

Dependent Development

Just as imperialism transformed political and social institutions in colonial areas, creating an amalgam of premodern and modern forms, economic change similarly occurred in a dramatic and uneven way.[4] The first important change in most imperial possessions was the replacement of a traditional agricultural economy with one driven by the needs of the industrializing capitalist home country. Systems based largely on subsistence agriculture and barter were transformed into cash economies, in which money was introduced as a means to pay for goods and labor.

Alongside this introduction of a cash-based economy came the transformation of economic production. Using a mercantilist political-economic sys-

IN FOCUS

**Economic Institutions
of Imperialism**

- Traditional agricultural economies were transformed to suit the needs of the imperialist power.
- Free trade was often suppressed as colonies were forced to supply goods only to the imperial country, creating extractive economies in the colonies.
- Economic organization under imperialism impeded domestic development in the colonies.

tem (see Chapter 4), empires sought to extract revenue from their colonies while at the same time using these territories and their people as a captive market for finished goods from the home country. Free trade thus did not exist for the colonies, which were obliged to sell and buy goods within the confines of the empire. In addition, colonial production was organized to provide those goods that were not easily available in the home country. Rather than finished goods, local economies were rebuilt around primary products such as cotton, cocoa, coffee, tea, wood, rubber, and other valuable commodities that could be extracted from the natural environment. Large businesses were established to oversee these so-called extractive economies, which were often dominated by a single monopoly. For example, in Indonesia, the United East India Company, a Dutch firm, gained control over lucrative spice exports while monopolizing the local market for finished goods from Europe, thereby destroying indigenous trade networks that had existed in the region for centuries. Similarly, the British East India Company functioned virtually as a state of its own, controlling a large portion of the Indian economy and much of its foreign trade. Export-oriented imperialism also led to the creation of large plantations that could produce vast quantities of rubber, coffee, or tobacco.

This form of economic organization was quite different from that of the home countries and in many respects was ill suited to domestic development. Infrastructure was often developed only to facilitate effective extraction and export rather than to improve communication or movement for the subject peoples; jobs were created in the extractive sector, but local industrialization and entrepreneurialism were limited; the development of agriculture for export instead of for subsistence damaged the ability of these peoples to feed themselves, and the creation of large-scale agricultural production drove many small farmers off the land. Many colonies saw a resulting boom in urbanization, typically centered around the colonial capital or other cities central to imperial politics and trade. By the late 1500s, for example, the Spanish had established more than 200 cities in Latin America, which to this day remain the central urban areas in the region.

Let us take a moment to summarize what we have considered so far. By virtue of their organizational strengths, modern states expanded their power around the globe, establishing new political, economic, and social institutions and displacing existing ones. In some cases, these institutions were reflections of the home country; in others, they were designed specifically to consolidate imperial rule. The result was an uneasy mixture of indigenous and foreign structures, premodern and modern. New political institutions and new societal identities were introduced or imposed while participation and citizenship were restricted; economic development was encouraged but in a form that would serve the markets of the home country. Imperialism thus generated new identities and conflict by classifying people and distinguishing between them—between rulers and ruled and between subject peoples themselves. At the same time, the contradictions inherent in this inequality and limitation on freedom became increasingly clear to subject peoples as they began to assimilate modern ideas and values. By the early twentieth century, the growing awareness of this system and its inherent contradictions helped foster public resistance to imperialism and would pave the way for eventual independence.

The Challenges of Postimperialism

Despite the power of empires to extend their control over much of the world, their time eventually came to an end. In Latin America, where European imperialism first emerged, Napoleon's invasion of Spain and Portugal in 1807–1808 led to turmoil in the colonies and a series of wars for independence, which freed most of the region by 1826. In Africa and Asia, where imperialism reached its zenith only in the nineteenth century, decolonization came after World War II. Numerous independence movements emerged within the Asian and African colonies, catalyzed by the weakened positions of the imperial powers and promoted by a Western-educated indigenous leadership able to articulate nationalist goals and organize resistance. Some imperial powers resisted bitterly: Portugal, for example, did not fully withdraw from Africa until 1975. Hong Kong was returned to China by the United Kingdom in 1997. For the most part, however, colonies in Africa and Asia gained independence in the 1950s and 1960s (Figure 9.1).

The elimination of imperialism, however, did not mean a sudden end to the problems of the newly industrializing and less-developed countries. Over the past half century, these countries have continued to struggle with political, social, and economic challenges to development and stability, freedom and equality. In many cases, these problems are a legacy of imperial rule, although in other cases they stem from particular domestic and international factors that have developed in the years since independence. But herein lies an important puzzle. If we consider the development of successful economic, social, and political institutions over the past fifty years, Asia has fared the best, Africa the worst, while the picture in Latin America is mixed. Why this

Figure 9.1   **THE DECOLONIZATION OF AFRICA**

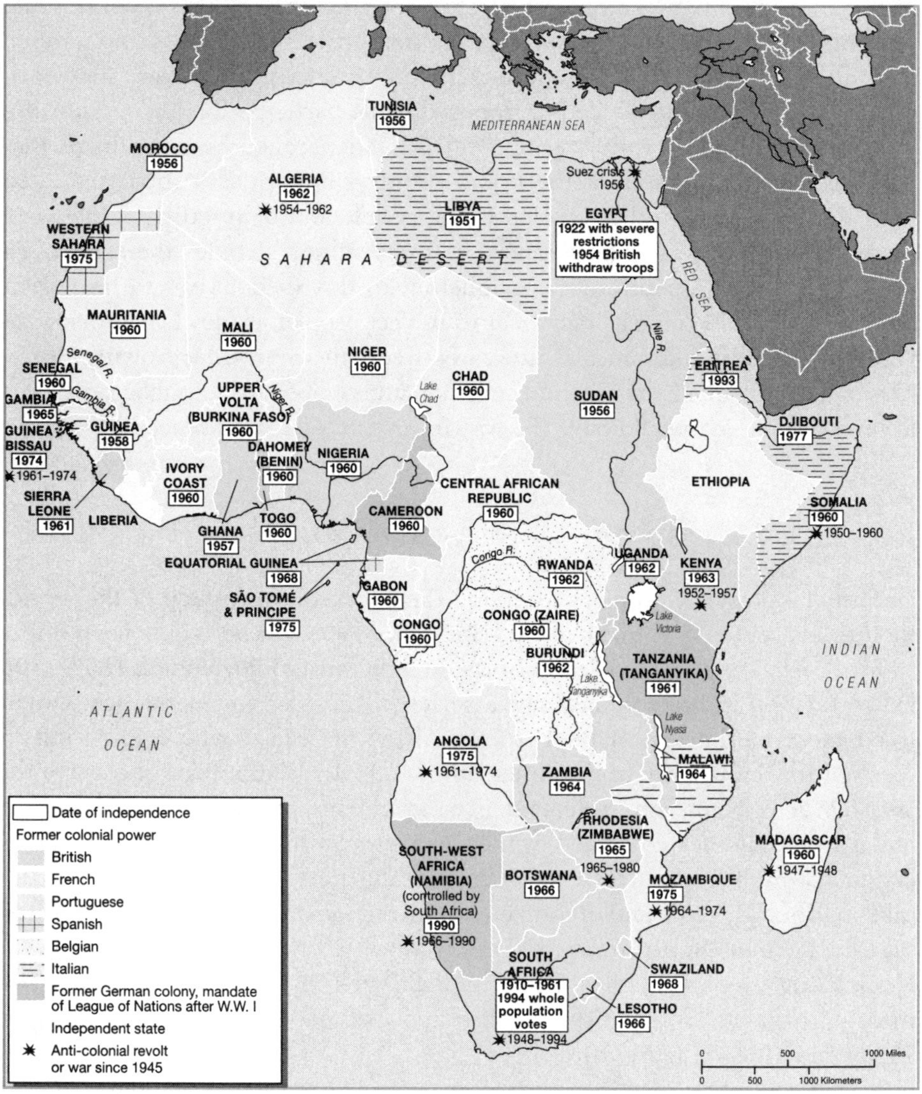

difference? Let's first consider some of the more common problems faced across postimperial countries, and then return to this question to see if the answer can provide some strategies for development and democracy.

Building State Capacity and Autonomy

One central problem that many newly industrializing and less-developed countries have faced in the years after imperialism has been the difficulty in creating effective political institutions. In Chapter 2, we distinguished between weak states and strong states and noted that many scholars look at state power by distinguishing between state capacity and state autonomy. Recall that capacity refers to the ability of a state to achieve basic policy tasks, and autonomy refers to the ability of a state to act independently of the public. Both are necessary to carry out policy, and both have been difficult for postimperial countries to achieve.

In terms of capacity, less-developed states are frequently unable to perform many of the basic tasks expected by the public, such as creating infrastructure, providing education and health care, or delivering other public goods. This lack of capacity stretches back to the absence of a professional bureaucracy; the foreigners who ran the imperial bureaucracies in the colonies typically left upon independence, precluding an effective transition to a local bureaucracy. These initial problems of capacity have since been further exacerbated by the politicization of the state; in many cases, the bureaucracy has become an important source of jobs, resources, and benefits that are doled out by political leaders as a way to solidify control. Civil servants thus become part of a system of clientelism, patrimonialism, and rent seeking, in which they assist in providing goods and benefits to certain members of the public in return for political support.[5]

Autonomy has been equally problematic in the postimperialist world. On the surface, many of these countries appear to be highly autonomous, able to function without consulting the population at all. The prevalence of nondemocratic regimes in much of the newly industrializing and less-developed world only seems to reinforce this impression. Indeed, many of these states can repress or terrorize the population as they see fit, but this autonomy is quite limited, built largely (and dangerously) around force alone. In many cases, the state is not a highly independent actor but is instead penetrated by actors and organizations that see the state as a resource to be exploited rather than a tool for achieving policy. Frequently, the result of such penetration is high levels of corruption—what has been termed *kleptocracy*, or government by theft. For example, during military rule in Nigeria in the 1990s, officials stole more than $1 billion from the state treasury. Studies of corruption indicate that the most corrupt countries in the world are less-developed and postcommunist countries, and there is a clear correlation between the level of development and the degree of corruption.

In addition to constraints on autonomy from domestic sources, the states of the newly industrializing and less-developed world are often also limited in their autonomy by international factors. Less-developed and newly industrializing countries are subject to pressure from other, more powerful states and international actors such as the United Nations, the World Bank, multinational corporations, and nongovernmental organizations such as Amnesty International and

Table 9.2 Corruption Index, 2007

Country	Score (10 = least corrupt)
Finland	9.4
Canada	8.7
United Kingdom	8.4
Japan	7.5
France	7.3
United States	7.2
Taiwan	5.7
Botswana	5.4
South Africa	5.1
South Korea	5.1
Mauritius	4.7
Brazil	3.5
China	3.5
India	3.5
Mexico	3.5
Bolivia	2.9
Mozambique	2.8
Uganda	2.8
Iran	2.5
Phillippines	2.5
Indonesia	2.3
Russia	2.3
Angola	2.2
Nigeria	2.2
Côte d'Ivoire	2.1
Ecuador	2.1
Kenya	2.1
Venezuela	2.0

The corruption index is based on national surveys regarding the overall extent of corruption (size and frequency of bribes) in the public and political sectors.

Source: Transparency International.

the Red Cross. Frequently wielding much greater economic and political power than the states themselves, these actors can significantly influence the policies of these countries, shaping their military and diplomatic alliances, trade relations, local economies, and domestic laws. Sovereignty is thus compromised.

IN FOCUS

Challenges to Building State Autonomy and Capacity in Less-Developed Countries

- Absence of professional bureaucracy (following departure of foreign imperial bureaucrats).
- Clientelism, rent seeking, and corruption in the struggle for state jobs and revenue.
- Sovereignty often compromised by external actors (other states, international organizations).

These constraints on state autonomy and capacity have clear implications for freedom and equality. A state with weak capacity and autonomy is unlikely to be able to establish the rule of law. Laws will not be respected by the public if the state itself is unwilling or unable to enforce and abide by them. Freedom is threatened by conflict and unpredictability, which in turn hinder economic development. A volatile environment and the absence of basic public goods such as roads or education will dissuade long-term investment. Wealth flows primarily into the hands of those who control the state, generating a high degree of inequality. There is no clear regime, and no rules or norms for how politics is to be played.

Unfortunately, where instability is so high, there is often only one institution with a great deal of autonomy and capacity: the military. Where states are weak, military forces often step in and take control of the government themselves, either to stave off disorder or simply to take a turn at draining the state. Military rule has been common in the newly industrializing and less-developed countries. Even where it has ended, as in many countries of Latin America, the military often remains a powerful actor in politics and economics.

Forging Social Identities

In the aftermath of colonialism, many less-developed and newly industrializing countries have struggled with the challenge of forging a single nation out of highly diverse societies. Initially, where centralized political authority did not exist prior to imperialism, societies were not homogenized. Their diversity became problematic when imperial powers began categorizing societal groups and establishing political boundaries and economic and social hierarchies. Migration within empires further complicated these relations. Upon independence, several problems rose to the surface.

First, group divisions often have economic implications, just as they did under colonial rule. Some ethnic or religious groups favored under colonialism continue to monopolize wealth in the postindependence society. For example, in Malaysia and Indonesia, ethnic Chinese continue to hold a disproportionate share of national wealth, generating resentment. Similarly, in some African countries like Kenya and Uganda, the Indian population, originally brought in by the British as indentured labor, came to control a large portion of the business sector. The resulting outbursts of violence appear on the surface to be ethnic in nature, but in fact their origins are economic. In 1972, the Ugandan government under the notorious dictator Idi Amin expelled all Indians from the country, seizing their lands and businesses. At other end of the spectrum, indigenous populations in Latin America are among the poorest, a situation that has sparked political movements in several of these countries. Many civil conflicts in the less-developed and newly industrializing countries are driven in large part by economic concerns overlaid onto ethnic or religious differences.

Second, ethnic and religious divisions can similarly complicate politics. In countries where populations are heterogeneous, the battle for political power often falls along ethnic or religious lines, with each side seeking to gain control over the state in order to serve its own group's particular ends. Each ethnic or religious group competes for its share of public goods or other benefits from the state. This struggle may foster authoritarian rule, for a group that gains control over the state may be unwilling to relinquish or share it, and no one group can be confident that it could successfully dominate politics simply through the democratic process. As a result, where ethnic or religious divisions are strong, we often see the state dominated by one group while others are effectively frozen out of the political process.[6] In some countries, a majority or plurality may dominate politics, as people of European origin do in Mexico, while the minority indigenous population has little political power. In still other cases, a minority may dominate a much larger minority; in Iraq, though the majority population is of the Shia sect of Islam, those in power have traditionally been members of the minority Sunni sect. With the overthrow of Saddam Hussein, conflict has emerged between Sunni and Shia over the future control of the country.

The economic and political difficulties that arise from such social divisions make the creation of a single national identity difficult. Amid such ethnic and religious diversity, many populations are much less inclined to see the postcolonial state as a true representation of their group's wishes, and states themselves have little beyond the initial struggle for independence on which to build a shared political identity for their people. At an extreme level, these ethnic and religious conflicts may take on the goal of secessionism, as disaffected groups seek to create their own autonomous or wholly independent territories.

Gender is another important social issue in less-developed and newly industrializing countries. Gender roles imposed or reinforced by colonial rule per-

sisted in many societies following independence, reinforced by
rapid urbanization and the
commercialization of agriculture, which tended to favor male
labor and property rights.
Because males are privileged in
this way, society tends to view
males as a more valuable addition to a family than females, an
attitude that can limit women's

**Challenges to Building a
Unified Nation-State**

- Arbitrary political boundaries imposed by imperial powers.
- Ethnic and religious divisions among different groups in heterogeneous societies (often exacerbated by economic inequality).

access to important resources such as education and, consequently, greater economic advancement. At an extreme level, this favoritism can be deadly, taking
the form of female infanticide. Estimates indicate that in India and China,
thousands of baby girls are killed each year, and an unknown number of female
fetuses are aborted once their sex has been determined by ultrasound examination. This has led to a gender imbalance in both countries, with potentially
dangerous implications. Some scholars have already noted that civil conflict
in part results when there is a large number of unemployed and unmarried
young men, and some have gone so far as to suggest that this can even spill
over into creating international conflict.[7]

We might conclude that sexist institutions in these countries are a result
of imperialism. But the situation is more complicated than that. Imperialism
also brought with it many liberal notions of female autonomy, which these
countries have since sought to reconcile with more traditional cultural values. For men, too, industrialization and urbanization have often meant a loss
of traditional roles, while new opportunities are circumscribed by a lack of
educational or economic opportunities. This can lead to marginalization and
humiliation, the tinder of domestic and international conflict.

Generating Economic Growth

It is economic growth that attracts the most focus among those who study
the less-developed and newly industrializing countries. Indeed, when we think
of development, typically it is economic progress that first comes to mind.
Because of imperialism, rather than undergoing economic modernization on
their own terms, these countries experienced rapid changes directed by the
imperial powers to serve their own needs. As a result, upon independence,
many of these countries found themselves in a continued state of economic
dependency on their former empire. But such dependent relationships did not
bode well for long-term development, since they stressed the production of
agricultural and other basic commodities in return for finished products. For

INSTITUTIONS IN

ACTION

IMPERIALISM, ISLAM, AND MODERNITY

Given the current focus on the Middle East, it can be instructive to look at the development of politics and faith in the region in light of our discussion of imperialism and its impact on social, political, and economic institutions. We cannot do justice to such a long and complex history in such a short space, but we can draw out a few important elements. Islam was founded in what is present-day Saudi Arabia in 610 C.E. by the prophet Muhammad and quickly spread as part of an Islamic empire. Within a century, this empire had spread across the Middle East and North Africa into central Asia and southern Europe. From the fourteenth century onward, the Ottomans, Turkish rulers who gained control over the lands of Islam, extended their empire further into Asia and Europe. During its 600-year rule, the Ottoman Empire was one of the largest and most technically sophisticated empires in the world—a reminder that imperial power did not always flow from Europe outward.

Eventually however, the Ottoman Empire began to decline in power, for reasons that are varied and contested. These include corruption, the decline of effective leadership, and the absence of a strong middle class or property rights. It has also been suggested that the consolidation of Islam under the Ottomans stunted religious and intellectual diversity, limiting outside ideas or challenges. Others suggest that it was not Ottoman authoritarianism but rather the empire's later decline that led to this intellectual orthodoxy. Interestingly, these arguments can be compared to similar processes in China around the same time. Whatever the reasons, by the eighteenth century, the Ottoman Empire retreated in the face of sustained European pressure, which was followed by internal revolts by its subject peoples in the following century. When the empire finally collapsed in the aftermath of World War I, the remaining Ottoman lands were divided into numerous new states in the Middle East, including Turkey, Iraq, Saudi Arabia, Syria, and Lebanon. Much of the former empire came under the direct or indirect control of Britain and France.

Many intellectuals in the Middle East questioned why their part of the world, once dominant in the region, had fallen behind the West, and what could be done about it. This debate resulted in a period of modernist reform, within which emerged the concept of *salafism* in the late nineteenth century. Salafism (based on the Arabic word *salaf*, meaning "predecessors") sought to revitalize the institutions of the Middle East by returning Islam to its original spirit and intent while selectively borrowing Western institutions, such as democracy and republicanism. This would create a modern faith and society where reason and religion would be reconciled. These views were not necessarily pro-Western but rather a response to Western imperialism, a way in which imperialism could be resisted and Islamic beliefs restored to their original intent. After World War I, salafism grew more hostile toward the West as imperialism deepened and societies in the Middle East experienced a bewildering array of changes. These included direct European control or local dictatorships backed by the European powers, competing ideologies and emergent nationalism, rapid changes in economic practices, and shifts and disruptions in traditional identities. For many, these were sources of confusion, humiliation, and spiritual emptiness. Faith in Western institutions declined, and salafists came to reject them as contrary to Islam. In addition, salafist thought was influenced by a more conservative version of Islam that dominates Saudi Arabia, known as Wahhabism. Rather than adapt their societies to modernity, as was the original intent, these salafists viewed Western modernity as alien, corrupt, and a rejection of God's authority. Islam became a center of resistance to this encroachment.

Most salafists are thus bound by a desire to resist Western culture and society by returning to what they see as the original spirit of Islam. For these practitioners, the emphasis is overwhelmingly social, focused on encouraging proper behavior. However, by the 1930s, a more politically oriented offshoot of salafism emerged, which explicitly sought to place Islam as the center of regime and state—what we would think of as fundamentalism. The main group behind this movement, the Muslim Brotherhood in Egypt, captured this idea in their slogan "The Koran is our constitution." Further offshoots of this fundamentalism came in the work of Sayyid Qutb (1906–1966). Qutb argued not only that Western institutions such as nationalism and democracy denied the sovereignty of God but that Muslim states and societies themselves had entered into a period of *jahiliyya*, or ignorance, akin to the time before the Prophet. This notion of jahiliyya mirrored Marx's idea of false consciousness: people had become blinded to the truth through the corrupt practices of the West. Qutb thus argued that such people or leaders were not "true" Muslims, having strayed from the path of Islam. Like Lenin, Qutb called for a vanguard to resist this ignorance, to wage war (jihad) and destroy the enemies of Islam.*

Qutb's ideas were far from mainstream salafism, and their radicalism inspired unsuccessful armed resistance against Middle Eastern governments. Qutb himself was eventually executed by the Egyptian government, and Islamic fundamentalists in many countries came to repudiate his views. During the 1980s, with the war in Afghanistan, these ideas took another turn. Jihad against the "near enemy"—the governments of the Middle East—would be ineffective so long as they were propped up by the "far enemy"—the United States and its allies. Jihad must therefore be used beyond the Middle East to set the stage for revolution in the Muslim world. This became the logic of bin Laden and his followers for September 11. This jihad approach is a far cry from the original ideas a century earlier, and in this change can be seen the tension of imperialism and its aftermath.

*See Sayyid Qutb, *Milestones* (Indianapolis: American Trust Publishers, 1990).

many less-developed countries, this unequal relationship was simply a new, indirect form of imperialism, or what has been called **neocolonialism**. Breaking this cycle of dependent development was thus the greatest concern for the less-developed countries following independence.

This need resulted in two distinct mercantilist economic policies that were applied throughout the less-developed world.[8] The first is known as **import substitution**. Under import substitution, countries restrict imports, with tariff or nontariff barriers to spur demand for local alternatives. New businesses to fill this demand could be built with state funds by creating subsidized or parastatal (partially state-owned) industries. Patents and intellectual property rights could also be weakly enforced to tap into foreign innovations. Eventually, these firms would develop the productive capacity to compete domestically and internationally. Following World War II, import substitution was commonly used across Latin America and was also taken up in Africa and parts of Asia.

How successful was import substitution? Most observers have since concluded that it did not produce the benefits expected, creating a kind of "hothouse economy." Insulated from the global economy, these firms could dominate the local market, but lacking competition, they were much less innovative or efficient than their international competitors. The idea that these economies would eventually be opened up to the outside world became hard to envision; the harsh climate of the international market would quickly kill off these less competitive firms.

Import substitution thus resulted in economies with large industries reliant on the state for economic support and unable to compete in the international market. Such firms became a drain on state treasuries, compounding the problem of international debt in these countries, for states had to borrow internationally to build and subsidize their industries. Uncompetitiveness was compounded by debt, leading to economic stagnation (Table 9.3).

Not all postcolonial countries pursued import substitution, however. In several Asian countries import substitution was eventually discarded in favor of what has been termed **export-oriented industrialization**. Countries that pursued an export-oriented strategy sought out technologies and developed industries that were focused specifically on export, capitalizing on what is known as the "product life cycle." Initially, the innovator of a good produces it for the domestic market and exports it to the rest of the world. As this product spreads, other countries find ways to make the same good more cheaply or more efficiently, eventually exporting their own version back to the country that originated the product. Thus, in South Korea, initial exports focused on basic technologies such as textiles and shoes but eventually moved into more complex areas such as automobiles and computers. This policy was not without its own issues: countries that pursued export-oriented industrializa-

Table 9.3 Import Substitution versus Export-Oriented Industrialization

Country	Economic System	GDP Per Capita (PPP, U.S. $)		Per Capita Annual Growth Rate, 1975–2005 (percent)
		1960	2005	
Ghana	Import substitution	1,049	2,480	0.7
Brazil	Import substitution	1,404	4,271	0.7
Argentina	Import substitution	3,381	14,280	0.3
South Korea	Export-oriented	690	22,029	6.0
Thailand	Export-oriented	985	8,677	4.9
Malaysia	Export-oriented	1,783	10,882	3.9

Source: *Human Development Report* 2004, 2007/2008.

tion also relied on high levels of government subsidies and tariff barriers. Yet overall, this strategy of development has led to much higher levels of economic development. Some export-oriented countries originally had per capita GDPs far below those of many Latin American and even some African countries.

Why did some countries choose import substitution while others opted for export-oriented industrialization? One important factor was geopolitical. In Latin America, import substitution was influenced by the region's economic domination by the United States. During the Great Depression, Latin America's market for raw materials and agricultural exports to the United States dried up, devastating many of its economies; later, during World War II, although markets for some exports improved, finished goods became scarce as the United States directed its industrial production toward the war effort. As a result of these dislocations, Latin American scholars and leaders concluded that import substitution would be a means to insulate their countries from this unpredictable and, in their eyes, neocolonial relationship. And in other parts of the world such as India, import substitution was seen as a way for a country to resist Western domination and ensure greater equality among its citizens by giving the state an important role in directing the economy and redistributing income.

In East Asia, however, development strategies were directly influenced by the Cold War and the role of the United States in this struggle. Backed by extensive American financial and technical support, many East Asian states specifically developed export-oriented industries; they were encouraged to tap into the American market as a way to industrialize their economies while protecting their own markets. The United States tolerated these more mercantilist policies as the price to pay for drawing these countries closer to the United States and preventing the spread of communism in the region. In short, the specific regional and geopolitical contexts of Latin America and Asia—and their countries' relationships with the United States in particular—influenced the paths of development they took.[9]

In recent years, both import substitution and export-oriented industrialization have been challenged. Although import substitution has long been criticized by liberals as inefficient and prone to corruption, the downturn of many Asian economies in the 1990s also led to critiques of export-oriented industrialization. In the wake of these economic difficulties, many less-developed and newly industrializing countries have adopted more liberal economic poli-

---

IN FOCUS

Three Paths to Economic Growth

Import substitution	Based on mercantilism.
	State plays a strong role in the economy.
	Tariffs or nontariff barriers are used to restrict imports.
	State actively promotes domestic production, sometimes creating state-owned businesses in developing industries.
	Criticized for creating "hothouse economies," with large industries reliant on the state for support and unable to compete in the international market.
Export-oriented industrialization	Based on mercantilism.
	State plays a strong role in the economy.
	Tariff barriers are used to protect domestic industries.
	Economic production is focused on industries that have a niche in the international market.
	Seeks to integrate directly into the global economy.
	Has generally led to a higher level of economic development than import substitution.
Structural adjustment	Based on liberalism.
	State involvement is reduced as the economy is opened up.
	Foreign investment is encouraged.
	Often follows import substitution.
	Criticized as a tool of neocolonialism and for its failure in many cases to bring substantial economic development.

cies, often at the behest of the advanced democracies or international agencies. These policies of liberalization—often known as **structural adjustment programs** or the Washington Consensus to reflect the wishes of Washington, D.C.–based institutions such as the World Bank and International Monetary Fund—have typically required countries to privatize state-run firms, end subsidies, reduce tariff barriers, shrink the size of the state, and welcome foreign investment. These reforms are controversial, and their benefits have been mixed. We will discuss this in greater detail when we consider future directions for economic prosperity in the poorer countries.

Puzzles and Prospects for Democracy and Development

We have covered some of the common challenges that postimperial countries face in developing institutions that will generate economic development and political stability. At the same time, we noted that in the face of these challenges, different parts of the world have had very different experiences. Asia has done the best, with rapid growth among many of these countries and a trend toward effective states and democratization. Latin America has seen similar progress in a number of countries, but this has also been accompanied by greater political difficulties and slower economic growth. Africa has done worst of all, with the lowest rankings on the Human Development Index, civil conflict, and corruption.

Why this variation? Scholars increasingly agree on some of the major factors at work, though they differ widely in what they mean in terms of solving the problems. One important factor that we have noted is that of ethnicity and borders. High degrees of ethnic division appear to correlate with greater economic and political instability. As we noted earlier, in such cases it may be much more difficult to forge a sense of national identity or national welfare, with economic and political institutions viewed as a means to dominate other groups rather than as instruments to share power and wealth. This can clearly be compounded by borders, which may exacerbate such differences by dividing ethnic or religious groups across international boundaries. Such conditions are particularly difficult in Africa, with ethnically fragmented states; for example, in Kenya, which recently saw severe ethnic conflict, no one group counts for more than a quarter of the population.

A second factor is that of resources. Recall that in Chapter 6 we spoke about the resource trap theory of development. In this argument, countries with natural resources are hindered from political and economic development as the state or political actors can rely on these resources and effectively ignore public demands or needs. This can further polarize politics when combined with ethnic divisions, since each side will seek to control those assets (like oil or diamonds) at the expense of others. Again, while natural resources are relatively scarce in Asia, they are a central part of African economies, where timber and diamonds not only lead to conflict, but fuel it as well, generating the revenue for private militias and civil war.

Third, there is the question of governance. This is the most problematic factor of the three to get a handle on, though perhaps the most important. It is evident to scholars that the obstacles discussed above, among others, cannot be addressed unless there is an effective state able to establish sovereignty and a monopoly of force and develop public goods and property rights, while resisting corruption and allowing for the transfer of power between governments over time. But what here is cause and what is effect? Are states weak because of ethnic division and/or resource traps, or do weak states facilitate these outcomes? This confusion has generated a great deal of controversy in the policy realm, as scholars remain divided over the extent to which political, social, and economic reforms need to be piecemeal and initiated locally or comprehensive and driven by international actors.[10] The remainder of our chapter will look at some of these possible solutions and the debates that surround them.

Forging States

The view of the state as a tool or obstacle to development in the postcolonial world has shifted over time. In the immediate postwar era, modernization theory focused on the importance of a state role in economic and political development, generating industrialization and modern citizens. Aid agencies and developed countries relied on these states to be conduits for aid, often directing funds toward large-scale, top-down development projects like dams or health care. Over the past fifty years some $2 trillion was funneled into Africa. However, many of these African states failed to live up to expectations, with corruption siphoning off resources and many development goals failing to be realized. A large but inefficient state, often abetted by foreign funds, was common. As a result, by the 1980s the Washington Consensus took a different track, encouraging (or pressuring) many less-developed countries to roll back state power, encourage private industry, and limit regulation in the belief that market forces could succeed where states had failed. But while these reforms viewed states as too big and interventionist, others noted that the real task needed to be redirecting, rather than reducing, the power of these states. Smaller would be little better if basic public needs could still not be met. As a result, attempts at liberalization have provided mixed results and skepticism of the Washington Consensus.[11]

What then to do? Scholars are increasingly looking at the configuration and location of state power in these countries, drawing from the experiences of recent democratization in Eastern Europe as well as changes in Latin America and Asia. In the past, studies of less-developed and newly industrializing countries were not particularly interested in how political institutions were themselves arranged, focusing instead on imperial legacies or these countries' position in the global economy. However, more focused studies of institutions have turned attention toward many of the concerns we have already addressed, such as executive-legislative relations and local versus national power.[12] A number of studies note that many of these countries rely on presidential rather than parliamentary systems, institutions which, as we noted in Chapter 5, are zero-sum offices that limit power sharing or the easy removal of those in office. While most of these offices are sufficiently institutionalized that they would be difficult to replace entirely, research indicates that factors such as whether the president is elected in one round or two can have a large impact on governability. Similarly, while there has been a great deal of interest in devolving power as a way to tackle corruption and increase state legitimacy, recall that in Chapter 7 we saw that devolution can in fact intensify conflicts if it encourages regional or ethnic parties that can increase political polarization.

Finally, at the most fundamental level, there are questions about the very nature of sovereignty in less-developed and newly industrialized countries. While the success of many newly industrialized countries may be due in part to effective states with a high degree of capacity, in many other cases these powers are weak, to such an extent that sovereignty is open to question—as in the case of civil conflicts and failed states. As a result, some scholars have raised the idea of "shared sovereignty," an arrangement in which international organizations would play a more direct role in building and maintaining political institutions.[13] For example, this can take the form of "conditionality," where other countries or organizations provide support (such as aid) only if particular outcomes have already been met. International organizations can also oversee the management of natural resources or taxation and the distribution of their revenue. At the most dramatic level, international institutions can also act in the core element of sovereignty, the monopoly of violence, intervening in domestic conflicts and serving, at least temporarily, as the central coercive power. The United Nations played this role in East Timor during its transition toward independence in 1999, and there have been similar calls in the Sudan. The expansion of the International Court of Justice can be seen in this light as well.

It is easy to see the difficulty involved here. While the term *shared sovereignty* may be new, many of the ideas suggested above are not and were often associated in the past with imperialism. Few countries welcome the role of foreign organizations or countries in domestic politics, and there is the danger that such practices could backfire. At the same time, such arrangements require that the international community not only commit resources but accept also that sovereignty—even their own—is not ironclad.

In the case of forging states, we can see some important differences in how reforms can be achieved. Some calls for institutional reform imply that less-developed countries can make political improvements with relatively small changes that could be led from within the country. Other arguments emphasize the role of international actors to drive a much larger process of state reform forward.

Building Society

While scholars and policy makers have been debating how to improve states, a similar discussion has concerned improving social conditions in the less-developed world. Much of this is rooted in discussions of economics, which we will consider next. But there is also the realization that improvements in society cannot always simply flow from economic development but must be dealt with simultaneously, as a foundation for political and economic progress. Earlier we spoke of the three central problems of ethnic conflict, resources, and governance. What steps can be taken at the societal level to address these concerns? Again, the debate turns in part on the scope and source of these changes.

A great deal of scholarship over the last decade or so has emphasized the role that small-scale social organization can play in improving governance and contributing to social stability. Influenced in part by experiences in Eastern Europe, this scholarship emphasizes building civil society in countries where social organization is poor and often polarized along ethnic, religious, class, or gender lines. Recall that in Chapter 5 we defined civil society as organized life outside the state. Civil society binds people together, creating a web of interests that cuts across class, religion, ethnicity, and other divisions; forms a bulwark through activism and organization against the expansion of state power that might threaten democracy; and inculcates a sense of democratic politics based on interaction, negotiation, consensus, and compromise. The state is also hampered by a lack of civil society, without which it can become enmeshed in clientelist relationships that prevent the formation of policies that serve society as a whole.

As in the case of state reform, building civil society has become a focal point for scholars and political actors involved in development.[14] No longer is the state seen as the sole instrument for democracy and development; public activity is now viewed as a vital part of the equation. A first step in the development of civil society is civic education, in which communities learn

their democratic rights and how to use those rights to shape government policy. Beyond education, organizational skills must also be strengthened so that
the public is able to mobilize effectively and make its voice heard. These efforts
need to go hand in hand with state reform; changes require participation not
just from local political elites but from the public as well, in league with similar organizations around the world.

Other scholars, however, have argued that this emphasis is for now mis-
placed. Stressing grassroots organization is well-meaning but unlikely to lead
to any real outcomes as long as the country's basic social conditions are dire.
Moreover, where civil society is built in the absence of political institutions
that can process people's desires and demands, the result can be frustration
and greater instability. Some scholars believe that responses to social issues
in the less-developed countries require a massive international effort rather
than a focus on local small-scale activism. The UN's Millennium Development
Goals (MDG) partly reflect this viewpoint, with proposals to improve education, health, agriculture, gender equality, and reduction of poverty. Already
the MDG has set up a dozen "Millennium Villages" in Africa to put these policies into practice, with the idea that these would eventually be scaled up to
regional and national projects. Such an ambitious goal is not cheap; each of
the villages requires $300,000 per year, and estimates are that a worldwide
implementation of the MDG would require between $75 and $150 billion per
year until 2015.[15] Critics of this program argue that such large-scale, top-down
programs are little different from the international programs tried in the past,
where billions poured into the less-developed world yielded limited results,
and that such large-scale programs fail to reflect real needs on the ground.[16]

Promoting Economic Prosperity

Economic prosperity is the third crucial need within the less-developed world.
Above all, the diverse countries that fall into this category are defined by their
lack of economic development and the pressing problems of poverty and
inequality. And as with political and social reform, there are sharply contrasting views over how to improve economic conditions in these countries.

A central problem is that for many less-developed countries, much of the
economy exists in the "informal" sector as opposed to the "formal" sector. By
informal sector we mean a segment of the economy that is not regulated, protected, or taxed by the state. Typically, the **informal economy** is dominated
by the self-employed or by small enterprises, such as an individual street
vendor or a family that makes or repairs goods out of its home. In some
cases, the informal economy may represent over half of a country's GDP, with
women playing a large role. According to some research studies, in many less-

developed countries up to 90 percent of women working outside the agricultural sector are part of the informal economy.

Why does the informal economy dominate many less-developed countries,
and why does this matter? Corrupt and highly bureaucratic state controls over
the economy often deter individuals from starting formal businesses; in addition, certain social institutions, such as hostility toward women in the workplace, may discourage employment outside of the home. And while informal
employment can be better than no employment at all, this gray market does
not generate tax revenue, is not subject to state protection or regulation, and
often lacks the capital necessary to grow since it lacks assets or collateral.
Businesses operating in the informal economy are thus unable to grow into
larger businesses and thereby enter the formal economy.

How to transform a small-scale informal economy into a larger formal
one? Some scholars emphasize the need for localized reform and opportunities within state and society to improve economic conditions. One important
argument is that economic underdevelopment has been in large part a function of weak property rights in many of these countries. This idea, pioneered
by the Peruvian economist Hernando De Soto, emphasizes the need to develop
stronger property rights in the less-developed world. In all informal
economies, De Soto argues, there is a vast amount of "dead capital"—land,
homes, businesses—that lack basic property rights such as clear title to ownership. Codifying existing informal institutions and ensuring effective state
protection of them would allow people to more easily tap into these resources.
Formal property rights would allow for the development of credit as well as
allow states to tax and regulate the economy. Here again we see a need not
for less state power but for its redirection toward establishing and institutionalizing property rights.[17]

Similarly, others scholars have emphasized the need to improve access to
capital normally unavailable to the informal economy at less than exorbitant
rates. A much discussed alternative is **microcredit** or **microfinance**, a system that makes small loans (less than $1,000) at reasonable interest rates to
small-scale businesses. Often these loans are funded through nonprofit organizations, and in some cases the borrower is also held accountable to other
borrowers in a local association, so that a failure to repay limits further loans
that can be taken out by that community. With globalization, microcredit too
has expanded; now organizations like Kiva allow individuals around the world
to make microcredit loans to those in need. As of 2008, Kiva had over a quarter million lenders, and loaned $27 million to 40,000 individuals.[18] The
Grameen Bank in Bangladesh, which first pioneered microcredit, has loaned
over $6 billion since its inception, and its founder, Muhammad Yunus, won
a Nobel Peace Prize in 2006 for his work.

As promising as these projects are, they are not a panacea. Critics of micro-credit note that while these small loans may help small entrepreneurs, they have not created a way for firms to grow and take on employees—a critical step in development and the creation of a middle class.[19] Similarly, an emphasis on property rights will be effective only insofar as there is a state with the capacity to delineate and defend those rights, something sorely lacking in most less-developed states. Not surprisingly, then, other scholars have focused more on large-scale economic issues as a solution to development. One particular focus has been on trade liberalization that would favor agricultural and other exports from the poorest countries, tied to the goals of the MDG. However, trade liberalization has been under negotiation within the World Trade Organization since 2001, and many countries, rich and poor alike, continue to oppose further opening up their markets, especially to agricultural imports—the most recent round of negotiations collapsed over just this issue in 2008. In the current global recession, less-developed countries are unlikely to see improved trade liberalization any time soon.

In Sum: The Challenges of Development

Although newly industrializing and less-developed countries differ in their levels of development, almost all share the legacies of imperial rule. The fusion of local institutions with those of the imperial power created challenges as these countries sought to chart their own independent courses. Weak states; conflicts over ethnicity, nation, religion, and gender; and incomplete and distorted forms of industrialization all contributed to instability, authoritarianism, economic stagnation, and overall low levels of freedom and equality. The newly industrializing countries seem to have overcome many of these obstacles, but it is unclear whether their strategies and experiences provide lessons that can be easily applied elsewhere in the world.

As of now, there is no consensus on how to tackle the most pressing problems of the less-developed world. Some emphasize the power of small-scale, piecemeal, local, and bottom-up solutions, arguing that the alternative of grand plans has consumed time and money with little to show for it. Others argue that the problem in the past was a lack of concerted effort and a unified vision of what needed to be done; they call for a new investment of resources to lift the poorest countries out of poverty. Who is right? Do the solutions lie in a patchwork of reforms, or a comprehensive plan for change? Both are competing for the attention of donors and policy makers to lead the way in the coming decades.

NOTES ────────────────────────────────────

1. For two excellent studies of imperialism in practice, see L. H. Gann and Peter Duignan, eds., *Imperialism in Africa, 1870–1960* (Cambridge: Cambridge University Press, 1969–75); and Nicolas Tarling, ed., *The Cambridge History of Southeast Asia* (Cambridge: Cambridge University Press, 1992).

2. A general discussion of the impact of colonialism can be found in Paul Cammack, David Pool, and William Tordoff, *Third World Politics: An Introduction* (Baltimore: Johns Hopkins University Press, 1993). See also Philip D. Curtin, *The World and the West: The European Challenge and the Overseas Response in the Age of Empire* (Cambridge: Cambridge University Press, 2000).

3. Georgina Waylen, *Gender in Third World Politics* (Boulder, CO: Lynne Rienner, 1996).

4. For a Marxist analysis of dependent development as it applies to Latin America, see Eduardo H. Galeano, *Open Veins of Latin America: Five Centuries of the Pillage of a Continent*, Cedric Belfrage, trans. (New York: Monthly Review Press, 1998).

5. See Joel S. Migdal, *Strong Societies and Weak States: State-Society Relations and State Capabilities in the Third World* (Princeton: Princeton University Press, 1988).

6. For a discussion of these issues, see Dennis L. Thompson and Dov Ronen, eds., *Ethnicity, Politics, and Development* (Boulder, CO: Lynne Rienner, 1986).

7. Valerie M. Hudson and Andrea M. Den Boer, *Bare Branches: The Security Implications of Asia's Surplus Male Population* (Cambridge, MA: MIT Press, 2005).

8. For a discussion of different paths of industrialization, see Stephan Haggard, *Pathways from the Periphery: The Politics of Growth in Newly Industrializing Countries* (Ithaca, NY: Cornell University Press, 1990).

9. Peter Evans, "Class, State, and Dependence in East Asia: Lessons for Latin Americanists," in Frederic C. Deyo, ed., *The Political Economy of the New Asian Industrialism* (Ithaca, NY: Cornell University Press, 1987), 203–226.

10. For a good overview of these issues and responses, see Paul Collier, *The Bottom Billion: Why the Poorest Countries Are Failing and What Can Be Done about It* (Oxford: Oxford University Press, 2007).

11. Francis Fukuyama, *State Building: Governance and World Order in the 21st Century* (Ithaca, NY: Cornell University Press, 2004).

12. See, for example, Seth Kaplan, *Fixing Fragile States: A New Paradigm for Development* (Westport, CT: Praeger, 2008).

13. Stephen Krasner, "The Case for Shared Sovereignty," *Journal of Democracy*, 16, no. 1 (January 2005), pp. 69–83.

14. Don Eberly, *The Rise of Global Civil Society* (New York: Encounter, 2008).

15. For more on the Millennium Development Goals, see www.unmillenniumproject.org.

16. See, for example, William Easterley, *The White Man's Burden: Why the West's Efforts to Aid the Rest Have Done So Much Ill and So Little Good* (New York: Penguin, 2006).

17. Hernando De Soto, *The Mystery of Capital: Why Capitalism Triumphs in the West and Fails Everywhere Else* (New York: Basic Books, 2000).

18. See www.kiva.org.

19. Karol Boudreaux and Tyler Cowen, "The Micromagic of Microcredit," *The Wilson Quarterly* (Winter 2008), pp. 27–31.

10 POLITICAL VIOLENCE

KEY CONCEPTS

- Political violence is violence outside of state control that is politically motivated.

- Individual, ideational, and institutional reasons may all contribute to political violence.

- Revolutions are public seizures of the state to overturn the government and regime.

- Terrorism is nonstate violence against civilians, often toward a revolutionary goal.

- Political violence may have a religious source when faith serves as an ideological force.

- Countering political violence raises questions about state power and individual liberty.

The turn of the century marked a new global threat. This danger was not surprising; for decades, loosely affiliated radicals had been staging attacks worldwide, killing civilians, government officials, and heads of state. These attacks drew from local grievances while bound by a common ideology that sought the destruction of states and regimes these radicals viewed as tyrannical and corrupt. Globalization helped facilitate the spread of these ideas and their followers, who moved from country to country, eluding detection and capture. The attacks in New York and Washington, D.C., directed at key symbols of America's national and global power, were another chapter in what had already been a long battle.

In response to these attacks, many citizens asked themselves to what extent freedom should be sacrificed for national security. Foreigners and those viewed as possible accomplices or sympathizers became subject to public scrutiny, deportation, and sometimes questionable prosecution. Around the world, governments stepped up similar controls, limiting civil liberties in democratic countries and increasing repression in authoritarian ones. Another concern was whether greater economic integration and immigration had made countries more vulnerable to such attacks.

The time we are speaking of is not today, and the danger is not that of religious violence. It took place over a century ago, and the danger then was anarchism and communism. In 1881, anarchists killed Russian czar Alexander II; in 1889, Empress Elizabeth of Austria; in 1894, French president Carnot; and in 1901, U.S. president William McKinley. In 1917, the Russian Revolution swept away the czarist regime, and short-lived revolutionary regimes followed in Hungary and Bavaria. In 1919, a series of mail bombs were sent to political and economic elites across the United States, and shortly thereafter there were explosions in seven American cities, including Washington, D.C., where the home of the attorney general was severely damaged. In 1920, a wagon carrying several hundred pounds of explosives and shrapnel was planted opposite 23 Wall Street, the headquarters of J. P. Morgan, in New York City, killing over thirty people. The government's response to this "Red Scare" was the Palmer Raids, in which thousands were arrested and many held without charge for long periods or deported.[1]

To this point, we have identified various institutions that define states, societies, and economic structure and regime type. We have also seen how these institutions are constructed and function in different parts of the world; power and legitimacy rest in these institutions, to varying degrees. What happens, though, when power escapes institutions altogether, or when people seek to take these institutions down by force?

It is the goal of this chapter to shed some light on this complex question, providing ways to think about political violence and its implications. We will begin by defining our terms: What do we mean by political violence, and how does this relate to the political institutions we have already covered? Next, we will look at some of the motivations of political violence, examining the differing (and often conflicting) explanations for why such violence occurs. From there we will concentrate on two important forms of political violence: revolution and terrorism. Each is an important phenomenon that can put governments, regimes, and states under threat. They are also highly loaded political terms that stir emotional responses, complicating analysis. We will look at some of the different ways revolution and terrorism can be defined and understood. In addition, we will explore the extent to which the two are related—how terrorism is often a tool to achieve revolution. Once we have these concepts and arguments before us, we will put them into some context by looking at contemporary forms of political violence motivated by religion. Finally, we will conclude with a discussion of how states and societies prevent or manage political violence and what this means for freedom and equality.

What Is Political Violence?

This textbook began with a focus on the state. This institution is the cornerstone of modern politics, one that we defined in its most basic terms as the monopoly of violence or force over a territory. Across human history, centralized political authority has been a part of this monopoly whereby states vanquish their domestic rivals, defend themselves from external threats, and establish order and security at home. This has been described as the shift from "private war" to "public war," meaning that individuals lose the freedom to use violence against one another, turning that right over to the state. This right is exchanged for a greater sense of security for all.

Of course, the state's monopoly of violence is never perfect or complete. Other states always represent a potential threat, given their own capacity for violence. Even at the domestic level, violence persists in such forms as murder and armed robbery. In many countries, such problems, though persistent, are manageable and do not threaten the stability and security of the state, society, or economy. But under certain conditions, this may not be true. Public violence may grow so pervasive or destructive that the state loses its control in this area. Governments, regimes, even states are subject to attack, and sovereignty is weakened or lost. We have already seen this in some detail in our discussion of ethnic and national conflict in Chapter 3.

It is this kind of violence, what we call **political violence**, or violence outside of state control that is politically motivated, that is the focus of this chapter. This is not to say that other forms of violence are not important in their own right. Endemic crime, for example, can threaten political stability, and many forms of violence at the domestic level may have political roots. Warfare, too, is clearly a violent and political act. But in the case of political violence, we are speaking of a phenomenon that operates beyond state sovereignty, neither war nor crime, and that seeks to achieve some political objective through the use of force. Such definitions are always cleaner in theory than in reality, of course. The lines between domestic and international and between war, crime, and politics are often quite blurry.

Why Political Violence?

Although defining political violence presents some challenges, a more controversial issue is why political violence occurs. What leads civilians to take up arms against a state or its citizens toward some political aim? The reasons given by scholars are diverse and have changed over time, but we can group them into three basic categories: institutional, ideational (based on ideas), and individual. These three explanations overlap to some degree; where one explanation ends and the other begins is not always clear. At the same time, such explanations are often in contention, with scholars or policy makers tending to favor one explanation over others. We will examine each of these before we look at how these explanations are used more specifically in studies of revolution and terrorism. In each of these cases, there is an underlying discussion of rationality. What is the incentive to use violence? What motivates political violence, and toward what end?

Institutional Explanations

As we have covered *institutions* at length, what we mean by this term should be relatively clear; we are referring to those self-perpetuating organizations or patterns of activity that are valued for their own sake. Institutions define and shape human activity, and institutional explanations argue that their specific qualities or combination are essential to political violence. The emphasis can be on political institutions, such as states or regimes; economic institutions, such as capitalism; or societal institutions, such as culture or religion. Moreover, this explanation can be based on either a constraining or an enabling argument. It may be that institutions contain certain values or norms that implicitly or explicitly encourage such violence or that certain institutions constrain human activity, thus provoking political violence. For example, in the chapter on democratic institutions we covered variations in executive structures and electoral systems; in both cases, it has been argued that variants that reduce the opportunity for power sharing—versions that produce "winner take all outcomes," like presidencies—increase the likelihood of marginalization and conflict. Under these conditions, political violence can be a logical reaction when other forms of participation are blocked. Institutional explanations can be seen as a quest for a "root source" for violence, a necessary condition for such actions to take place, and presume that changes in the institutional structure would eliminate the motivation for this violence.

Ideational Explanations

If institutional explanations emphasize the impact of fixed organizations and patterns in fostering political violence, ideational explanations focus more on the rationale behind that violence. By **ideational** we simply mean having to do with ideas. Ideas may be institutionalized—concepts rooted in some institution such as a political organization or a religion—but just as often they are

Explanations for Political Violence

Explanation	Reasoning	Example
Institutional	Existing institutions may encourage violence or constrain human action, creating a violent backlash.	Presidentialism
Ideational	Ideas may justify or promote the use of violence.	Some forms of religious fundamentalism; nationalism
Individual	Psychological or strategic factors may lead people to carry out violence.	Humiliation

uninstitutionalized, with no real organizational base. The argument here is that ideas play an important role in political violence in the way they set out a worldview, diagnose a set of problems, provide a resolution, and describe the means of getting there. Any or all of these elements can be bound up with a justification of violence. For example, scholars of suicide terrorism have focused on the ways in which groups use particular ideas, such as self-sacrifice and glory, to motivate individuals, binding them to a greater cause. These ideas can draw on religious beliefs, as in the case of violent Islamic fundamentalists linked to Al Qaeda. Or they may draw on secular ideas such as nationalism, as with the Tamil Tigers in Sri Lanka, who have used large numbers of suicide attackers in their quest for national independence.

These ideational factors take us back to our discussion of political attitudes in Chapter 3. As we noted there, political violence is more likely to be associated with attitudes that are radical or reactionary, since each attitude views the current institutional order as bankrupt and beyond reform. This reminds us that it is not only the content of the ideas that matters but the place of those ideas relative to the domestic political status quo. Ideas seen as conservative in one context may become a source of radicalism, and thus violence, elsewhere.

Individual Explanations

Finally, individual explanations center on those who carry out the violence themselves. Here the scholarship emphasizes the personal motivations that allow people to contemplate and carry out violence toward political ends. Scholars who study individual explanations of political violence usually follow one of two paths. One emphasizes psychological factors, conditions that lead individuals toward violence. Such factors can be a function of individual experiences or they may be shaped by broader conditions in society, such as standard of living, level of human development, or gender roles. Such an approach tends to concentrate on how people may be driven to violence as an expression of desperation, liberation, or social solidarity. For example, some scholars of religious violence emphasize the role of humiliation as a motivating force, a sense that one's own beliefs are actively marginalized and denigrated by society. Revolutionaries or terrorists, in this view, see violence as a way to restore meaning to their lives and may in many ways be largely unconcerned with whether they are effectively achieving their goals.[2] A contrary approach, however, rejects this view, seeing political violence as a rational act, carried out by those who believe it to be an effective political tool. Strategy, rather than despair, drives these actions. Political violence is in this view not an expression of deviancy but a strategy that is carefully wielded by those who understand its costs and potential benefits.[3]

One important element of comparison across these three explanations is how they approach free will—that is, to what extent people are the primary actors in political violence. Institutional explanations often are quite deterministic, seeing people shaped and directed by larger structures that they do not control. An individual's recourse to violence is simply the final step in a much larger process. In contrast, individual explanations place their focus squarely on people; they are the primary makers of violence because they choose to be. Ideational explanations lie somewhere in between. Ideas are influenced by institutions but are also actively taken up and molded by individuals to justify political violence.

A second element of comparison concerns universal versus particularistic explanations. Institutional explanations tend to be more particularistic, stressing the unique combination and role of institutions in a given case that are not easily generalized elsewhere. Individual explanations tend to center on those personal or psychological attributes common to all humans that can lead to violence. Ideational explanations, again, lie somewhere in the middle, generalizing the importance of ideas while noting the very different lessons that different ideas impart.

Which explanation is most convincing: institutional, ideational, or individual? These explanations are often placed in competition with each other, but it may be that they actually work in conjunction. Institutional factors provide a context in which particular preconditions, problems, and conflicts may emerge. Ideational factors help describe and define those problems, ascribe blame, and provide solutions by calling for the transformation of the status quo. These ideas in turn influence and are shaped by individuals and groups who may already be prone to violent activity. In the case of the Basque independence group Euskadi Ta Askatasuna (ETA) in Spain, institutional factors include a long period of repression under authoritarian rule and its effects on the region; ideational factors include a belief among ETA members and supporters that the Basque people face cultural extermination at the hands of the Spanish; and individual factors include the role and motivations of many Basque youth in conducting "kale borroka" (urban struggle) in their quest for an independent, revolutionary Basque state. This example helps illustrate the interconnection of these three factors and why political violence is relatively unpredictable and has emerged in a variety of contexts. We will consider these various explanations next as we look specifically at revolution and terrorism.

Forms of Political Violence

So far, we have spoken of political violence in fairly general terms, defining it as violence that is outside state control and politically motivated. Even under this definition, political violence can manifest itself in many different forms: assassinations, riots, rebellions, military coups, civil war, and ethnic conflict, to name a few. We will concentrate on two forms of political violence: revolution and terrorism. Revolution is important to study because of its profound effects. Revolutions have ushered in sweeping changes in modern politics, overturning old institutions and dramatically transforming domestic and international relations. Terrorism, while less sweeping, holds our attention as a similar challenge to modern political institutions whose impact on domestic and international politics has spiked in recent years. Both are forces that seek dramatic change. Yet in many ways, revolution and terrorism are the opposite of one another. Revolution conjures up the image of a spontaneous uprising of the masses, who take to the streets, seize control of the state, and depose the old regime. In contrast, terrorism is much more secret and hidden, a conspiratorial action carried out by a small group. But there are similarities in their sources and goals. As we analyze and compare the dynamics of revolution and terrorism, we will draw out some of these elements as well as show how these seemingly disparate forms of political violence can be linked.

Revolution

The term *revolution* has many connotations. Although we speak of revolution as a form of political violence, the word is also used in a much more indiscriminate manner. Any kind of change that is dramatic is often described as revolutionary, whether the change is political or a trend in clothing. Related to this, the term *revolution* has a generally positive connotation, one that speaks of progress. People speak of dramatic change as positive, and "counterrevolution" is seen as an attempt to turn back the clock to a darker time. This should not be surprising; across much of the world, significant political change has been a result of revolution, and in these countries, revolution is often associated with independence, sovereignty, and development. Thus, revolution is a loaded term, albeit with positive connotations.

For our purposes, we shall speak of revolution in a more limited manner. **Revolution** can be defined as a public seizure of the state in order to overturn the existing government and regime. There are several factors at work here. First, revolutions involve some element of public participation. To be certain, there are typically leaders, organizers, and instigators of revolution who play a key role. But unlike a coup d'état, where elites overthrow the government, in revolutions the public plays an important role in seizing power. Russia is an interesting example. While we typically speak of communism's triumph in 1917 as a revolution, some scholars call it a coup, with Lenin and a handful of followers seizing control of the state rather than some mass action toppling the government. Second, revolutions seize control of the state. This distinguishes these actions from such violence as ethnic conflicts, where groups may gain local control or even seek independence but do not or cannot take over the entire state. Finally, the objective of revolution is not simply the removal of those in power but the removal of the entire regime itself. Protests or uprisings to pressure a leader to leave office are not necessarily revolutionary. At their core, revolutions seek to fundamentally remake the institutions of politics and often economic and societal institutions as well. As a result, scholars sometimes speak of "social revolutions" to indicate that they are referring to events that completely reshape society.

Must revolutions be violent? This is a tricky question. Given the dramatic goals of revolution, violence is often difficult to avoid. Governments will resist overthrow, and such conflict can often lead to the fragmentation of the monopoly of violence, with parts of the state (such as elements of the military) often siding with revolutionaries. The immediate aftermath of revolutions can also be very bloody, as the losers are killed or carry out a counterrevolutionary struggle against the new regime.

However, not all revolutions are violent. In 1989, communist regimes in Eastern Europe collapsed in the face of public pressure, sweeping away institutions that many thought immovable. In most cases, violence was limited; Romania is the only country that experienced a violent struggle between the communist regime and revolutionaries that led to numerous deaths. Because of this absence of violence, many scholars would resist calling the collapse of communism in Eastern Europe revolutionary, preferring instead to speak of these changes as political transitions. Yet in most important ways, these events did fulfill our definition of revolution. South Africa, too, is a case where we see a change in regime from apartheid to multiracial democracy, but the elite-driven, largely nonviolent, and slowly negotiated process makes most scholars uncomfortable with calling this a revolution.

What causes revolution? There is no agreement on this question, and the consensus has changed over time, with scholars grouping studies of revolution into three phases. In the first phase prior to World War II, scholars tended to describe rather than explain revolution. When causes were ascribed, explanations were often unsystematic, blaming bad government policies or leaders. With the behavioral revolution of the 1950s and 1960s (see Chapter 1), social scientists sought more generalized explanations. These new research efforts took on varied forms and areas of emphasis, but they shared a common view that dramatic economic and social change or disruption, such as modernization, was central in sparking revolutionary events. The views tended to focus on the role of individuals as potential revolutionaries, seeking to understand what motivated them.

For example, one of the main arguments that emerged out of this work was a psychological approach known as the **relative deprivation model**. According to this model, revolutions are less a function of specific conditions than the gap between actual conditions and public expectations. Improving economic or political conditions might still lead to revolution if, for example, such change leads to increased public demands that are eventually unmet, fostering discontent. It has sometimes been suggested that the 1979 Iranian Revolution is an example of relative deprivation at work. As Iran experienced rapid modernization in the decades prior to the revolution, this only increased expectations for greater freedom and equality, especially among young adults. This is what is meant by relative deprivation: it is not the absolute conditions that influence revolution but rather how the public perceives them.

By the 1970s, these studies of revolution began to lose favor. Critics argued that theories of revolution predicated on sudden change could not explain why some countries could undergo dramatic change without revolution (as in Japan during the early twentieth century) or what levels of change would be enough to trigger revolution. In the specific case of the relative deprivation model, there was little evidence that past revolutions were in fact preceded by rising expectations or discontent. Similarly, there were many cases when both expectations and discontent rose but revolution did not result. New studies of revolution took a more institutional approach, moving away from a focus on public reactions to a focus on the target of revolutions: the state.

Most influential in this regard has been the work of Theda Skocpol and her landmark book *States and Social Revolutions*. Focusing on France, China, and Russia, Skocpol argued that social revolutions required a very specific set of conditions. First is competition between rival states as they vie for military and economic power in the international system through such things as trade and war. Such competition is costly and often betrays the weakness of those states that cannot match their rivals. Second, as a result of this competition, weaker states often seek reform in order to increase their autonomy and capacity, hoping to change domestic institutions in order to boost their international power. This can include greater state centralization and changes in agriculture, industry, education, and taxation. Such changes, however, can threaten the status quo, undermining the power of entrenched elites, sowing discord among the public, and creating resistance as a result. The result is discontent, political paralysis, and an opening for revolution. In this view, it is not change per se that is central to revolution, but the power and actions of the state. Other actors are of relatively little importance.

The institutional approach to revolution became the dominant view during the 1980s, paralleling a wider interest in institutions and the power of the state. Yet institutional approaches themselves became subject to questions and criticism. Some argued that an overemphasis on institutions ignored the role played by leadership or ideas in helping to catalyze and direct revolutionary action. In addition, if earlier approaches did not seem to fit with the historical record, institutional approaches were themselves hard to disprove, essentially asserting that if there were a revolution, the state must have been weak and under international pressure.

Shifting Views of Revolution

Phase	Approach	Criticisms
First: pre–World War II	Studies of revolutionary events	Unsystematic and descriptive
Second: post–World War II; behavioral revolution	Studies of disruptive change, such as modernization, as driving revolutionary action	Not clear why change or rising discontent leads to revolution in some cases and not others
Third: 1970s–present	Studies of domestic and international state power as providing the opening for revolution	Too focused on institutions, to the neglect of ideas and individual actors

These concerns were underscored by the revolutions in Eastern Europe in 1989. There can be no doubt that changes in the international system, specifically the Cold War and the Soviet Union's loosening of control over Eastern Europe, led to conflict and paralysis within these states. At the same time, however, public action was mobilized and shaped by opposition leaders who were strongly influenced by the ideas of liberalism, human rights, and nonviolent protest. In addition, mass protest appeared influenced by strategic calculation: successful public opposition in one country changed the calculations of actors elsewhere, increasing their mobilization and demands. Drawing on these events, some scholars have moved back toward more individual and ideational approaches. While state actions do matter, so do the motivations of opposition leaders and the public as a whole, their views regarding political change, and their ability to bring this change about. Small shifts in ideas and perceptions may have a cascading effect, bringing people into the streets when no one would have predicted it the day before—including the revolutionaries themselves.[4]

As important as the cause of revolution is its impact. If a revolution does manage to sweep away the old regime and install a new one, the effects can be profound, but also with surprising continuities from the past. The first major impact is that revolutionary regimes often institutionalize new forms of politics, transforming the existing regime. Revolutions help pave the way for new ideas and ideologies: republicanism, secularism, democracy, liberalism, communism, and Islamism were all marginal ideas until revolutions helped place them at the center of political life. Revolutions have served to destroy well-entrenched regimes and legitimize new and radical alternatives. They have also been responsible for dramatic economic and societal changes, such as the end of feudalism and the development of capitalism. This is why we tend to think of revolutions as positive events: from hindsight, their effects are often seen as progressive. If ideational factors are often underplayed as a source of revolution, it is certainly true that these factors are central in the successful institutionalization of revolutionary regimes.

Though revolutions may be instruments of progress, it is important to note what they do not achieve. In spite of the call for greater freedom or equality that is a hallmark of revolution, the result is often the reverse. Revolutionary leaders who once condemned the state quickly come to see it as a necessary tool to consolidate their victory, and they often centralize power to an even greater extent than before. This is not necessarily bad if this centralization of power can facilitate the creation of a modern state with a necessary degree of autonomy and capacity. Revolutions are often the foundation of a modern state. However, revolutionary leaders may seek a high degree of state power, rejecting democracy as incompatible with the sweeping goals of the revolution. Cuba, China, Russia, France, and Iran are all cases in which public demands for more rights ended with yet another dictatorship with uncanny echoes of the previous authoritarian order. Mexico is another good example. The 1910 revolution swept away the previous corrupt dictatorship but was soon replaced by a one-party regime, itself corrupt and dictatorial, that held power until 2000.

A second impact is that revolutionary change often comes at a high cost. Revolutions are often destructive and bloody. The events that bring revolutionaries to power may themselves not claim many lives, but in the immediate aftermath, revolutionary leaders and their opponents often use violence in their struggle over the new order. The Mexican Revolution led to the death

INSTITUTIONS IN ACTION

THERMIDOR: THE INSTITUTIONALIZATION OF REVOLUTION

Our discussion of revolutions has emphasized the degree to which these events are driven by a desire to sweep away old institutions and create some new, often utopian order. Great creative as well as destructive energies are unleashed by such revolutions in this quest for radical change. In spite of this, revolutionary zeal inevitably exhausts itself, as people grow disenchanted with perpetual turmoil, insecurity, the reappearance of mundane problems, and politics. Inevitably, **thermidor** sets in, or a period of conservatism and the loss of revolutionary idealism and zeal. This word refers to the eleventh month in the French Revolutionary calendar, when the French Reign of Terror came to an end in 1794 and a more conservative regime came to power. Across all revolutions one finds this tension between those who would seek to keep the spirit of the revolution alive, no matter what the cost, and those who would rather consolidate the revolution through new and old institutions. The former are accused of zealotry while the latter are accused of betraying the revolution. Revolutions often devour themselves because of this tension. For example, in China in the 1960s, Mao unleashed the Cultural Revolution against the Communist Party itself, which he saw as having lost sight of its original revolutionary goals. Similar conflicts can be seen in the early years of the Russian and Mexican revolutions, and such battles continue to deeply influence contemporary Iranian politics. The end result can be a deep sense of disappointment, disengagement, and cynicism among the population, who feel that they have been betrayed. This can play into the hands of authoritarian leaders, who rely on such disengagement as a way to maintain control. Revolutions by their very nature seek to escape the oppressive weight of existing institutions, but in the end they find they are unable to escape them, as their radicalism becomes the new conservative status quo.

of a million and a half people; the Russian Revolution and subsequent civil war may have claimed well over 5 million. This violence can become an end in itself, as in the case of France's Reign of Terror after 1789. Enemies, supporters, and bystanders alike may all be consumed by an indiscriminate use of violence. In addition, it has been suggested that revolutionary states are also more likely to engage in interstate war, whether to promote their revolutionary ideology or because other countries feel threatened and/or see an opportunity to strike during this period of turmoil.[5] The long war between Iran and Iraq (1980–1988) can be cited here. Iraq attacked Iran in part because it hoped to take advantage of Iran's domestic turmoil, and the length of the war itself can be attributed to Iran's hope to use the war as a platform to export its revolution. Given the fragmentation of state power and the loss of the monopoly of force associated with revolution, greater violence is not surprising.

Terrorism

The word *terrorism* is, like revolution, loaded with meaning and used rather indiscriminately. However, these conceptual difficulties stem from issues that are the opposite of those surrounding revolution. While revolution's conceptual fuzziness comes in part from its inherently positive connotation (leading people to associate the term with all sorts of things), the word *terrorism* is highly stigmatized, a term no one willingly embraces. As a result, terrorism has become confused with a variety of other names, many of which are misleading, while others use the term indiscriminately to describe any kind of political force or policy they oppose. This has led some to conclude that it is effectively impossible to define terrorism, falling back on an old cliché: "One man's terrorist is another man's freedom fighter." Such a conclusion runs against the whole purpose of political science, which is to define our terms in an objective manner. We should therefore seek out a definition as precise as possible and use it to distinguish terrorism from other forms of political violence with which it might be confused. Certainly, one thing we should note is that terrorism has claimed far fewer lives than revolution, in spite of its recent increase (Figure 10.1 and Table 10.1). It is not so much the scale of the violence that holds our attention, but rather whom that violence is directed toward.

Terrorism can be defined as the use of violence by nonstate actors against civilians in order to achieve a political goal. As with revolution, there are several components at work in this definition, and we should take a moment to clarify each. First, there is the question of nonstate actors. Why should the term not be applied to states as well? Do they not also terrorize people? Indeed,

Figure 10.1
DEATHS FROM TERRORISM WORLDWIDE, 1998–2007

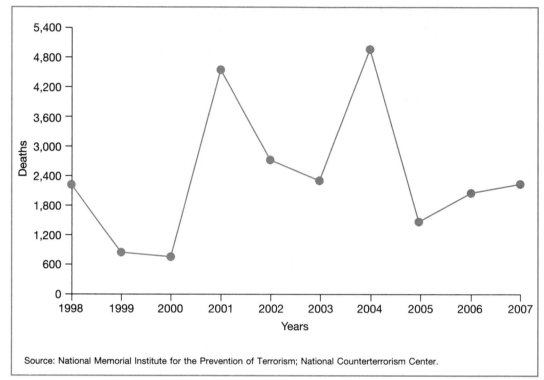

Source: National Memorial Institute for the Prevention of Terrorism; National Counterterrorism Center.

as we shall discuss later, the very concept of terrorism originally referred to state actions, not those of nonstate actors. Over time, the term came to be associated with nonstate actors who used terrorism in part because conventional military force was not available to them. This, however, does not mean that states cannot terrorize. Rather, other terms have come to stand in for such acts. When states use violence against civilian populations, we speak of war crimes or human rights violations, depending on the context. Both can include such acts as genocide and torture. Finally, there is **state-sponsored terrorism**. States do sometimes sponsor nonstate terrorist groups as a means to extend their power by proxy, using terrorism as an instrument of foreign policy. For example, India has long faced terrorist groups fighting for control over Kashmir, a state with a majority Muslim population (unlike the rest of India, which is majority Hindu). These terrorists are widely thought to be trained and armed by Pakistan, whose state leaders contend that Kashmir should be joined to their country. In short, we speak of terrorism as a nonstate action not because states are somehow above such violence but rather because other terminology exists to describe these actions (Figure 10.2).

Table 10.1 Terrorist Incidents by Region, 2007

Region	Incidents	Fatalities
Middle East	7,540	14,010
East Asia and Pacific	1,429	1,119
Europe	606	227
South Asia	3,067	4,737
Africa	835	2,187
Western Hemisphere	482	405
TOTALS	13,959	22,685

Source: National Counterterrorism Center, 2007 Report on Terrorism.

Second, our definition of terrorism emphasizes that the targets of violence are civilians. Here the issue of intentionality is important. In violent conflicts, there are often civilian casualties. But terrorists specifically target civilians, believing that such actions are a more effective way to achieve their political ends than by attacking the state. As a result, we can make a distinction between terrorism and **guerrilla war**. In contrast to terrorism, guerrilla war involves nonstate combatants who largely accept traditional rules of war and target the state rather than civilians. Often the line between these two can be blurry: Is killing a policeman or a tax collector an act of terrorism or a guerrilla warfare? Still, the central distinction remains, not only to observers but also to those carrying out the violence. We will speak more of this in a moment.

Finally, there is the issue of the political goal. It is important to recognize that terrorism has some political objective; as such, it is not simply a crime or a violent act without a larger goal. Here, too, the lines can be less than clear: terrorists may engage in crime as a way to support their activities, while criminal gangs may engage in terrorism if they are under pressure from the state. But in general, terrorism and other forms of violence can be sorted out by the primacy of political intent.

What are the causes of terrorism? As with revolution, there are varied and conflicting hypotheses, and these have changed over time as the nature of terrorism has shifted. In addition, because terrorism is so amorphous and shadowy, we find few comprehensive theories as we do in studies of revolution, though we can again group these in terms of institutional, ideational, and individual explanations.

Figure 10.2 **FORMS OF STATE AND POLITICAL VIOLENCE**

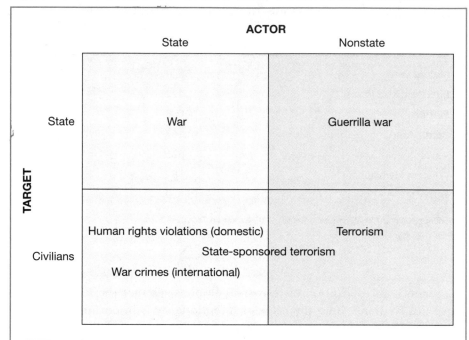

This chart distinguishes between forms of political violence, depending on who carries out the violence and who is the target of that violence. This includes both state and nonstate actors.

One of the most common responses to terrorism is to see it in institutional terms, often with the assertion that economic conditions are critical to understanding terrorist motivations. Poverty and the lack of education are commonly cited in this regard, with terrorism viewed as a tool of desperation by those who have no other opportunities before them. These arguments, while intriguing (and consistent with our discussions of the struggle over freedom versus equality) don't have a great deal of evidence to back them up. Educational explanations do not appear to be a strong explanation for terrorism; on the contrary, terrorists tend to come from more educated backgrounds compared with the population as a whole, and universities have frequently been centers of terrorist organization and recruitment. Economic explanations are equally problematic. We know that terrorists are not necessarily impoverished; Osama bin Laden's personal wealth is estimated to be in the millions of dollars. Although it may seem reasonable that poverty would be a motivation for terrorism, research on this topic finds instead that poverty tends to foster apolitical views and a detachment from political action. Here, too, research indicates that terrorists tend to come from economically advantaged backgrounds and that terrorist activity is not clearly correlated with low or deteriorating economic conditions, just as we saw in the case of revolution.[6] Explanations regarding the role of political institutions may be on firmer ground. Where state capacity and autonomy are weak and mechanisms for public participation poorly institutionalized, terrorism may find both the rationale and opportunity to use force.[7]

Ideational explanations are similarly useful and problematic. It has been commonplace to explain terrorism by blaming some ideology, religion, or set of values. However, given the way in which terrorism has shifted and morphed over time, these explanations often cannot explain cause and effect particularly well. This having been said, ideas thsmselves are important as they can provide justification for terrorist acts; such violence needs to have a political goal to motivate its members.

Some have asserted that irrespective of the particular set of ideas, what is crucial is their connection to nihilist or apocalyptic views. By **nihilism**, we

---

IN FOCUS

Regime Type and Terrorism

Regime Type	Effect on Terrorism	Result	Risk of Terrorism
Authoritarian	Authoritarianism may foster terrorism, but the state can repress domestic terrorists; the state is unhindered by civil liberties.	Limited terrorism, but may be redirected outside of the country toward more vulnerable targets	Lower
Democratic	Participatory institutions and civil liberties are likely to undercut public support for terrorism.	Domestic terrorism less likely, but country may be a target of international terrorism generated in nondemocratic regimes	Moderate
Illiberal/transitional	Weak state capacity, instability, and limited democratic institutions may generate both opportunities and motivations for terrorism.	Terrorism more likely, with domestic and/or international support	Higher

mean a belief that all institutions and values are essentially meaningless and that the only redeeming value one can embrace is that of violence. In this view, violence is desirable for its own sake. Nihilism can also be combined with utopian and apocalyptic views, whereby violence can destroy and thus purify a corrupted world, ushering in a new order. Interestingly, then, the actual content of the ideas themselves can change, even dramatically, so long as the justification for violence and the call for utopia remain intact. Indeed, in many cases terrorist organizations lack a clear articulation of the actual outcome they want to achieve.

Finally, individual explanations for terrorism have been a consistent source of focus, with researchers seeking to understand the personal motivations of terrorists. As mentioned earlier, one common explanation centers on feelings of injustice coupled with humiliation—that an individual or community's self-worth has been denigrated by others. Such feelings can generate frustration, anger, and, most important, a desire for vengeance. In addition, terrorist groups can play a role in providing a sense of identity and solidarity for otherwise alienated or humiliated individuals. Political violence can be a source of meaning, giving one a sense of greater purpose. In fact, it has been argued that terrorist groups resemble religious cults, with an emphasis on community, the purity of the cause, faith in the rectitude of the group's own beliefs and actions, and the conviction that retribution paves the way toward some utopian outcome.[8]

The effects of terrorism are harder to discern than the effects of revolutions. The first question to ask is whether terrorists are able to achieve their goals. In the case of revolution, the political violence is by definition successful—we study cases in which regimes have been successfully overthrown. In the case of terrorism, however, we are looking at the acts and actors rather than the events or outcomes.

One general observation we can make is that terrorists are mostly unsuccessful in achieving their stated long-term outcomes. Terrorists often seek some dramatic change in the existing domestic and/or international order, and their actions usually do not achieve this particular objective. In that sense, then, terrorism is not particularly strategic if its primary outcome is to usher in political change. However, this is not to say that terrorism has no impact. Economically, terrorism can be highly successful in depressing tourism, foreign direct investment, stock markets, and other sectors of the economy. Society can be similarly impacted, not just from the effects of a weakened economy but also by increasing anxiety and insecurity that undermines people's sense of well-being.

Terrorism can also have a distinct effect on politics. Countering terrorism can be a costly and frustrating process with little to show for it, diverting national resources while failing to address public concerns. An eroded sense of confidence in the state can be the result. In the quest for greater security, governments and their citizens may also favor increasing state power and curtailing civil liberties in the hope that such steps will limit terrorists' scope for action. However, this can lead to a weakening of democratic institutions and civil rights. The result can be less trust in government and less public control over it. At an extreme, terrorism can help bring down a regime. In 1992, Alberto Fujimori, the president of Peru, dissolved the legislature and suspended the constitution, acts that he justified in part as necessary to battle two separate terrorist groups that had destabilized the country. Much of the public supported this action, seeing it as the only way to reestablish order. Terrorism in Russia by Chechen separatists similarly helped pave the way for Vladimir Putin to win the presidency in 2000, and subsequent attacks were used as a justification for removing democratic institutions and limiting civil liberties.

This destruction of a regime, of course, is precisely what terrorism seeks— justification for their violence and another step toward destabilizing existing institutions. Terrorism uses violence against civilians as a way to disrupt the institutional fabric of state, society, and economy, calling into question all those things we take for granted, including stability, security, and predictability. By disrupting these most basic elements of modern life and instilling fear, terrorists believe they will help pave the way for revolution.

Terrorism and Revolution: Means and Ends

The question of what terrorists want leads us to consider terrorism and revolution as related forms of political violence. While we might think of these two as quite separate, it was not always this way. In modern politics, the concepts of terrorism and revolution were initially bound together as parts of a single process, having their origins in the French Revolution. For revolutionary leaders like Maximilien Robespierre, terror was an essential part of revolution. Robespierre argued that "terror is nothing other than justice, prompt, severe, inflexible; it is therefore an emanation of virtue" in the service of revolutionary change.[9] Thus, terror was not only a positive act, but a tool in the service of the revolutionary state.

Over time, this concept of terrorism and revolution began to shift. Revolutionaries who embraced the lessons of Robespierre concluded that terror need not be a tool to consolidate revolution once a regime has been overthrown but could in fact be the means toward that revolutionary end. A small group could speak for and lead the masses, instigating violence as a way to spark revolution. These revolutionaries thus openly embraced the name "terrorist" as an expression of their desire to use violence to achieve their political goals. Although the terrorist label has become stigmatized over time, this relationship between terrorism and revolution remains in place.

Terrorism can therefore be understood not simply in terms of who is directing political violence and toward whom but also in its revolutionary nature. Terrorists rarely seek limited goals, such as political or economic reform, since the entire system is seen as illegitimate. Rather, they believe that through their seemingly indiscriminate use of violence, all the dominant institutions can be shattered, overthrown, and remade. Consider, for example, this passage from an early manifesto of the Peruvian terrorist group Shining Path:

> The people rise up, arm themselves and rebel, putting nooses on the necks of imperialism and reaction. The people take them by the throat, threaten their lives and will strangle them out of necessity. The reactionary meat will be trimmed of fat, they will be torn to tatters and rags, the scraps sunk into mire, and the remainders burned. The ashes will be thrown to the winds of the world so that only the sinister reminder of what must never return will remain.[10]

This link between terrorism and revolution also helps to distinguish between terrorism and guerrilla war. We mentioned earlier that the line between these two forms of political violence is blurry, but that we can distinguish between the two in terms of their targets. (Guerrilla war seeks to abide by traditional rules of war, avoiding the targeting of civilians.) This decision is driven by political goals. Guerrillas typically accept that their opponents are legitimate actors, and they themselves seek to be regarded as legitimate by their opponents and the international community. Demands, while sometimes extensive (such as greater civil rights or independence for an ethnic group) do not deny the legitimacy of the other side, as is normally the case with terrorism. These distinctions matter, as such differences in means and ends will affect the degree to which states can negotiate with such groups to bring an end to conflict.

For example, during the civil conflict in Algeria in the 1990s, two nonstate groups were operating: the Islamic Salvation Front (FIS) and the Armed Islamic Group (GIA). Both opposed the Algerian regime, which suppressed Islamic fundamentalist groups, but took very different forms of opposition. The FIS created an armed wing that targeted specific parts of the state seen as directly supporting the regime. The FIS, which began as a nonviolent political movement, simultaneously declared that they could come to a compromise with the regime if certain demands were met, such as holding democratic elections. In contrast, the GIA rejected the entire regime and political process as un-Islamic and argued that anyone they viewed as having cooperated with the state in any manner, such as voting, deserved to be killed. The GIA's killing was thus much more indiscriminate and widespread, directed at state, society, and the FIS. Jihad, they argued, was the only means to an Islamic state.[11]

In short, revolution and terrorism have close connections. Terrorists often have revolution as their ultimate goal and use violence more widely in the belief that this will help set the stage for revolution. More limited use of force, as in guerrilla war, reflects a desire to participate in or work with existing institutions rather than overthrow them. The issue, then, for nonstate wielders of violence is whether they desire a seat at the political table or seek to knock the table over.

Political Violence in Context: Faith, Terrorism, and Revolution

Now that we have considered different ways to approach political violence, particularly revolution and terrorism, let us apply these ideas to the most pressing example in contemporary domestic and international politics: religious violence. As we discussed in Chapter 3, in recent decades we have seen the rise of movements that view religion as absolute and without error and that seek to make faith the sovereign authority over states and people. This religious fundamentalism is a major challenge to traditional ideologies in part because it is modeled after ideology itself. But while such fundamentalism may be uncompromising (as with many ideologies), it is not necessarily violent. Many fundamentalists may believe that reestablishing God's sovereignty can be done through nonviolent engagement in politics or by withdrawing from politics altogether. But as with ideologies, within this strain of thought there is also a violent approach.

What are the conditions under which religion becomes a source of political violence? The factors here echo much of our earlier discussion, including institutional, ideational, and individual factors. First, one common factor is hostility to modernity. In this view, modern institutions, driven by states and nations, capitalism, ideology, secularism, individualism, and material prosperity, have stripped the world of greater meaning and driven people to alienation and despair. Indeed, political violence is often embraced by those who initially enjoyed modernity but at some point turned away from its "corrupt" lifestyle. These antimodernist views have emerged in many different contexts but seem to be most powerful in societies where modern institutions are foreign in nature and poorly grafted onto traditional structures and values. It is at this border between traditional and modern institutions that the contradictions can be sharpest, which may explain why adherents of an antimodern mind-set are often urban and well-educated individuals: such persons are often most deeply immersed in modernity and may feel its contradictions most sharply.

A second factor is what the sociologist Mark Juergensmeyer calls "cosmic war."[12] In this view the modern world not only actively marginalizes, humiliates, and denigrates the views of the believers but also seeks their outright extermination. Those who hold this view see themselves as soldiers in a struggle between the righteousness of faith and its enemies (modernity), a war that transcends space and time. This is often bound up in conspiracy theories that point to shadowy forces in league to exterminate the good. With these views, violence against civilians can be rationalized because the conflict is seen not in terms of civilians versus combatants but of the guilty versus the innocent: those who do not stand on the side of righteousness are by definition on the side of evil. Scholars note that this dehumanization of the enemy is an important component in justifying violence against civilians, as social or religious taboos against murder must be overcome.

Third, religion as a source of political violence is often connected to messianic, apocalyptic, and utopian beliefs. Although the forces of darkness (modernity) have gained the upper hand, the role of the righteous is to trigger events that will lead to the destruction of the modern world. Evil will be destroyed and justice served. These views of violent apocalypse are often tied to some messianic belief that links the apocalypse to the savior's return. Following the apocalypse, a new utopian order will be established, re-creating the sovereignty of God and reuniting humanity with the true faith. Violence is therefore not only acceptable but is a form of ritual, whether in the form of self-sacrifice (martyrdom) or the sacrifice of others.

Such groups or movements are an extreme form of fundamentalism, since their path to violence requires a dramatic reinterpretation of the faith in a way that sharply divorces it from its mainstream foundations. These groups thus tend to break away from the mainstream faith and other fundamentalists, whom they accuse of having lost their way, presenting their radical alternatives as a restoration of religious truth. Muslim, Christian, or other fundamentalists would thus find many of these views as horrific and far removed from their view of faith. To reiterate, it is a mistake to confuse fundamentalism with violence. Now that we have outlined some of the most significant factors involved in religiously motivated political violence, let us consider some specific examples to see these factors at work.

Within Al Qaeda and similar jihadist groups, individuals like Osama bin Laden or Muhammed Atta (one of the leaders of the September 11 attacks) were steeped in modernity before turning to religion and religious violence. This violence is understood as part of a global struggle against infidels that goes back centuries. Hence, when bin Laden refers to the West as "Crusaders" in his 1996 manifesto, he is reaching back to the battles between the Islamic and Christian worlds in the Middle Ages. In the modern world, bin Laden argues, this crusade against Islam and its followers continues, though the

West's conspiracies are often cloaked by international organizations like the United Nations. In the September 11 attacks, we can see how the logic of cosmic war also fits into apocalyptic beliefs. Al Qaeda carried out these attacks not simply to weaken the United States but to provoke a backlash that they believed would intensify the conflict between the Islamic and non-Islamic worlds and would in turn lead to the overthrow of "un-Islamic" regimes in the Middle East and the eventual collapse of the West.

In these circumstances, not only are civilians fair targets, but Muslim civilians as well, whether in the United States, Europe, or the Middle East. This is justified because their "collaboration" with the forces of evil means by definition that they are not true Muslims and therefore can be killed, sacrificed to the cause. Recalling our discussion of the GIA in Algeria, its leader justified their widespread violence against the public by stating that "all the killing and slaughter . . . are an offering to God."[13]

Such views have strong parallels to certain violent strains drawn from Christianity. In the United States, racist groups assert that Western Christianity has been corrupted and weakened by a global Jewish conspiracy, and they seek to rebuild Western society on the basis of a purified white race. One particularly important figure in this ideology was William Pierce, who died in 2002. Pierce, who held a Ph.D. in physics and was at one time a university professor, formed the National Alliance in 1974. Pierce departed from Christianity altogether as a faith tainted by its association with Judaism, offering instead a "cosmotheist" faith that viewed whites as a form of superior evolution on the road to unity with God. In his novel *The Turner Diaries*, Pierce described the creation of a dedicated underground that would attack symbols of American authority, seize territory, and eventually launch a nuclear attack against the country itself. This apocalypse destroys the state, allowing the revolutionaries to exterminate all nonwhites and those who do not accept the new order. This genocide is eventually extended worldwide.[14] Timothy McVeigh's bombing of the federal courthouse in Oklahoma City in 1995, which killed 167 people, was directly inspired by *The Turner Diaries* and Pierce's argument that terrorism could trigger revolution. Pierce, while dissociating himself from McVeigh's act, nevertheless stated that McVeigh was

> a soldier, and what he did was based on principle. . . . He was at war against a government that is at war against his people. . . . In this war the rule is: Whatever is good for our people is good, and whatever harms our people is evil. That is the morality of survival.[15]

Pierce's views and those of related movements continue to attract followers throughout North America and Europe; it is estimated that several hundred thousand copies of *The Turner Diaries* have been sold, and the book has been translated into a number of European languages.

This violence extends outside the monotheistic religions of the West. In the 1980s, Japan saw the emergence of a new religion, Aum Shinrikyo ("Supreme Truth"). Aum was headed by Shoko Asahara, a partially blind mystic who claimed that he had reconnected with the true values of Buddhism that had been lost in the modern world. Asahara claimed that the world had gone through a series of thousand-year stages since the time of Buddha, with each one moving further away from his teachings until the contemporary period of moral degeneration. Aum attracted thousands well-educated members in Japan and Russia, including scientists and doctors, who felt alienated and in search of spiritual meaning. Asahara initially believed that the group should try to engage Japanese politics and fielded candidates for parliamentary elections in 1990. When all these candidates were defeated, however, Aum took on a more apocalyptic tone. Asahara claimed that a global war triggered by the United States would destroy the planet by the end of the decade, and he began to investigate how to construct weapons of mass destruction to trigger this event. The use of violence against civilians was justified with the argument that those who had not embraced Aum had already experienced a "karmic death," making violence more akin to a mercy killing.[16] In 1995, members of Aum placed bags of the nerve gas sarin in the Tokyo subway, killing twelve and injuring several thousand. Had the poison been more refined, the casualties would have been much higher.

In these three cases we see important similarities. First, these groups radically reinterpret an existing faith by arguing that it has departed from the true path. Osama bin Laden, William Pierce, and Shoko Asahara each claimed for themselves the ability to reinterpret traditional faith in a new, overtly ideological manner. Second, through this interpretation, they recast the world in terms of an final showdown between good and evil, purity versus corruption. Third, as the defenders of truth, they placed themselves in the role of warriors in the service of faith, able to mete out justice against all those who are seen as the enemy, whether state or society. Fourth, this violence was described not as an unfortunate necessity but as a sacrifice to the cause that would purify humanity and bring forth utopia.

These kinds of religiously motivated political violence have many parallels with similar acts carried out by nonreligious groups. The failures and humiliations of modernity, the creation of a group of "true believers" who see the world in stark terms of good versus evil, the idea of a global apocalypse that will destroy the old order and usher in a utopia can all be ascribed to many forms of secular, even antireligious political violence.

Do such conclusions give us any better understanding of future manifestations of political violence? In this regard there has been a sharp debate among scholars about environmental and animal rights groups and whether they might become more violent in the future. Some assert that these are inherently peaceful movements that would never tolerate such activity, while others point to arson and other property damage already committed by groups such as the Animal Liberation Front. In fact, many of the elements we have considered—hostility to modernity, a struggle in which the fate of the planet hangs in the balance, the belief in apocalypse and utopia, and the need for violence—can be found in the writings of the more radical environmentalists.[17] Again we can see the similarities between ideology and religion and the similar ways in which both can be used to justify violence.

Countering Political Violence

Our discussion indicates that political violence is a varied and constantly shifting force in the modern world. So long as states monopolize force, there will be actors who seek to wrest this power from the state so they can use it to pursue their own political objectives. Violence can be motivated by institutional, ideational, and individual factors—most likely some combination of the three. Though religious violence is currently at the forefront of concern, we see that in many ways the distinctions between ideological and religious violence are not as great as we might have supposed.

Given the amorphous nature of political violence, what can states do to manage or prevent it? This is difficult to answer, since the response partly depends on the nature of the political violence itself. Although violence differs across time and from place to place, we can nevertheless make a few tentative observations, understanding that these are not ironclad answers.

One observation is that regime type does appear to make a difference; terrorism and revolution are less likely in democratic societies. Why? The simplest answer is that democracies allow for a significant degree of participation among a wide enough number of citizens to make them feel that they have a stake in the system. While democracies produce their own share of cynicism and public unrest, including political violence, they also appear to co-opt and diffuse the motivations necessary for serious organized or mass violence against the state and civilians. Again, this is not to say that democracies are impervious to political violence; Timothy McVeigh and Shoko Asahara have recently proved otherwise. Our observation is merely that democracies appear to be more effective at containing and limiting such groups.

Of course, one of the dangers is that in an interconnected world, terrorism and revolution sparked by one kind of regime can easily spill beyond its borders. While democracy may be an important factor in preventing domestic violence, this will not necessarily prevent the development of political violence elsewhere. Indeed, the paradox here is that open democratic societies may limit domestic conflict but make for a much more tempting target for political violence that is globalized.

One might then conclude that if regime type is an important factor, then regime change should be a central goal for reducing political violence. Perhaps. However, such a policy is fraught with problems. First, research indicates that the successful institutionalization of democracy is predicated on how that regime change takes place. Regime changes that are top down (such as external intervention) or involving societal violence are less likely to produce a democratic outcome in the long run (Figure 10.3).[18]

The result instead is more likely to be an illiberal regime where democracy is weakly institutionalized, or even a failed state. And as we noted earlier, condi-

Figure 10.3   REGIME CHANGE AND FREEDOM

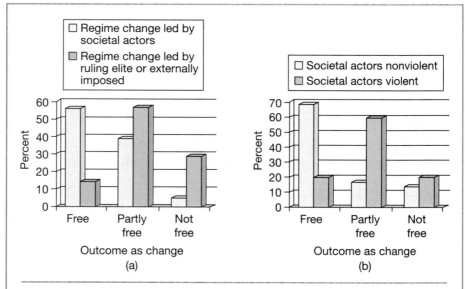

These charts look at nearly seventy cases of regime change from authoritarianism between 1973 and 2002. Chart (a) shows that in those cases where societal actors led the transition, over 50 percent resulted in a free country with full civil and political rights. In contrast, less than 15 percent of transitions controlled by those in power or imposed by other states led to a free political regime. Chart (b) indicates that in those cases where societal actors refrained from violence, nearly 70 percent of transitions resulted in a free country with full civil and political rights. In contrast, only 20 percent of transitions with societal violence resulted in a free political regime.

Source: Freedom House.

tions with low institutionalization, instability and insecurity can provide both the motivation and the opportunity for political violence to emerge. In short, regime change can in fact increase, not reduce, the number of regimes that foster political violence. Iraq and Afghanistan would appear to be sad evidence of this.

What about states that are already liberal democracies and yet face political violence from domestic or international actors? In this case, the classic dilemma of freedom versus security raises its head. In the face of threats, democratic states and their citizens will often favor limiting certain civil liberties and increasing state autonomy and capacity in order to bring an end to political violence (Figure 10.4). In the United States, the 2001 Patriot Act

Figure 10.4 **VIEWS ON COUNTERING TERRORISM: CANADA AND THE UNITED STATES**

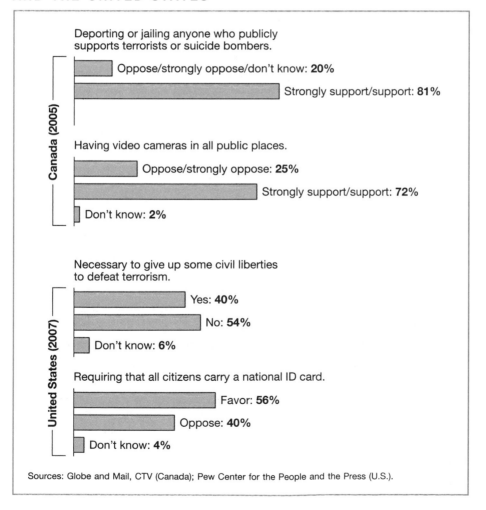

Sources: Globe and Mail, CTV (Canada); Pew Center for the People and the Press (U.S.).

is an example of such counterterrorism, with its increased powers to conduct public surveillance. Since 2006, suspects in the United Kingdom can be detained up to twenty-eight days without charge, and individuals arrested for inciting or "glorifying" terrorism.

There are several dangers here. First, an excessive focus on security over freedom may be dangerous to democracy. Placing too much power in the hands of the state to observe and control the public could seriously threaten to erode individual rights and with them democracy. Second, such actions can in fact contribute to political violence, since they confirm the idea that the state is conspiring to destroy its opponents, thus justifying violent resistance. Third, the increase of state control typically means greater centralization of power, which may not increase security. For example, many countries have suggested national ID cards as a way to thwart terrorism. However, such a move raises several concerns. Identity cards created to counter terrorism can be used to track a variety of actions, many unrelated to national security, and they introduce the risk that a centralized national ID database could be hacked into or disabled, easing the way for terrorists or paralyzing transactions altogether.[19] However, people and politicians often seek dramatic and visible solutions because they provide a sense of security, although in reality they may have limited or even counterproductive effects. The old adage attributed to Benjamin Franklin is worth recalling: "Those who would give up essential liberty to purchase a little temporary safety deserve neither liberty nor safety."[20]

In Sum: Meeting the Challenge of Political Violence

Political violence is a complex issue for scholars, states, and societies. Often its objectives are cast in idealistic terms as a part of necessary historical change. At the same time, this violence often comes at a tremendous cost of human life, with violence often becoming an end in itself. Because political violence is a response to existing institutions, it is difficult to pin down exactly how it emerges, what motivates it, and how states should respond. Like a virus, it may suddenly emerge in unexpected places, ravaging the population before disappearing again. Or it may lie dormant for many years, only to break out when certain conditions come together.

There is clearly no one way to stop or prevent political violence. Each case is different and requires its own approach. However, we have noted that in general, democracies have been effective at limiting political violence. If we accept the analogy of political violence as a virus, one means of response to political violence may be immunization. Countries may be able to immunize themselves by maintaining and strengthening social ties and organizations that help reduce the appeal or societal impact of political violence.[21] While such actions will never eradicate the danger, they may be able to limit its spread and damage by undercutting the motivations behind it. To think of political violence as a public health issue may provide new ways of countering this danger in the future. In our final chapter, we will consider how these and other questions of comparative politics may be shaped by the ongoing process of globalization.

NOTES

1. M. J. Heale, *American Anticommunism: Battling the Enemy Within, 1830–1970* (Baltimore: Johns Hopkins University Press, 1990).
2. Max Abrams, "What Terrorists Really Want," *International Security*, 32, no. 4 (Spring 2008), pp. 78–105.
3. Robert Pape, *Dying to Win: The Strategic Logic of Suicide Terrorism* (New York: Random House, 2005).
4. Timur Kuran, "Now Out of Never: The Element of Surprise in the East European Revolution of 1989," *World Politics*, 44, no. 1 (October 1991), pp. 7–48.
5. Stephen M. Walt, *Revolution and War* (Ithaca, NY: Cornell University Press, 1996).
6. Alan B. Krueger and Jitka Malečková, "Education, Poverty and Terrorism: Is There a Causal Connection?" *Journal of Economic Perspectives*, 17, no. 4 (Fall 2003), pp. 119–144.
7. Alberto Abadie, "Poverty, Political Freedom, and the Roots of Terrorism," NBER Working Paper No. W10859, October 2004, http://papers.ssrn.com.
8. Randy Borum, *Psychology of Terrorism* (Tampa: University of South Florida, 2004).
9. Maximilien Robespierre, *On Political Morality*, 1794.
10. *We Are the Initiators*, Shining Path Manifesto, Shining Path Central Committee, 1980.
11. Mohammed M. Hafez, "Armed Islamist Movements and Political Violence in Algeria," *Middle East Journal*, 54, no. 4 (Autumn 2000), pp. 572–591.
12. Mark Juergensmeyer, *Terror in the Mind of God: The Global Rise of Religious Violence* (Berkeley: University of California Press, 2003).
13. Quoted in Hafez, "Armed Islamist Movements," p. 590.
14. Brad Whitsel, "The Turner Diaries and Cosmotheism: William Pierce's Theology," *Nova Religio*, 1, no. 2 (April 1998), pp. 183–197.
15. William Pierce, "The Morality of Survival," May 2001, www.natvan.com.
16. Daniel A. Metraux, "Religious Terrorism in Japan: The Fatal Appeal of Aum Shinrikyo," *Asian Survey*, 35, no. 12 (December 1995), pp. 1140–1154.
17. Gary Ackerman, "Beyond Arson? A Threat Assessment of the Earth Liberation Front," *Terrorism and Political Violence*, 15, no. 4 (Winter 2003), pp. 143–170; see also Craig Rosebraugh, *The Logic of Political Violence: Lessons in Reform and Revolution* (Portland: Arissa, 2003).
18. "How Freedom Is Won: From Civic Resistance to Durable Democracy," Freedom House Special Report, 2005, www.freedomhouse.org.

19. Stephen T. Kent and Lynette I. Millett, eds., *IDs—Not That Easy: Questions about Nationwide Identity Systems* (Washington, DC: National Academy Press, 2002).

20. Anonymous, *An Historical Review of the Constitution and Government of Pennsylvania* (London, 1759), p. i.

21. Ami Pedazhur, "Struggling with the Challenges of Right Wing Extremism and Terrorism within Democratic Boundaries: A Comparative Analysis," *Studies in Conflict and Terrorism*, 24 (2001), pp. 339–359.

11 GLOBALIZATION AND THE FUTURE OF COMPARATIVE POLITICS

KEY CONCEPTS

- Globalization is a process whereby extensive and intensive webs of relationships connect people across time and space.

- Political globalization challenges sovereignty.

- Economic globalization can transform markets and property within and between countries.

- Societal globalization may undermine old identities and create new ones.

- Scholars debate whether globalization is new, exaggerated, or irreversible.

The central theme of this textbook has been the struggle to balance freedom and equality. Market forces can generate tension in this relationship; when societies clash over how to reconcile these two values, states must confront the problems using their capacity to generate and enforce policy. Democratic institutions presume that freedom and equality are best reconciled through public participation, whereas nondemocratic regimes significantly restrict such rights. The variety of institutional tools available has led to a diverse political world, where freedom and equality are combined and balanced in many different ways. Here, in essence, is the core of comparative politics: the study of how freedom and equality are reconciled around the world.

But over the past decade this dynamic has become more international in scope. Of course, domestic politics has always been shaped by international forces, such as war and trade, empires and colonies, migration and the spread of ideas. But to some observers, this interconnection between countries is changing in its scope, depth, and speed. Linkages between states, societies, and economies appear to be intensifying, and at an increasingly rapid pace, challenging long-standing institutions, assumptions, and norms. This process, still ill defined and unclear, is commonly known as **globalization**, a term that fills some with a sense of optimism and others with anxiety or dread. Although the extent of globalization and its long-term impact remain unclear, behind it lies the sense that the battle over freedom and equality is becoming internationalized, no longer a concern to be solved by each country in its own way. What does this mean for comparative politics—how we study and compare domestic politics across countries? To be more blunt about it, is there even such a thing as domestic politics any longer? Is everything that we've read in this book up to this point becoming obsolete or irrelevant? And if so, how are we to study politics in a globalized world?

In this chapter, we will look at the concept of globalization and its potential impact on comparative politics and the ongoing struggle over freedom and equality. We will begin by defining globalization, sorting out what this term means and how we might measure it. Next, we will consider some of the possible effects of globalization, and how globalization may change political, economic, and societal institutions at the domestic level. We will also ask some questions about the progress of globalization—whether it is in fact something fundamentally new, profound, and inevitable. We will then conclude with a discussion of how the old dilemma of freedom and equality may change in a globalized world.

What Is Globalization?

We could argue that we have lived in a globalized world for many thousands of years. Even as early humans dispersed around the world tens of thousands of years ago, they maintained and developed long-distance connections between one another through migration and trade. Such contacts helped spur development through the dissemination of knowledge and innovations; for example, it is speculated that the technology of written language was created independently only three or four times in human history: in the Americas, in Asia, and in the Middle East. All other written languages were essentially modeled after these innovations as the idea of writing things down spread to other communities.[1] Thousands of years ago empires stretched from Asia to Europe, and people moved between these areas, exchanging goods and ideas. Trade routes forged even more far-flung connections between people who were only dimly aware of each other's existence. For example, in the first century C.E., the Romans treasured silk imported from distant China, although they did not fully understand how it was made or where it came from. Were these, then, "globalized" societies?

When we speak about globalization, we don't simply mean international contacts and interaction, which have existed for tens of thousands of years.

According to the political scientists Robert Keohane and Joseph Nye, one important distinction between globalization and these age-old ties is that many of these longtime relationships were relatively "thin," involving a small number of individuals. Although such connections may have been extensive across a vast region, the connections were not intensive in their volume or personal impact. In contrast, globalization can be viewed as a process by which this web of global connections becomes increasingly "thick," creating an extensive and intensive web of relationships between many people across vast distances. In the twenty-first century, people are not distantly connected by overland routes plied by traders, diplomats, and missionaries; they are directly participating in a vast and complex international network through travel, communication, business, and education. Globalization is a system in which human beings are no longer part of isolated communities that are themselves linked through narrow channels of diplomatic relations or trade (Figure 11.1). Entire societies are now directly connected to global affairs. Thus, globalization represents a change in human organization and interconnection, but these are a function of technological changes that have made it possible.[2]

Globalization presents a number of potential implications for comparative politics. First, because of the thickening of connections between people across countries, globalization breaks down the distinction between international relations and domestic politics, making many aspects of domestic politics subject to global forces. Debates over environmental policy become linked to global warming; struggles over employment are framed by concerns about trade, outsourcing, and immigration; health care is influenced by pandemics like AIDS or avian flu. As a result, political isolation becomes difficult or even impossible, and the line between domestic and foreign policy is blurred.

Second, globalization can also amplify politics in the other direction, essentially "internationalizing" domestic issues and events. Given that globalization deepens and widens international connections, local events, even small ones, can have ripple effects throughout the world. Computer hackers in China can bring down websites in the United States; a panicky stock market in Russia can trigger an economic downturn in Brazil. These interconnections across space are further amplified by the speed of today's world. Whereas technological change once took years or centuries to spread from region to region, today a new piece of software or video can be downloaded or viewed globally at the same time everywhere. The Internet allows the rapid dissemination of news and information from every corner of the globe, no matter how remote. The world lives increasingly in the same moment—what happens in one place affects others around the world soon after.

In short, globalization is a process that creates intensive and extensive international connections, which in the process change traditional relationships of time and space. Will globalization overturn or transform the very

Figure 11.1   **MEASURING GLOBALIZATION: THE GLOBAL TOP 20, 2007**

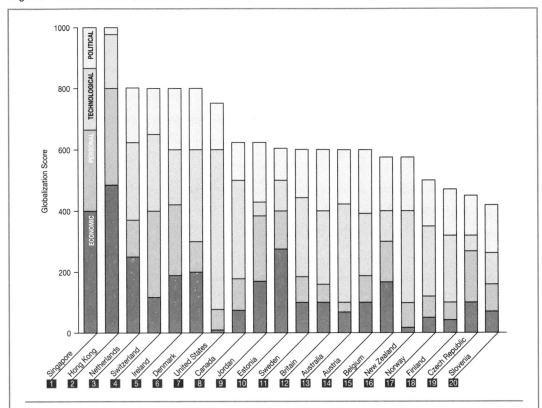

This figure shows the top twenty globalized countries in the world in terms of economics (trade and foreign direct investment), people (travel and other forms of international contact), technology (Internet penetration), and politics (treaties with other states and membership and participation in international organizations).

Source: Foreign Policy/A. T. Kearney.

foundations of politics? Would such a change make the world a better place—more prosperous, stable, and democratic—or just the opposite? And finally, is any of this inevitable? These are big questions of profound significance with little consensus. Let us first consider how we can think about the nature of institutions in a globalizing world.

Institutions and Globalization

We have spoken of globalization as a process, one that creates more extensive and intensive connections across the globe. These changes can, in turn, change the institutions of economics, politics, and societies. At the start of this textbook, we spoke of institutions as being a key reference point for modern life. Institutions are organizations or patterns of activity that are self-perpetuating and valued for their own sake. The modern world is a world codified by institutions. Institutions such as states, culture, property, and markets establish borders, set boundaries for activity and behavior, and allocate authority, norms, rights, and responsibilities. Moreover, by doing so, they establish local identity and control—a particular state, religion, or set of cultural values holds sway over this land and people, but not the ones over there. Space and time are thus understood and measured through institutions.

The question we now ask is whether this will still be true in the future. It may be that before long, domestic institutions will no longer be the most important actors in people's lives. Long-standing institutions like states, cultures, national identities, or political economic systems now face a range of international forces and organizations that transform, challenge, or threaten their traditional roles. Let's look at some of the reasons this might be the case.

To begin with, globalization is associated with the growing power of a host of nonstate or suprastate entities. Most can be grouped in three categories that we have already touched on in previous chapters: **multinational corporations (MNCs)**, **nongovernmental organizations (NGOs)**, and **intergovernmental organizations (IGOs)**. All three organizational forms are decades if not centuries old, but the argument is that their role and impact are rapidly expanding as they benefit from and contribute to globalization. MNCs are firms that produce, distribute, and market in more than one country. Multinational corporations such as Microsoft wield assets and profits far larger than the gross domestic products (GDPs) of most countries in the world and are able to influence politics, economic developments, and social relations through the goods and services they produce and the wealth at their disposal. Nongovernmental organizations, as we discussed in the last chapter, are national and international groups, independent of any state, that pursue policy objectives and foster public participation. Some, such as Greenpeace and Amnesty International, also wield influence in their ability to shape domestic and international politics by mobilizing public support across the globe. Intergovernmental organizations, groups created by states to serve particular policy ends, include the United Nations, the World Trade Organization, the European Union, and the Organization of American States. They vary widely in their objectives, membership, and powers, but they tend to exert some form of authority over their member states.

In addition to these entities, there are organizations that are largely technological in nature. This is not new; all earlier waves of human interconnection were themselves dependent on technological changes, such as the domestication of plants and animals, the creation of the wheel, seafaring, and the telegraph. Most recently, globalization has been profoundly influenced by the Internet. Originally created by the U.S. government as a way to decentralize communications in the event of a nuclear war, the Internet has grown far past this initial limited objective to become a means through which people exchange goods and information, much of it beyond the control of any one state or regulatory authority. Unlike MNCs, NGOs, or IGOs, the Internet has no single "location" to speak of, and so discussions of authority, sovereignty, and control become problematic. But as technological change facilitates nonstate or suprastate actors, these actors in turn tend to foster further technological change.

Are these organizations, whether the UN or the Internet, institutions? This is an important question, for as we have noted, institutionalization carries with it authority and legitimacy. Many would argue that yes, these organizations do have a life of their own. Many MNCs, IGOs, and NGOs are legitimate and highly valued, such that they have become a seemingly indispensable part of the global system. The same could be said of the Internet or other forms of technology, such as satellite television or global positioning systems (GPS). As institutions, then, they carry and can call on a degree of influence and power. This may augment and improve the workings of domestic institutions; it may also conflict with or undermine them. Let us consider this idea further through the familiar categories of states, economies, and societies.

IN FOCUS

Nonstate Organizations and Globalization

Organization	Definition	Example
Multinational corporations (MNCs)	Firms that produce, distribute, and market their goods or services in more than one country	Microsoft, General Electric
Intergovernmental organizations (IGOs)	Groups created by states to serve particular policy ends	United Nations, European Union
Nongovernmental organizations (NGOs)	National and international groups, independent of any state, that pursue policy objectives and foster public participation	Greenpeace, Red Cross

Political Globalization

In Chapter 2, we noted that in historical terms, the state is relatively new, a form of political organization that emerged only in the past few centuries. Because of their unique organization, states were able to quickly spread across the globe, supplanting all other forms of political organization. Yet we also noted that if states have not always been with us, it then stands to reason that there may come a time when states are no longer the dominant political actor on the face of the earth. States may at some time cease to exist. Some see globalization as the very force that will bring about this dramatic political change, but whether such a change is to be welcomed or feared is uncertain.

At the core of this debate is the fact that globalization and globalized institutions complicate the ability of states to maintain sovereignty. In some cases, this loss of sovereignty is intentional, as states may give up authority to IGOs to gain some benefit or alleviate some existing problem. The European Union is an excellent example of this, though as we have seen, even under these conditions sovereignty is often given up reluctantly and contested. In other cases, the loss of sovereignty may be unintentional and wholly unwanted. The growth of the Internet, for example, has had important implications for states regarding legal authority in many traditional areas, given the fact that the Internet does not easily conform to international boundaries or rules. Thus, software may be easily copied and shared, in spite of property rights or national security restrictions. Similarly, legal restrictions on certain forms of speech can be circumvented in a way in which traditional newspapers or television cannot, through e-mail, websites, social networks, or blogs. Developments such as electronic currency may further erode the powers of states by undercutting their ability to print money, levy taxes, or regulate financial transactions—all critical elements of sovereignty.

What do these changes mean for state autonomy and capacity? One possible scenario is that the state will become bound to numerous international institutions that will take on many of the tasks that states normally conduct. In this scenario, a web of organizations, public and private, domestic and international, would shape politics and policy, set standards, and enforce rules on a wide range of issues where states lack effective authority. The rule of law would become less a preserve of individual states than a set of global institutions created for and enforced by a variety of actors.

Under this diffusion of responsibility, sovereignty would decline. States would be "hollowed out," no longer able to act independently within their own territory; they would be constrained within the international system by their reliance on the globalized world. Some argue that many of the vital issues that modern-day people face—environmental degradation, drugs, trade, technological innovation—cannot be dealt with through force. One cannot arrest computer viruses or enact sanctions against global warming, and despite the U.S. call for a "war on drugs" and a "war on terror," even here one cannot declare war in the conventional sense. For globalized states, then, war may become less viable, largely ineffective, and likely to undermine vital international connections. This narrowing of state sovereignty as a result of globalization is what the *New York Times* columnist Thomas Friedman has referred to as a "golden straitjacket."[3] In this view, political globalization may bring about a more peaceful world order, constraining the tendencies toward violent conflict by dispersing sovereignty among numerous actors while constraining the capacity and autonomy of states.

It has also been argued that globalization will change not only the utility of force but also the nature of public participation and democracy. The increasing interconnection between domestic and international institutions makes it more difficult for sovereign actors to function without oversight from other organizations and to hide their actions from others. The development of the International Criminal Court could be seen as an example here, where the enforcement of international laws and judicial authority opens the door to hold states and their leaders accountable for such things as human rights violations in the former Yugoslavia or in Sudan. Nongovernmental organizations can play a similarly powerful watchdog role, as such groups as Transparency International (an anticorruption NGO) already do. Globalization will thus make politics less opaque and more open to scrutiny by domestic and international communities.

In contrast to these optimistic views, others see political globalization not as a pathway to peace and participation but as a source of dangerous fragmentation and weakened democracy. First, violence will not lose its utility in the international system as optimists hope; it will simply change form, much as it did when states themselves first appeared. According to this argument, globalization is fostering not only new organizations that may foster cooperation but also violent international actors that in many ways are the exact opposite of the modern state. These groups are decentralized and flexible, hold no territory and exercise no sovereignty, and are able to draw financial and other support from across the globe. In many ways, then, they are not unlike other nonstate actors. Yet unlike NGOs or MNCs, these groups seek to achieve their objectives through the acquisition and use of force, applying it in ways that may be difficult for states or other international actors to counter. Globalized criminal organizations or terrorist groups are perfect examples of this new threat.[4]

For example, in the case of Al Qaeda, we see a group that is highly decentralized, in which a leadership provides resources, guidance, and inspiration but allows for a great deal of individual initiative and responsibility among individual operators. Such decentralization makes it very difficult for state intelligence agencies to surveil or destroy such networks. The death of a leader, although a potential setback, will not destroy the group itself since it does not depend on a hierarchical structure of command and control. This decentralization is further aided by globalized technology, such as cell phones, encrypted e-mail, websites, and satellite television, which allows terrorists to communicate, disseminate propaganda, access money, and recruit new followers. Indeed, such groups look more like an online social network than any formal nonstate actor. Although states may at times be able to use conventional force against such groups where they have a physical presence, there is no central location to attack nor any easy way to keep such individuals and information from simply dispersing and regrouping elsewhere. States, the military capacity of which is geared toward fighting other states, may be ill equipped to battle small groups that can take advantage of globalization to attack and undermine existing institutions.[5]

Second, many question how a more globalized political system can be more democratic. Although increased connections may increase transparency, this does not necessarily lay out a mechanism by which individuals can act on that information. As we noted in Chapter 5, modern liberal democracy is based on republicanism, the ability to choose one's representatives through a competitive process. But who votes for international organizations? These bodies may be indirectly elected or appointed from the member states—or they may not be directly accountable to anyone at all. Thus, while one may laud the work of Greenpeace or the World Wildlife Fund, it is instructive to note that these organizations are not subject to popular democratic control nor necessarily more transparent than states themselves. This raises the concern of a "democratic deficit," an idea first raised with regard to the EU. If power moves to global institutions, representation and democratic control may grow weaker as citizens lack the ability to control these bodies, and these institutions grow distant from the citizenry and their preferences. At an extreme, this could lead to a new form of global illiberalism, such as we discussed in Chapter 6, where representative institutions exist but have been hollowed out by the loss of sovereignty and by the power of global technocratic institutions and elites.[6]

These are two starkly different visions of politics in a globalized world. In both scenarios, states and state functions become more diffused as power shifts to the global level. For optimists, international cooperation follows, with these developments undermining the logic of war and increasing transparency. For pessimists, deepening international connections facilitate new violent organizations as well as weaken democratic ties between the people and their representatives. Some combination of both scenarios is also possible.

Economic Globalization

Politics is not the only realm in which globalization may be taking place; in fact, when many people think about globalization, economics is what typically comes to mind, and it is this area that generates the most controversy and debate. In the area of economic globalization, there are in fact two distinct but interrelated processes at work. The first is the globalization of international trade. This means that trade, which has always had a strong international component, is increasingly extensive and intensive, tying markets, producers, and labor together in a way that had not existed previously. The second facet of economic globalization is less visible but no less profound. Financial globalization is the integration of capital and financial markets— markets for money—around the world. Banking and credit, stocks and foreign direct investment all fall under this category. Over the past few decades, the world has seen a rapidly developing system of trade and financial globalization, fostered by technological change and dramatic shifts in world politics, such as the collapse of communism and the spread of liberalism.

Some examples can provide perspective on the growth of economic globalization In 1992, world exports in merchandise was approximately $3 trillion U.S.; in 2007, it had grown to $13 trillion. **Foreign direct investment** (the purchase of assets in a country by a foreign firm) was under $200 billion U.S. in 1992; as of 2006 it had reached $1.3 trillion.[7] As mentioned earlier, economic globalization is also associated with the emergence of a number of MNCs that dominate global markets. Assisted by more open markets and reduced costs for transportation, large firms such as IBM, Honda, McDonald's, and Johnson & Johnson control assets and make profits in the billions of dollars, often rivaling the GDPs of many countries in which they do business. For example, General Electric's total profits in 2007 were approximately $21 billion, which is roughly equal to the Congo's entire GDP at purchasing-power parity (Figure 11.2).

These economic developments are compounded by expanding global communications. Recent economic difficulties notwithstanding, the development of electronic commerce, with its ability to link far-flung businesses globally, is transforming the way in which markets, firms, and individuals interact. Technological innovations have reduced many of the traditional barriers to trade. Firms and people are able to buy goods and services from around the world using fewer or no intermediaries. As a result, markets are more open and firms face greater competition. A business in China or Chile, for example, can market its goods and services directly to other firms or individuals anywhere in the world. In the area of investment, too, online banking and investment allow people to move their money internationally with a few mouse clicks. Many people liken the significance of the development of the Internet to that of the creation of railroads and the telegraph in the nineteenth cen-

Figure 11.2 **FOREIGN DIRECT INVESTMENT, 1980–2006**

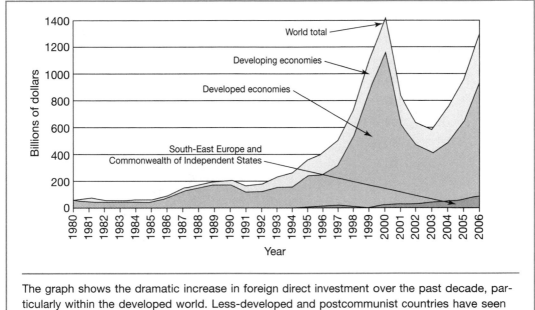

The graph shows the dramatic increase in foreign direct investment over the past decade, particularly within the developed world. Less-developed and postcommunist countries have seen more modest investment.

Source: UN Conference 2007, www.unctad.org/en/docs/wir2007_en.pdf.

tury, which helped transform the way goods could be produced, marketed, and delivered.

Finally, economic globalization also applies not just to trade, firms, or finances but also to labor. Globalization may shift not only where things are made but also where labor is located. As noted in Chapter 7, the globe is currently experiencing a huge wave of migration, both between countries and within them, as people move from countryside to city (Figure 11.3). For example, in China, it is estimated that the country's "floating population"—individuals migrating, often illegally, from countryside to city and interior to the coast—is projected to reach 200 million by 2015, nearly half the population of the European Union.

Perhaps the best-known example of this intersection between globalized labor, technology, and markets is offshore outsourcing. Outsourcing has long existed, as it is simply a process by which a firm moves some of its work to a secondary business that can do the work more efficiently or cheaply. However, in the past, much of this outsourcing was done inside domestic or regional economies. The rise of a postindustrial and information-based economy, however, has meant that much of this outsourcing may now go a great

Figure 11.3 **WORLD MIGRATION TRENDS**

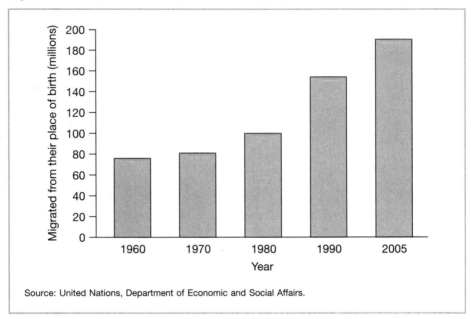

Source: United Nations, Department of Economic and Social Affairs.

distance, to wherever the cost advantage can be found. Examples include call centers, data processing, animation, and software programming. In 2002, offshore outsourcing amounted to about $1.3 billion; by 2007 the number rose to nearly $300 billion. India is often noted as a major player in these areas, but Eastern Europe, China, and even Africa have all been active as well.

For optimists, economic globalization contains within it the means for global prosperity. Recalling our discussion of political-economic systems in Chapter 4, consider that globalization looks very much like the internationalization of a liberal economic system, with its emphasis on open markets and competition for goods and labor. Through the expansion of international economic connections, goods and services, labor, and other resources can be allocated more effectively through a broader market, unfettered by tariff barriers and other obstacles that states might erect. Countries are able to export what they produce best, encouraging innovation, specialization, and lower costs. Jobs are also created as capital flows and transnational corporations take advantage of new markets and new opportunities. People, too, can move to where there is work, whether domestically or internationally (see Figure 11.3). In the end, wealth is diffused more effectively through open markets for goods, labor, and capital, increasing standards of living worldwide. Globalization is thus viewed as a positive trend, a global division of labor that can lift billions out of poverty and generate greater prosperity by allowing more people to be a part of an international marketplace for goods and labor (see Figure 11.4).[8]

Figure 11.4 GLOBALIZATION AND LIFE EXPECTANCY

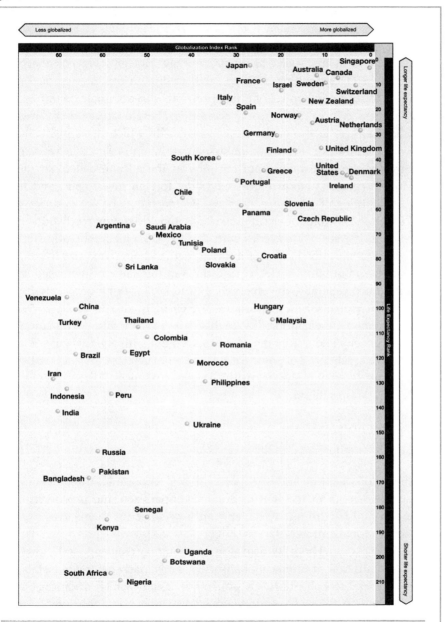

Studies indicate that the most globalized countries are also those with the highest life expectancy. This is true not only of advanced democracies but also of less-developed and newly industrializing countries as well.

Source: Foreign Policy/A. T. Kearney.

Others view economic globalization with more suspicion, particularly those who are less enamored of a liberal political economy. Some equate increased trade with increased dependence, arguing that trade creates conditions whereby some countries will gain monopoly control over particular goods vital in the international economy, such as software, energy, biotechnology, or pharmaceutical products. The resulting unequal relationships in the international system will allow countries in control of crucial resources to dominate countries whose goods are less critical to the world economy. The globalization of investment and labor markets is also criticized as a system in which firms invest in countries with cheap labor and weak labor regulations in order to increase profits; these moves eliminate manufacturing jobs in the advanced democracies and undermine organized labor. Increased trade, foreign investment, and the offshore outsourcing of jobs hurts workers around the globe as countries engage in a "race to the bottom," lowering standards and weakening regulations to keep or attract businesses. For societies with developed social democratic systems in particular, globalization is seen as a threat, demanding a "one size fits all" set of weak states and minimal social expenditures in the name of increased competitiveness. More generally, the emergence of large, far-flung corporations raises the fear that globalized businesses are increasingly able to avoid government oversight and public accountability. In this view, as economic globalization weakens state capacity and autonomy, it is replaced not with a global rule of law but rather with a small cartel of powerful corporations that lack any national or democratic control—what one writer calls "disaster capitalism."[9] Freedom and equality are thus compromised.

Societal Globalization

Whether globalization and the political and economic transformations it brings becomes an instrument of greater cooperation and prosperity or one of conflict and hardship may depend on how societies themselves are transformed by globalization.

We have explored how political globalization may challenge state sovereignty and power and how economic globalization binds markets for goods, labor, and capital. Societal globalization is a similar process, in which traditional societal institutions are weakened, creating new identities that do not belong to any one community or nation. As we know from previous chapters, in the premodern world, people's identities were rather limited and narrow, focused on such things as family, tribe, village, and religion. Only with the rise of the state did national identities begin to emerge, such that individuals began to see themselves tied to a much larger community of millions, strangers bound together by complex myths and symbols—flags, legends, symbols, anthems, culture. This transfor-

mation coincided with the development of sovereignty, whereby borders and citizenship reinforced the notion of national identity—one people, one state.

Some argue that as globalization proceeds, these central aspects of individual and collective identity are giving way. Just as the state and domestic
economic institutions are being challenged, so, too, are the traditional identities of the past. New technologies, waves of migration, trade, and communication link people across vast distances, forging relationships between
people on the basis of common interests and ideas rather than shared national
symbols. Many find the Internet particularly powerful in this regard, in its
ability to spread information, ideas, and cultural products to billions of individuals around the globe (Table 11.1). As the Internet continues to grow by

Table 11.1 Percentage of Population That Uses the Internet, 2000 and 2007

	2000	2007	Growth in Percent
Sweden	44.9	76.7	70.8
United States	61.2	71.4	16.7
Japan	36.9	68.0	84.3
South Korea	40.0	67.1	67.8
United Kingdom	44.5	66.4	49.2
France	21.5	54.7	154.4
Malaysia	22.9	52.7	130.1
Czech Republic	13.6	50.0	267.6
Kuwait	8.1	29.9	269.1
Iran	0.4	25.6	6300.0
Peru	19.9	25.5	28.1
Brazil	3.6	22.8	533.3
Mexico	3.2	21.3	565.6
Russia	2.5	19.5	680.0
China	2.3	12.3	434.8
South Africa	10.0	10.3	3.0
India	0.5	5.3	960.0
Nigeria	0.2	4.9	2350.0
Worldwide	*9.1*	*19.1*	*109.9*

Source: www.internetworldstats.com

leaps and bounds, people find ways to connect to one another across time and space, building and deepening connections to one another. E-mail and text messaging, websites and blogs, social networks and virtual reality spaces such as World of Warcraft or Second Life are all examples of virtual interconnections that have become integral to, or have even displaced, physical spaces and relationships.

How might this process shape societal institutions and identities? We can point to two directions. The first is that societal globalization may engender global multiculturalism. The deepening of international connections between people and the exchange of ideas between them will transfer the dynamics of multiculturalism from the national level to the international one, with different cultures connecting and combining more through connections that are not bound by traditional barriers of time and space. This means not only that a globalized society will draw from many sources but also that the interconnection of such institutions at the global level will create new values, identities, and culture—a "creative destruction" that will enrich all cultures.[10] One result of this outcome could be a *global cosmopolitanism*—a term that comes from the Greek *kosmos*, or universe, and *polis*, or state. Cosmopolitanism is thus a universal, global, or "worldly" political order that draws its identity and values from everywhere. Historically, the cosmopolis was that physical space where such ideas usually came together, notably the city. In a globalized world, however, there is the potential for an international cosmopolitanism that binds people together irrespective of where they are.[11]

Parallel to a global cosmopolitanism is the idea of global democracy. We have already spoken of how globalization might shape political institutions at the domestic and international levels, though we focused largely on the development of nonstate and suprastate organizations as rivals to the state itself. When we focus on societal globalization and its effects on democracy, however, we return to our notion of civil society. The argument here is that growing international connections at the societal level would generate not only a form of cosmopolitanism but also a civic identity that stretches beyond traditional barriers and borders. This global civil society—organized life not simply beyond the state but above it—can take shape in such formal organizations as NGOs but also in such informal manifestations as social movements or more basic grassroots connections between people drawn by shared interests and values. This global civil society could in turn shape politics by creating new opportunities for concerted public action and new ways of thinking about politics and participation at the domestic and international levels.[12] Finally, this development of global cosmopolitanism and civil society has the potential to eliminate international conflict, though for reasons quite different from those outlined in the discussion of political globalization. Whereas political globalization imagines a "golden straitjacket" that makes war too costly for states to

pursue, societal globalization would undercut national, patriotic, and other identities that states call on to justify war. Political globalization may make war
unbeneficial, but societal globalization would make it unthinkable.[13]

As you might expect, there are critics of such views, skeptical of the notion
that increased globalization will be beneficial to social progress. These criticisms are twofold. First, some contend that the onslaught of globalization will
overwhelm people with innumerable choices, values, ideas, and information
that they are unable to understand, evaluate, or escape—especially those not
part of the globalized elite. They predict confusion, alienation, and a public
backlash as people seek to hold on to their traditional identities in the face
of these changes. Nationalism and fundamentalism could be a reaction to a
globalized society that people find alien and hostile to their own way of life.
This countervailing trend against globalization has been described by the political theorist Benjamin Barber as "jihad," the impulse across many societies
(Islamic or otherwise) to violently resist these alien ideas and values.[14] The
September 11 attacks can be viewed in this light—as a strike against the values (and perceived source) of globalization rather than against the United
States itself.

A second criticism emphasizes not the reaction to societal globalization
but rather the eventual outcome. Even in the absence of resistance, the critics contend, societal globalization will not generate a richer global culture
and cosmopolitanism but rather a cultural and intellectual race to the bottom. Akin to the criticism of economic globalization, societies will trade their
own cultures, institutions, and ideas for a common global society shaped not
by values or worldliness but by speed and consumption. Those things that
make each society unique—languages, food, music, history, customs, values,
and norms—will be absorbed, rationalized, and packaged for mass consumption everywhere. This outcome has been described by Barber as
"McWorld," where what is most attractive in each society is sterilized, repackaged, and sold to the rest of the planet and where those things that lack mass
appeal are thrown away or driven out, replaced by what satisfies the widest
public and the lowest common denominator. What is distinct and cannot be
globalized is lost; what is globalized are those things that have been stripped
of any distinctiveness or identity. One scholar calls this "the globalization of
nothing."[15]

Finally, although the emergence of a homogenized world may promise
greater prosperity and even cooperation, it may also come at the cost of foundations of democratic society. When there are no longer any meaningful differences in ideas and when choices are limited to the realm of consumption
rather than that of values, participation and debate lose their meaning. Both
freedom and equality become, in essence, meaningless concepts, since they
are not goods or services that can be marketed, bought, or sold.

Taking Stock of Globalization

Clearly, these heated debates over globalization show that it remains a highly controversial issue. At the most optimistic, globalization will be the instrument of dramatic human progress, spreading prosperity, enriching cultures, and expanding democracy, peace, and civil society. This utopian view has its dystopian alternative, in a vision of globalization marked by poverty and inequality, violence, tyranny, and the destruction of culture. Embedded in both of these visions is the idea that globalization is a major, and inevitable, turning point in history. But what is the evidence? Our task now is to match research against argument and consider what impact globalization has had on the world to date, and whether, as is often assumed, this is truly something new that will transform humanity and politics.

Is Globalization New?

One thing we can begin with is the assumption that globalization is a fundamentally new development in human history, a change in institutions that is without precedent. As we noted earlier, for thousands of years humanity was linked across great distances, spreading people, goods and ideas around the world. Scholars, however, have noted that such connections were often extensive but not intensive. But we should not underestimate how deep many of these connections were for their time. Medieval Europe was tightly interconnected through political, economic, and societal institutions, while a thousand years earlier, the Persian Empire bound people from Europe to North Africa and as far as India. In many of these cases, war was an important component of globalization, disrupting old institutions and propelling change.[16]

Let us look at a more recent phenomenon: the development of modern imperialism. The spread of European power into Latin America, Africa, the Middle East, and Asia profoundly reshaped domestic and international relations as Western political, economic, and social systems were transplanted into these parts of the world. Within Europe, too, imperialism and the declining costs of transportation helped facilitate the migration of millions of people to North and South America and parts of Africa and Asia. By comparison, the current world of passports, visas, and immigration in some ways constrains human mobility far more than just a century ago. It was during the late nineteenth century that we begin to see the rise of the first nongovernmental and intergovernmental organizations, such as the International Telegraph Union (ITU), founded in 1865, and the Red Cross, in 1863. And those who marvel at the advent of Internet communication forget that the first transatlantic cable connected Europe and North America by telegraph in 1866, spurring a global system of rapid communications and trade.[17] In his famous

GOLD FARMING: THE GLOBALIZATION OF GAMING

For about a decade, one of the interesting elements of globalization has been the rise of massively multiplayer online role-playing games, often known by the unwieldy acronym MMORPGs. These games or spaces (such as Second Life, World of Warcraft, or EVE Online) emerged with the Internet as a way in which individuals could play traditional role-playing games online with individuals scattered around the country or around the world. These games encapsulate many of the facets of globalization that we have discussed to date. First, they represent purely synthetic or artificial worlds in which the typical structures of nations, territory, ethnicity, or citizenship play a completely different role. While these games generate hundreds of millions of dollars for their owners, they also have internal economies with their own currencies, forms of labor specialization, and even rates of exchange and black or gray markets for goods and services. Civic organization and political action, including protests and riots, have emerged in these virtual worlds. At the same time, while individuals may don identities that are far removed from their real selves, political and national or ethnic identities have expressed themselves in these spaces as well.

One of the more interesting examples of the intersection between globalization, gaming, and the physical and virtual worlds is gold farming. Gold farming is an activity within a MMORPG such as World of Warcraft where an individual plays not for enjoyment but to collect benefits ("gold" in World of Warcraft or Interstellar Kredits in EVE Online) or build up characters that then can be sold for real money to other players. Although most MMOPRGs attempt to prevent the use of real money to buy virtual goods, a large secondary market has emerged for online credit and complete characters. Much of this gold farming takes place in China, where there are firms that employ young gamers to build up credits and characters. The credits or characters are then sold on the global market, largely to consumers in North America and Europe. Gold farmers have even offered "guided tours" of more dangerous parts of online worlds, so that inexperienced gamers could benefit from the protection of these more seasoned players—not unlike novice climbers on Everest using Sherpas to guide the way.

The rise of gold farming has created conflict within the MMORPG community, as many players believe that gold farmers and those who buy from them are subverting the purpose of the games. As a result, gamers often seek out and kill gold farmers in their virtual worlds, posting the exploits on YouTube, and these "vigilante" activities often have racist overtones. Gold farmers (who call themselves professional gamers) explain that they are simply doing a job that provides a service other gamers want, and they fail to understand why others would want to kill their characters. Online games have become a fascinating nexus where national, economic, real, and virtual identities and institutions intersect.

work *The Economic Consequences of the Peace*, economist John Maynard Keynes wrote of the dramatic impact of such changes:

> The inhabitant of London could order by telephone, sipping his morning tea in bed, the various products of the whole earth, in such quantity as he might see fit, and reasonably expect their early delivery upon his doorstep; he could at the same moment and by the same means adventure his wealth in the natural resources and new enterprises of any quarter of the world, and share, without exertion or even trouble, in their prospective fruits and advantages; or he could decide to couple the security of his fortunes with the good faith of the townspeople of any substantial municipality in any continent that fancy or information might recommend.[18]

Sound like the new global economy? The time period Keynes wrote about was prior to World War I. Indeed, the rise of Internet commerce, often heralded as a central piece of globalization, would not be possible without the previous establishment of such institutions as the telephone, national postal services, passable roads, ports, and commercial shipping—all things that far predate globalization.

At that time, many observers believed that globalization would lead to the abolition of war and the spread of international law and world government. For others, however, these rapid changes also brought with it concerns and dangers not unlike those discussed today. Migration and trade brought fears of cultural destruction and violent resistance in response, including nationalism and eventually fascist ideas. And as we saw in the last chapter, Marxist and anarchist ideas also attracted followers around the world, some of whom sought revolution and engaged in terrorism. In these confusing and often violent developments, some saw an imminent collapse of Western society.

These examples suggest that it may be shortsighted of us to think that today's global interconnections are more dramatic than any before or that they portend changes that are beyond our power to control. History may help us better understand the present; we should not assume that what is occurring now is so unique that the past has nothing to teach us.

Is Globalization Exaggerated?

We have asked earlier what the evidence is with regard to globalization's impact on political, economic, and societal institutions, whether for good or ill. Is globalization making the world better or worse, however we might measure this? More generally, is globalization's impact as great as many of its supporters or critics assert?

As is often the case, the data present a mixed picture. Let us begin with political globalization: some have suggested it would lead to greater transparency and global democratic institutions, while others have worried that the result would be an important loss of democratic participation and the rise of nonstate and nondemocratic actors. In both of these cases the assumption is essentially that globalization means the eclipse of the state; yet in both scenarios, there is still not a great deal of evidence that shows this is in fact taking place. At the most basic level, even as globalization has spread, so too have the number of states; sovereignty has remained a critical demand for people around the world, from East Timor to Kosovo. While observers of globalization commonly point to the European Union as evidence of this change, they fail to point out that fifty years on, no other part of the world has shown an interest or ability to replicate this model.

Indeed, over the past decade there has been a resurgence in sovereign authority in some areas, most notably national security, as countries have tightened controls to combat terrorism or secure themselves against other state rivals. The U.S. invasion of Iraq, Russian military action in the Caucasus, the growth of the Chinese military, and the nationalization of certain industries around the world in response to economic recession are all examples of traditional state power unconstrained by global institutions. On the opposite end, the idea that stateless actors such as terrorists are beyond the reach of states seems exaggerated. In new areas, as well, states have shown themselves capable of asserting authority. Many assumed in the early days of the Internet that this stateless, almost anarchic institution would displace the state, yet states have found ways to regulate content, limit access, and control electronic transactions. China and Iran's censorship of websites, European privacy laws, or American controls over Internet radio and TV are all good examples, puncturing what some scholars have called "the illusion of a borderless world."[19] There is little comprehensive evidence that states are becoming more transparent or hollowed out under globalization; rather, it seems that the nature of their capacity and autonomy is changing to meet new challenges and needs. For now, at least, states still matter.

If the picture of states and globalization is not clear, one might expect that in the area of economic globalization our evidence would be more comprehensive. While people may not agree on the effects of economic globalization, even the limited data we showed regarding trade and foreign direct investment would seem to indicate a profound change over the last two decades. But here too, caveats are in order. For example, in spite of impressive growth, the total levels of international trade represent only about a quarter of global GDP; for the United States, it is closer to 11 percent.[20] In addition, international economic relations remain less "virtual" than we might think. For example, international trade drops to near zero at a distance of over 4,000 miles

(7,000 kilometers). Foreign direct investment (FDI), too, is hardly globalized to the degree we might imagine. In spite of our image of FDI riding a wave of globalization to penetrate every corner of the globe, over 60 percent of such investments stay inside the advanced democracies, with the largest single recipient being the United States (see Figure 11.2). State boundaries, economic barriers, cultural linkages and physical distance still appear to have powerful impact on global economic integration.

With those caveats in place on the limits of economic globalization, what impact has it had to date? Recall our discussion in Chapter 4; worldwide poverty has fallen by several hundred million since the 1980s. Most of this reduction has occurred in Asia, particularly China, while in Latin American poverty has declined only modestly, and it has risen in sub-Saharan Africa. This could be correlated with globalization, indicating that countries that have integrated into the global economy have seen the greatest benefits in poverty reduction. At the same time, however, inequality as measured by the Gini index has risen within some countries, such as the United States and China. So once again, we might correlate economic globalization with greater domestic inequality. But at the same time, inequality *between* countries overall appears to have declined—this again being disproportionately shaped by the rise of wealth in China. Indeed, some scholars suggest that much of what we think of as economic globalization has been driven by domestic reforms in China and its integration into the global market, and that much of China's reform (which began in the 1980s) occurred well before the current wave of economic globalization. Finally, when one removes China from the discussion, globalization does not appear to be generating greater poverty, nor is it likely to reduce it.[21] In short, then, much of what we think about in terms of economic globalization may be the result of domestic politics and reforms in a single, albeit very large, country; past that, globalization's effects are not uniform or unambiguous.

So far we've found no "smoking guns" in terms of political or economic globalization. What about at the level of society? Here, too, we confront the limitations of our data. Both supporters and opponents of societal globalization agree with the proposition that national and local identities are giving way in the face of a broader global identity. Whether this will be a peaceful process and whether this is a positive outcome are the basis of their disagreement. But again we must ask: Are these processes actually taking place? A 2003 global survey of over forty countries indicated that while many people feel that globalization has increased, in less than a third of those countries did a majority say they had become more connected to others outside of their own country.[22] Similarly, national identity continues to remain strong in the face of globalization. The 2001 World Values Survey of over eighty countries similarly indicated that on average around 10 percent of individuals see their primary identification with their continent or the world as a whole, over town, region, or country. This figure has not moved significantly in the past twenty-five years (Table 11.2). Such data seem to run counter to a more interconnected and postnational world.

But if we look at this data more selectively, we may see some potential impact. Some recent studies find that young people in highly globalized societies show a weaker identity with nation and state. What is unclear is whether these values are life-cycle or generational in nature—in other words, whether they are values that people feel when they are young (but will discard as they grow older), or ones inherent to a generation that will stay with them as they age. If they are generational, this finding would be potent evidence for those who believe in the emergence of global cosmopolitanism or a global civil society.

However, this societal globalization may come with a price. The data that show a generational change away from national and state identity also find that this change is correlated with a weaker emphasis on citizenship as well. Going back to our discussion of nations, states, and citizenship in Chapter 3, we recall how strong the connections between these institutions are. If young people are turning away from traditional identities like nation and state, it may come at the cost of a commitment to civic participation and the responsibilities of citizenship. And if this is the case, the democratic problem of globalization may not be that global institutions lack the mechanisms for public participation but that a coming generation will show little interest in civic responsibility, global or domestic.[23] Whether these changes are permanent will require more time to track the rise of this globalized generation.

Is Globalization Inevitable?

Let us for the sake of argument, reject all of the qualifiers raised above and assume that globalization is fundamentally different from the past and

Table 11.2 Globalization and Societal Identities

	1981	1990	2001
Strong national or local identity	75%	73%	77%
Weak supranational identity	14%	15%	12%
Strong supranational identity	11%	12%	11%

World Values Survey Question: "To which of these geographical groups do you belong to first of all?" (Compilation of answers given in United Kingdom, France, West Germany, Italy, Spain, Belgium, Netherlands, Denmark, Sweden, Iceland, Ireland, Finland, United States, Canada, Mexico, Argentina, South Africa, and Japan between 1981 and 2001.)

could be profound in its effects. Accepting this, it often follows that glob-alization is a juggernaut that people, groups, societies, and states cannot control or resist. Is globalization so unstoppable? The recent global eco-nomic downturn has been a stark reminder that globalization is somehow an inexorable process that cannot be stopped. To illustrate this point, let us again return to history, and to Keynes. After noting the profound changes that occurred before World War I, he remarked that above all, the average individual

> regarded this state of affairs as normal, certain, and permanent, except in the direction of further improvement, and any deviation from it as aberrant, scandalous, and avoidable.[24]

Yet this was not to be the case. The onset of World War I disrupted inter-national trade; its effects were further compounded by a subsequent world depression. History suggests, then, that globalization is not unstoppable; deglobalization can occur as well, as it has in the past.

Globalization could be limited or reversed in a number of ways. One is eco-nomic crisis. The heady period of economic development a hundred years ago was finally undermined by financial collapse in the 1930s. In its immediate aftermath, trade, investment, and migration declined, often as a result of new national barriers that reflected increased isolationism, protectionism, and nationalism. Many of these barriers persist to this day, in spite of recent lib-eralization. For example, between 1901 and 1910, the United States accepted nearly 9 million immigrants, but it would not again reach even half that level until the 1970s. Prolonged global recession could create pressure to roll back many of the elements of globalization that have developed over the past decade, reducing economic ties, migration, or other forms of globalization.

Indeed, recent global economic turmoil has pointed to this very possibil-ity. As we have noted in previous chapters, much of what has developed in comparative politics over the past decade has taken place within the context of rapid global economic growth. The rise of China as a major exporting power, Russia as a supplier of energy and other natural commodities, India as a hub for outsourcing, and the integration of global markets for investment are a few examples of this rapid economic growth that has had important political implications. Now a good portion of this development has been blunted by an economic crisis unseen since the 1930s. Energy prices have slumped from record levels as demand has decreased; exporters have seen their overseas markets dry up; foreign investments in the developed and developing world have lost much of their value; businesses and banks large and small have reeled and some collapsed; migration flows have, in some cases, reversed and global travel declined. Who will be hit hardest by this crisis is uncertain, but more generally, it portends a weakening of the web of interconnections that define globalization. This may last only a short time, or stretch on for many years.[25]

This crisis may, in turn, contribute to a second major challenge to globalization, which is public opposition. Many people's concerns about how globalization might affect such things as the environment, labor standards, and democratic practices around the world are being translated into antiglobalization activism—aided, ironically, by new technology such as the Internet. The protests against the World Trade Organization (WTO) in Seattle in 1999 are perhaps the most notable example of such activism: there, for the first time in the WTO's history, members were unable to begin negotiations on a new round of trade liberalization measures. Although this failure was not simply, or even primarily, due to public protests, widespread opposition in the street by activists from around the world certainly helped to complicate matters.[26] Since 1999, the WTO has failed to regain momentum and faced another collapse of trade talks in 2008. Opposition to EU reforms also helped scuttle the proposed constitution in 2005 and 2007 (see Chapter 7). Such opposition to increased integration and globalization can be found across the political spectrum and around the world. A 2007 survey over the pace of globalization found that a majority in the United States, Canada, and a number of European countries believed it was moving too fast. In China the response was closer to 70 percent, which is particularly interesting given that we tend to regard that country as being one of the greatest beneficiaries of this rapid change.[27]

These concerns all echo the past. The historian Niall Ferguson has suggested several causes for the collapse of globalization a century ago, among them the overstretch of one dominant power, unstable alliances and rivalry, rogue states, and the spread of revolutionary ideologies opposed to capitalism. In one form or another, Ferguson argues, all of these factors are again at work.[28] Throughout human history, societies have gone through periods of international connection and isolation. Some of these contacts have been relatively thin, involving relatively few people, but in other cases, many millions became directly connected to and a part of a larger world. Although today's globalization may look qualitatively different from waves of globalization in the past, what we are experiencing now may not be an unprecedented or irreversible force. Globalization may stall through its own flaws or concerted action against it. Nothing is set in stone.

In Sum: Freedom and Equality in a Globalized World

Our world may now be undergoing a profound shift in the face of globalization, though this is subject to debate. If it does in fact become truly globalized, the struggle over freedom and equality could shift from the domestic to the international arena. Both values will be measured not just within states, but between them: Does one country's freedom or equality come at the expense of another's? How can freedom or equality be balanced globally in the absence of any single sovereign power or dominant regime? Under these conditions, the very meanings of freedom and equality may evolve as new ways of thinking about individual choice and collective aspirations emerge. These changes could lead to greater stability, peace, and prosperity. They may also lead to greater conflict and chaos. However, it is still far too early to write off the power of domestic politics. States and nations, regimes and ideologies, culture and political organizations continue to play the dominant role in driving domestic politics, and domestic politics in driving the content of world affairs. Whatever the outcome, comparative politics gives us the power to analyze the present, glimpse the future, and play a role in shaping the course of human progress.

NOTES

1. Jared Diamond, *Guns, Germs and Steel: The Fate of Human Societies* (New York: Norton, 1997).
2. See Robert O. Keohane and Joseph S. Nye, Jr., "Introduction," in Joseph S. Nye, Jr., and John D. Donahue, eds., *Governance in a Globalizing World* (Washington: Brookings Institution Press, 2000), pp. 1–41.
3. Thomas Friedman, *The Lexus and the Olive Tree* (New York: Farrar, Straus and Giroux, 2000).
4. John Arquilla and David Ronfeldt, eds., *Networks and Netwars: The Future of Terror, Crime, and Militancy* (Washington: RAND, 2001).
5. Mare Sageman, *Leaderless Jihad: Terror Networks in the Twenty-First Century* (Philadelphia: University of Pennsylvania Press, 2008).
6. John Fonte, "Democracy's Trojan Horse," *National Interest,* 76 (Summer 2004), pp. 117–127.
7. *World Investment Report 2007,* www.unctad.org.
8. Martin Wolf, *Why Globalization Works* (New Haven, CT: Yale University Press, 2005).
9. Naomi Klein, *The Shock Doctrine: The Rise of Disaster Capitalism* (New York: Picador, 2008).
10. Tyler Cowen, *Creative Destruction: How Globalization Is Changing the World's Cultures* (Princeton, NJ: Princeton University Press, 2004).
11. David Held, *Democracy and the Global Order* (Cambridge: Polity Press, 1995).
12. Mary Griffiths, "e-Citizens: Blogging as Democratic Practice," *Electronic Journal of e-Government,* 2, no. 3 (December 2004), www.ejeg.com.
13. Mary Kaldor, *Global Civil Society: An Answer to War* (Cambridge: Polity Press, 2003); *New and Old Wars: Organized Violence in a Global Era* (Stanford, CA: Stanford University Press, 2007).

14. Benjamin Barber, *Jihad versus McWorld: How Globalism and Tribalism Are Reshaping the World* (New York: Random House, 1995).

15. George Ritzer, *The Globalization of Nothing* (Thousand Oaks, CA: Pine Forge Press, 2007).

16. Ronald Findlay and Kevin H. O'Rourke, *Power and Plenty: Trade, War, and the World Economy in the Second Millennium* (Princeton, NJ: Princeton University Press, 2007).

17. Tom Standage, *The Victorian Internet: The Remarkable Story of the Telegraph and the Nineteenth Century's On-Line Pioneers* (New York: Berkley, 1998).

18. John Maynard Keynes, *The Economic Consequences of the Peace,* (New York: Harcourt, Brace and Howe, 1920), pp. 11–12.

19. Jack Goldsmith and Tim Wu, *Who Controls the Internet? The Illusions of a Borderless World* (Oxford: Oxford University Press, 2006).

20. World Bank, *World Development Indicators 2007*, www.worldbank.org.

21. Martin Ravallion, "Looking Beyond Averages in the Trade and Poverty Debate," *World Development*, 34, no. 8 (August 2006), pp. 1374–1392.

22. Pew Center for the People and the Press, "Views of a Changing World 2003," http://people-press.org.

23. Wendy Rahn, "Globalization, the Decline of Civic Commitments, and the Future of Democracy," in Peter F. Nardulli, ed., *International Perspectives on Contemporary Democracy*, (Chicago: University of Illinois Press, 2008), pp. 134–157.

24. Keynes, *The Economic Consequences of the Peace*, p. 12.

25. Roger C. Altman, "The Great Crash, 2008: A Geopolitical Setback for the West," *Foreign Affairs*, (January/February 2009), pp. 2–14.

26. Jeffrey J. Schott, "The WTO after Seattle," in Jeffrey J. Schott, ed., *The WTO after Seattle* (Washington: Institute for International Economics, 2000), p. 5.

27. "Widespread Unease About Economy and Globalization—Global Poll," BBC World Service Program on International Policy Attitudes Poll, February, 2008. www.worldpublicopinion.org/pipa/pdf/feb08/BBCEcon_Feb08_rpt.pdf.

28. Niall Ferguson, "Sinking Globalization," *Foreign Affairs*, 84, no. 2 (March/April 2005), pp. 64–77.

GLOSSARY

abstract review   Judicial review that allows the constitutional court to rule on questions that do not arise from actual legal disputes.

advanced democracy   A country with institutionalized democracy and a high level of economic development.

anarchism   A political ideology that stresses the elimination of the state and private property as a way to achieve both freedom and equality for all.

authoritarianism   A political system in which a small group of individuals exercises power over the state without being constitutionally responsible to the public.

autonomy   The ability of the state to wield its power independently of the public.

behavioral revolution   A movement within political science during the 1950s and 1960s to develop general theories about individual political behavior that could be applied across all countries.

bicameral system   A political system in which the legislature comprises two houses.

bureaucratic authoritarianism   A system in which the state bureaucracy and the military share a belief that a technocratic leadership, focused on rational, objective, and technical expertise, can solve the problems of the country without public participation.

capacity   The ability of the state to wield power to carry out basic tasks, such as defending territory, making and enforcing rules, collecting taxes, and managing the economy.

capitalism   A system of production based on private property and free markets.

central bank   The state institution that controls how much money is flowing through the economy, as well as how much it costs to borrow money in that economy.

Central Committee   The legislature-like body of a communist party.

central planning   A communist economic system in which the state explicitly allocates resources by planning what should be produced and in what amounts, the final prices of goods, and where they should be sold.

charismatic legitimacy   Legitimacy built on the force of ideas embodied by an individual leader.

citizenship   An individual's relationship to the state, wherein citizens swear allegiance to that state and the state in return is obligated to provide rights to those citizens.

civil liberties   Individual rights regarding freedom that are created by the constitution and the political regime.

civil rights Individual rights regarding equality that are created by the constitution and the political regime.

civil society Organizations outside of the state that help people define and advance their own interests.

clientelism A process whereby the state co-opts members of the public by providing specific benefits or favors to a single person or a small group in return for public support.

coercion Compelling behavior by threatening harm.

colonialism An imperialist system of physically occupying a foreign territory using military force, businesses, or settlers.

communism (1) A political-economic system in which all wealth and property are shared so as to eliminate exploitation, oppression, and, ultimately, the need for political institutions such as the state. (2) A political ideology that advocates such a system.

comparative advantage The ability of one country to produce a particular good or service more efficiently relative to other countries' efficiency in producing the same good or service.

comparative method The means by which social scientists make comparisons across cases.

comparative politics The study and comparison of domestic politics across countries.

concrete review Judicial review that allows the constitutional court to rule on the basis of actual legal disputes brought before it.

conservatives Those with a political attitude that is skeptical of change and supports the current order.

constituency A geographical area that an elected official represents.

constitutional court The highest judicial body in a political system that decides whether laws and policies violate the constitution.

co-optation The process by which individuals are brought into a beneficial relationship with the state, making them dependent on the state for certain rewards.

corporatism A method of co-optation whereby authoritarian systems create or sanction a limited number of organizations to represent the interests of the public and restrict those not set up or approved by the state.

correlation An apparent relationship between two or more variables.

country Term used to refer to state, government, regime, and the people who live within that political system.

coup d'état A move in which military forces take control of the government by force.

culture Basic institutions that define a society.

deductive reasoning Research that works from a hypothesis that is then tested against data.

deflation A period of falling prices and values for goods, services, investments, and wages.

democracy A political system in which political power is exercised either directly or indirectly by the people.

devolution A process in which political power is "sent down" to lower levels of state and government.

direct democracy Democracy that allows the public to participate directly in government decision making.

economic liberalization   Changes consistent with liberalism that aim to limit the power of the state and increase the power of the market and private property in an economy.

electoral system   A set of rules that decide how votes are cast, counted, and translated into seats in a legislature.

empire   A single political authority that has under its sovereignty a large number of external regions or territories and different peoples.

endogeneity   The issue that cause and effect are not often clear, in that variables may be both cause and effect in relationship to one another.

equality   A shared material standard of individuals within a community, society, or country.

ethnic conflict   A conflict in which different ethnic groups struggle to achieve certain political or economic goals at each other's expense.

ethnicity/ethnic identity   Specific attributes and societal institutions that make one group of people culturally different from others.

executive   The branch of government that carries out the laws and policies of a state.

export-oriented industrialization   A mercantilist strategy for economic growth in which a country seeks out technologies and develops industries focused specifically on the export market.

failed state   A state so weak that its political structures collapse, leading to anarchy and violence.

fascism   A political ideology that asserts the superiority and inferiority of different groups of people and stresses a low degree of both freedom and equality in order to achieve a powerful state.

federalism   A system in which significant state powers, such as taxation, lawmaking, and security, are devolved to regional or local bodies.

first past the post   An electoral system in which individual candidates compete in single-member districts; voters choose between candidates, and the candidate with the largest share of the vote wins the seat.

foreign direct investment   The purchase of assets in a country by a foreign firm.

freedom   The ability of an individual to act independently, without fear of restriction or punishment by the state or other individuals or groups in society.

fundamentalism   A view of religion as absolute and inerrant that should be legally enforced by making faith the sovereign authority.

game theory   An approach that emphasizes how actors or organizations behave in their goal to influence others. Built upon assumptions of rational choice.

Gini index   A statistical formula that measures the amount of inequality in a society; its scale ranges from 0 to 100, where 0 corresponds to perfect equality and 100 to perfect inequality.

glasnost   Literally, openness. The policy of political liberalization implemented in the Soviet Union in the late 1980s.

globalization   The process of expanding and intensifying linkages between states, societies, and economies.

government   The leadership or elite in charge of running the state.

gross domestic product (GDP)   The total market value of all goods and services produced by a country over a period of one year.

guerrilla war   A conflict whereby nonstate combatants who largely abide by the rules of war target the state.

head of government   The executive role that deals with the everyday tasks of running the state, such as formulating and executing policy.

head of state   The executive role that symbolizes and represents the people both nationally and internationally.

human development index (HDI)   A statistical tool that attempts to evaluate the overall wealth, health, and knowledge of a country's people.

hyperinflation   Inflation of more than 50 percent a month for more than two months in a row.

ideational   Having to do with ideas.

illiberal/hybrid regime   Rule by an elected leadership through procedures of questionable democratic legitimacy.

imperialism   A system in which a state extends its power to directly control territory, resources, and people beyond its borders.

import substitution   A mercantilist strategy for economic growth in which a country restricts imports in order to spur demand for locally produced goods.

indirect democracy   Democracy in which representatives of the public are responsible for government decision making.

inductive reasoning   Research that works from case studies in order to generate hypotheses.

inflation   An outstripping of supply by demand, resulting in an increase in the general price level of goods and services and the resulting loss of value in a country's currency.

informal economy   A segment of the economy that is not regulated or taxed by the state.

initiative   A national vote called by members of the public to address a specific proposal.

institution   An organization or activity that is self-perpetuating and valued for its own sake.

integration   A process by which states pool their sovereignty, surrendering some individual powers in order to gain shared political, economic, or societal benefits.

intergovernmental organization (IGO)   Group created by states to serve certain policy ends.

intergovernmental system   A system in which two or more countries cooperate on issues.

judicial review   The mechanism by which courts can review the actions of government and overturn those that violate the constitution.

laissez-faire   The principle that the economy should be "allowed to do" what it wishes; a liberal system of minimal state interference in the economy.

legislature   The branch of government charged with making laws.

legitimacy   A value whereby an institution is accepted by the public as right and proper, thus giving it authority and power.

less-developed country (LDC)   A country that lacks significant economic development or political institutionalization or both.

liberal democracy   A political system that promotes participation, competition, and liberty and emphasizes individual freedom and civil rights.

liberalism   (1) A political attitude that favors evolutionary transformation; (2) An ideology and political system that favors a limited state role in society and the economy, and places a high priority on individual political and economic freedom.

market   The interaction between the forces of supply and demand that allocates resources.

marketization   The creation of the market forces of supply and demand in a country.

mercantilism   A political-economic system in which national economic power is paramount and the domestic economy is viewed as an instrument that exists primarily to serve the needs of the state.

microcredit   A system in which small loans are channeled to the poor through borrowing groups whose members jointly take responsibility for repayment.

military rule   Rule by one or more military officials, often brought to power through a coup d'état.

mixed electoral system   An electoral system that uses a combination of single-member districts and proportional representation.

modern   Characterized as secular, rational, materialistic, technological, and bureaucratic, and placing a greater emphasis on individual freedom than in the past.

modernization theory   A theory asserting that as societies developed, they would take on a set of common characteristics, including democracy and capitalism.

monopoly   A single producer that is able to dominate the market for a good or service without effective competition.

multimember district (MMD)   An electoral district with more than one seat.

multinational corporation (MNC)   Firm that produces, distributes, and markets its goods or services in more than one country.

nation   A group of people bound together by a common set of political aspirations, the most important of which is self-government.

national conflict   A conflict in which one or more groups within a country develop clear aspirations for political independence, clashing with others as a result.

national identity   A sense of belonging to a nation and a belief in its political aspirations.

nationalism   Pride in one's people and the belief that they have a unique political destiny.

nation-state   A state encompassing one dominant nation that it claims to embody and represent.

neocolonialism   An indirect form of imperialism in which powerful countries overly influence the economies of less-developed countries.

neocorporatism   A system of social democratic policy making in which a limited number of organizations representing business and labor work with the state to set economic policy.

newly industrializing country (NIC)   A historically less-developed country that has experienced significant economic growth and democratization.

nihilism   A belief that all institutions and values are essentially meaningless and that the only redeeming value is violence.

nomenklatura   Politically sensitive or influential jobs in the state, society, or economy that were staffed by people chosen or approved by the Communist Party.

nongovernmental organization (NGO)   A national or international group, independent of any state, that pursues policy objectives and fosters public participation.

nontariff regulatory barriers   Policies and regulations used to limit imports through methods other than taxation.

one-party rule   Rule by one political party, with other parties banned or excluded from power.

parastatal   Industry partially owned by the state.

parliamentary system   A political system in which the roles of head of state and head of government are assigned to separate executive offices.

party-state   A political system in which power flows directly from the ruling political party (usually a communist party) to the state, bypassing government structures.

patrimonialism   An arrangement whereby a ruler depends on a collection of supporters within the state who gain direct benefits in return for enforcing the ruler's will.

patriotism   Pride in one's state.

perestroika   Literally, restructuring. The policy of political and economic liberalization implemented in the Soviet Union in the late 1980s.

personality cult   Promotion of the image of an authoritarian leader not merely as a political figure but as someone who embodies the spirit of the nation and possesses endowments of wisdom and strength far beyond those of the average individual and is thus portrayed in a quasi-religious manner.

personal/monarchical rule   Rule by a single leader, with no clear regime or rules constraining that leadership.

Politburo   The top policy-making and executive body of a communist party.

political attitude   Description of one's views regarding the speed and methods with which political changes should take place in a given society.

political culture   The basic norms for political activity in a society.

political-economic system   The relationship between political and economic institutions in a particular country and the policies and outcomes they create.

political economy   The study of the interaction between states and markets.

political ideology   The basic values held by an individual about the fundamental goals of politics or the ideal balance of freedom and equality.

political violence   Violence outside of state control that is politically motivated.

politics   The struggle in any group for power that will give one or more persons the ability to make decisions for the larger group.

populism   A political view that does not have a consistent ideological foundation, but that emphasizes hostility toward elites and established state and economic institutions and favors greater power in the hands of the public.

postindustrialism   The shift during the last half century from an economy based primarily on industry and manufacturing to one in which the majority of people are employed in the service sector, which produces the bulk of profits.

postmodern   Characterized by a set of values that center on "quality of life" considerations and give less attention to material gain.

presidential system   A political system in which the roles of head of state and head of government are combined in one executive offices.

privatization   The transfer of state-owned property to private ownership.

property   Goods or services that are owned by an individual or group, privately or publicly.

proportional representation (PR)   An electoral system in which political parties compete in multimember districts; voters choose between parties, and the seats in the district are awarded proportionally according to the results of the vote.

public goods   Goods, provided or secured by the state, available to society and which no private person or organization can own.

purchasing-power parity (PPP)   A statistical tool that attempts to estimate the buying power of income across different countries by using prices in the United States as a benchmark.

qualitative method   Study through an in-depth investigation of a limited number of cases.

quantitative method   Study through statistical data from many cases.

quota   A nontariff barrier that limits the quantity of a good that may be imported into a country.

radicals   Those with a political attitude that favors dramatic, often revolutionary change.

rational choice   Approach that assumes that individuals weigh the costs and benefits and make choices to maximize their benefits.

rational-legal legitimacy   Legitimacy based on a system of laws and procedures that are highly institutionalized.

reactionary   Someone who seeks to restore the institutions of a real or imagined earlier order.

referendum   A national vote called by a government to address a specific proposal, often a change to the constitution.

regime   The fundamental rules and norms of politics, embodying long-term goals regarding individual freedom and collective equality, where power should reside, and the use of that power.

regulation   A rule or order that sets the boundaries of a given procedure.

relative deprivation model   Model that predicts revolution when public expectations outpace the rate of domestic change.

rent seeking   A process in which political leaders essentially rent out parts of the state to their patrons, who as a result control public goods that would otherwise be distributed in a nonpolitical manner.

republicanism   Indirect democracy that emphasizes the separation of powers within a state and the representation of the public through elected officials.

revolution   Public seizure of the state in order to overturn the existing government and regime.

rule of law   A system in which all individuals and groups, including those in government, are subject to the law, irrespective of their power or authority.

selection bias   A focus on effects rather than causes, which can lead to inaccurate conclusions about correlation or causation.

semipresidential system   An executive system that divides power between two strong executives, a president and a prime minister.

separation of powers   The clear division of power between different branches of government and the provision that specific branches may check the power of other branches.

service sector   Work that does not involve creating tangible goods.

shock therapy   A process of rapid marketization.

single-member district (SMD)   An electoral district with one seat.

social democracy (socialism)   (1) A political-economic system in which freedom and equality are balanced through the state's management of the economy and the provision of social expenditures. (2) A political ideology that advocates such a system.

social expenditures   State provision of public benefits, such as education, health care, and transportation.

society   Complex human organization, a collection of people bound by shared institutions that define how human relations should be conducted.

sovereignty   The ability of a state to carry out actions or policies within a territory independently from external actors or internal rivals.

state   (1) The organization that maintains a monopoly of force over a given territory. (2) A set of political institutions to generate and execute policy regarding freedom and equality.

state-sponsored terrorism   Terrorism supported directly by a state as an instrument of foreign policy.

strong state   A state that is able to fulfill basic tasks, such as defending territory, making and enforcing rules, collecting taxes, and managing the economy.

structural adjustment program   A policy of economic liberalization adopted in exchange for financial support from liberal international organizations; typically includes privatizing state-run firms, ending subsidies, reducing tariff barriers, shrinking the size of the state, and welcoming foreign investment.

suffrage   The right to vote.

supranational system   An intergovernmental system with its own sovereign powers over member states.

tariff   A tax on imported goods.

terrorism   The use of violence by nonstate actors against civilians in order to achieve a political goal.

theocracy   A nondemocratic form of rule where religion is the foundation for the regime.

thermidor   A period of conservatism and declining zeal or idealism following a revolution.

totalitarianism   A nondemocratic regime that is highly centralized, possessing some form of strong ideology that seeks to transform and absorb fundamental aspects of state, society, and the economy, using a wide array of institutions.

traditional legitimacy   Legitimacy that accepts aspects of politics because they have been institutionalized over a long period of time.

unicameral system   A political system in which the legislature comprises one house.

unitary state   A state in which most political power exists at the national level, with limited local authority.

vote of no confidence   Vote taken by a legislature as to whether its members continue to support the current prime minister. Depending on the country, a vote of no confidence can force the resignation of the prime minister and/or lead to new parliamentary elections.

weak state   A state that has difficulty fulfilling basic tasks, such as defending territory, making and enforcing rules, collecting taxes, and managing the economy.

CREDITS

Table 2.1: From "The Failed States Index 2008," *Foreign Policy*, July/August 2008, p. 67. Copyright 2008, The Fund for Peace and the Carnegie Endowment for International Peace. Reproduced with permission of Foreign Policy (www.foreignpolicy.com) in the format Textbook via Copyright Clearance Center.

Figure 3.4: "Inglehart-Welzel Cultural Map of the World," Ronald Inglehart and Christian Welzel, *Modernization, Cultural Change and Democracy*, p. 63. © Ronald Inglehart and Christian Welzel 2005. Reprinted with the permission of Cambridge University Press.

Figure 4.2: "Measuring Satisfaction," David Leonhardt, "Maybe Money Does Buy Happiness After All," *The New York Times*, April 16, 2008. Copyright 2008 The New York Times Company. Reprinted with permission.

Figure 11.1: Jared Schneidman, "A.T. Kearney/Foreign Policy Globalization Index," *Foreign Policy*, March/April 2004. Copyright 2004, A.T. Kearney, Inc. and the Carnegie Endowment for International Peace. Reproduced with permission of Foreign Policy (www.foreignpolicy.com) in the format Textbook via Copyright Clearance Center.

Figure 11.4: Jared Schneidman, "A.T. Kearney/Foreign Policy Globalization Index," *Foreign Policy*, March/April 2004. Copyright 2004, A.T. Kearney, Inc. and the Carnegie Endowment for International Peace. Reproduced with permission of Foreign Policy (www.foreignpolicy.com) in the format Textbook via Copyright Clearance Center.

INDEX

abortion, 173, 247
abstract review, **121**
advanced democracies, **167**–95
  countries classified as, *170, 171,* 172
  defining of, 166–72
  devolution in, 184–86, 187
  economic change in, 190–95
  as First World, 168, 230
  freedom and equality in, 168, 172–75,
    176, *176*
  immigration in, 188–90, 193–95
  integration in, 177–84, *181,* 187
  life expectancy in, *303*
  modernity in, 176, 187
  political competition in, 174, 175
  political participation in, 173, 175
  postindustrialism in, 191–92, *191*
  postmodern values and organization
    in, 186–88
  as problematic term, 167
  social change and conflict in, 186–90
  states and sovereignty in, 177–86
  in transition, 195
  welfare state maintenance in, 192–95
Afghanistan:
  Al Qaeda in, 218, 225, 298–99
  civil war in, 218, 249
  ethnic conflict in, 56
  postcommunist social transition in,
    224–25

  Soviet invasion of, 211, 212
  state power in, 40
  theocracy in, 161
Africa, 31
  aid to, 254, 257
  colonialism in, 238
  communist regimes in (1980s), *199*
  decolonization of, 241, *242*
  empire in, 29
  ethnic fragmentation in, *58*
  imperialism in, 33, 235, 236, 238, 241,
    308
  import substitution in, 250
  military rule in, 158
  political culture in, 73, *73*
  rise of states in, 33–34
  state power in, 42
  terrorist incidents in, *275*
  see also specific countries
agriculture:
  employment in (1960–2004), *191*
  imperialism and, 239–40
  rise of, 27–28, 29
aid, 254, 255
Albania, *217*
  economic indicators in (1993–2004),
    221
Alexander II, Czar of Russia, 262
Algeria, civil conflict in (1990s), 280,
    283

Page numbers in **boldface** refer to in-text glossary definitions. Page numbers in *italics* refer to figures
and tables.